(1)
AF182231
1
54

PRODUCT LIABILITY ACTIONS BY FOREIGN PLAINTIFFS IN THE UNITED STATES

9789065443250

Product Liability Actions by Foreign Plaintiffs in the United States

by

Warren Freedman

Kluwer Law and Taxation Publishers
Deventer • Antwerp • London • Frankfurt • Boston • New York

Distribution in the USA and Canada
Kluwer Law and Taxation Publishers
101 Philip Drive
Norwell, MA 02061
USA

Library of Congress Cataloging-in-Publication Data
Freedman, Warren.
Product liability actions by foreign plaintiffs in the United States

Includes index.
1. Products liability—United States. 2. Conflict of laws—Products liability—United States. 3. Products liability. 4. Conflict of laws—Products liability.
I. Title.
KF1296.F725 1987 346.7303'8 87-32471
ISBN 90-6544-325-8 347.30638

Cover design: Bert Arts

D/1987/2664/101

ISBN 90 6544 325 8

©1988 Kluwer Law and Taxation Publishers, Deventer, The Netherlands

All rights reserved. No part of this publication may be reproduced, stored in a retrieval system, or transmitted in any form or by any means, mechanical, photocopying, recording or otherwise, without the prior written permission of the publishers.

Foreword

The large and open doors to litigation in the courts of the United States are especially attractive to foreign plaintiffs who have sustained personal injury, property damages, or economic loss as a result of the use or misuse of a product manufactured or marketed by an American corporation, even though located in the foreign country.

The liberality of US courts in recognizing the claim of injured party means liberal compensation brought about by liberal legal rules for the promotion of the litigation. Consumer advocates and consumer advocates in foreign countries are thrilled by the success of foreign plaintiffs in achieving satisfactory compensation for injuries sustained by the use or misuse of the product.

The book also details the defensive measures taken by US manufacturers and US marketers of products, principally under the doctrine of *forum non conveniens* (successfully used by Union Carbide Corporation in the pending Bhopal, India, litigation in the courts of India).

Table of Contents

Table of Cases

Chapter 1. Why Foreign Plaintiffs Bring Product Liability Actions in the United States

Section 1. Introduction

Products liability is today recognized as having important international dimensions, for there literally are no physical boundaries that a given consumer product may not cross during the course of its manufacture, marketing, distribution and ultimate use by the consumer. Frequently the consumer must place his health and well-being in the hands of the foreign entity manufacturing, marketing, and distributing the product, a foreign entity that may be an individual, local company, multinational corporation, or even a State-controlled enterprise. Under local law that foreign entity may or may not be responsible for the injury, death, damage, or economic loss caused by defects in or the hazardous nature of the very product. What are product defects in one country may well be unrecognized as defects in another country. There are innumerable 'contacts' that the product, as well as the foreign entity, may have with innumerable jurisdictions that will endeavor to apply their own law of products liability to the situation at hand. Some countries profess great interest, while other countries profess little or no interest in protecting the product consumer from injury, death, damage or economic loss. The consequence is a profusion of confusion with little predictability as to whether the consumer or the foreign entity will prevail once a claim arises.

The United States is one country where predictability has taken root, and the product consumer is afforded the greatest protection against the tortfeasor who manufactures or distributes an unsafe product. The United States is indeed the mecca or El Dorado for injured plaintiffs because the American tort system is geared to full recognition of the rights of consumers.[1] The rule of liability is liberal; there is procedural ease in serving defendants,[2] in obtaining pre-trial discovery, and in promoting the jury system to answer questions of fact, *inter alia*, all of which characteristics appeal to plaintiffs everywhere. The contingency fee system where plaintiffs do not have to put their money up front,[3] also contributes to the euphoria which plaintiffs experience under the American tort system.

The US Supreme Court in 1981 was itself aware of how favorable to plaintiffs was the American law of products liability: 'First, all but six of the 50 American states . . . offer strict liability. Rules roughly equivalent to American strict liability are effective in France, Belgium and Luxembourg . . . However, strict liability remains primarily an American innovation. Second, the tort plaintiff may choose, at least potentially, from among 50 jurisdictions if he decides to file suit in the United States. Each of these jurisdictions applies its own set of malleable choice-of-law rules. Third, jury trials are almost always available in the United States, while they are never provided in civil law jurisdictions . . . Fourth, unlike most foreign jurisdictions, American courts allow contingent attorney's fees and do not tax losing parties with their opponent's fees . . . Fifth, discovery is more extensive in America than in foreign courts.'[4]

The frequency of excessively high judgments and huge monetary awards in US courts have also been a magnet for the injured foreign consumer to bring his or her case into US courts. In Kahn *v.* United Technologies Corp,[5] decided by the Connecticut Superior Court in 1981, the plaintiffs represented all victims of a helicopter crash in the North Sea off the coast of Norway, i.e., a British citizen residing in Norway, two Norwegians, and one American citizen. The defendants were an American helicopter manufacturer from Connecticut and a Norwegian helicopter operator. [Similar litigation had been dismissed in 1980 on *forum non conveniens* grounds by the US Court of Appeals for the District of Columbia in Pain *v.* United Technologies Corp.[6]] When the current action was filed in the Connecticut Superior Court, the Connecticut-based helicopter manufacturer again moved to dismiss the suit on *forum non conveniens* grounds, despite the fact that it was being sued on 'home turf' before a jury of Connecticut citizens. The Connecticut state court refused dismissal, enunciating a number of factors weighing heavily in favor of its retention of jurisdiction, to wit:

1. the claim was a product liability claim and US law should apply;
2. the helicopter had been designed, manufactured, assembled, tested, and inspected in Connecticut by employees of the Connecticut-based defendant, and all evidence relevant to such product was located in Connecticut;
3. representatives of that defendant who had inspected parts of the helicopter wreckage in Norway were in Connecticut as were their investigatory reports;
4. the state of Connecticut has a strong public interest in addressing a product liability claim where the allegedly defective product had been technologically created in Connecticut; and
5. the Federal Aviation Administration, a part of the US Department of Transportation, had issued a safety certificate to that defendant for the helicopter involved in the crash, so the FAA had a consuming interest in having the litigation take place in the US. Thus, the state of Connecticut retained jurisdiction here as against the alternate forum of Norwegian courts, the site of the helicopter crash. The attractiveness of suit in the US in the eyes of the foreign plaintiffs was thus accepted by the US court.

It should also be observed that the United States Government itself can readily be sued by foreign plaintiffs under the Federal Tort Claims Act.[7] Also it should be noted that American courts are not free to interfere with any prior suit by foreign plaintiffs pending in foreign courts.[8] The accessibility of US courts to aliens has a positive effect upon American foreign relations for it becomes part of the goodwill and excellence conveyed by the US imprimatur on consumer products and on the reputations of American companies.[9]

Opening US courts to claims by foreign plaintiffs also has a sanguine effect upon US regulation of the foreign operations of multinational corporations headquartered in the United States: 'Forcing the corporate defense of foreign claims in US courts in front of US jurors implies clear pressure to comply with US regulations'. On the other hand, the US judiciary, by entertaining jurisdiction over foreign claims, might infringe upon the right of the foreign country to self-determination and to regulation over the event giving rise to the liability. US interests are not served by judicial intermeddling, and the foreign policy of the United States which falls into executive hands can be adversely altered by injudicious conduct of US courts. Yet there is a universal value in promoting product safety worldwide, and the joint concern of the United States and the foreign country should be welcomed.

The adoption in May 1986 by the American Law Institute of a 'Revised Statement of the Foreign Relations Law of the United States' (to be published in 1987) promises that foreign plaintiffs bringing suit in the United States will be accorded greater recognition. For example, Section 437(1) enhances foreign discovery by sanctioning adverse findings of fact by courts and federal agencies in the United States where disclosure of information located abroad is prohibited under foreign law, although sanctions will not be applied against the party failing to comply with the order under such circumstances. Section 469 restates the Act of State doctrine, and requires courts in the United States to refrain from passing judgment on the acts of a foreign state but only where such acts are done within the territory of the foreign state. However, the Act of State doctrine does not apply if there is a relevant treaty or other international agreement that governs the very issues being adjudicated. And Section 402 of Part IV on 'Jurisdiction and Judgments' sets forth the jurisdictional bases necessary for a state to prescribe its laws, i.e., conduct within the territory of the state, the status of persons present within its territory, and conduct outside the territory that has a substantial effect within its territory. But under Section 403 the state may not take jurisdiction if the exercise of such jurisdiction has extraterritorial consequences that are 'unreasonable'. Section 414 creates a presumption of jurisdiction over foreign branches of US corporations but limits jurisdiction over foreign subsidiaries to certain defined circumstances. Section 416 subjects certain categories of conduct and effects in the United States to jurisdiction by courts in the United States. A repudiation or a breach of an international contract is treated as a violation of international law under Section 712(2), which also prescribes that the compensation must be an amount equivalent to value of the property, paid at the time of the tort, and in a form economically usable by the foreign national. The 'Revised Statement of the Foreign Relations Law of the United States' will undoubtedly have a profound effect upon the developing international law applicable to the product liability law suit in the United States by the foreign plaintiff.

Section 2. Commencement of Suit by the Foreign Plaintiff in US Court

The law suit by the foreign plaintiff in the US court is generally commenced with the service of process within the United States or abroad, in which latter event Rule 4 of the Federal Rules of Civil Procedure, or the 1965 Hague Convention on the Service Abroad of Judicial and Extrajudicial Documents in Civil and Commercial Matters[10] will apply. Rule 4 provides for service outside a state when a federal statute or federal order authorizes such service or when the federal statute or rule of the particular federal district court authorizes service abroad. There are also alternative methods of service of US process in a foreign country, to wit:

a. in the manner prescribed by the foreign country;
b. in response to letter rogatory;
c. service upon the individual or company personally;
d. service by any form of mail; and
e. service as directed by order of the US court.

The Hague Convention[11] applies 'in all cases, in civil and commercial matters', but under Article 1 such service of process does not apply where the address of the person to be served is not known at the time of service; Article 2 requires each contracting country to designate a Central Authority to receive and carry out such service of process, and the method of service requires the Central Authority to serve the papers or documents either by a method prescribed by the internal law of that country,[12] by a method requested by the applicant,[13] or by any other method if voluntarily accepted by the addressee.[14] The Hague Convention, as cumbersome as it is, reflects the procedure of the signatory countries which include the United States, United Kingdom, Sweden, Turkey, Portugal, The Netherlands, Italy, Japan, Israel, West Germany, France, Finland, Denmark and Belgium, *inter alia*.

Rule 30 of the Federal Rules of Civil Procedure provides that once the action has commenced, any party 'may take the testimony of any person, including a party, by deposition upon oral examination'. These depositions can be taken 'on notice before a person authorized to administer oaths in the place in which the examination is held, either by the law thereof or by the law of the United States, or ... before a person commissioned by the court ... or pursuant to a letter rogatory'.[15] However, it should be noted that many foreign countries are hostile to allowing depositions to be taken in their countries since it represents an incursion into their sovereignty and is, moreover, extraterritorial.

Taking evidence abroad is delineated by The Hague Convention on Taking of Evidence Abroad in Civil or Commercial Matters,[16] to which Convention the United States, the United Kingdom and thirteen other countries are signatories. The executing authority in the foreign country is required to use whatever means of compulsion are available under its internal law to obtain the evidence,[17] and the foreign country is required to execute the letter of request expeditiously.[18] But US courts have not hesitated to follow the Convention procedure in some cases[19] and to reject the Convention procedure in other cases.[20] One of the prime difficulties is that many foreign courts regard the taking of evidence as the prerogative of the judiciary and not of the parties to the law suit. The Convention respects this notion of judicial sovereignty and does not ease the path of the party seeking to obtain evidence abroad. But the letters of request mandated under the

Convention are effective instruments since the Convention increases the powers of consuls to secure evidence and also supports the concept of commissions to obtain evidence.[21] In Volkswagenwerk *v.* Superior Court[22] the California trial court issued discovery orders to compel the defendant foreign corporation to allow its West German employees to be deposed in West Germany by an appointed commissioner, and also to open its West German property to inspection under threat of US court sanctions. The West German Embassy protested to the California court that the orders constituted an encroachment on West German sovereign rights, but nevertheless the Embassy would accept discovery procedures accomplished by a Letter of Request. The California appellate court overturned the trial court's discovery orders and held that courts ordering discovery abroad must conform to the channels and procedures established by the host nation where the evidence is located; and that this restriction may rest on theories of Comity, curtailed discretion, or implied statutory qualifications. Years later in Pierburg GmbH & Co. *v.* Superior Court[23] (137 Cal App3d 238) the California appellate court opined that the parties should exhaust the Evidence Convention's procedures before resorting to other devices to obtain evidence abroad.

Treaties and international agreements which allow citizens of those countries signatories to the treaties and international agreements equal access to each country's courts are prime factors in encouraging commencement of suits such as the foreign plaintiff in US courts. The United States has entered into many bilateral treaties providing for reciprocal court access; these documents are called Treaties of Friendship, Commerce and Navigation, for the lack of a better name.[24] The Second US Court of Appeals in Farmanfarmaiain *v.* Gulf Oil Co[25] expressly declared that US courts should not discriminate against foreign plaintiffs when a treaty ensuring access to US courts exists between the United States and the plaintiff's home country. The United States, as a member of the United Nations, is bound to recognize, for example, Article 7 of the Universal Declaration of Human Rights[26] which reads in part: 'All are equal before the law and are entitled without any discrimination to equal protection of the law. All are entitled to equal protection against any discrimination in violation of this Declaration and against any incitement to such discrimination.' It would appear that this universal declaration restricts somewhat US authority to limit a foreigner's access to US courts.[27]

Section 3. Form of Complaint Against Product Manufacturer by Foreign Plaintiff in Federal Court

Count 1

Plaintiff for Count 1 of her Complaint states as follows:

1. Plaintiff is an individual citizen of Great Britain and the United Kingdom, and resides on Grosvenor Square in the City of London; defendant is a

corporation organized and existing pursuant to the laws of the State of New York with its principal offices for the transaction of business on Stratford Road in New Rochelle, New York, so that defendant being a citizen of the State of New York and not a citizen of Great Britain permits complete diversity of citizenship between the parties.

2. The amount in controversy exceeds Ten Thousand Dollars exclusive of interest and costs, to wit: One Million Dollars, and this court has jurisdiction in the first instance pursuant to Title 28, Section 1332(a) US code.

3. At all times hereinafter alleged defendant was duly authorized to transact business in the State of New York and have offices and distribution centers for its products in Great Britain and the United Kingdom, and also in the State of New York and within the Southern District of the State of New York.

4. On or about 1 January 1984, a widget manufactured by defendant and assembled and inflated by a person other than the plaintiff exploded in the City of London in Great Britain and the United Kingdom while the plaintiff was handling the product, causing the plaintiff to suffer total and permanent blindness.

5. At the time of the manufacture of the widget by defendant, said widget was defective in that it had a proclivity to blow apart and explode when it was put to ordinary, normal use as intended and anticipated by the defendant; and defendant failed to warn of said defect in the product, and failed to recall, retrofit, or otherwise remedy the design defects in the product.

6. At the time of the explosion which blinded plaintiff the widget product was in substantially the same condition as when manufactured by defendant, and was being used by plaintiff as the product was reasonably intended to be used and as defendant anticipated its use; and because of the aforesaid defect in said product, the widget broke apart and exploded, totally and permanently blinding the plaintiff.

7. At the time of the design, development, manufacture, distribution, and sale of the subject widget product and prior to plaintiff's injury, defendant knew or had reason to know that the design, the materials and the construction of the product, presented an extreme and unusual hazard to the consuming public; in spite of the existence of known hazards and numerous serious and fatal injuries over the period of many years, the defendant negligently, willfully or intentionally

(a) failed and refused to redesign the widget;
(b) failed to recall such defective widgets from the market;
(c) failed to develop, test and incorporate in the widget safety devices to prevent explosive separation of the widgets;
(d) failed to warn adequately of the hazards involved in the use of the widget;
(e) failed to notify users of such widgets of the risk involved;
(f) failed to notify and fully inform the proper federal and state agencies of the existence of the hazard in the widget product;
(g) deliberately withheld information and gave misinformation with respect to the nature, extent, cause, and serious consequences of the defects in such widget products; and
(h) failed to discontinue production of the defective widget products.

8. Plaintiff's left eyeball was traumatically removed and her right eyeball was partially disgorged, as a consequence of defendant's conduct; plaintiff is rendered totally blind, which injury caused her great pain, mental anguish, psychological and emotional derangement and suffering.

9. Plaintiff has also been deprived of the ability to support and maintain herself, and is thereby damaged in the amount of One Million Dollars.

10. Plaintiff states that the conduct and failures of defendant were in willful, wanton, reckless and grossly negligent disregard for the safety of the public and particularly the plaintiff herein, and as result plaintiff is entitled to exemplary or punitive damages in the sum of One Million Dollars.

WHEREFORE, PLAINTIFF PRAYS JUDGMENT AGAINST DEFENDANT IN COUNT 1 IN THE SUM OF ONE MILLION DOLLARS ACTUAL DAMAGES AND ONE MILLION DOLLARS IN PUNITIVE DAMAGES, TOGETHER WITH THE COSTS OF THIS ACTION.

Count 2

Plaintiff for Count 2 of her Complaint states as follows:

11. Realleges each and every allegation set forth hereinabove in paragraphs numbered 1, 2, 3 and 4 with the same full force and effect as if specifically set forth.

12. Defendant defrauded plaintiff by failing to notify properly plaintiff and others of the consuming public as to the inherent dangers in the use of the widget product.

13. Defendant deliberately and fraudulently understated and minimized the number of known incidents, claims and law suits involving the widget product in its response to the demands for accurate information by federal and state agencies;

14. Defendant deliberately and fraudulently conspired with others at secret and clandestine meetings at the ABCD Hotel in the City of London to remain silent and avoid adequate warnings to users of the widget product by failing to attach a warning sticker to the product.

15. As a result of the foregoing fraudulent misrepresentation of defendant, plaintiff is entitled to exemplary or punitive damages of One Million Dollars.

16. Most of the acts, omissions and misrepresentations of the defendant occurred or were planned at defendant's principal places of business in New Rochelle, New York. Plaintiff requests that the Court take judicial notice of the law of the State of New York which provides for the recovery of compensatory and punitive damages for tortious conduct of the defendant in failing to redesign or recall the widget product or to warn the public when defendant knew the design of the product posed a grave danger to the lives or property of consumers.

WHEREFORE PLAINTIFF PRAYS JUDGMENT AGAINST DEFENDANT IN COUNT 2 IN THE SUM OF ONE MILLION DOLLARS ACTUAL DAMAGES AND IN THE SUM OF ONE MILLION DOLLARS

PUNITIVE DAMAGES TOGETHER WITH COSTS HEREIN EXPENDED.

By:
Attorneys for Plaintiff
Address:

DEMAND FOR TRIAL BY JURY

Plaintiff demands trial by jury.

Section 4. Form of Complaint Against Product Manufacturer by Foreign Plaintiff in State Court

1. At all times relevant herein the plaintiff is and was a citizen and resident of the State of Israel, and defendant is and was a domestic corporation organized and existing under the law of the State of ABCD.

2. Defendant designed, tested, researched, promoted, manufactured, distributed, marketed, sold, and advertised a product known as Widget.

3. Defendant's conduct was negligent in all respects, as shown hereinafter.

4. The aforementioned product Widget was permitted by defendant to be sold and advertised in the State of Israel.

5. Defendant expressly and impliedly warranted and represented to the public and to the plaintiff in particular that the product Widget was fit, safe, and effective for consumption.

6. The product Widget was not fit for the purpose for which it was designed, was not of merchantable quality, and was neither fit, safe nor effective for consumption.

7. Plaintiff relied to his detriment upon the express and implied warranties and representations made to plaintiff by defendant.

8. Plaintiff relying upon the aforesaid warranties and representations permitted the insertion of the product Widget into his person.

9. On or about 1 January 1984, a Widget, manufactured by defendant, was inserted into the person of the plaintiff by Michael S. Stiebel, M.D.

10. The Widget was inherently dangerous and deleterious to the health and safety of users thereof and, in particular, to the person of the plaintiff, contrary to defendant's aforesaid warranties and representations; and defendant knew or in the exercise of reasonable care should have known of the dangerous and deleterious nature of the product Widget.

11. Although defendant became aware of the potential hazard and danger in the product Widget, defendant failed to advise plaintiff and/or his physician thereof.

12. Defendant was grossly negligent, wanton, willful and reckless in the design,

testing, researching, promoting, manufacturing, distributing, marketing, selling and advertising the product Widget.

13. Defendant is subject to the imposition of punitive damages.

14. Defendant is strictly liable in tort to the plaintiff for the damages sustained by the plaintiff herein alleged.

15. Defendant's conduct, delineated hereinabove, caused plaintiff on or about 1 July 1985, to be admitted to the XYZ Hospital where competent medical examination and surgical treatment revealed that the Widget, inserted within the person of the plaintiff, had embedded itself within and had perforated plaintiff's stomach.

16. As a direct and proximate result of defendant's aforesaid conduct, plaintiff has suffered serious and permanent physical and mental disability, expenses for the medical and surgical attention necessary to remove defendant's product Widget from the person of the plaintiff, limitation of activity, and other serious damage as may be later established.

WHEREFORE PLAINTIFF PRAYS THAT JUDGMENT BE ENTERED IN HIS FAVOR AND AGAINST DEFENDANT AS FOLLOWS:

1. General damages in the amount of $1,000,000.
2. Special damages in an amount as shall be proved at time of trial.
3. Punitive damages in the amount of $1,000,000.
4. Costs of suit and such other and further relief as to which plaintiff may be entitled.

By:
Attorneys for Plaintiff
Address:

DEMAND FOR TRIAL BY JURY

Plaintiff demands trial by jury.

Section 5. Form of Complaint Against Product Manufacturer by Foreign Plaintiff in New York Court

First Cause of Action

1. Plaintiff is a resident and citizen of Switzerland, and was at all times set forth hereinafter a Swiss resident and a Swiss citizen with his residence in Geneva, Switzerland; defendant is a New York corporation and was at all times hereinafter set forth doing business in the State of New York and elsewhere in the world.

2. Upon information and belief, the defendant manufactured, assembled, and

fabricated all the parts of a certain motorcycle that was sold to the plaintiff for valuable consideration on 1 July 1984 in Geneva, Switzerland.

3. Upon information and belief, defendant caused to be brought into Switzerland for purpose of sale a motorcycle sold to the plaintiff.

4. On or about 15 July 1984, while plaintiff was lawfully operating the motorcycle on a public highway, the motorcycle was struck by an automobile operated by ABC, and as a result of the negligence of ABC, plaintiff suffered severe and permanent injuries as set forth herein.

5. The motorcycle had been negligently and carelessly designed, manufactured and assembled by defendant, in that a luggage rack had been in a dangerous position on the motorcycle, about three inches above and front of the saddle. The negligent design, manufacture, and assembly of the motorcycle greatly aggravated, enhanced, and contributed to plaintiff's serious and disabling injuries.

6. Defendant negligently and carelessly put an inherently dangerous product on the market, failed to provide a reasonably safe vehicle in which to travel and otherwise failed to exercise a degree of care and caution which a reasonably prudent manufacturer of motorcycles would have exercised with regard to protecting the safety and welfare of the user of its product.

7. The alleged defect in the design of the motorcycle was latent in nature and plaintiff did not perceive the danger incident to the design, and could not have perceived the danger by any means known to him.

8. The defendant furthermore was negligent in delivering and distributing to plaintiff the aforesaid motorcycle that was dangerously and carelessly manufactured, designed and assembled by defendant.

9. By reason of the foregoing, plaintiff suffered severe, personal, painful, and permanent injuries, internal as well as external.

10. Due to his injuries plaintiff has been and will be required to expend large sums of money for medical and hospital care; plaintiff has been and will be incapacitated from performing his usual duties for a long period of time, and will be incapable of fathering children for the rest of his life, all to plaintiff's damages in the sum of One Million Dollars.

Second Cause of Action

11. Plaintiff repeats with same force and effect paragraphs 1 through 9.

12. By reason of the above plaintiff has been and will be deprived of his wife's services, companionship, support and consortium for a long period of time, and will suffer the consequences of his sterility, resulting from his injuries, all to plaintiff's damages in the sum of One Million Dollars.

Third Cause of Action

13. Plaintiff repeats with the same force and effect paragraphs 1 through 9.

14. By reason of the above, defendant breached both express and implied

warranties extended to plaintiff including the warranty of merchantability and of fitness for particular purpose, in that defendant's product was not of the fair average quality and standard; these warranties were made in order to induce plaintiff to purchase the product of the defendant, and plaintiff relied on the warranties to his detriment.

15. By reason of defendant's breach of warranties which resulted in injury to the plaintiff, the plaintiff has been injured and damaged as set forth above, all to his damage in the sum of One Million Dollars.

Fourth Cause of Action

16. Plaintiff repeats with the same force and effect paragraphs 1 through 9.

17. The defendant is strictly liable in tort for plaintiff's injuries and damages because the defect was a substantial factor in bringing about the injuries and damages; the injured plaintiff could not by the exercise of reasonable care have discovered the defect in the product nor perceived of its danger.

18. The product was being used for the purpose for which it was intended at the time of the accident.

19. By reason of the above, plaintiff has been injured and damaged in the sum of One Million Dollars.

[Demand for relief, indorsement by attorney, and verification]

Section 6. Factors Favoring US Forum

The foreign plaintiff will choose a forum such as a US forum after he or she has fully assessed the probability of the court in the United States accepting jurisdiction. This pessimistic attitude is a pragmatic response, for the foreign plaintiff is of the belief that suit in the United States will be successful once the court has decided to accept jurisdiction and not dismiss the action under *forum non conveniens.*[28] Perhaps these very thoughts were in the mind of the Swedish citizen in Carlenstolpe *v.* Merck & Co, decided by the federal district court for the Southern District of New York on 12 August 1986. He allegedly suffered serious injury in the form of disabling arthritis after he received two doses of defendant's hepatitis vaccine in Sweden. Defendant moved to dismiss the suit on the ground that Sweden had the paramount interest in determining products liability for drugs sold in Sweden, although the drugs were manufactured in the United States. Judge Motley rejected defendant's argument, and ruled that 'where an allegedly defective drug has been developed, tested, and manufactured in the United States and is being distributed to and presumably used by American citizens, including citizens of the forum, the forum's interest in litigating the controversy is at least equal to that of the foreign citizen's home forum'. Indeed, the foreign plaintiff's suit in the United States 'challenges defendant's conduct in distributing the drug, both in Sweden and in America, allegedly without adequate testing and warning of its risks'.

On 7 July 1986 the US Supreme Court in Merrell Dow Pharmaceuticals Inc *v.* Thompson gave more hope to foreign plaintiffs that their product liability suits against US manufacturers will not be summarily dismissed on *forum non conveniens* grounds within the federal court system and that the litigation may ever remain within the state court system. Here, Canadian and Scottish plaintiffs sued in an Ohio state court the Ohio product manufacturer of 'Bendectin', a drug product ingested during pregnancy by mothers, which drug allegedly brought about multiple deformities in their children. Among the counts in negligence, breach of warranty, strict liability, fraud, and gross negligence was a count which alleged that the drug product was 'misbranded' under the Federal Food Drug and Cosmetic Act, as amended (21 USC 301 *et seq*). It was this innocent, additional count that the defendant product manufacturer seized upon and filed a timely motion for removal from the Ohio state court to the federal district court, upon the basis that a 'federal question' was involved. After removal the product manufacturer again moved successfully to dismiss upon *forum non conveniens* grounds. The Sixth US Court of Appeals, however, reversed (766 F2d 1005, 1985), holding that the cause of action under the FFDC Act did *not* create or imply a private cause of action, and therefore there was no 'federal question' involved which could serve as the basis for removal from the state to the federal court. But the court did retain jurisdiction.

The highest court, in affirming, agreed that no 'federal question' was involved, particularly where, as here, the court would not be doing justice to plaintiffs' choice of a state forum. Mr Justice Steven writing for the majority concluded that for the FFDC Act 'Congress did not intend a private federal remedy for violations of the statute that it enacted . . .

> 'Given the significance of the assumed congressional determination to preclude federal private remedies, the presence of the federal issue as an element of the state tort is not the kind of adjudication for which jurisdiction would serve congressional purposes and the federal system. This conclusion is fully consistent with the very sentence relied on so heavily by petitioner. We simply conclude that the congressional determination that there should be no federal remedy for the violation of this federal statute is tantamount to a congressional conclusion that the presence of a claimed violation of the statute as an element of a state cause of action is insufficiently "substantial" to confer federal-question jurisdiction.'

Accordingly, the product manufacturer should not have able to remove the Ohio state court action to the federal district court based upon the presence of a 'federal question'. Indeed, there was no claim asserted by the plaintiffs which arose 'under the Constitution, laws, or treaties of the United States' (28 USC 1331). The four dissenters (Justices Brennan, White, Marshall and Blackmun) seemed to believe that the foreign plaintiffs had put all their eggs in one basket, to wit: violation of FFDC Act was negligence *per se*, and was the proximate cause of plaintiffs' injuries. Therefore, the dissenters argued that there was federal jurisdiction:

> 'Both 28 USC 1331 and the enforcement provisions of the FDCA reflect Congress' strong desire to utilize the federal courts to interpret and enforce the FDCA, and it is therefore at odds with both these statutes to recognize a private state law remedy for violating the FDCA but to hold that this remedy cannot be adjudicated in the federal courts.'

Indeed, legal factors such as the required elements of proof, the substantive rules of liability, and the varied theories of recovery all play a role in this selection process of the foreign plaintiff, as does the likelihood of high awards or judgments. An international aircraft accident, for example, involving a US or even a foreign carrier doing business in the United States, will encourage the foreign plaintiff to sue in the United States not only because of the competence of US tribunals and other favorable factors but also because of the liberality of discovery rules.[29]

The amount of potential recovery in a US court is a special factor favoring the choice of US forums; the jury system and the recognition of numerous elements of damages produce awards for personal injury or death which are much higher than in any other national jurisdiction. Juries tend to be more emotional and sympathetic to an injured plaintiff than a judge or tribunal. Survival and wrongful death statutes in virtually all States recognize elements of damages far beyond those recognized in many foreign jurisdictions;[30] these elements include loss of future earnings, loss of society, loss of parental guidance, pain and suffering, and even fear of impending death.[31] Punitive damages are readily obtainable where the injury is willfully or wantonly inflicted.[32]

The discovery rules of both the federal and even many State courts are exceptionally liberal, and enable a foreign plaintiff to procure readily a broad array of information from defendants. On the other hand, England, for example, severely restricts pre-trial discovery, limiting discovery to documents only.[33] Virtually every signatory to The Hague Convention on the Taking of Evidence Abroad in Civil or Commercial Matters,[34] except the United States, has elected not to permit 'common law pre-trial discovery of documents'.[35]

The availability of contingency fees for attorneys representing foreign plaintiffs is also a factor favoring US forums. The financially weak plaintiff is given the means to pursue redress for injuries or damages sustained, even against the multinational corporate giant.[36] It is counsel for the foreign plaintiff who bears the financial risk, and earns his fee only if he wins, then taking generally one-third of the award for his legal services. The losing party is not generally required to pay his opponent's attorney fees nor costs of the action.

Undoubtedly, the availability of Strict Liability in Tort as a theory of liability makes the US forum especially attractive to the foreign plaintiff.[37] Section 402A of Restatement (Second) of Torts provides that 'One who sells any product in a defective condition unreasonably dangerous to the user or consumer or to his property is subject to liability for physical harm thereby caused to the ultimate user or consumer [even though] the seller has exercised all possible care in the preparation and sale of his product'. This doctrine of Strict Liability in Tort is respected in at least 44 of the 50 States.[38]

There are other innumerable factors why foreign plaintiffs bring their product liability suits into US courts such as the inadequacy of the foreign forum, the unavailability of local counsel at reasonable fees, and the reluctance of foreign courts to recognize liability based upon the use or misuse of a product. It is the foreign forum that in reality is more responsible for driving the foreign plaintiff into US courts than all the 'magnetism' of the American El Dorado. Justice denied in a foreign country means that foreign plaintiffs will seek relief in other courts including those in the United States.

Section 7. An Illustrated New York Decision

The New York Supreme Court, New York County, in Bewers *v.* American Home Products Corp.[39] expounded at great length in 1982 why a New York court should not dismiss a products liability suit by foreign plaintiffs against an American defendant corporation. Justice Taylor rested her decision on Justice, Fairness, and Convenience in supporting the right of three British wives (and their husbands) to sue for personal injuries allegedly attributed to their ingestion of prescribed oral contraceptive products manufactured and distributed in England by the American defendant. The gravamen of these three suits was not only the contention that these prescriptive drug products were sold in England without proper warnings, but that defendant was aware of the medically recognized risks from the ingestion of the oral contraceptives, and yet did not warn English users of the drug product. The American defendant argued that, since the injuries occurred in England and the oral contraceptive product had been manufactured and distributed by its English subsidiary, these suits must be litigated in England. Furthermore, the English subsidiary had tested and marketed the drug product in England, and not in the United States; therefore the US court should not entertain jurisdiction. At the outset of her opinion Justice Taylor stated:

> 'The doctrine of *forum non conveniens* allows local courts to dismiss cases in which both subject matter and personal jurisdiction technically exist, but which have so minimal a relationship with the forum state that the burden on the forum's judicial resources is not justified . . . The court's inquiry must evaluate both the private interests at stake—the parties' interest in litigating the matter conveniently and justly—and the public interests—the states' interest in conserving judicial resources, the burden of applying foreign law if applicable, and the policies relevant to the substantive issues raised in the law suit.'

Justice Taylor observed and found no difficulty with the fact that suits in the US by the three British plaintiffs 'may be a tactical decision designed in part to secure the procedural and substantive advantages of suing in the United States . . . There is nothing amiss with choosing one *bona fide* case among several possible ones with a view to securing the benefits of favorable laws.'[40] Indeed, 'forum-shopping' by either plaintiffs or defendants is not an evil especially since US law is more favorable to plaintiffs, and English law is more favorable to defendants where there is no Strict Liability in Tort doctrine to be applied against the product manufacturer.[41] Justice Taylor pointed out that the defendants seeking to move the case to English courts, 'do not maintain that they could have been sued in English courts', and therefore England was not an alternative forum, for the defendants might not be suable in England, and plaintiffs would be left without a remedy. Furthermore, 'a transfer of this case to England would result in a forfeiture of plaintiffs' strongest cause of action, i.e., its strict products liability claims . . . Plaintiffs are understandably troubled by the fact that, if relegated to suing in Great Britain, they will be denied a trial by jury, pre-trial discovery will be severely curtailed, the possibility of recovering punitive damages will be diminished, and the contingency fee representation by counsel will not be permitted'. Therefore, declared the New York court, 'from a procedural point of view, Britain is not an adequate alternative forum for the plaintiffs in this case'.[42]

The burden of proof, according to the New York court, was upon the defendants 'clearly (to) establish that New York is an inconvenient forum and that another forum is available which will best serve the ends of Justice, Fairness and Convenience of the parties: 'A forum is not necessarily inconvenient because of its distance from pertinent parties or places if it is readily accessible in a few hours of air travel. It will be often quicker and less expensive to transfer a witness than to transfer a law suit.'[43] Justice Taylor further supported her thesis that New York and not English courts were entitled to jurisdiction by her statement that the alleged 'tortious conduct' derived from defendants' efforts to 'dump unsafe products'[44] onto a specific foreign market and further to do so without warning of the disproportionate dangers of using them as birth control pills . . . The instant cases do not arise out of an accident which can happen as readily in one place as another. The tortious acts here alleged involve calculation and decision, that is, intentional and deliberate conduct. This conduct, the making of defendants' relevant corporate decisions, is claimed, without contradiction, to have occurred not in England but in New York. In short, the nexus between these cases and New York is not merely that defendant corporations as legal entities are amenable to process in New York but rather their officials and employees, costs and benefits, weighed alternatives and made decisions here. It is those decisions and the actions taken in New York to implement them that are the subject matter of these suits.'[45]

Justice Taylor of the New York Supreme Court, New York County, urged that 'serious consideration' be given to 'the substance and theories' of 'the proposal of the United States to The Hague Conference of 1972 with regard to choice of law rules for products liability cases', to wit:

> 'The plaintiff should be given the choice of any one of these laws or forums; the law or forum of the state of injury, the law or forum of the state where the plaintiff acquired the product, the law or forum of the state of manufacture, or the law or forum of the state of defendants' main office or principal place of business; provided that in the case of

> the state of injury or of acquisition, the defendant could reasonably foresee that the particular product, or products of similar type which it decided to manufacture or sell, would come into the state through commercial channels. An injured person should be able to sue the primary tortfeasor—the decision-maker—on its home-turf. The Federal Tort Claims Act, 28 USC Sec. 2672, for example, applies the law of the place where the tortious act or omission occurred, not the place of injury. These rules would merely allow an injured person to test before a judge or a jury whether, under all the circumstances, the company's behavior relating to the distribution of the alleged defective product was reasonable or unreasonable. By allowing plaintiffs to choose, *inter alia*, the law of a defendant's state, these rules would significantly increase the uniformity of result among cases brought by plaintiffs who have been injured in different states by the same product of the same supplier, as well as among cases where the products of suppliers from the same state cause injury in two or more different states. Predictability of result would be enhanced, as would be the possibility of reasonable insurance by suppliers. These rules would be fair to plaintiffs since plaintiffs would have a choice, though limited, of forum and law. They would be fair to defendants because plaintiffs' choices would be rigorously circumscribed by defendants' prior operating and marketing choices. By the time plaintiffs have the unenviable occasion to choose which forum and law should apply, defendants have long since chosen where to operate and where to market their goods. Thus, applying the proposed choice of law solution would not only be fair to plaintiffs and defendants, but would also be in line with the trend of products liability legislation and case law in the great majority of countries.'[46]

The English interest in protecting the English subsidiary of the American parent company must fall aside, the court declared, because 'individuals have certain rights which are superior to and transcend a government policy of encouraging local industries . . . The least they should be permitted to do is to sue in forums which will apply laws more favorable to their claims if such forums have some relation to the dispute.'[47] Accordingly, 'it is settled law that so long as a case has a substantial nexus with the forum state, plaintiffs' choice of forum should not be disturbed unless the balance of convenience is strongly in favor of defendants . . . The balance of private convenience favors plaintiffs' choice of forum. In addition, the nexus to New York is plain and substantial, and the availability of an alternative forum is uncertain.'[48]

The brilliant analysis of Justice Taylor was, however, on 5 March 1984, overturned and reversed by the New York Appellate Division, First Dept.[49] The appellate court ruled that New York was not the proper forum to litigate the claims for personal injuries suffered by the three English plaintiffs from the use of oral conceptive products manufactured and marketed by the British subsidiary of the American pharmaceutical parent company: 'It seems quite clear that the

United Kingdom would have a greater interest in determining whether pharmaceuticals which were licensed, manufactured, marketed and distributed therein, were appropriately tested and labeled in that country . . . Nor do we perceive any unfairness to the plaintiffs in requiring that they prosecute those actions in the United Kingdom. Indeed, it clearly appears that all of the facts and circumstances surrounding these law suits, except for the alleged decision by the defendants, allegedly made in New York, to market the drugs in the United Kingdom without adequate warnings respecting known dangerous side effects, occurred in the United Kingdom.'[50] What is most surprising about the 1984 reversal by the New York appellate court is how crystal-clear the facts of manufacturing, distribution, testing, and marketing the prescriptive drug product appeared to the appellate court that rendered its determination solely upon a record, written and detailed by the parties. The prime decision to market the drug product without adequate labeling was made not in England but in New York, a 'fact' noted by the appellate courts as 'alleged' despite clear testimony at the trial level. Indeed, the New York appellat court was merely following a precedent recently established by neighboring state courts in Pennsylvania, New Jersey, Illinois and even California, to keep foreign plaintiffs out of US courts[51] on the parochial grounds of '*forum non conveniens* doctrine and principles of international comity'.[52] It is ironic that 'international comity' should be invoked in the same context with the isolationist viewpoint that jurisdiction should be denied where foreign plaintiffs seek to have their cases heard in a forum of their choice. Justice, Fairness and Convenience, as delineated by Justice Taylor, have been swept aside as the case is transfered to English courts with the following probabilities:

a. the subsidiary of the American product manufacturer will not be held liable or accountable to US government agencies which approved and regulated the prescriptive drug product from its very beginning; nor will the English subsidiary be required to explain its behavior in marketing the unlabeled drug product to the Food and Drug Administration in Washington, DC;[53]
b. if the English court does not apply US law (and there is every likelihood that the court will apply English substantive and procedural law) the defendant American parent company will circumvent liability for in England there is no Strict Liability doctrine, no pre-trial discovery, no jury trial, no contingent fee system for plaintiffs' attorneys, and no punitive damages;
c. the *forum non conveniens* doctrine will be a lame excuse for an American defendant to avoid liability, although the thrust of that doctrine was fundamentally to give the defendant 'home turf' in the very first instance;
d. defendants may, in fact, not waive the statute of limitations defense, as required by the New York appellate court, and hence defy the New York judiciary;[54]
e. the law of the place of the tort, or *lex loci delicti*, will not be applied, for the tort, being the deliberate decision to market the unlabeled product in England, was actually made in New York and US law should be applicable, not the law of England;[55]
f. there will be uncertainty and nonconformity of decisions with respect to the

particular drug product, depending upon the results of applying varying foreign laws in subsequent cases which will be tried in various foreign jurisdictions;

g. there is little nexus with England other than the English plaintiffs who had actually preferred to sue in the United States until frustrated by the New York appellate court; and
h. plaintiffs simply may not have the front money to litigate in England where contingency attorneys' fees are non-existent, and hence the plaintiffs may be deprived of their day in court.

It should be noted, however, that the 1984 ruling by the New York appellate court required the defendants, within 90 days of the service of the order, to agree in writing:

> '1. to waive objection to suit being brought in the United Kingdom for the relief sought in the complaints herein and to waive objection to the jurisdiction of the courts of the United Kingdom in this matter;
> 2. to accept the service of process in the United Kingdom;
> 3. to waive objection to compulsory process requiring the appearance of witnesses and production of documents and to make the same available at their own expense;
> 4. to consent to full faith and credit of any judgment obtained against them in the United Kingdom and to consent to pay the same; and
> 5. to waive any defence of limitations of time, whether statutory or otherwise, provided, however, that the suit in the United Kingdom be commenced within 90 days from the date of service of the defendants' stipulation upon counsel for the plaintiffs'. The ruling concluded: 'In the event of defendants' failure to comply with the foregoing conditions, the order of Supreme Court is affirmed without costs'.

This disturbing decision of the New York appellate court was on 23 July 1984 affirmed by the highest court in the state of New York, as the New York Court of Appeals simply dismissed the appeal pursuant to the Rules of Practice of the Court of Appeals.[56] The irony is that the United States, having rejected The Hague Convention on the Law Applicable to Products Liability (1973),[57] had reserved the discretionary right to afford foreign plaintiffs the benefits of US law when the foreign plaintiffs sue American product manufacturers in US courts for injuries sustained in a foreign country. A possible political reason behind the transfer of such a case back to the home court of the foreign plaintiffs here is the United Kingdom Protection of Trading Interests Act (1980).[58] This vindictive piece of Parliament legislation was probably motivated by what England saw as American interference with English jurisdictional prerogatives. Section 1 of the Act forbids compliance by English citizens and English businesses with orders of foreign judicial authorities that have extraterritorial effect and are prejudicial to English trading interests. Section 5 of the Act prohibits enforcement by courts in the United Kingdom of foreign judgments awarding multiple damages and certain other type judgments touching upon the control of restrictive practices. And Section of the Act establishes the right of English citizens and the English businesses against whom foreign courts have awarded multiple damages to recover in English courts the noncompensatory portion of damages from the original plaintiff who sued the English citizen or the English business in the foreign court. The United Kingdom Protection of Trading Interests Act (1980)[59] has made US courts hypersensitive to all foreign plaintiffs and their interests, as demonstrated historically by Timberland Lumber Co *v.* Bank of America[60] and by Mannington Mills, Inc *v.* Congoleum Corp,[61] where both federal appeals courts adopted the position that US courts should decline to exercise jurisdiction where the vital national interests of foreign states outweigh the interests of the United States.[62]

In passing, it might be prudent to note that the State of New York has hardly been receptive to the foreign plaintiff, probably due in part to the crowded court dockets and the reluctance of the New York judiciary to decide questions of foreign law, unless necessary. On 7 May 1987 the same New York appellate court, as in the Bewers case declared: 'We do not reach the merits of the decision below, but dismiss the complaint *sua sponte*, on the ground of foreign conveniens. Apart from the fact that appellant is a domestic corporation, the transaction at issue has no other substantial tie to this state which would warrant adjudication in New York's courts. The doctrine of *forum non conveniens* exists for the convenience of both the parties and the court. It is a flexible doctrine which requires the court, in the exercise of its discretion, to determine whether it should retain jurisdiction. Where, as here, an action which has only minimal contact with the state is instituted in New York, the court is not obliged to await the motion of counsel but may invoke the doctrine *sua sponte*'[62.1] (i.e., of its own accord).

Section 8. The Multinational Corporation

A creature of the present international economic system is the multinational corporation, or MNC, which is a business enterprise employed in the movement internationally of products, information, people, and/or services of every kind.[63] There are perhaps a thousand or more MNCs operating today across national borders with annual sales far in excess of billions of dollars and with currency reserves at their disposal in excess of the currency reserves of many countries. MNCs are generally secretive about organizational structure, finances and policy formation, and are frequently insensitive to the needs of governments and of consumers. Many MNCs dump unsafe products in foreign markets and commit toxic torts and cause hazardous waste. Efforts at meaningful regulation by governments have been unsuccessful as have foreign plaintiffs in their efforts to sue MNCs in US courts.[64]

A typical MNC may do business internationally through such complex business forms as subsidiaries, branches, licensees, franchisees, joint-ventures, and the like. Complete control, horizontally and vertically, is considered the *summum bonum* by these global entities which often utilize both private and public funds to dominate an industry or even control a country. The MNC is regarded by some economists as the next great step beyond the national state in the human societal revolution.[65]

Jurisdiction over MNCs frequently runs afoul of the territorial principle of a state's jurisdiction under international law, so that the MNC, a target defendant usually, is frequently non-responsive to a state's jurisdiction.[66] Both the United Nations and the International Labour Organisation in 1973 recognized the problem: 'The multinational corporation, by definition, is established and has activities in more than one state. If a strict territorial approach is adopted, each state may regulate only those activities within its borders. Such an approach would have serious effects. It might make it impossible for the corporation to do business by subjecting it to contradictory or confusing legal regimes, or, on the other hand, it might allow the corporation to escape liability for conduct whose components are legal in each of the states in which they take place but which, taken as a whole, is illegal under the laws of some or all of the states concerned . . .'[67]

One solution to the problem of jurisdiction over the MNC is that the state where the adverse effects or results are experienced, is entitled to jurisdiction over the subsidiaries or branches or licensees or franchisees of the MNC located in that state.[68] Foreign plaintiffs would be relieved of the jurisdictional problem in suing the MNC within the US courts. Section 418(1) of Restatement (Second) of the Foreign Relations Law of the United States declares that 'the United States has jurisdiction to apply its law to foreign branches of corporations organized under the laws of the United States',[69] but that declaration does not necessarily solve the jurisdictional problem of the MNC organized under the laws of a foreign country. However, Section 418(2) amplifies that jurisdiction to include 'corporations (or similar juridical entities) organized under the laws of a foreign state that are substantially owned or controlled by nationals of the United States (including corporations organized under the laws of the United States)'.[70] Under Section 402(2) of the same Restatement US law is applicable to subsidiaries of US corporations under the principle of nationality. But it remains to be seen what controls or regulations over MNCs will, in fact, be exercised by the United States, particularly MNC defenses in the products liability situation.[71]

Interestingly, the notewriter in 37 Stanford Law Review 155 (1984) points out that the rise of multinational business transactions and the concomitant growth in transnational litigation have created opportunities for parties to bring suit on the same issue in more than one country. As a result the unhappy party may move for an injunction against the prosecution of litigation in the forum that he finds inconvenient. An international anti-suit injunction prohibits a party from proceeding with his suit in a foreign forum that has concurrent jurisdiction over the case. An international jurisdiction-protecting injunction, on the other hand, does not bar a party from litigating a parallel suit; it simply protects a court's jurisdiction against a foreign action designed not to reach a judgment on the merits but only to halt proceedings before the enjoining court. The notewriter believes that courts in the United States too frequently enjoin foreign proceedings, and recommends that the US court before issuing its injunction makes certain that *forum non conveniens* defense will not apply and that the foreign court has had an opportunity to dismiss or stay the case on similar grounds.

Section 9. Alienage Jurisdiction of US Courts

Traditionally the alien, the foreigner, and the stranger in our midst have been welcome to seek redress for grievances in the courts of the United States.[72] Under Article III, Section 2, of the US Constitution, 'the judicial power shall extend . . . to Controversies . . . between a State, or the Citizens thereof . . . and foreign States, Citizens, or Subjects'.[73] Allowing aliens or foreign plaintiffs to enjoy access to the federal courts was, however, encumbered over the years, despite the mandate expressed in the US Constitution and in 28 USC 1332 (a)(2) and (3) to the effect that the federal courts shall have jurisdiction over actions between citizens of the US and citizens or subjects of a foreign state, or actions in which citizens or subjects of a foreign state are additional parties.[74] Indeed, under 28 USC 1331 federal courts are given 'original jurisdiction of all civil actions arising under the Constitution, laws or treaties of the United States'.[75]

Fundamentally there are several reasons for such accessibility of aliens to US federal courts, to wit: aliens from states that are friendly to the forum state are accorded the rights and privileges of suit (and the hazard of being sued); and such aliens with such rights and corresponding duties are more readily assimilated as citizens or residents of the forum state.[76] The Civil Rights Act of 1870 prohibited the several states from denying to 'any person' (which would include aliens or foreign plaintiffs) within their jurisdiction due process and equal protection of the laws.[77] Non-resident aliens under Lord Campbell's Act, adopted in New York[78] and most states, are entitled to maintain wrongful death actions in New York and those states. In 1949 the New York Court of Appeals ruled that New York courts are bound to try an action for a foreign tort when either the plaintiff or the defendant is a resident of the state of New York.[79] In the federal courts the foreign plaintiff or alien may sue the US citizen or corporation only in the district in which that defendant resides or has its principal office or is doing business in that particular district.[80]

The US Government has entered into international agreements, conventions, and treaties with friendly nations and with the United Nations,[81] authorizing equal access of foreign plaintiffs and aliens to domestic US courts but with certain restrictions.[82]

A foreign plaintiff or alien is a citizen or subject of a foreign state, as defined by the law of that foreign state and by the recognition given the alien or foreign plaintiff by that foreign state.[83] A foreign state is defined as a political entity recognized by other states as a sovereign and independent state.[84] A stateless person, for example, cannot sue under the alienage jurisdiction of the US federal courts.[85] A foreign corporation is a citizen of that foreign state of incorporation as are its stockholders,[86] although since 1958 the foreign corporation can also be a citizen of the state 'where it has its principal place of business'.[87] But in Eisenberg *v.* Commercial Union Assurance Co.[88] the foreign corporation was deemed only a citizen of the country in which it was incorporated.

In 1976 in the Foreign Sovereign Immunities Act [89] the US Congress established a procedure for actions by or against foreign states, and removed foreign states from the general alienage statutes.[90] Congress changed the language of the statute so as to provide the jurisdiction only when 'citizens or subjects of a foreign state' are parties to the suit; but this language change does not defeat jurisdiction even when aliens from different foreign states are on the same side of the litigation, provided that a US citizen or US corporation is on the other side of the litigation. Where aliens are on both sides of the litigation, even without the presence of a US citizen or corporation, the federal courts may retain jurisdiction.[91] As a general rule, unrecognized foreign governments and their instrumentalities, citizens, and subjects are not granted access to US courts.[92]

Notes

1. *See* W. Freedman, International Products Liability, 2 vol., Kluwer 1987. *Also see* Gibson, 'Products Liability in the United States and England: The Difference and Why.' 3 Anglo-Am L Rev 493 (1974); Kennelly, 'Transitory Tort Litigation—The Need for Uniform Rules Pertaining to In Personam Jurisdiction, *Forum Non Conveniens*, Choice of Law, and Comparative Negligence', 22 Trial Law Guide 422 (1979); Park, 'International Products Liability Litigation': Choosing the Applicable Law, 12 Int Law 845 (1978); and Reese, 'American Trends in Private International Law: Academic and Judicial Manipulation of Choice of Law Rules in Tort Cases', 33 Van L Rev 717 (1980).
2. *See* Lamb *v.* Volkswagenwerk A.G., 104 FRD 95 (SD Fla., 1986) where service on a foreign corporation was effected by serving its American subsidiary since the foreign corporation exerted sufficient control over the subsidiary. The court rejected the argument that service could only be made under The Hague Convention on International Service (20 UST 361, TIAS No. 6638), holding that the Convention provisions were only applicable to service abroad, not to service on a foreign subsidiary within the United States.
3. The contingency fee system is an arrangement between an attorney and client in which the payment for attorney services is based upon the condition precedent of his success in litigation or settlement. The system, it is said, promotes litigation, is a form of speculation undignified to the legal profession, and is close to one of the common law crimes of champerty or maintenance. But the contingency fee system, it was argued, was 'the poor man's key to the court house', and the US Supreme Court in 1853 upheld its validity in Wylie *v.* Coxe, 56 US 415 (1853). The Code of Professional Responsibility, which governs the conduct of attorneys in the United States, provides in Ethical Consideration 2–20 the following:

'Contingent fee arrangements in civil cases have long been commonly accepted in the United States in proceedings to enforce claims . . .

'Although a lawyer generally should decline to accept employment on a contingent fee basis by one who is able to pay a reasonable fee, it is not necessarily improper for a lawyer, where justified by particular circumstances of a case to enter into a contingent fee contract in a civil case with any client who, after being fully informed of all relevant factors, desires that arrangement.'

Disciplinary Rule 5-103, which is entitled Avoiding Acquisition of Interest in Litigation, provides the following:

'(A) . . .A lawyer should not acquire proprietary interest in the cause of action or the subject matter of litigation he is conducting for a client except that he may:
(1) . . .
(2) contract with a client for a reasonable contingent fee in a civil case.'

The contingent fee is subject to court supervision in most jurisdictions of the United States.

4. Piper Aircraft Co *v*. Reyno, 102 S Ct 252 (1981).
5. 16 Av CAS (CCH) 17,651, Conn Super (1981).
6. 637 F2d 775 (DC Cir., 1980).
7. 28 USC 1346(b), *See* Chapter 3, Section 3, herein.
8. *See* Gannon *v*. Payne, decided by the Texas Supreme Court on 12 March 1986. Under the principle of judicial comity, a single parallel proceeding filed in a party's home country, cannot justify issuing an anti-suit injunction.
9. H.R. Rep No. 893. 95th Sess. 708 note 25 (1978).
9.1. *See* Trial Magazine (Oct. 1986) at pp. 63–66.
9.2. *Id*. at p. 64.
10. 20 UST 361, TIAS No. 6638, effective 20 February 1969.
11. *Id*.
12. Article 5 thereof.
13. Article 5(b) thereof.
14. *See* Tamari *v*. Bache & Co (Lebanon) SA, 431 F Supp 1226 (Ill, 1977), aff 565 F2d 1194 (7th Cir, 1977), cert den 435 US. 905 (1978).
15. Note Rule 28(b) of FRCP.
16. 23 UST 2555, TIAS No 7444, effective in 1970.
17. Article 10 thereof.
18. Article 9 thereof.
19. *See* Schroeder *v*. Lufthansa German Airlines,—F Supp—18 Av CAS (CCH) 17, 222 (Ill, 1983).
20. *See* Lasky *v*. Continental Products Corp, 569 F Supp 1227 (Pa, 1983).
21. *Supra* note 16.
22. 33 Cal App3d 503 (1973).
23. 137 Cal App3d 238 (1981).
24. The FCN treaty with Belgium is 14 UST 1284, TIAS No. 5432, and is dated 21 December 1961. The FCN treaty with West Germany is 7 UST 1839, TIAS No. 3593, and is dated 14 July 1956. Between 1946 and 1953 the United States concluded similar

bilateral treaties with Italy, Ireland, Uruguay, Colombia, Greece, Israel, Ethiopia, and Denmark, *inter alia.*

25. 588 F2d 880 (2nd Cir., 1978).
26. GAO Res 217, UN Doc A/810.
27. Professor Moore in his 'International Law Digest' (Section 536) in 1906 has observed: 'The policy of the United States in all cases of complaints made by foreigners is to extend to them the same means of redress as is enjoyed by our own citizens'. Indeed, resident aliens are entitled to protection under the Fourteenth Amendment. (Graham *v.* Richardson, 403 US 365, 1971).
28. *See* Chapter 4 herein.
29. *See* 7 Boston College Internat & Comp L Rev at pp. 38 *et sq* (1984).
30. *See*, for example, NJ Stat Ann 2A:31–1 (1952).
31. *See* Hemmelgarn *v.* Boeing Co., 106 Cal App3d 586 (1980).
32. *See* In Re Air Crash Disaster Near Chicago, 644 F2d 594 (7th Cir., 1980), cert den 454 US 878 (1981).
33. *See* Aboujdid *v.* Gulf Aviation Co., 437 NYS2d 219 (1980).
34. 23 UST 2555, TIAS No. 7444, effective 1970.
35. *See* Note 16 Internat Lawyer 575 (1982) at p. 579.
36. For example, *see* Fiorenza *v.* US Steel Corp., 311 F Supp 117 (SDNY, 1969).
37. *See* W. Freedman, Strict Liability (Hanrow Press, 1986).
38. *See* Prosser On Torts (4th edn., 1971) at pp. 657–658.
39. 459 NYS2d 666 (1982).
40. *Id.*
41. *See* Donaghue *v.* Stevenson, (1932) AC 562; and Daniels *v.* White & Sons & Tarford, (1938) 4 All ER 258.
42. Note that the English 3-year statute of limitations might also bar the suit, although the court could condition the transfer of the case to English courts upon a waiver by defendants of the statute of limitations.
43. 'In sum, it appears that the larger number of witnesses is in New York, not in England, and that the vastly larger part of exceedingly bulky documentary evidence is also to be found in New York or within a 100-mile radius of New York. Defendants have failed to show that it would be more onerous for them to defend these cases in New York than in England. *A fortiori*, they have failed to show that they would be more inconvenienced by trial in New York than plaintiffs would be by trial in England.'
44. Note footnote 24 of the opinion which points out that

    > 'the marketing abroad by American pharmaceutical companies of alleged unreasonably dangerous drugs has increasingly become a matter of public controversy and concern. In some cases companies market the drugs directly; in other instances, through wholly-owned subsidiaries. It is claimed that these sales account for a large part of such companies' profits. Suits arising from these activities are bound to proliferate and New York courts must develop fair, principled and predictable ways of handling them.'

45. The Court then answered the argument that

    > 'in view of Britain's pervasive drug regulatory scheme, it would be presumptuous of the United States to apply its law to a case where the injuries took place in Britain and the manufacture, sale and distribution of the drugs also took place in Britain'

to wit:

> 'The courts have failed to develop reliable standards by which to balance the conflicting private and public interests so as to ensure reasoned and predictable *forum non conveniens* decisions.'

And,

> 'The problems of unsettled standards is especially acute in international products liability cases in which various policy considerations and the lack of uniform tort laws complicate the application of normal *forum non conveniens* rules. Actions brought by foreign plaintiffs for injuries incurred abroad necessarily involve courts in complex choice of law determinations. There are no uniform standards for determining which law will apply . . .'

Furthermore,

> 'it would seem unwise to base choice-of-law and *forum non conveniens* decisions on the nebulous standard of the extent of the pervasiveness of a particular government's regulatory policies. Such a standard would re-institute in a different form, all the chaos presently existing in determining competing 'governmental interests'. Courts should not be required to speculate on just how pervasive a foreign government's regulatory scheme must be to trigger presumptiousness on the part of New York courts . . . Further, there is no convincing or reliable evidence that Britain would consider a holding that AHP was subject to suit in New York under New York's strict product liability doctrine an improper interference with its drug regulation scheme. This argument is based on nothing more concrete than conjecture by the defendants and various courts as to what they think they were presented with the problem. For the purposes of these motions, the court assumes compliance with English drug statutes (excepting, of course, plaintiffs' allegations of fraud). But compliance with minimum government requirements, even our own state government's, does not necessarily constitute compliance with the duty of care owing to consumers . . .'

Justice Taylor rejected the rule of *lex loci delecti* in tort cases;

> 'If there is one consistent thread throughout all conflicts chaos and confusion, it is the almost unanimous opinion of courts and scholars that a rigid application of the *lex loci* rule was in the past, is now and would be in the future, unsound, unfair and unjust, particularly in the new world of extensive multinational travel and trading. The very reason for the conflicts chaos in tort law was the strong feeling of the courts that strict adherence to the traditional conflicts rule of *lex loci delecti* in tort cases

46. *Id.*
47. The New York court summarized:

> 'In adopting the doctrine of strict products' liability New York has committed itself to a policy of holding local industries accountable for their

unconscionable decisions to profit from products that create unreasonable risks to the health of consumers anywhere. That commitment should not end at the state's geographical boundaries. The realities of modern technology, travel and communication are such that a business with international operations could make a mockery of a strict products liability doctrine confined to territorial effect. This court should not permit a local corporation to circumvent and flount the law and social policy of this state for its own economic benefit by deflecting onto a foreign subsidiary all liability for the decisions and products funneled through that subsidiary but conceived at home. *It is alleged that the defendants deliberately chose to find a foreign market for these drugs after the Food and Drug Administration regulations precluded its distribution at home.* The United States and the State of New York clearly have an interest in deterring such alleged unconscionable business decisions on the part of its corporate residents. Organizations may choose New York as the focus of their activities for a variety of financial, political, social or legal considerations, among others. Once these organizations choose to operate within New York's borders, and their activities in New York give rise to legal obligations, New York has a continuing strong interest in the regulation of their activities. There would be little question, for example, of the legitimacy of New York's interest in regulating physical acts of a tortious nature by such organizations—even where the consequences of such tortious acts are felt outside the state. When decisions of a tortious nature to act—or to refrain from acting—are formulated in New York, this state's interest in the regulation of these decisions is equally legitimate.'

48. *See* footnote 5 of the court opinion to the effect that 'English case law suggests that plaintiffs would not have been permitted to serve these American defendants. English courts may grant leave for service outside their jurisdiction only where the tort is alleged to have been committed within their jurisdiction.'

    See Temple by Romano *v.* Temple, 468 NYS2d 389 (AD2, 1983) which held that once a substantial nexus has been found with the forum state, plaintiff's choice of forum will not be disturbed unless the balance of convenience is strongly in favor of the defendants'.
49. 472 NYS2d 637 (1984).
50. According to the appellate court,

    'Such a determination should be made pursuant to that country's own regulatory scheme and in accordance with its laws . . . It would, in the circumstances (of these cases) constitute as unnecessary burden on our courts to be compelled to apply foreign law, as the case demands in our courts. (Crown Cork & Seal Co, Inc, *v.* Rheem Manufacturing Co, Inc, *et al.*, 64 AD2d 545).'

51. 'The vast majority of witnesses and documentation regarding the testing, labelling and marketing of these drugs in the United Kingdom are in England, as well as the witnesses and documentary evidence respecting the medical treatment of plaintiffs. Thus not only would continued prosecution of these cases here unduly burden our courts, it would not serve the convenience of the parties. (Silver *v.* Great American Insurance Co., 29 NY2d 356).'
52. 'Although not in any way critical to our decision, we note that cases brought in the

Federal courts in New York and Pennsylvania and in the state courts of Pennsylvania, New Jersey, Illinois and California, by similarly situated plaintiffs were also dismissed by those courts pursuant to the *forum non conveniens* doctrine and principles of international comity. (*See* e.g. Purser *v.* American Home Products Corp., 80 Civ No 710 (SDNY 30 Jan. 1981) (Cannella J.]; Harrison *v.* Wyeth Laboratories, 510 F Supp 1 (ED Pa 1980), aff'd mem., 676 F2d 685 (3d Cir 1982); Jones *v.* Searle Laboratories, No 79-L 13115 (Ill. Cir Ct Cook County 30 May 1980), aff'd 93 Ill2d 366, 444 NE157 (1982); Holmes *v.* Syntex Laboratories, Inc, No. 425268 (Cal. Super. Ct. 15 July 1982); In Re British Oral Contraceptive Cases, No. L-44473-78 (NJ Super Ct. Morris County 20 July 1982), aff'd No. A-348-81T3 (NJ App Div 23 Dec 1982). cert den, No. C-459 (NJ 21 April 1983).'

53. In Dahl *v.* United Technologies Corp, 632 F2d 1027, United States Third Circuit Court of Appeals on 7 August 1980 affirmed a dismissal under the doctrine of *Forum Non Conveniens* of a suit by Norwegian plaintiffs against an American manufacturer of a helicopter which crashed off the coast of Norway. The Court ruled that both private and public interest militated in favor of jurisdiction by a Norwegian court, to wit: witnesses and materials, were available in Norway; the Norwegian plaintiffs had no contact with American law, and it was therefore more appropriate to apply Norwegian law; and Norway's interest in helicopter accidents occurring over its territorial waters should be superior to the American interest therein. It should be noted that the State of Delaware in which this federal action was brought had no contact with the defendant except as its state of incorporation. (In addition to considering public interest factors, the court in Dahl identified and discussed the following private interest factors, to wit: no evidence was located in Delaware; the defendant agreed to make witnesses and documents under its control available in Norway; the defendant's last contact with the product was 7 years prior to the crash; site of the crash was located off the Norwegian coast; defendant was unable to implead the Norwegian helicopter owner-operator in an American court; and defendant accepted the burden of translating documents. The Court concluded that the private interests indicated that Norway was the most appropriate forum. Indeed, Delaware's interest in the outcome of the litigation was relatively slight, and thus the decision correctly rejected the notion that foreign citizenship presupposes a presumption against foreign litigants in American courts. *See* Danser *v.* Firestone Tire & Rubber Co, 86 FRD 120, 123 (SDNY, 1980): here New York's interest in regulating the manufacture of tires within its borders did not outweigh the Netherland's interest in products used by its citizens within its borders.
54. *See* In Re Air Crash Disaster Near Bombay, India, on 1 January 1978, 531 F Supp 1175 (1982).
55. *See* Reese, Further Comments on the Hague Convention on the Law Applicable to Products Liability, 8 Ga J Int'l & Comp L 331, 312 (1978). Applying New York's law to test defendants' liability is consistent with well-established choice of law principles. For example, when the law of the State in which an act or omission occurs selects an admonitory policy, the defendant will be held liable if that act causes harm in another State. When a plaintiff from a nonrecovery State is involved in an accident with a defendant from a recovery State, recovery will generally be allowed irrespective of where the accident occurs. Sedler, Rules of Law Versus Choice of Law Rules: Judicial Method in Conflicts Tort Cases. 44 Tenn L Rev 975 1038 (1977).
56. 63 NY2d 677 (1984).
57. 15 UST 2228, TIAS No. 5710.
58. 1980 Parliament.

59. *Id.*
60. 549 F2d 597, on remand 574 f Supp 1453, aff 749 F2d 1378 (1979).
61. 595 F2d 1287 (3rd Cir, 1979).
62. However, when an American defendant can show that the foreign plaintiff's home country pervasively regulates the product in question, the foreign government's interest in conducting litigation in its own courts may override the interest of a different American regulatory scheme. In Harrison *v.* Wyeth Laboratories, 510 F Supp 1, the United States District Court for the Eastern District of Pennsylvania in 1980 dismissed a suit brought by British plaintiffs against the American pharmaceutical manufacturer of oral contraceptives. This drug product was manufactured, packaged and labelled in England by a wholly owned subsidiary of the American company. The subsidiary had obtained product licenses for the drugs under the laws of the United Kingdom, and make marketing, packaging, and labelling decisions in light of prevailing British regulation and law. The drugs were prescribed, purchased, and ingested in the United Kingdom, the country in which all of the alleged injuries occurred. These substantial contacts with the United Kingdom led the Harrison court to conclude that, under Pennsylvania choice of law rules, British law should prevail. Citing the Medicines Acts of 1968 and 1971, the defendants had argued that the British government pervasively regulates the licensing, manufacture, and distribution of all pharmaceuticals in the United Kingdom. The Harrison court agreed, stating that the United States should not impose its own standards of safety, warning, and duty of care upon a foreign country. In addition, the Court stated that Pennsylvania's interest in regulating the conduct of its resident drug manufacturers does not extend to the regulation of their conduct in foreign countries. Similarly, Pennsylvania's interest in the safety of drugs produced and distributed within its borders does not encompass drugs manufactured and distributed in foreign countries. Because production, distribution, and consumption of the pharmaceuticals at issue were subject to the regulatory scheme of Great Britain and not that of Pennsylvania, the Court concluded that it would be inappropriate to apply Pennsylvania law. Thus, the heavier weight accorded the regulatory interests of the foreign forum tipped the *Forum Non Conveniens* balance toward dismissal, and spared the American court the possibility of indirectly calling into question the adequacy of foreign regulatory mechanism. Considerations of Comity also support the Harrison decision to dismiss the complaint.

    Of course, here there was an absence of legitimate US interest for the defendant was an independent American subsidiary. When the defendant can show that the foreign subsidiary acts independently in manufacturing, marketing, packaging, and distributing a product, or controls a major portion of the production process, policy dictates that the *Forum Non Conveniens* inquiry should focus upon the subsidiary rather than the parent company. But if a foreign subsidiary merely distributes products that the parent company manufactured, tested, and labeled in the United States, the parent company would have maintained primary control over and responsibility for the product. In that case evidence relating to production and even decision-making presumably would be located in the United States, and *Forum Non Conveniens* dismissal would not be justified. The Harrison case illustrates the interplay that exists between the presence of pervasive foreign regulations and the operational independence of foreign subsidiaries. Although the subsidiary in Harrison manufactured, packaged and labeled the oral contraceptives in England, the plaintiffs argued that the fundamental manufacturing and marketing decisions made by the parent company in the United States constituted the primary tortious acts. But the Court held that the defendant's most significant activities occurred abroad, and therefore a foreign court applying foreign standards should evaluate defendant's actions.

62.1 VSL Corporation *v.* Dunes Hotel and Casino, Inc, —NYS2d— (1987).

63. *See* generally Wilson, International Business Transaction in a Nutshell (1984), Introduction.

64. The UN Economic and Social Council is working on a set of minimum guide-lines for consumer protection. The UN Commission on Transnational Corporations has assigned top priority to drafting a code of conduct for the MNC. The UN Conference on Trade and Development (UNCTAD) is preparing a code of conduct for the transfer of technology.

65. *See* Sweeney, Oliver & Leech, The International Legal System (1980), pp. 1180–1194. It is argued that the MNC raises the standard of living in less developed countries; aids in reducing world tension; fosters development of managerial techniques around the world; makes a major contribution to balance of payments; and stimulates exports. Others maintain that the MNC is responsible for exporting jobs; that it makes for much corporate giantism; and that, having no allegiance to any sovereign state, the MNC is more or less a stateless monster.

66. *See* Starke, Introduction to International Law (London, 1977), pp. 271–272.

67. 'Multinational Corporations in World Development' (UN) and 'Multinational Enterprises and Social Policy' (ILO), Dept. of State Bulletin, 12 October 1970, p. 429.

68. *See* US *v.* Aluminum Corporation of America, 148 F2d 416 (1945).

69. *See* Imperial Chemical Industries, Ltd *v.* EC Commission, CMLR 557, 629 (1972).

70. Subject to Section 403 which limits jurisdiction where 'conduct, relations, status, or interests' have 'connections with another state or states when the exercise of such jurisdiction is unreasonable'.

71. *Supra* note 70.

72. *See* generally Rubinstein, 'Alienage Jurisdiction in the Federal Courts', 1982 International Lawyer, pp. 283–307. *Also see* 9 Holdsworth, A History of English Law 97 (7th Ed 1956).

73. In Van Der Schelling *v.* US News & World Report, 213 F Supp 756 (1963), it was held that the word 'subject' and the word 'citizen' were identical in meaning. Here plaintiff, a citizen of the US had been a permanent and continuous resident of Mexico since 1950. She owned no property in the US, had not sought renewal of her US passport since 1952, and had the status in Mexico of an 'immigrado' which gave her the right of a definitive residence, but did not confer Mexican citizenship. She brought a libel action in 1963 in the federal court against the magazine publisher, a Delaware corporation which had its principal place of business in the District of Columbia. Federal jurisdiction was based on diversity of citizenship under Section 1332. Defendant moved to dismiss the complaint, arguing that plaintiff was not a citizen of any state because of her Mexican domicile and therefore there was no diversity. Plaintiff pointed out that diversity exists whether she is a citizen of a state or of a foreign state. But the court granted defendant's motion to dismiss, concluding that, although plaintiff was a citizen of the US she was not a citizen of any state because of her Mexican domicile, and so diversity of citizenship did not exist. Note that she was not a citizen of a foreign state either! Historically, 'subject' means 'citizen' and plaintiff did not satisfy the requirement of citizenship of a state.

74. Note 28 US Code, Section 1350 as to actions by aliens for torts committed in violation of the law of nations. Furthermore, 'an alien may select a federal court in which to sue a citizen of any state', Ex Parte Edelstein, 30 F2d 636, 638 (2nd Cir 1929).

75. Other federal statutes include 28 US Code, Section 1333 on Admiralty and Maritime Cases; 8 US Code, Section 1329 on Immigration; and 8 US Code, Section 1421 on Naturalization of Aliens.
76. *See* Dunlop & Co. *v.* Ball, 6 US (2 Cranch) 180 (1804), and Taylor *v.* Carpenter, 11 Paige (NY) 292 (1844) 'The policy of the US in all cases of complaints made by foreigners is to extend them the same measure of redress as is enjoyed by our own citizens', 4 Moore, International Law Digest, Sec. 536 (1906).
77. 16 Stat 144.
78. New York Estates Powers & Trusts Law, Section 5–4.1.
79. De La Bouillerie *v.* de Vienne, 300 NY 60, 89 NE2d 15 (1949). Cf. Douglas *v.* New Haven Railroad, 279 US 377 (1929) holding that a New York statute granting the court discretion to dismiss actions by non-residents against foreign corporations on foreign-based tort actions was not in violation of Article IV, Section 2 of the US Constitution on Privileges and Immunities. And in De Sairingna *v.* Gould, 83 F Supp 270 SDNY, 1949), the Court opined: 'No alien has a constitutional right to sue in the US courts', particularly where suit would precipitate a deluge of cases that would clog the court calendar.
80. *See* 28 US Code, Section 1391, and note Prudencia *v.* Hanselmann, 178 F Supp 887 (D Minn, 1959).
81. Article 7 of the Universal Declaration of Human Rights declares that 'all are equal before the law and are so entitled without any discrimination to equal protection of the law', GA Res 217, UN Dir A/8110 (1948).
82. *See* Farmanfarmaian *v.* Gulf Oil Co, 588 F2d 880 (2nd Cir, 1978). *See* 'American Law Institute Study of the Division of Jurisdiction Between State and Federal Courts', Dept. of State File No. P82 0127–1417, at p. 108:— 'Whether state courts in fact generally render full, fair, and speedy justice to alien litigants is largely beside the point. It is important in the relations of this country with other nations that any possible appearance of injustice or tenable ground for resentment be avoided. This objective can best be achieved by giving the foreigner the assurance that he can have his cases tried in a court with the best procedures the federal government can supply and with dignity and prestige of the US behind it.'
83. *See* Klausner *v.* Levy, 83 F Supp 599 (ED Va 1949), to the effect that citizens of Palestine prior to 1948 when the State of Israel was created again were not citizens of a foreign state.
84. *See* US *v.* Wong Kim Ark, 169 US 649 (1898), and Blair Holdings Corp *v.* Rubinstein, 133 F Supp 496 (SDNY 1955).
85. *See* Shoemaker *v.* Malaxa, 241 F2d 129 (2nd Cir 1957).
86. Louisville Railroad Co *v.* Letson, 2 How (42 US) 497 (1844).
87. *See* 28 US Code, Section 1332(c), and Arab International Bank & Trust Co *v.* National Westminster Bank, 463 F Supp 1145 (SDNY 1979).
88. 189 F Supp 500 (SDNY 1960). *Also* Salomon *v.* Israel Discount Bank, 494 F Supp 914 (SDNY 1980).
89. P.L. No. 94-583 (1976) 28 US Code, Section 1602 *et seq*. See Chapter 3, Section 2, herein.
90. 28 US Code, Section 1332.
91. *See* Strawbridge *v.* Curtiss, 7 US (3 Cranch) 267 (1806). Also Tsitsinakis *v.* Simpson Spence & Young, 90 F Supp 578 (SDNY 1950). *See* generally Owen Equipment & Erection Co *v.* Kroger, 437 US 365 (1978).
92. *See* Republic of Vietnam *v.* Pfizer, Inc, 556 F2d 892 (8th Cir, 1977) and Russian Socialist Federated Soviet Republics *v.* Cibrario, 235 NY 255, 139 NE 259 (1923) Cf. Transportes Aereos de Angola *v.* Ronair, Inc, 544 F Supp 858 (D Del, 1982).

Chapter 2. Jurisdiction of Courts and the Foreign Plaintiff

Section 1. Nature of the US Judicial System: Federal and State

The United States is a federal system of government whereby autonomous states are unified with a division of powers between the federal government and the 50 State governments. Both the federal and State systems operate within assigned spheres upon all persons and upon all property within their assigned spheres or jurisdictions. Article III, Section 2, of the US Constitution sets forth the areas to which federal judicial power shall extend: (a) the federal courts have power over all cases in law or equity arising under the US constitution, the laws of the United States, and the treaties signed by the United States, i.e., jurisdiction based on the prevalence of a federal question; (b) federal courts have jurisdiction over all cases affecting ambassadors and consuls; (c) federal courts exercise jurisdiction over all admiralty and maritime cases; (d) federal courts' jurisdiction extends to all cases to which the United States is a party; (e) federal court jurisdiction extends to controversies between two or more States, or between a State and citizens of another State; and (f) federal courts have jurisdiction over cases between citizens of different States or between citizens and foreign nationals, i.e., jurisdiction based upon diversity of citizenship. Federal law limits such jurisdiction to cases involving more that $10,000.

The federal judicial system is based upon the principle that federal courts are courts of limited jurisdiction, while State courts are courts of general jurisdiction with a presumption of jurisdiction over a particular controversy. Federal courts have only the judicial powers that are conferred upon them by the US Constitution or by the Acts of Congress. At the apex of the federal judiciary is the US Supreme Court, which is the only constitutionally mandated federal court. It has limited jurisdiction including appellate jurisdiction over the lower federal courts and over final judgments of the highest State courts where judgment turns on a substantial federal question.[1] The intermediate federal appellate courts are the Courts of Appeals for the eleven judicial circuits established by Congress. With the exception of limited cases where there is a right of direct appeal from a district court to the US Supreme Court, the Courts of Appeals are vested with appellate jurisdiction over the decisions of the federal district courts.

Despite the insistence of the US Supreme Court that State courts are as obligated and as competent as the federal courts to decide federal constitutional claims, the federal courts have greater expertise and the litigants generally stay within the federal court system.[2] The fifty State courts generally entertain jurisdiction unless they are specifically prohibited from exercising jurisdiction[2.1] over a particular type of action by a valid Act of Congress or by the US Constitution. Indeed, in theory State courts have concurrent jurisdiction with the federal courts; a State court may entertain an action based entirely on a federal question. Congress has, however, given the federal courts exclusive jurisdiction on bankruptcy matters, on admiralty, on patents and copyrights and trademarks, as well as on antitrust matters arising under federal statutes.

Federal court expertise is perhaps demonstrated by Competex, SA *v.* LaBow,[3] where the Second US Court of Appeals ruled that a commodities trader must satisfy a judgment for 188,000 English pounds levied against him in England by an English court and enforced in the federal district court in New York by paying dollars rather than English pounds. The effect of the ruling was that it cost the commodities trader $236,000 more than he had already paid in England, because the proper date to be used for converting the English judgment was deemed to be the day the judgment was entered in England. The suit here was by the Swiss broker who had obtained a default judgment in 1981 in England against the commodities trader: 'It would be anomalous to suggest that New York would allow its creditor's preference rule to be undercut by giving the judgment debtor the opportunity to satisfy his New York judgment by paying the underlying judgment in depreciated pounds'. The federal court applied state law which identified the conversion rate on the date judgment was entered on the original foreign judgment.

Another illustration of the expertise of the federal courts is found in Pitts *v.* Ciba-Geigy Corp,[4] decided by the federal district court in Massachusetts. Here plaintiffs brought suit against a Swiss corporation, its two subsidiaries and the distributor of foam housing insulation, to recover for injuries allegedly caused by the product. The subsidiary manufacturer of the product defaulted, and the parent company and the other Swiss subsidiary moved for summary judgment on the basis that the liability, if any, was on the subsidiary manufacturer. The federal court agreed pointing out that the corporate identities were not a sham, that the subsidiary manufacturer of the product had no minimum contacts with the jurisdiction, and that the parent company and the other Swiss subsidiary as well as the product manufacturer were entitled to summary judgment. Only the distributor of the product remained as a defendant in the law suit.

Section 2. Venue

The prerequisite of venue may be an obstacle to the foreign plaintiff, for, at least in the federal court system, venue must be established or waived as to each defendant and each separate cause of action.[5] The general statutory rules relating to venue embrace the following: if the sole basis for jurisdiction in a transitory civil action is diversity of citizenship (unless otherwise provided by law), then the action may be brought only in the judicial district where all plaintiffs reside, or where all defendants reside, or in the judicial district in which the claim arose.[6] Thus, venue is proper in any of the three districts unless defendants reside in different States and plaintiffs reside in different States or foreign countries, in which event venue is proper only in the judicial district where the cause of action arose. But a corporation may be sued in any judicial district in which it is incorporated, licensed to do business, or is in fact doing business.[7]

An alien or foreign person may be sued in any district, according to 28 USC 1391(d); indeed the US Supreme Court in Brunette Machine Works *v.* Kockum Industries[8] stated that the Section 'is properly regarded, not as a venue restriction at all, but rather as a declaration of the long established rule that suits against aliens are wholly outside the operation of the federal venue law, general and special'.[9] A civil action against a foreign state or a political subdivision thereof[10] may be brought

a. in any judicial district in which (i) 'a substantial part of the events or omissions giving rise to the claim occurred';[11] (ii) 'a substantial part of the property that is the subject of the action is situated'; or (iii) 'the vessel or cargo of a foreign state is situated as the claim is asserted under Section 1605(b) of this title';[12] or (iv) 'the agency or instrumentality is licensed to do business or is doing business, if the action is brought against an agency or instrumentality of a foreign state as defined in Section 1603(b) of this title';[13] or
b. in the United States District Court for the District of Columbia, if the suit is brought against a foreign state or a political subdivision thereof'.[14]

It should be noted that 28 USC 1391(f) was added as part of the Foreign Sovereign Immunities Act[15] and provides the venue rules for cases thereunder.[16]

Pursuant to Rule 12(h)(1) of the Federal Rules of Civil Procedure, a defense of improper venue is waived if omitted from a Rule 12 motion or is neither made by a Rule 12 motion nor interposed in a responsive pleading. According to Manley *v.* Engram,[17] 'the right to object to improper venue may be waived in any of several ways: by express waiver, by conduct amounting to waiver as a matter of law, or by failure to interpose a timely and sufficient objection'.[18]

The principal federal statute on change of venue is 28 USC 1404,[19] illustrated in Van Dusen *v.* Barrack,[20] where a commercial airliner scheduled to fly from Boston to Philadelphia plunged into Boston Harbor, and over 150 law suits were commenced against the airline, various US manufacturers and the Massachusetts Port Authority. (The cause of the crash was apparently the ingestion of birds by the aircraft's engines.) Forty of these wrongful death actions were brought in the federal court in Pennsylvania, and the defendant moved to transfer the venue under Section 1404(a) to the federal court in Massachusetts where over 100 wrongful death actions were pending. The Pennsylvania court approved the transfers, but the US Supreme Court reversed:

> 'There is nothing . . . in the language or policy of § 1404(a) to justify its use by defendants to defeat the advantages accruing to plaintiffs who have chosen a forum which, although it was inconvenient, was a proper venue. In this regard the transfer provisions of § 1404(a) may be compared with those of § 1406(a). Although both sections were broadly

> designed to allow transfer instead of dismissal, § 1406(a) provides for transfer from forums in which venue is wrongly or improperly laid, whereas, in contrast, § 1404(a) operates on the premise that the plaintiff has properly exercised his venue privilege. . . . The legislative history of § 1404(a) certainly does not justify the rather startling conclusion that one might "get a change of law as a bonus for a change of venue". Indeed, an interpretation accepting such a rule would go far to frustrate the remedial purposes of § 1404(a). If a change of law were in the offing, the parties might well regard the section primarily as a forum-shopping instrument. And, more importantly, courts would at least be reluctant to grant transfers, despite considerations of convenience, if to do so might conceivably prejudice the claim of a plaintiff who had initially selected a permissible forum. We believe, therefore, that both the history and purposes of § 1404(a) indicate that it should be regarded as a federal judicial housekeeping measure, dealing with the placement of litigation in the federal courts and generally intended, on the basis of convenience and fairness, simply to authorize a change of courtrooms.'[21]

This federal transfer statute, 28 USC 1404(a),[22] has been construed to apply to proceedings in admiralty as well as to ordinary civil actions.[23] In Hoffman *v.* Blaski[24] the US Supreme Court held that the statute authorized transfer only to a federal district in which jurisdiction over the defendant could have been obtained and in which venue was proper at the time the suit was commenced, regardless of the defendant's consent. In 1964 in Van Dusen *v.* Barrack[25] the highest court stressed the fact that State law governed the capacity of the plaintiff to bring the suit, while Section 1404(a) referred only to the defendant's ability to sue under the federal laws of venue, service and jurisdiction.

In Quandt *v.* Beech Aircraft Corp[26] the plaintiffs were citizens and residents of West Germany, and they brought an action in the federal district court of Delaware where the defendant aircraft manufacturer was incorporated; the plane crash occurred in Italy. At the defendant's request the court transferred the action under Section 1404(a) to the federal district court in Kansas where the aircraft was manufactured. The transfer was based upon the convenience of the witnesses; the court observed that plaintiffs would still have an inconvenient forum whether trial was held in Delaware or in Kansas. But some cases point up that the convenience of expert witnesses, as well as the convenience of counsel, are not bases for determining transferability under Section 1404(a), as illustrated by Wright *v.* American Flyers Airline Corp[27] and by Cressman *v.* United Airlines,[28] in which the court opined:

> 'It will almost always be the case that the granting of a transfer motion will inconvenience counsel in the transferor district or necessitate the engagement of new counsel. Were this fact to be accorded much weight in motions of this type, Section 1404(a) would be rendered virtually nugatory.'[29]

Plaintiff's choice of forum is given great deference under Section 1404(a) transfer, as shown in Bush *v.* United Airlines[30] where the court stated:

> 'The defendant is engaged in an extensive nationwide business of transporting passengers by air. In operating a business of this nature, it is reasonable to expect the defendant to anticipate the hazard and expense of suits filed against it at various points over the territory in which it operates. Moreover, the defendant should expect that such suits will require the transportation of such of its employees as it must call as witnesses to the places of trial. The matter of the transportation of witnesses would pose a problem more easily solved by the defendant than by the plaintiff. The fortuitous circumstances that this accident occurred through a collision with a mountain in Wyoming should not operate to deprive the plaintiff of her choice of forum.'

But where there are other actions involving the same accident or same incident and the same defendant or defendants, courts will in the interest of justice either transfer or not transfer the case, depending upon the possibilities of consolidation with related actions in the designated forum. The federal district court for the Southern District of New York in Rodgers *v.* Northwest Airlines, Inc.[31] in 1962 expressed the problem in these terms:

> 'The benefits and advantages to all parties in having the related actions considered in one jurisdiction under one judge are obvious. Pre-trial proceedings can be conducted more efficiently, duplication of time and effort can be avoided and the benefit to witnesses and to the parties calling them and having them attend only once at one location is plain. Furthermore, to require defendants to re-litigate the issue of liability in a number of forums would be vexatious and would not serve the ends of justice. The transfer of this case to the District Court sitting in Chicago is in the interest of sound judicial administration as well as speedier and more efficient disposition of the mass of litigation arising out of this accident. The phrase in § 1404(a) 'in the interest of justice' requires that [b]oth the interest of the parties to the lawsuit as well as society in general should be considered.'[32]

In Lehman *v.* Humphrey Cayman, Ltd[33] the federal district court in Iowa was the scene of a suit brought by the surviving widow whose husband was presumed dead after a sailing accident in Jamaica; plaintiff and decedent were residents of Iowa, and the defendants were the Jamaican franchisee of a Tennessee corporation. The trial court initially granted defendants' motion to dismiss on *forum non conveniens* grounds, but the Eighth US Court of Appeals reversed, finding an abuse of discretion on the part of the trial court in the following respects:

a. the trial court failed to weigh the relevance of plaintiff's residence or her choice of forum;

b. defendants' burden of producing witnesses was not any greater than plaintiff's burden;
c. defendants' inability to implead the local Jamaican diving school was not due such great weight;
d. both the State of Iowa and the Cayman Islands, Jamaica, had an interest in the controversy, and therefore the latter's interest did not prevail over Iowa's interest;
e. the law of Iowa may apply, and the federal court in Iowa can also apply Cayman Islands law; and
f. the trial court did not consider the consequences of forcing the plaintiff widow to litigate in a foreign forum.

It would appear, however, that, from a pragmatic viewpoint, the foreign forum might be found more convenient for all the parties except the surviving widow. Under such a factual conclusion, no issue as to the federal transfer statute was presented, and so the trial would take place in the State of Iowa, unless appropriately transferred to another federal district court. Where another federal court is more convenient, transfer under 28 USC 1404(a) is the exclusive remedy and dismissal under *forum non conveniens* is inappropriate.[34]

There are differences in venue rules between federal and State courts, for example: State courts delineated counties and local districts, while federal courts describe venue in terms of districts or divisions; improper venue cannot be waived in a State court, but can be waived in a federal court; a State court cannot dismiss an action for improper venue, but a federal court can do so unless the defense is not properly interposed; and a corporation in State courts is deemed a resident of the county or district specified as its principal place of business in the certificate of incorporation or its application for authority to do business in the State, while in the federal courts, except with respect to certain causes of action, the residence of the defendant corporation for venue purposes is deemed to be the district in which it is incorporated, licensed to do business, or is doing business.[35]

Venue under State statutes in State courts may be described by reference to the New York picture: CPLR 503 provides in part that the place of trial 'shall be in the county in which one of the parties resided' at the time of the commencement of the action. But CPLR 510 provides the grounds for change of venue as follows: 'The court, upon motion, may change the place of trial of an action where: the county designated for that purpose is not a proper county; or there is reason to believe that an impartial trial cannot be had in the proper county; or the convenience of material witnesses and the ends of justice will be prompted by the change.'[36] And Rule 327(a) CPLR provides:

> 'When the court finds that in the interest of substantial justice the action should be heard in another forum, the court, on the motion of any party, may stay or dismiss the action in whole or in part on any conditions that may be just. The domicile or residence in this state of any party to the action shall not preclude the court from staying or dismissing the action.'

A 1984 amendment added a new subsection (b) that precludes dismissal if the suit arises out of a claim to which Section 5-1402 of the New York General Obligations Law applies, as exemplified by a commercial contract involving at least $1 million, which means that the parties thereto may assure themselves of a New York forum if the choice of law agreement covered by Section 5-1401 of the New York General Obligations Law is contained in the contract as well as an agreement by the non-resident or foreign corporate party to submit to New York jurisdiction. New York courts in making their discretionary determination[37] must nevertheless consider the convenience of the litigants, the convenience of the courts, and the availability of another forum. However, recent New York decisions like Broida *v.* Bancroft[38] have fortified the presumption that New York residents are entitled to a New York forum: 'We conclude that, in light of the substantial nexus of this litigation with New York, it was an improvident exercise of discretion to decline jurisdiction.' Justice Titone of the New York Appellate Division, 1st Department, had relied upon the holding of the US Supreme Court in Koster *v.* Lumbermens Mutual Casualty Co[39] to the effect that the 'internal affairs' rule about corporations 'is not entitled to separate status and should be treated as one facet under general principles of *forum non conveniens*'. Furthermore, 'consideration of all relevant factors compels the conclusion that plaintiffs should not be deprived of their chosen forum':—

> 'Plaintiffs, as New York residents, are presumptively entitled to utilize their judicial system for dispute resolution (McLaughlin, Practice Commentaries, McKinney's Cons Laws of NY, Book 7B, CPLR C 301:4, p 5; C 327:1, pp 238–239, 1983–1984 pocket part; Slaughter *v.* Waters, 41 AD 2d 810). In fact, New York has a special responsibility to protect its citizens from questionable corporate acts when a corporation, though having a foreign charter, has substantial contacts with this State (e.g., Western Airlines *v.* Sobieski, 191 Cal App 2d 399; Dudley *v.* Jack Waite Mining Co., 49 Wash 2d 867; see Latty, Pseudo-Foreign Corporations, 65 Yale L J 137; Reese & Kaufman, The Law Governing Corporate Affairs: Choice of Law and the Impact of Full Faith & Credit, 58 Col L Rev 1118; cf. Rakaric *v.* Croatian Cultural Club Cardinal Stepinac Organization, 76 AD 2d 619, app dsmd 52 NY 2d 1072).'

Indeed, the residence of the parties and the situs of the cause of action are but single factors to be considered by the courts in ruling on a motion to dismiss based on *forum non conveniens*. In Christoao *v.* Unisul-Uniao,[40] without explanation the highest New York court dismissed the action although the plaintiff was a New York resident and the cause of action arose in New York. Similarly, in United States Aviation Underwriters *v.* United States Fire Insurance Co[40.1], both insurers being incorporated in the State of New York, the New York court granted defendant's motion to dismiss on *forum non conveniens* grounds since the issue of residency was no longer controlling in such motions and furthermore there was no substantial nexus with the State of New York. Here the plaintiff, the secondary carrier, claimed that defendant, the primary carrier, had used improper settlement procedures in a wrongful death action brought about by an aircraft accident which took place in Texas where all the parties resided. According to the court,

> 'The burden of proof on this issue rests upon the defendant challenging the forum to demonstrate relevant private or public interest factors which militate against accepting the litigation. . . . The former rigid and inflexible rule which prohibited the doctrine of *forum non conveniens* from being invoked if one of the parties was a New York resident has been relaxed and replaced by a discretionary consideration of the many factors involved . . . Although the residence of the parties remains as one of the factors to be considered the doctrine may now be invoked even in cases where all the parties to the action are New York residents . . . Other factors to be considered include the difficulty for the defendant in litigating the claim in this state, the burden on the New York courts in entertaining the suit, the availability of another more convenient forum, and the choice of law to be applied.'

Section 3. Subjectmatter Jurisdiction

Jurisdiction generally comprises two separate and necessary elements, subject-matter jurisdiction and personal jurisdiction. The former is concerned with the authority of the court to entertain a particular type or subjectmatter of action, regardless of the nature or relationships of the parties to the action. State courts generally have subjectmatter jurisdiction over virtually any case, but the federal courts have limited jurisdiction and the foreign plaintiff may invoke the subjectmatter of a federal court under (a) federal question jurisdiction;[41] (b) admiralty jurisdiction;[42] or (c) diversity jurisdiction.[43]

The US Supreme Court in 1986 in Merrell Dow Pharmaceuticals, Inc *v.* Thompson [43.1] defined very narrowly the parameters of the 'federal question' prerequisite to federal jurisdiction. Here plaintiff's alleged violation of the Federal Food, Drug and Cosmetic Act [43.2] was argued by the defendant product manufacturer as the very basis for federal court jurisdiction, enabling the defendant to remove the case into the federal courts. But the highest court did not agree with defendant's argument, to wit: respondent's cause of action did not necessarily depend upon a question of federal law, and therefore the prime cause of action did not arise under federal law. Accordingly, the foreign plaintiffs from Scotland and Canada could retain their suit in the Ohio state courts without fear that defendant would remove the suit to the federal courts.

The 'federal question' jurisdiction exists when the US Constitution, laws or treaties of the United States apply to the controversy, as set forth in 28 USC 1331:—

§ 1331. *Federal question; amount in controversy; costs*

(a) The district courts shall have original jurisdiction of all civil actions wherein the matter in controversy exceeds the sum or value of $10,000, exclusive of interest and costs, and arises under the Constitution, laws, or treaties of the United States.

(b) Except when express provision therefor is otherwise made in a statute of the United States, where the plaintiff is finally adjudged to be entitled to recover less than the sum or value of $10,000, computed without regard to any setoff or counterclaim to which the defendant may be adjudged to be entitled, and exclusive of interests and costs, the district court may deny costs to the plaintiff and, in addition, may impose costs on the plaintiff.

It should be noted that under the 'federal question' jurisdiction the defendant may remove the suit from a state court to a federal court, for example, whether the defendant is a resident of the district or not.[44]

'Diversity of citizenship' requirement brings the foreign plaintiff into US courts, except when both parties are aliens or where both parties reside in the same State;[45] the addition of a US resident as a party will not cure the jurisdictional defect,[46] as is clear from reading 28 USC 1332:

§ 1332. *Diversity of citizenship; amount in controversy; costs*

(a) The district courts shall have original jurisdiction of all civil actions where the matter in controversy exceeds the sum or value of $10,000, exclusive of interest and costs, and is between—

(1) citizens of different States;
(2) citizens of a State, and foreign states or citizens or subjects thereof; and
(3) citizens of different States and in which foreign states or citizens or subjects thereof are additional parties.

(b) Except when express provision therefor is otherwise made in a statute of the United States, where the plaintiff who files the case originally in the Federal courts is finally adjudged to be entitled to recover less than the sum or value of $10,000, computed without regard to any setoff or counterclaim to which the defendant may be adjudged to be entitled, and exclusive of interest and costs, the district court may deny costs to the plaintiff and, in addition, may impose costs on the plaintiff.

(c) For the purposes of this section and section 1441 of this title, a corporation shall be deemed a citizen of any State by which it has been incorporated and of the State where it has its principal place of business: *Provided further*, That in any *direct action against the insurer of* a policy or contract of liability insurance, whether incorporated or unincorporated, to which action the insured is not joined as a party-defendant, *such insurer shall be deemed a citizen of the State of which the insured is a citizen, as well as of* any State by which the insurer has been incorporated and of the State where it has its principal place of business.

(d) The word 'States', as used in this section, includes the Territories, the District of Columbia, and the Commonwealth of Puerto Rico.

Diversity of citizenship requisites are satisfied, in general, when the foreign plaintiff alleges more than $10,000 in damages and is from a state or country other than the state or country of the defendant. In Macedo *v.* Boeing Co[47] the federal district court held that the foreign plaintiffs could not sue a foreign airline along with a US product manufacturer, although in the particular suit the US plaintiffs were suing both the foreign airline and the US product manufacturer. And in Dixon Chok *et al v.* S & W Beresford, PLC *et al*[48] the federal district court for the Southern District of New York opined: 'When there are alien parties on both sides of the controversy, jurisdiction will be found lacking even though they are citizens of different countries or one is a resident or domiciliary of the United States'. A partnership poses a different problem: 'For purposes of diversity, a partnership is a citizen of each jurisdiction of which a partner is a citizen ... Therefore, under the requirements of complete diversity, ... a court does not have diversity jurisdiction over a suit by a plaintiff against a partnership in which any partner's citizenship is identical to that of the plaintiff'.[49]

Admiralty jurisdiction of the federal courts requires a 'maritime nexus'[50] to sustain jurisdiction; a court must assess the 'points of contact between the transaction and the states or governments whose competing laws are involved'.[50] 'Admiralty jurisdiction' is another facet of subjectmatter jurisdiction, and for the federal court to entertain the suit, plaintiff must show that the cause of action has a 'maritime nexus', although proof of the nexus under admiralty does not dictate the application of US law; the choice of applicable law depends upon the following seven points set forth in the landmark case of Lauritzen *v.* Larsen[52]:—

1) the place of the wrongful act;
2) the law of the flag (under which the ship operates);
3) the allegiance or domicile of the injured party;
4) the allegiance of the shipowner;
5) the place of the making of the contract (e.g., shipping);
6) the inaccessibility of the foreign forum; and
7) the law of the chosen forum.

An eighth point, to wit, the base of the ship operations, was delineated in Hellenic Lines, Ltd, *v.* Rhoditis[53].

Subjectmatter jurisdiction, it should be noted, is subject to collateral attack, as delineated in Section 451(2) of Restatement (Second) of Conflict of Laws:

'Where a court has jurisdiction over the parties and determines that it has jurisdiction over the subject matter, the parties cannot collaterally attack the judgment on the ground that the court did not have jurisdiction over the subject matter, *unless* the policy underlying the doctrine of *res judicata* is outweighed by the policy against permitting the court to act beyond its jurisdiction. Among the *factors* appropriate to be considered in determining that collateral attack should be permitted are that

(a) the *lack of jurisdiction over* the *subject matter* was clear;

(b) the determination as to jurisdiction depended upon a *question of law* rather than of fact;

(c) the *court was one of limited* and not of general jurisdiction;

(d) the question of *jurisdiction was* not *actually litigated;*

(e) *the policy against the court's acting beyond its* jurisdiction is strong.'

And it was in Durfee *v.* Duke[54] that the highest court observed:

> 'While it is established that a court in one State, when asked to give effect to the judgment of a court in another State, may constitutionally inquire into the foreign court's jurisdiction to render that judgement, the modern decisions of this Court have carefully delineated the permissible scope of such an inquiry. From these decisions there emerges the general rule that a judgment is entitled to full faith and credit—even as to questions of jurisdiction—when the second court's inquiry discloses that those questions have been fully and fairly litigated and finally decided in the court which rendered the original judgment. This Court soon made clear in a series of decisions that the general rule is no different when the claim is made that the original forum did not have jurisdiction over the subject matter. Davis *v.* Davis, 305 US 32; Stoll *v.* Gottlieb, 305 US 165; Treinies *v.* Sunshine Mining Co, 308 US 66; Sherrer *v.* Sherrer, 334 US 343. In each of these cases the claim was made that a court, when asked to enforce the judgment of another forum, was free to retry the question of that forum's jurisdiction over the subject matter. In each case this Court held that since the question of subjectmatter jurisdiction had been fully litigated in the original forum, the issue could not be retried in a subsequent action between the parties. . .'

Thus, the decision clearly foreclosed the issue of subjectmatter jurisdiction: however, even when the issue has been fully litigated, there is authority that certain issues of subjectmatter jurisdiction may not be foreclosed, as illustrated in Kalb *v.* Feuerstein[55] where a farmer had lost his farm through State foreclosure proceedings while a petition was pending under Section 75 of the Bankruptcy Act which deprived State courts of jurisdiction. Plaintiff's attack collaterally on the foreclosure judgment was allowed because Congress had expressed a strong policy on bankruptcy that would be thwarted by an impermissible exercise of jurisdiction.

Section 4. Personal Jurisdiction

Personal jurisdiction or jurisdiction *in personam*, also known as jurisdiction over a party, deals with the authority of a court over the person or presence of a party to the action by reason of his contacts with a territorial jurisdiction or the activity which he undertakes within that jurisdiction. Also included in the concept of personal jurisdiction is jurisdiction over some asset or property in which such a person or party has an interest, i.e., jurisdiction *in rem* and *quasi in rem* jurisdiction.

The methods of acquiring and challenging personal jurisdiction are regulated in great detail by local statutes and by court rules; even the apparatus of challenging personal jurisdiction by a special appearance and waiver by a general appearance is subject to complex regulation. Due Process of Law under the Fourteenth Amendment requires a method of notice reasonably calculated to afford parties interested in the judicial proceedings the opportunity to appear and be heard. Another aspect of personal jurisdiction is that the State or federal government cannot authorize its courts to affect a person's or a company's interests unless there is some rational basis for the exercise of judicial power, i.e., there must be a relationship of the litigants and the subjectmatter in dispute to the forum in some significant manner.

A century ago in Pennoyer *v.* Neff[56] the common law concept of personal jurisdiction stressed the physical presence of the defendant and/or his property within the jurisdiction exercising the judicial power. But that requisite of personal service within the state or jurisdiction eroded with the passing of time and by the year 1945 in International Shoe Co *v.* Washington,[57] personal jurisdiction, like notice, was deemed to be an element of the fair-trial requirement, and due process of law restricted personal jurisdiction only when the exercise of that jurisdiction would be unfair to the defendant.[58] Subsequently in 1957 the US Supreme Court in McGee *v.* International Life Insurance Co[59] simplified the requisite by declaring that it was 'sufficient for purposes of due process that the suit was based on a contract which had substantial connection with that State'.[60] The next year in Hanson *v.* Deckla[61] the highest court emphasized that 'however minimal the burden of defending in a foreign tribunal, a defendant may not be called upon to do so unless he has had the minimum contacts with that State that a prerequisite to its exercise of power over him ... We fail to find such contacts in the circumstances of this case ... The cause of action in this case is not one that arises out of an act done or transaction consummated in that forum State.'

Other aspects of personal jurisdiction are the 'long-arm statute' and the 'doing business' aspect, which confer personal jurisdiction upon the court over the parties. Section 302 of New York's CPLR is an example of a 'long-arm statute' whereunder New York courts may exercise jurisdiction based on specified acts of out-of-State defendants and their agents; if the cause of action arises from the specified acts, a non-domiciliary may be subject to jurisdiction in New York when, in person or through an agent, the non-domiciliary transacts any business within New York or contracts to supply goods or services in New York, commits a tortious act within New York, commits a tortious act outside New York causing injury in New York under certain circumstances, or owns, uses, or possesses any real property situated in New York.

A frequently litigated issue is whether the transacting or doing business nexus has been satisfied; the inquiry tends to be heavily factual as the court attempts to determine whether there was 'purposeful activity' in the State of New York, in person or through an agent, with a sufficient causal relation to the cause of action. In Hoffritz for Cutlery, Inc *v.* Amajac Ltd[62] the Second US Court of Appeals reviewed the issues, holding that the jurisdictional issue is determined by reference to the law of the State in which the federal court is sitting, that the burden of establishing personal jurisdiction is on the plaintiff, and that the cause of action arose out of defendant's transaction of business in New York. Here plaintiff alleged that its franchisee had acted improperly with respect to a lease for a store in Georgia and thereby breached its franchise agreement; the fact that the lease at issue was for property in Georgia did not change the character of the New York transaction:

> 'Viewing the totality of the circumstances surrounding defendants activities in New York in connection with the matter giving rise to the law-suit, we conclude that there is a substantial nexus between these activites, including the preliminary contract negotiations in New York and the frequent later visits to New York, and the alleged breach of the franchise agreement.'[63]

The US Supreme Court in 1980 in the leading case of World-Wide Volkswagen *v.* Woodson[64] held that a retailer and regional product distributor with no demonstrable shipments, sales or other business in the forum state, cannot constitutionally be held amenable to the forum's personal jurisdiction in an action for personal injuries allegedly caused by a design defect in the product. The action was instituted in an Oklahoma state court by plaintiffs against the manufacturer, importer, regional distributor and retailer of their Audi automobile after an accident in the forum state. The highest US court rejected the concept[65] that the foreseeability of a product finding its way into the forum state provided a sufficient basis of the assertion of *in personam* jurisdiction: 'Having interred the mechanical rule that a creditor's amenability to a *quasi in rem* action travels with his debtor, we are unwilling to endorse an analogous principle in the present case.'[66] Rather, the court held, foreseeability was relevant only in determining whether the defendant's conduct and contact with the forum state was sufficient to cause him to anticipate an exercise of jurisdiction by that state's courts.[67]

Quasi-in-rem jurisdiction is another method for subjecting a non-resident to suit in a given State; it may be exercised when the property owned by the defendant is found within the State and is attached for purposes of suit. This procedure enables a court to adjudicate a controversy unrelated to the attached property, but the judgment or award is only effective to the extent of the property's value. In Shaffer *v.* Heitner[68] the US Supreme Court held that the 'minimum contacts' analysis applied to actions involving *quasi-in-rem* as well as *in personam* jurisdiction. Consequently, property serving as the basis for jurisdiction must relate to the cause of action in the event that there are no contacts between the defendant, the forum and the litigation itself. In effect, the court limited severely the exercise of jurisdiction predicated solely upon attachment of a non-resident's property that is located within the State.

The 'long-arm' jurisdiction exercised by both federal and state courts in the products liability situation enhance the potential recoveries of plaintiffs by giving plaintiffs greater opportunities to be heard. When a foreign corporation qualifies to do business in any State, it appoints an agent for service of process and at least implicitly submits itself to the jurisdiction of the courts of that State as if it were a resident. Thus, the plaintiff has a target defendant within the control of the local courts. But a German woman who had purchased the notorious and dangerous drug thalidomide in West Germany and who subsequently gave birth in New York to a deformed infant, had no right to be heard against the German seller who had no reason to believe that the purchaser would use the product in the United States.[69] Most recently in Celton Man Trade, Inc *v.* Utex, S.A.[69.1] the federal district court for the Southern District of New York rejected an attempt in a breach of contract action to predicate transnational jurisdiction over a nonresident based on telephone calls and telexes: 'A defendant who merely places telephone calls or sends telexes to persons in New York is not thereby subject to personal jurisdiction here.' But the same court in ORM Publishing Co, Inc *v.* Reed[69.2] denied a motion to dismiss an action for trademark and copyright infringement for lack of personal jurisdiction; the defendant, the publisher of a newsletter in California with 15 out of 300 subscribers in New York, argued that he was not subject to personal jurisdiction in New York. The court observed that defendant would be subject to New York jurisdiction even if he had no New York subscribers since he had solicited subscriptions from 500 New York residents: 'The offering of allegedly infringing goods for sale within the state constitutes a tortious act . . . even if no actual sales occur.'

The wide range of jurisdictional contacts are delineated in the proposed Uniform Interstate and International Procedure Act (1962),[70] adopted by a few states. Jurisdiction is allowed if the claim arises from such contacts as the transaction of any business in the forum State, the contracting to supply services or products in the forum State, or the causing of tortious injury in the forum State by an act or omission outside the State, if the person regularly does or solicits business or engages in any persistent course of conduct or derives substantial revenue from products used or consumed or services rendered in the forum State.

The 1985 decision of the US Supreme Court in Phillips Petroleum Co *v.* Shutts[71] held unanimously that the exercise of personal jurisdiction over absent class members in a class action (absent class members having no contact with the State of Kansas here) was not barred by the Fourteenth Amendment. The court recognized that cases where personal jurisdiction is asserted over absent members of a plaintiff class are different for due process purposes from cases where personal jurisdiction is asserted over a single defendant:

'The burdens placed by a State upon an absent class-action plaintiff are not of the same order or magnitude as those it places upon an absent defendant. An out-of-state defendant summoned by a plaintiff is faced with the full powers of the forum State to render judgment *against* it. The defendant must generally hire counsel and travel to the forum to defend itself from the plaintiff's claim, or suffer a default judgment. The defendant may be forced to participate in extended and often costly discovery, and will be forced to respond in damages or to comply with some other form of remedy imposed by the court should it lose the suit. The defendant may also face liability for court costs and attorney's fees. These burdens are substantial, and the minimum contacts requirement of the Due Process Clause prevents the forum state from unfairly imposing them upon the defendant ... In sharp contrast to the predicament of a defendant haled into an out-of-state forum, the plaintiffs in this suit were not haled anywhere to defend themselves upon pain of a default judgment.'[72]

The highest court continued:

'Besides this continuing solicitude for their rights, absent plaintiff class members are not subject to other burdens imposed upon defendants. They need not hire counsel or appear. They are almost never subject to counterclaims or cross-claims, or liability for fees or costs. Absent plaintiff class members are not subject to coercive or punitive remedies. Nor will an adverse judgment typically bind an absent plaintiff for any damages, although a valid adverse judgment may extinguish any of the plaintiff's claim which was litigated. Unlike a defendant in a normal civil suit, an absent class-action plaintiff is not required to do anything. He may sit back and allow the litigation to run its course, content in knowing that there are safeguards provided for his protection. In most class actions an absent plaintiff is provided at least with an opportunity to 'opt out' of the class, and if he takes advantage of that opportunity he is removed from the litigation entirely.'[73]

However, the court did not exclude absent plaintiff class members from all due process protection:

'If the forum State wishes to bind an absent plaintiff concerning a claim for money damages or similar relief at law, it must provide minimal procedural due process protection. The plaintiff must receive notice plus an opportunity to be heard and participate in the litigation, whether in person or through counsel. The notice must be the best practicable, 'reasonably calculated, under all the circumstances, to apprise interested parties of the pendency of the action and afford them an opportunity to present their objections'. Mullane [*v.* Central Hanover Bank & Trust], 339 US [306] at 314–315 [1950]; cf. Eisen *v.* Carlisle & Jacquelin, 417 US 156, 174–175 (1974). The notice should

> describe the action and the plaintiffs' rights in it. Additionally, we hold that due process requires at a minimum that an absent plaintiff be provided with an opportunity to remove himself from the class by executing and returning an 'opt out' or 'request for exclusion' form to the court. Finally, the Due Process Clause of course requires that the named plaintiff at all times adequately represent the interests of the absent class members.'[74]

Section 5 The Alien Tort Claims Act (1789)

The Alien Tort Claims Act was enacted as part of the first Judiciary Act of 1789, and provided that 'the district courts shall have original jurisdiction of any civil action by an alien for a tort only, committed in violation of the law of nations or a treaty of the United States'.[75] Admittedly, this Act is obscure and poorly understood, and only in relative recent years has the Act been given attention by the courts. On but four occasions have aliens and foreign plaintiffs successfully maintained federal subject matter jurisdiction:

1. in 1795 in Bolchos *v.* Darrel[76] in a federal court in South Carolina a Spanish citizen had mortgaged slaves to a British citizen who then placed them on a Spanish ship which was seized by Bolchos, a French privateer, who brought the ship into South Carolina; a British agent of the morgagee sued for restitution, and the court ruled that property of friendly nations found aboard an enemy vessel was deemed forfeited;
2. Adra *v.* Clift,[77] filed under the Act in the federal court in Maryland in 1961;
3. in 1984 in DeBlake *v.* The Republic of Argentina[78] in a California federal district court seeking compensation for torture committed in Argentina; and
4. in Filartiga *v.* Pena-Irala[79] in 1984 compensating the victims of torture committed in Paraguay.

The Filartiga case represents the high point in favorable construction of the Alien Tort Claims Act, for the Second US Court of Appeals held that the Act conferred subjectmatter jurisdiction on the federal courts for the wrongful death action brought by two Paraguayan citizens residing in the State of New York against a third Paraguayan who was present in New York on a visitor's visa. The court found that torture in Paraguay was a tort which violated international law and that the foreign plaintiffs could properly assert federal subjectmatter jurisdiction under the Alien Tort Claims Act. Each plaintiff was awarded $5 million in punitive damages plus $10,364 for expenses incurred in bringing the action. According to the court,

> 'it is not extraordinary for a court to adjudicate a tort claim arising outside of its territorial jurisdiction. A state or nation has a legitimate interest in the orderly resolution of disputes among those within its borders . . . Although the Alien Tort Statute has rarely been the basis for jurisdiction during its long history, in light of the foregoing discussion, there can be little doubt that this action is properly brought

> in the federal court. This is undeniably an action by an alien, for a tort only, committed in violation of the law of nations.'

[In closing the court observed that 'we do not reach the critical question of *forum non conveniens*, since it was not considered below'.]

In Tel-Oren *v.* Libyan Arab Republic [80] the District of Columbia Circuit Court of Appeals in 1984 refused to accept jurisdiction by the federal courts, pointing out that the Act does not provide a private cause of action for violations of international law,[81] and that the issue involved a political question which was non-justiciable.

The judicial construction of the Act leaves much to be desired,[82] and it would appear that jurisdiction should be extended to alien tort claims in which it is alleged that international law was violated in the course of committing the tort, regardless of whether the tort itself constitutes an international violation of law. Courts should not, however, decide political questions which admittedly are not justiciable; important foreign policy issues similarly do not belong in the federal courts.

The Act was delineated in 1975 by Judge Friendly in IIT *v.* Vencap, Ltd[83] as a 'legal Lohengrin', referring to the medieval German hero who championed the cause of a young maiden who was falsely accused of murdering her brother; when the maiden sought to learn his identity, Lohengrin disappeared as mysteriously as he had come to save her. Indeed, the Act is obscure both in origin and in purpose, although it seems clear that aliens may bring actions for common law torts in federal courts without regard for diversity of citizenship or for jurisdictional amounts so long as the aliens allege a violation of the law of nations or a treaty of the United States. Thus, the key to invoking the Act is that the tort which forms the basis of plaintiff's cause of action must be a violation of international law, i.e., the law of nations and/or a treaty of the United States. But in IIT *v.* Vencap,[84] the court held that a claim by a Luxembourg international investment trust for fraud, conversion and corporate waste did not allege a violation of international law. Judge Friendly there remarked that the Eighth Commandment, 'Thou shalt not steal', apparently had not been incorporated into the law of nations! Other instances of torts not constituting violations of international law include Benjamins *v.* British European Airways[85] where the court in 1978 declined jurisdiction under the Act on the ground that an airplane crash even if caused by willful negligence did not constitute a violation of international law; Huynh Thi Anh *v.* Levi,[86] where the court ruled that a grandmother's suit for custody of her children did not find approval under the Act; Dreyfus *v.* von Finck[87], holding that expropriation of Swiss property by West German citizens in Nazi Germany in 1938 did not violate international law; and Lopes *v.* Reederei Richard Schroder[88] to the effect that the unseaworthiness of a vessel was not a tort in violation of international law. Yet the US Supreme Court in 1820 in United States *v.* Smith[89] had stated that international law 'may be ascertained by consulting the works of jurists, writing professedly on public law, or by the general usage and practice of nations, or by judicial decisions recognizing and enforcing that law'.

On 11 September 1987 the Second US Court of Appeals in Amerada Hess Shipping Corp *v.* Argentine Republic[89.1] ruled that jurisdiction existed in a US court for a claim that Argentina, in violation of international law, attacked on the high seas a neutral ship engaged in US domestic trade. In reversing the federal district court the federal appellate court declared:

> 'Although seldom employed, the Alien Tort Statute means what it says. If an alien brings a suit, for a tort only, that sufficiently alleges a violation of the law of nations, then the district court has jurisdiction. All of these requirements are met in the instant case. Appellants are aliens, they are Liberian corporations. This suit is for a tort only—the bombing of a ship without justification.'

The court observed that

> 'not only is the legislative history of the Foreign Sovereign Immunities Act devoid of any indication that Congress intended the FSIA to bar jurisdiction under the unusual circumstances of this case, a suit under the Alient Tort Act for a violation of international law, but in our view, construing the FSIA to require that result would actually frustrate Congress's purpose.'

The court also pointed out

> 'the modern view . . . is that sovereigns are not immune from suit for their violations of international law. . . . That international law currently denies immunity for violations of international law is not surprising, when one considers that international law consists primarily of rules guiding the conduct of nations. If sovereign acts were immunized today from scrutiny under international law, the exception would nearly swallow the rule. For example, the emerging international law prohibiting genocide . . . would make little sense, even in theory, if sovereign states were not covered by the prohibition. Indeed, the sovereign immunity defense raised by Nazi war criminals at the Nuremberg trials was rejected by the international tribunal. . . . Since the sinking of a neutral vessel on the high seas without justification violates a substantive principle of international law, no matter who does the sinking, there is no immunity under international law in this case. We hold therefore that the Alien Tort Statute provides jurisdiction over Argentina.'

Section 6. Alienage Jurisdiction Revisited

The desirability of providing aliens and foreign plaintiff with access to the federal courts was recognized by the founders of the United States and they expressly granted aliens and foreign plaintiffs the right to have their cases heard in the federal courts.[90] Federal courts were above local prejudices against foreigners, it was believed, and furthermore, there was concern that foreign nations might take offense if the affairs of their citizens were not treated at the national level of courts in the United States. In DiFrischia *v*. New York Central Railroad Co[91] the Third US Court of Appeals bent over backwards to protect the interest of the foreign plaintiff; it seems that the defendant played 'fast and loose with the judicial machinery' and almost 'deceived the court' as the defendant inserted one defense after another to the utter consternation of the foreign plaintiff!

Bringing an action into federal courts pursuant to the court's alienage jurisdiction is accomplished under 28 USC 1332(a)(2) or 1332(a)(3):

> 'The district courts shall have original jurisdiction of all civil actions where the matter in controversy exceeds the sum or value of $10,000 exclusive of interest and costs, and is between . . . citizens of a State and citizens or subjects of a foreign state; or citizens of different States and in which citizens or subjects of a foreign state are additional parties.'

In determining whether an individual is a citizen or subject of a foreign state for purposes of alienage jurisdiction, the court must look to the law of the foreign nation involved and whether the foreign nation recognizes the person as one of its citizens or subjects.[92] A foreign corporation is considered a citizen of the foreign state in which it is incorporated;[93] after 1958 the foreign corporation is also a citizen of the country where it has its principal place of business.[94] However, one New York federal court holds that foreign corporations are only citizens of the country in which they are incorporated.[95] Fourteen years later that same court in Bergen Shipping Co, Ltd *v*. Japan Marine Services, Ltd[96] held that when a foreign corporation has its principal place of business in the United States, it should be considered only a US corporation and its foreign citizenship should be disregarded. Nevertheless, the court stated that alienage jurisdiction existed in the action between a Liberian corporation with its principal place of business in New York and a Japanese corporation.

Where aliens are on both sides of the action the US Constitution does not authorize the exercise of alienage jurisdiction. As stated in Tsitsinakis *v*. Simpson, Spence & Young:[97]

> 'It is well settled that in order to sustain jurisdiction of an action based on diversity of citizenship in the federal court, each plaintiff must be capable of suing each defendant in that court . . . The courts of the United States have no jurisdiction of a case in which both parties are aliens . . . if both a party plaintiff and party defendant are aliens, the district court lacks jurisdiction, even though there are other parties in the action, as plaintiffs or defendants, who are citizens of the United States . . . Since in this action the plaintiff and the two individual defendants (who, it seems, are indispensable to the action) are aliens, the court has no jurisdiction to entertain the action.'

But there is respectable authority to the contrary that alienage jurisdiction does exist.[98]

Suit by an alien in US courts involves the prerequisites of Standing and Lack of Political Question. As the US Supreme Court stated in 1908 in Disconto Gesellschaft *v.* Umbreit,[99] aliens 'are ordinarily permitted to resort to the courts for the redress of wrongs and the protection of their rights'. But US courts have been reluctant to grant Standing to aliens who sue the US Government, for example, for allegedly unconstitutional actions, as illustrated by Berlin Democratic Club *v.* Rumsfeld[100] where the federal district court in the District of Columbia denied Standing to a non-resident alien. However, in Bivens *v.* Six Unknown Federal Narcotic Agents[101] the highest court held that a 'person' could sue a federal official for damages based on violation of his Fourth Amendment rights. And in Cardenas *v.* Smith[102] it was held that a non-resident alien can satisfy Article III Standing requirements by showing 'injury in fact' that 'fairly can be traced' to wrongful US governmental activity abroad, which wrong is 'likely to be redressed by a favorable decision'. The court lumped US citizens and aliens in the same ball of wax: 'It is the injury and not the party that determines . . . Standing'. The second hurdle that an alien must overcome before being entitled to bring suit in US courts is the Lack of a Political Question. In Baker *v.* Carr[103] the court listed the following elements as indicative of a non-justiciable political question, *equally referable to the alien and the US citizen:*

> 'commitment of the issue to a coordinate political department; lack of judicially measurable standards; impossibility of deciding the case without an initial policy determination of a kind clearly for nonjudicial discretion; an unusual need for unquestioning adherence to a political decision; potential of embarassment due to multifarious pronouncements by various departments over one question; or impossibility of deciding the issue without expressing lack of respect for a coordinate political department.'[104]

Notes

1. *See* Article III, Section 1, of the US Constitution.
2. *See*, for example, Huffman *v.* Pursue, 420 US 592 (1975), reh den. 421 US 971 (1975) 2.1. The State of New York in 1984 took a bold step to entertain jurisdiction in favor of foreign plaintiffs by enacting Section 5–1401 of the New York General Obligations Law, which provides that parties to a contract involving at least $250,000, may choose New York law as the governing law of the contract 'whether or not such contract . . . bears a reasonable relation' to the State of New York. Under Section 5–1402, if the

transaction involves more than $1 million, both non-New York corporations and non-residents of the State of New York may be sued in New York if the contract includes a Section 5–1401 clause, as above elucidated, as well as a consent by the defendant to be subject to New York jurisdiction. New York CPLR 327 was also amended to prohibit the defendant from pleading that New York is not a convenient place to try the case.

3. —F2d—(2nd Cir, 1986).
4. 616 F Supp 1495 (1985).
5. *See* Textor *v.* Board of Regents of Northern Illinois University, 87 FRD 751 (ND Ill, 1980), and Beattue *v.* US, 756 F2d 91 (DC Cir, 1985).
6. 28 USC 1391(a). The pertinent provision is part of 28 USC 1391 which reads as follows:

> § 1391. *Venue generally*
>
> (a) A civil action wherein jurisdiction is founded only on diversity of citizenship may, except as otherwise provided by law, be brought only in the judicial district *where all plaintiffs or all defendants reside, or in which the claim arose.*
>
> (b) A civil action wherein jurisdiction is not founded solely on diversity of citizenship may be brought only in the judicial district where *all defendants* reside, or in which the claim arose, except as otherwise provided by law.
>
> (c) A corporation may be sued in any judicial district in which it is incorporated or licensed to do business or is doing business, and such judicial district shall be regarded as the residence of such corporation for venue purposes.
>
> (d) An alien may be sued in any district.
>
> (e) A civil action in which each defendant is an officer or employee of the United States or any agency thereof acting in his official capacity or under color of legal authority, or an agency of the United States, may, except as otherwise provided by law, be brought in any judicial district in which: (1) a defendant in the action resides, or (2) the cause of action arose, or (3) any real property involved in the action is situated, or (4) the plaintiff resides if no real property is involved in the action.
>
> The summons and complaint is such an action shall be served as provided by the Federal Rules of Civil Procedure except that the delivery of the summons and complaint to the officer or agency as required by the rules may be made by certified mail beyond the territorial limits of the district in which the action is brought.'

7. 28 USC 1391(c).
8. 406 US 706 (1972).
9. *Id.*, at p. 714.
10. 28 USC 1603; *see* Chapter 3 herein.
11. 28 USC 1391(f)(1).
12. 28 USC 1391(f)(2).
13. 28 USC 1391(f)(3).
14. 28 USC 1391(f)(4).
15. *See* Chapter 3 herein; Pub L 94–583, 90 Stat 2891 (1976), codified at 28 USC 1330 *et seq.*

16. *See* Schmidt *v.* Polish People's Republic, 579 F Supp 23 (SDNY, 1984), aff 742 F2d 67 (2nd Cir, 1984).
17. 755 F2d 1463 (11th Cir, 1985).
18. *Id* at p. 1468.
19. '§ 1404.*Change of venue*

    (a) For the convenience of parties and witnesses, in the interest of justice, a district court may transfer any civil action to any other district or division where it might have been brought.

    (b) Upon motion, consent or stipulation of all parties, any action, suit or proceeding of a civil nature or any motion or hearing thereof, may be transferred, in the discretion of the court, from the division in which pending to any other division in the same district. Transfer or proceedings *in rem* brought by or on behalf of the United States may be transferred under this section without the consent of the United States where all other parties request transfer.

    (c) A district court may order any civil action to be tried at any place within the division in which it is pending.

    (d) As used in this section, "district court" includes the United States District Court fo the District of the Canal Zone; and "district" includes the territorial jurisdiction of that court.'
20. 376 US 612 (1964).
21. In Parsons *v.* Chesapeake & Ohio Railroad Co (375 US 71, 1963) an action dismissed by an Illinois State court because of *forum non conveniens* was later filed in a federal court in Illinois. The US Supreme Court held that the Illinois decision did not require the federal court to transfer the case under Section 1404(a):

    > 'Since different factual considerations may be involved in each court's determination, we hold that a prior state court dismissal on the ground of *forum non conveniens* can never serve to divest a federal district judge of the discretionary power vested in him by Congress to rule upon a motion to transfer . . . .'

22. *Supra* note 19. *See* Harrison *v.* United Fruit Co, 141 F Supp 35 [1948], and Norwood *v.* Kirkpatrick 349 US 29 [1955]. Obviously the federal transfer statute has no applicability where the only alternative forum is a State court (Gross *v.* Owen, 221 F2d 94, DC Cir, 1955) or where the alternative forum is in a foreign country. (Vanity Fair Mills *v.* Eaton Co, 234 F2d 633, 2nd Cir, 1956; cert den 352 US 658, 1956).
23. *See* Cessna Aircraft Co *v.* Brown, 348 F2d 689 (10th Cir, 1965).
24. 363 US 335 (1960).
25. *Supra* note 20.
26. 317 F Supp 1009 (Del, 1970).
27. 263 F Supp 865 (SC, 1967).
28. 158 F Supp 404 (SDNY, 1958).
29. *See* generally 46 J of Air L & Com 941 (1981).
30. 148 F Supp 104 (SDNY, 1956).
31. 202 F Supp 309 (SDNY, 1962).
32. Note that consolidation is not always the *summum bonum* for on occasions the benefits may be achieved without transfer where a verdict unfavorable to the defendant in the transferee forum may be determinative of the liability issues in the transferor forum under Collateral Estoppel principles, as shown in Schmidt *v.* American Flyers Airline Corp, 260 F Supp 813 (SDNY, 1966).

Generally the motion to transfer under Section 1404(a) will be made prior to the motion to dismiss under *forum non conveniens*, and therein lies a hidden hazard because the transferee court may very well conclude that the defendant (or plaintiff) seeking the transfer was content to continue the action in the home forum and therefore should not be interested in subsequent dismissal based on *forum non conveniens*. In Reyno *v*. Piper Aircraft Co (*supra*) and Third US Court of Appeals had observed in 1980 that the party requesting the transfer could be equitably estopped from moving subsequently to dismiss the action.

33. 713 F2d 339 (8th Cir, 1983).
34. *See* Dangerfield *v*. Bachman Foods, Inc, 515 F Supp 1383 (ND, 1981).
35. § 1406. *Cure or waiver of defects*

(a) The district court of a district in which is filed a case laying venue in the wrong division or district shall dismiss, or if it be in the interest of justice, transfer such case to any district or division in which it could have been brought.

(b) Nothing in this chapter shall impair the jurisdiction of a district court of any matter involving a party who does not interpose timely and sufficient objection to the venue.

(c) If a case within the exclusive jurisdiction of the Court of Claims is filed in a district court, the district court shall, if it be in the interest of justice, transfer such case to the Court of Claims, where the case shall proceed as if it had been filed in the Court of Claims on the date it was filed in the district court.

(d) As used in this section, 'district court' includes the United States District Court for the District of the Canal Zone; and 'district' includes the territorial jurisdiction of that court.

§ 1441. *Actions removable generally*

(a) Except as otherwise expressly provided by Act of Congress, any civil action brought in a State court of which the district courts of the United States have original jurisdiction, may be removed by the defendant or the defendants, to the district court of the United States for the district and division embracing the place where such action is pending.

(b) Any civil action of which the district courts have original jurisdiction founded on a claim or right arising under the Constitution, treaties or laws of the United States shall be removable without regard to the citizenship or residence of the parties. Any other such action shall be removable only if none of the parties in interest properly joined and served as defendants is a citizen of the State in which such action is brought.

(c) Whenever a separate and independent claim or cause of action, which would be removable if sued upon alone, is joined with one or more otherwise non-removable claims or causes of action, the entire case may be removed and the district court may determine all issues therein, or, in its discretion, may remand all matters not otherwise within its original jurisdiction.

36. Note that CPLR 511 provides:

> '(a) *Time for motion or demand*. A demand under subdivision (b) for change of place of trial on the ground that the county designated for that purpose is not a proper county shall be served with the answer or before the answer is served. A motion for change of place of trial on any other ground shall be made within a reasonable time after commencement of the action.
>
> '(b) *Demand for change of place of trial, upon ground of improper venue, where motion made*. The defendant shall serve a written demand that the action be tried in a county he specifies as proper. Thereafter the defendant

may move to change the place of trial within fifteen days after service of the demand, unless within five days after such service plaintiff serves a written consent to change the place of trial to that specified by the defendant. Defendant may notice such motion to be heard as if the action were pending in the county he specified, unless plaintiff within five days after service of the demand serves an affidavit showing either that the county specified by the defendant is not proper or that the county designated by him is proper.'

37. *See* Bult *v*. Kornspan, 37 AD2d 672, 322 NYS2d 366 (1980).
38. 103 AD2d 88, 2nd Dept, 1984.
39. 330 US 518 (1947).
40. 41 NYS2d 338 (1937).
40.1 —NYS2d— 1 May 1987
41. 28 USC 1331.
42. 28 USC 1333.
43. 28 USC 1332.
43.1 106 S Ct 3229 (1986).
43.2 21 USC 301–392.
44. *See* Avco Corp *v*. Aero Lodge, 390 US 557 (1968).
45. *See* Montalet *v*. Murray, 8 US 14 (1807).
46. *See* Owen Equipment & Erection Co *v*. Kroger, 437 US 365 (1978).
47. 15 Av Cas (CCH) 18,032 (ND Ill, 1980).
48. 583 F Supp 927 (SDNY, 1985).
49. *See* Murphy *v*. Gutfreund, 583 F Supp 957 (SDNY, 1985).
50. *See* In Re Air Crash Disaster Near Bombay, India, 531 F Supp. 1175 (WD Wash, 1982), defining 'maritime nexus'.
51. *See* Lauritzen *v*. Larsen, 345 US 571 (1953) at p. 582.
52. *Id*.
53. 398 US 306 (1970). *See* Puerto Rico Maritime Shipping Authority *v*. Luallipam, Inc, 631 F Supp 1472 (PR, 1986), where Greek law was applied under the Lauritzen-Rhoditis choice of law rules. The Greek seaman was injured in a US port by a fall while painting the mast on a Greek-flag vessel owned by a Liberian corporation. The federal district court in Puerto Rico asserted jurisdiction over the plaintiff's good faith wage claim under 46 USC 591 as well as over his non-wage claim as there were no special circumstances for refusal. The Greek law that the court applied was a comparative workers' compensation statute that provided for automatic recovery.
54. 375 US 106 (1963).
55. 308 US 433 (1940).
56. 95 US 714 (1878).
57. 326 US 310 (1945).
58. Mr Chief Justice Stone spelled it out in these classic words:

'It is evident that the criteria by which we mark the boundary line between those activities which justify the subjection of a corporation to suit, and those which do not, cannot be simply mechanical or quantitative. The test is not merely, as has sometimes been suggested, whether the activity, which the corporation has seen fit to procure through its agents in another state, is a little more or a little less. . . . Whether due process is satisfied must depend rather upon the quality and nature of the activity in relation to the fair and orderly administration of the laws which it was the purpose of the due process clause to insure. That clause does not contemplate that a state may make binding a judgment *in personam* against an individual or corporate defendant with which the state has no contacts, ties or relations. . . But to the extent that a corporation exercises the privilege of conducting activities within a state, it enjoys the benefits and protection of the laws of that state. The exercise of that privilege may give rise to obligations; and, so far as those obligations arise out of or are connected with the activities within the state, a procedure which requires the corporation to respond to a suit brought to enforce them can, in most instances, hardly be said to be undue. . . . Applying these standards, the activities carried on in behalf of appellant in the State of Washington were neither irregular nor casual. They were systematic and continuous throughout the years in question. They resulted in a large volume of interstate business, in the course of which appellant received the benefits and protection of the laws of the state, including the right to resort to the courts for the enforcement of its rights. The obligation which is here sued upon arose out of those very activities. It is evident, that these operations establish sufficient contacts or ties with the state of the forum to make it reasonable and just according to our traditional conception of fair play and substantial justice to permit the state to enforce the obligations which appellant has incurred there. Hence we cannot say that the maintenance of the present suit in the State of Washington involves an unreasonable or undue procedure.'

59. 355 US 220 (1957).
60. 'The contract was delivered in California, the premiums were mailed from there and the insured was a resident of that State when he died. It cannot be denied that California has a manifest interest in providing effective means of redress for its residents when their insurers refuse to pay claims. These residents would be at a severe disadvantage if they were forced to follow the insurance company to a distant State in order to hold it legally accountable. When claims were small or moderate individual claimants frequently could not afford the cost of bringing an action in a foreign forum—thus in effect making the company judgment proof. Often the crucial witnesses—as here on the company's defense of suicide—will be found in the insured's locality. Of course there may be inconvenience to the insurer if it is held amenable to suit in California where it had this contract but certainly nothing which amounts to a denial of due process. Cf. Travelers Health Ass'n *v.* Commonwealth of Virginia ex rel. State Corporation Comm, 339 US 643. There is no contention that respondent did not have adequate notice of the suit or sufficient time to prepare its defenses and appear.'
61. 357 US 235 (1958).
62. 763 F2d 55 (2nd Cir, 1985).
63. Another example involving the State of Hawaii is seen in Duple Motor Bodies Inc *v.* Hollingsworth, 417 F2d 231 (9th Cir, 1969) where the Ninth US Court of Appeals ruled that the federal district court in Hawaii properly asserted personal jurisdiction over an English corporation, Duple Motor, which furnished bus bodies in England to another English company, Vauxhall, which, in turn, assembled the buses and shipped them to the Hawaiian customer. Duple Motor had not previously done business in Hawaii, had maintained no office in Hawaii, and did not advertise in Hawaii; its sole contact with Hawaii was the contract to supply bus bodies in England to an English bus manufacturer for transportation in Hawaii. The court observed, however, that

Duple Motor knew when it sold the bus bodies to Vauxhall that the assembled bus would be sold to a Hawaiian customer for use in Hawaii. This knowledge 'was sufficient to meet the requirements of due process . . . We do not regard it as offensive to fair play or substantial justice or an undue burden on foreign commerce to require a manufacturer to defend his product wherever he himself has placed it, either directly or through normal channels of trade'. (It should be pointed out that all parties had agreed that Vauxhall was subject to the personal jurisdiction of the court in Hawaii.)

64. 100 S Ct 559 (1980).
65. In Lasky *v.* Continental Products Corp, 569 F Supp 1225 (Pa, 1983) Datsun vehicles manufactured by a Japanese company were marketed and sold in Pennsylvania. The court held that the foreign manufacturer was not shielded from personal jurisdiction because it marketed and distributed its vehicles by a independent dealership distribution system since the defendant expected its vehicles to be sold in the State of Pennsylvania. Accordingly, the defendant should expect to be subject to the jurisdiction of courts in Pennsylvania.
66. At pp. 566 and 567, citing Shaffer *v.* Heitner, 433 US 186 (1977).
67. 'When a corporation "purposefully avails itself of the privilege of conducting activities within the forum State," Hanson *v.* Denkla, [357 US at 253] it has clear notice that it is subject to suit there, and can act to alleviate the risk of burdensome litigation by procuring insurance, passing the expected costs on to customers, or, if the risks are too great, severing its connection with the State. Hence if the sale of a product of a manufacturer or distributor such as Audi or Volkswagen [the national distributor] is not simply an isolated occurrence, but arises from the efforts of the manufacturer or distributor to serve, directly or indirectly, the market for its product in other States, it is not unreasonable to subject it to suit in one of those States if its allegedly defective merchandise has there been the source of injury to its owners or to others. [p. 567]
68. 433 US 186 (1977).
69. *See* Harvey *v.* Chemie Grunenthal, 354 F2d 428 (2nd Cir, 1965); cert den 384 US 1001 (1966).

69.1 —F Supp.— (SDNY, Aug. 1987).

69.2 —F Supp.— (SDNY, Aug. 1987).

70. 9B Uniform Laws Ann.
71. 53 USLW 4879 (1985).
72. *Id.* at p. 4883. For lower court decision, *see* 235 Kan 195, 679 P2d 1159 (1984).
73. *Id.* at p. 4882.
74. *Id.* at p. 4882.
75. 28 USC 1350, based on 1 Stat 73 (1789).
76. 3 F Case 810 (D SC, 1795).
77. 195 F Supp 857 (D Md, 1961).
78. —F Supp—(ED Cal, 1984).
79. 630 F2d 876 (2nd Cir, 1980), on remand 577 F Supp 860 (EDNY, 1984) *See* Siderman *v.* Republic of Argentina, —F Supp— (CD Cal, 1985), holding that neither the Alien Tort Claims Act nor the Foreign Sovereign Immunities Act provided an exception to the defendant government's immunity from suit. *Also see* Berkovitz *v.* Islamic Republic of Iran, 735 F2d 329 (9th Cir, 1984), to the effect that the wrongful death action could not be brought against the government of Iran.
80. 726 F2d 774 (DC Cir, 1984) cert den 470 US 1003 (1985).
81. According to Judge Bork at p. 799.
82. *See* 27 Ariz L Rev 438 (1985).
83. 519 F2d 1001 (2nd Cir, 1975).

84. *Id.*
85. 572 F2d 913 (2nd Cir, 1978).
86. 586 F2d 625 (6th Cir, 1978).
87. 534 F2d 24 (2nd Cir, 1976).
88. 225 F Supp 292 (D Pa, 1963).
89. 18 US 153 (1820).
89.1 —F2d— (2nd Cir, 1987).
90. *See* Farrand, The Framing of the Constitution 154 (1913).
91. 279 F2d 141 (3rd Cir, 1960).
92. *See* United States *v.* Wong Kim Ark, 169 US 649 (1898) at p. 668.
93. *See* National Steamship Co *v.* Tugman, 106 US 118 (1882) at p. 121.
94. *See* 28 USC 1332(c).
95. *See* Eisenberg *v.* Commercial Union Assurance Co, 189 F Supp 500 (SDNY, 1960).
96. 386 F Supp 430 (SDNY, 1974).
97. 90 F Supp 578 (SDNY, 1950).
98. *See* State Farm Fire & Casualty Co *v.* Tashire, 386 US 523 (1967) at pp. 530 and 531.
99. 208 US 570 (1908).
100. 410 F Supp 144 (1976).
101. 403 US 388 (1971).
102. 733 F2d 909 (DC Cir, 1984).
103. 369 US 186 (1962).
104. *See* generally 17 Internat L and Pol 287 (1985).

Chapter 3. Sovereign Immunity and the Foreign Plaintiff

Section 1. The Sovereign Immunity Doctrine

The foreign plaintiff bringing his products liability suit into US courts against a government must face the recognized universal legal principle that a government and all its subdivisions and agencies accept liability for acts or omissions only by consent or by waiver.[1] The underlying premise harkening back to the earliest of times is that the 'king can do no wrong', and hence governments are simply immune from liability for their acts or omissions unless the governments [in enlightened times] have consented or waived this right of sovereign immunity. However, in recent times an increasing number of nations have applied a doctrine of limited immunity under which a sovereign or government enjoys immunity only where the sovereign or government was exercising authority in a purely government, non-commercial capacity.[2] In the United States the Foreign Sovereign Immunities Act (1976), as delineated hereinafter in Section 2, controls and determines whether the foreign sovereign or government is or is not immune from liability.[3] The Federal Tort Claims Act (1946), as delineated in Section 3 hereinafter, provides that the United States government may be held liable in tort for injuries caused by the negligent acts or omissions of the government, its agencies and employees.[4] Municipal liability, frequently tested under the civil rights legislation at 42 USC 1983, may not be based upon the doctrine of respondent superior;[5] and municipal bodies may not be found liable simply for having employed a tortfeasor, but only liable when unconstitutional action implements or executes a municipal custom or policy.[6] However, public officials at all levels of government have in recent years become amenable to lawsuits under 42 USC 1983, the civil rights statute which states, 'Every person who . . . subjects . . . any citizen of the United States . . . to the deprivation of any rights, privileges or immunities secured by the Constitution and laws, shall be liable to the party injured . . .'. Suit is brought against the public official in his official capacity[7] or against him in his individual capacity.[8] Since municipalities are generally immune from punitive damages,[9] public officials sued in their official capacities are likewise immune from punitive damages.[10] The public official sued in his individual capacity is potentially liable not only for damages and injunctive relief but also for attorney's fees.[11]

A private company may even take advantage of the limited liability of a sovereign or government, as demonstrated in Lerakol *v.* Pan American World

Airways,[12] where the Second US Court of Appeals found that the airline was an agent of the US Postal Service and therefore its liability was limited by an international treaty; the court held that Pan American was performing services 'pursuant to its bailment relationship with sender', and therefore can invoke the particular treaty limiting its liability; and application of the limited liability was 'appropriate in light of the reasoning of this and other courts . . . holding that the liability limitations for air carriers under the Warsaw Convention should be extended to employees and agents of such carriers.'

The Restrictive Theory of Sovereign Immunity had its origins in the earliest US decisions which simply did not do justice in the situation. In 1926, for example, the US Supreme Court in Berizzi Brothers Co *v.* The Pesaro[13] stubbornly upheld the defendant Italian government which operated a vessel engaged in the commercial carriage of goods: 'We know of no international usage which regards the maintenance and advancement of the economic welfare of a people in time of peace as any less a public purpose than the maintenance and advancement of a naval force.' It was the US State Department that actually insisted upon the sovereign immunity of the defendant; courts had allowed the executive branch of government to control the grant of immunity to foreign countries under the guise of fostering international relationships. But in 1952 the so called 'Tate Letter', issued by the US State Department,[14] confirmed that the United States had decided to distinguish between 'public' and 'private or commercial' acts of sovereign nations, holding that only the former acts were entitled to sovereign immunity. In 1976 this Restrictive Theory of Sovereign Immunity was codified in the Foreign Sovereign Immunities Act,[15] delineated hereinafter under Section 2.

The theory of sovereign immunity was tested recently in 1985 in Sanchez-Espinoza *v.* Reagan,[16] where 12 citizens of Nicaragua and 12 members of the US House of Representatives brought suit against President Reagan and other governmental officials and organizations, asserting constitutional, statutory, tort and international law claims based on the defendants' support of the rebel forces in Nicaragua. The federal district court in the District of Columbia[17] dismissed the suit primarily on the ground that it presented a nonjusticiable, political question, and the District of Columbia Court of Appeals affirmed, adding other reasons for dismissal of the suit, such as the court's power to withhold discretionary injunctive relief and the absence of a private right of action. The court also pointed out that, while the suit was nominally against individual officials, it was in fact challenging actions of the United States Government whose sovereign immunity was intact unless waived; the Alien Tort Claims Statute[18] did not serve as a waiver of US sovereign immunity. The court declined to reach the question of whether the protections of the US Constitution extend to all non-US citizens residing abroad, but the court did state that 'as a general matter the danger of foreign citizens using the courts . . . to obstruct the foreign policy of our government' required the court to deny monetary relief.[19] Thus, it would appear that US courts must show deference to the executive branch of government in areas related to US foreign policy.[20] The court found no implied private action for damages for violation of numerous statutes such as the War

Powers Resolution,[21] the Department of State Authorization Act,[22] the National Security Act,[23] or the Neutrality Act.[24]

The 'commercial activity' of the sovereign State is not entitled to immunity from suit, but what constitutes 'commercial activity' is not always clear. Under Section 1603(d) of FSIA,[25] 'commercial activity means either a regular course of commercial conduct or a particular commercial transaction or act. The commercial character of an activity shall be determined by reference to the nature of the course of conduct or particular transaction or act rather than by reference to its purpose.' Section 1605 specifically removes immunity for such defined 'commercial activity'. In Sugarman *v.* Aeromexico[26] the Third US Court of Appeals in 1980 held that the Mexican government airline was not immune from suit for wrongs allegedly suffered by plaintiff in Acapulco, Mexico, as he was waiting in the airport for his delayed homeward flight. The defendant government agency was held to be conducting airline operations as a common, commercial carrier engaged in 'commercial activity'. There must be a 'nexus' between the 'commercial activity' and the cause of action, as illustrated in Gibbons *v.* Udaras na Gaeltachta.[27] 'Commercial activity' means that not only is the act carried on in the particular forum State but the act 'has a substantial contact' with the forum State.[28] Torts committed by a foreign State or government in the absence of a commercial contract or sales transaction but in connection with some form of 'commercial activity' fall within the provisions of FSIA as 'commercial activity'.[29]

Sovereign immunity may be waived under Section 1605(a)(1) of FSIA[30] 'either explicitly or by implication'. The legislative history of Section 1605 expressly states that an agreement to arbitrate[31] or an agreement to submit the matter to the law of another State[32] constitutes an implicit waiver of sovereign immunity. In essence, there has been an intentional and knowing relinquishment of the legal right of immunity, as shown in Castro *v.* Saudi Arabia.[33] Explicit waivers of sovereign immunity may also be found in treaties and international agreements between the parties.[34]

States within the United States have generally asserted sovereign immunity, and any waiver thereof must be accomplished by the legislature of the State. In New York the 1929 enactment of the New York Court of Claims Act expressly made municipalities in the State of New York liable for torts which occurred in the exercise of their governmental or 'public' acts or functions.[35] Section 8 of the New York Court of Claims Act provides in part: 'The state hereby waives its immunity from liability and action and hereby assumes liability and consents to have the same determined in accordance with the rules of law as applied to actions . . . against individuals or corporations . . .' Initially, the specific effect of this waiver by the State of New York as applied to municipalities confused the courts, but in Bernadine *v.* City of New York[36] the New York Court of Appeals held that 'civil subdivisions of the State are answerable equally with individuals and private corporations'. However, since 1945 New York courts have generally been reluctant to accept the avowed legislative intent of waiving such governmental liability.[37]

Section 2. Foreign Sovereign Immunities Act (1976)

Prior to the year 1976 actions by and against foreign states or countries were governed by the same jurisdictional statute as actions by and against citizens or subjects of foreign states, to wit: 28 USC 1332(2), which gave federal district courts original jurisdiction of all civil actions

> 'where the matter in controversy exceeds the sum or value of $10,000 exclusive of interest and costs, as is between
> 1. citizens of different States;
> 2. citizens of a State, and foreign states or citizens or subjects thereof; and
> 3. citizens of different States and in which foreign states or citizens or subjects thereof are additional parties.'

The determination of whether sovereign immunity was applicable often depended upon the recommendation of the US Department of State.[38] But in 1976 the US Congress enacted FSIA[39] which removed the provision regarding foreign states from the alienage jurisdiction statute and enacted separate jurisdictional sections for actions involving foreign states. Under FSIA a foreign state includes not only the government of the foreign country, but also subdivisions, agencies and instrumentalities.[40] A foreign plaintiff may even maintain a suit against a foreign state or country in a federal district court on a non-federal cause of action, as illustrated by the US Supreme Court's ruling in Verlinden B V *v.* Central Bank of Nigeria.[41] The highest court ruled in 1983 that Congress in granting such subject matter jurisdiction, did not exceed the scope of its authority under Article III of the US Constitution. Thus, it appears likely that the federal courts as well as state courts will increasingly be chosen as the forum for disputes between foreign plaintiffs and foreign states or countries.[42]

In the Verlinden case[43] the court dwelt upon 28 USC 1605 which provides in part:

> '(a) A foreign state shall not be immune from the jurisdiction of courts of the United States or of the States in any case—
> 1. in which the foreign state has waived its immunity either explicitly or by implication, notwithstanding any withdrawal of the waiver which the foreign state may purport to effect except in accordance with the terms of the waiver;
> 2. in which the action is based upon commercial activity carried on in the United States by the foreign state; or upon an act performed in the United States in connection with a commercial activity of the foreign state elsewhere; or upon an act outside the territory of the United States in connection with a commercial activity of the foreign state elsewhere and that act causes a direct effect in the United States.'

The Second US Court of Appeals[44] had earlier dismissed the complaint by the foreign plaintiff on the ground that the immunity of the foreign state had been rebutted, but the US Supreme Court reversed, upholding the constitutionally valid grant of subjectmatter jurisdiction. The decision potentially enlarged the role of American courts in promoting the integrity of the world's financial markets, thereby conferring substantial benefits upon US banking interests.[45]

The New York Court of Appeals on 3 June 1986 in Aboujdid *v.* Singapore Airlines, Ltd[46] had occasion to interpret the waiver of immunity under FSIA. The court declared that an entity otherwise entitled to sovereign immunity under FSIA[47] which serves an answer asserting not only a number of affirmative defences other than sovereign immunity but also a counterclaim against plaintiff and their counsel, and in furtherance of its position utilizes a number of procedural devises before attempting some four and half years after commencement of litigation to amend its answer to assert the immunity defense, waives immunity and the grant of permission to serve an amended answer including such a defense does not preclude a finding on the merits that the defense has been waived.' The highest New York court affirmed that 'neither the reasonableness requirement of international law nor the due process requirements of our constitutional law foreclose an action, though brought upon activities wholly unrelated to the United States, against a foreign state agency doing business in the United States and which has waived its immunity and submitted to the jurisdiction of the court. Thereafter dismissal may be obtained only on *forum non conveniens* grounds . . . or on the merits.'

FSIA eliminated prejudgment attachment in most suits against foreign states[48] and also deleted *quasi in rem* jurisdiction by substituting specific methods of service of process by which to obtain *in personam* jurisdiction over the defendant foreign state.[49] Other provisions of FSIA provide for post-judgment attachment to satisfy judgment.[50] The service of process provisions of FSIA are complex and have been the source of an inordinate number of lawsuits over the years.[51]

It is self evident that the United States government itself requires the assistance of the judiciary to protect itself against liability and to accord the United States government some degree of sovereign immunity. In United States *v.* Varig Airlines,[52] for example, the US Supreme Court ruled unanimously that no liability could attach to the United States for certification of aircraft later involved in an air crash: 'Congress could not have intended to impose liability for the regulatory enforcement activities of the Federal Aviation Administration challenged in this case'. The court held that FAA activity was 'discretionary' and therefore protected by the 'discretionary function exception' in the Federal Tort Claims Act.[53] Earlier in Raymer *v.* US[54] the Sixth US Court of Appeals, in a case involving a federal mine safety and health act, held that the federal government was not liable for the failure of its mine inspector to order removal of a hazard from the mine; the court found that no plaintiff had relied on the inspector's action or inaction, and that in any event such reliance would have been unjustifiable since the statute imposed the duty to comply with the statutory provision upon the mine operator and not upon the federal government.

Another very popular defense utilized by those defendants working for or in association with the federal government is the 'government contractor' defense. It is argued that, because of the special relationship with the federal government the contractor doing government work is an extention of the government and therefore immune from liability. The Seventh US Court of Appeals in Tillett *v.* J. I. Case Co[55] upheld the 'government contractor' defense in a case where the plaintiff-widow of a serviceman sued the manufacturer of a front end loader. Her husband was killed in West Germany while operating the machine that overturned and crushed him. [The machine was manufactured in Indiana by the defendant Delaware corporation whose principal place of business was in Wisconsin]. The United States Government had provided the defendant with specifications for various component parts of the machine, the most important specification being the lack of a roll bar for protection of the driver. Suit was filed nearly 3 years after the serviceman's death, and under Indiana law the suit was barred by Indiana's two-year statute of limitations. But the federal appellate court stated that it would have applied Wisconsin's three-year statute of limitations under conflicts of laws rules *but for* the fact that the death did not occur in Wisconsin. The 'government contractor' defense broke the widow's case wide open, since under the Feres case[56] the federal government is not liable for injuries to servicemen where the injuries arise from activity incident to military service, and the federal government's immunity would be undermined if the same immunity was not extended to military suppliers who could impose the costs upon the United States Government through contractual mechanisms. The appellate court also opined that to hold these contractors liable for 'design defects' created or approved by the federal government would thrust the judiciary into the decision-making process of the military. Still another basis for the decision to deny damages to the widow was the argument that government contractors often possess no negotiation leverage and are compelled by federal law to produce products under contracts of adhesion. Finally, the extension of government immunity to contractors provides incentives for suppliers to consult and collaborate with the Government in developing and testing equipment.

The 'government contractor' defense has apparently been limited to 'design defect' cases and has not been extended to manufacturing flaw or failure to warn cases in products liability.[57]

In Sanner *v.* Ford Motor Co[58] Ford manufactured a jeep without a seat belt, and the plaintiffs were injured allegedly due to the absence of the seat belt. Ford defended successfully on the ground that the jeep was made to government specifications which did not include such safety features as a seat belt. Accordingly, there was no defect in design and no liability could be predicated against Ford. Thus, Ford was able to hide behind the cloak of the 'government contractor' defense. But in O'Keefe *v.* Boeing Co[59] the court acknowledged the military involvement in the design of the aircraft, but this fact alone 'neither exonerates the defendant nor has it in any way altered the defendant's duty as a manufacturer.' Still the 'government contractor' defense represents majority opinion in the US today.

In Lockheed Aircraft Corp *v.* US[60] there was a claim by a civilian employee of the US against Lockheed for damages arising out of a military accident of the Lockheed aircraft near Saigon, Vietnam. (Damages against the US Government were limited, however, by the Federal Employee's Compensation Act or FECA.) The highest US court held in 1983 that Lockheed could claim indemnity from the US government on the grounds that FECA does not bar such claims against the federal government even under the Federal Tort Claims Act.[61] Thus, it would appear that, as a result of this decision, the US Government is already subject to suit for indemnification where the facts indicate that the US Government may have responsibility for the accident. The federal government here had made admissions of responsibility in connection with the motion seeking indemnity during the pre-trial period. The Lockheed case may also expose the federal government to various state law standards of comparative negligence.

Section 3. Federal Tort Claims Act (1946)

The foreign plaintiff has ample opportunity to bring suit in the US against the federal government, its agencies and instrumentalities under the Federal Tort Claims Act[62] which since 1946 provided that the government may be held liable in tort for injuries caused by the negligent acts or omissions of its employees. This waiver of sovereign immunity reflects the sentiment of Congress that the US Government should be held legally responsible for its negligent conduct.[63] Section 1346(b) of 28 USC sets forth the gist of the statute[64] but Section 2680(a) provides that FTCA 'shall not apply to any claim based upon an act or omission of an employee of the government, exercising due care, in the execution of a statute or regulation, whether or not such statute or regulation be valid, or based upon the exercise or performance or the failure to exercise or perform a discretionary function or duty on the part of a federal agency or an employee of the government, whether or not discretion involved be abused.' In addition there are a number of other exceptions to FTCA such as the loss of mail by the US Government, the negligence of government tax or customs officers, admiralty claims, any claim arising out of a quarantine by the United States; and claims arising out of false imprisonment, assault and battery, malicious prosecution, deceit, or interference with contract rights by federal law enforcement officers. But it is the 'discretionary function' exception that has given plaintiffs the most difficulty. In Dalehite *v.* US[65] the US Supreme Court held that the United States was not liable for damages arising out of an explosion because the program leading to the explosion was discretionary and because the negligence occurred at a policy level within the meaning of the provisions of FTCA. But in 1955 in Indian Towing Co *v.* US[66] the same highest court held the United States liable under FTCA for the US Coast Guard's negligence in operating a lighthouse because the negligence was operational and did not involve policy-making discretion. In 1984 in United States *v.* SA Empresa de Viacao Aerea Rio Grandense, Varig Airlines,[67] where a Boeing aircraft caught fire due to a smoldering cigarette that was not extinguished when placed in a lavatory trash receptacle, the court held that the United States was not liable for the 135 deaths and other damages resulting from the negligent decision of the Federal Aviation Administration not to inspect a lavatory disposal unit in the Boeing aircraft. The FAA determination was discretionary, and therefore the federal government was not liable under FTCA. On the other hand, the Eighth US Court of Appeals in 1985 in McMichael *v.* US[68] ruled that the deaths and injuries caused by an explosion at a Government-supervised munitions plant involved the US Defense Department as a proprietor who had failed to perform mandatory inspections by on-site government inspectors, and therefore the Government was liable under FTCA. The inspections involved no judgment nor agency policy, according to the court. But generally sovereign immunity of the federal government is readily upheld. Civilians who lived downwind from the federal government's Nevada test and who sustained severe injuries therefrom were held not to be entitled to compensation in Allen *v.* United States.[68.1] Military personnel exposed to radiation in the federal government's A-bomb tests had their suits dismissed in In Re Consolidated Atmosphere Testing Litigation,[68.2] even though military contractors working for the federal government had caused the radiation. (Under 42 USC 2212 the federal government is required to substitute itself for the military contractors as a defendant; the 'discretionary exception' under the FTCA immunized both defendants from liability.)

The case of United States *v.* Brown[69] involved a discharged veteran who had been a victim of malpractice by the Veterans Administration; the federal government's defense was the Feres doctrine[70] which involved servicemen on active duty, and recognized the sovereign immunity of the federal government. But here in 1955 plaintiff recovered[71] and the US Supreme Court explained the Feres doctrine in these terms: 'The peculiar and special relationship of the soldier to his superiors, the effects of the maintenance of such suits on discipline, and the extreme results that might obtain if suits under the Federal Tort Claims Act were allowed for negligent orders given or negligent acts committed in the course of military duty, led the court to read that Act as excluding claims of that character.'[72] However, in United States *v.* Lee[73] the Ninth US Court of Appeals subsequently denied any serviceman on active duty the right to sue the government under FTCA, irrespective of whether military discipline was involved. But in Johnson *v.* US[74] the Eleventh US Court of Appeals in 1985 held that where elements of military discipline were not involved a serviceman or his estate could sue the United States under FTCA; upon rehearing the decision was affirmed,[75] giving a helicopter pilot for the US Coast Guard who had been dispatched to search for a civilian boat and who died as a result of the negligence of civilian air traffic controllers employed by the Federal Aviation Administration, the right to sue the federal government. Obviously here no military discipline was involved, and therefore suit under FTCA was possible.[76]

The first step in suit against the United States Government is the presentation of an administrative claim on 'Standard Form 95' to the responsible federal agency prior to the initiation of the suit.[77] The purpose behind this step is clearly to afford the Government an opportunity to settle the claim, if possible. The step is jurisdictional and cannot be waived; the filing of the administrative claim must occur within 2 years of the date of accident. The second step is the six-months' wait for the federal government agency to act on the claim; failure to act indicates rejection, and the claimant then has six months to institute suit in the federal courts. Many federal courts have held that providing insufficient information to allow the federal government agency to process a claim is tantamount to failure to file a proper administrative claim, and the subsequent law suit may be dismissed for lack of jurisdiction.[78] But the filing of the prior administrative claim is not required under 28 USC 2675(a) for third party claimants, cross-claimants, or counter-claimants; this waiver applies only to 'compulsory' counter-claims or third party complaints or cross-claims which arise out of the same transaction or occurrence that is the subjectmatter of the opposing party's claim.[79]

Suit under FTCA must be brought in the federal judicial district where the plaintiff resides or where the negligent act or omission occurred. The United States Government as a defendant has 60 days within which to answer the complaint. There is no right to jury trial.[80] The applicable law is the law of the place where the negligent act or omission occurred, i.e., the whole law of the State or country including its conflicts of laws rules.[81]

Citizens as well as subjects of any foreign state or country which accord US citizens the right to prosecute claims against its government in its courts may, based on reciprocity, also sue the United States in the United States Claims Court.[82]

Notes

1. On the consent basis, *see* The Schooner Exchange *v.* McFadden, 11 US (7 Cranch) 478 (1812) at pp. 481 and 482. On the waiver basis, *see* Terrell *v.* US, decided by the 11th US Court of Appeals on 13 March 1986, in which case the Florida State Department of Transportation was deemed to have waived its immunity from tort actions filed in state court.

   In general, however, the Act of State doctrine, while a matter of federal law, as opposed to a principle of international law, was first articulated by the US Supreme Court in 1897 in Underhill *v.* Hernandez, 168 US 250 (1897), holding that every sovereign State 'is bound to respect the independence of every other sovereign State'. *See* Allied Bank International *v.* Banco Credito Agricola de Cartago, 757 F2d 516 (2nd Cir, 1985) to the effect that the Act of State doctrine was not applicable to Costa Rican decrees suspending payments by Costa Rican banks on the ground that interests affected were situated outside of Costa Rica, thereby rendering the Act of State extraterritorial. On the other hand, in Braka *v.* Bancomer, SNC, 762 F2d 222 (2nd Cir, 1985) the Mexican exchange controls were territorial in scope insofar as they affected plaintiffs' certificates of deposit since the certificates of deposit had their situs in Mexico. The court found it unnecessary to address the existence of a 'commercial activity' exception to the Act of State doctrine because the promulgation of exchange controls clearly constituted sovereign activity. In Callejo *v.* Bancomer, SA,—F2d—(5th Cir, 1985) confirmed that the sovereign action of a foreign government affecting debts situated in the foreign country is generally beyond the scope of judicial review by US courts: 'Both the sovereign immunity and act of state doctrines are rooted in principles of international comity; both involve a balancing of interests in providing a forum to injured parties against our interest in maintaining amicable relations with other nations by respecting their sovereign acts.'

2. *See* 42 Modern L Rev 72 (1979).
3. Pub L 94–583, 90 Stat 2891, at 28 USC 1330, 1332(a)(2), 1391(f), 1441(d), 1602–1611. Great Britain's State Immunity Act (1978) is described in 13 Internat Lawyer 619 (1979).
4. 28 USC 1346(b), 2671, 2680(a) to (n).
5. *See* Monell *v.* Department of Social Services, 436 US658 (1978).
6. *See* Pembaur *v.* City of Cincinnati, 105 S Ct 2427 (1985).
7. *See* Brandon *v.* Holt, 105 S Ct 873 (1985).
8. *See* Lake Country Estates, Inc *v.* Tahoe Regional Planning Agency, 99 S Ct 1171 (1979).
9. *See* City of Newport *v.* Fact Concerts, Inc, 101 S Ct 2748 (1981).
10. *See* Smith *v.* Wade, 103 S Ct 1625 (1983) and also Carey *v.* Piphus, 98 S Ct 1042 (1978).
11. 42 USC 1988.
12. Decision by the 2nd US Court of Appeals on 5 February 1986.
13. 271 US 562 (1926).
14. 26 Dept. of State Bullėtin 984–985.
15. 28 USC 1330 *et seq.*
16. 770 F2d 202 (DC Cir, 1985).
17. 568 F Supp 596 (D DC, 1983).
18. 28 USC 1350; *also* Chapter 2, Section 5 herein.
19. *Supra* note 16 at p. 209.
20. *See* 80 Am J Internat L 350 *et seq* (1986).
21. 50 USC 1541–1548.
22. 50 USC 1546(a).
23. 50 USC 401 *et seq.*
24. 18 USC 960.
25. *See* Section 2 herein.
26. 626 F2d 270 (3rd Cir, 1980).
27. 549 F Supp 1094 (SDNY, 1982)

    The US jurisdictional 'nexus' was deemed to be tenuous in Tchacosh Co *v.* Rockwell International Corp, 766 F2d 1333 (9th Cir, 1985). Here an Iranian corporation brought suit to recover payment under a subcontract with the defendant for construction work at an airport in Iran. Both the federal district court and the federal appellate court found that plaintiff, *inter alia*, lacked authority to bring suit since that authority had been removed by the Act of State of the government of Iran. (Note that the case was not pre-empted by the jurisdiction of the Iran–US Claims Tribunal since the Tribunal's jurisdiction did not extend to claims brought by Iranian nationals against US nationals.) The debt in question was deemed not to be a debt within the United States, and the court refused to embrace the extraterritorial exception under the Act of State doctrine.
28. *See* Gemini Shipping, Inc *v.* Foreign Trade Organization, Inc, 647 F2d 317 (2nd Cir, 1981).

29. *See* Matter of Sedco, Inc, 543 F Supp 561 (Tex, 1982). But Section 1605(a)(5) of FSIA provides that suit for damages based upon an alleged non-commercial tort committed by a foreign government in the United States is actionable in the federal district court. (Renchard *v.* Humphreys & Harding, Inc, 381 F Supp 302, DC, 1974).
30. *See* Section 2 herein.
31. *See* Maritime International Inc *v.* Republic of Guinea, 692 F2d 1094 (DC Cir, 1982).
32. *See* Ipitrade International, Inc *v.* Federal Republic of Nigeria, 465 F Supp 824 (DC, 1978).
33. 510 F Supp 309 (Tex, 1980).
34. *See* Libra Bank *v.* Banco Nacional de Costa Rica, 676 F2d 47 (2nd Cir, 1982).
35. *See* Steitz *v.* City of Beacon, 64 NE2d 704 (NY, 1945).
36. 62 NE2d 604 (NY, 1945).
37. *See* Murrain *v.* Wilson Lines, Inc, 59 NYS2d 750 (1946), aff 72 NE2d 29 (NY, 1947).
38. *See*, for example, Mexico *v.* Hoffman, 324 US 30 (1945).
39. *Supra* note 3.
40. 18 USC 1603. In Colonial Bank *v.* Compagnie Generale Maritime Et Financiere,—F Supp—(Civ 85–7830, SDNY, 15 Oct. 1986) the court dismissed the action for tortious interference and abuse of process on the ground that the court lacked subjectmatter jurisdiction; the court found that defendant was an instrumentality of a foreign state and entitled to a foreign state's immunity: 'To extend jurisdiction to claims brought by all persons indirectly injured by commercial acts of foreign states would subject them to jurisdiction of the United States in an enormously expanded number of cases . . . Given the proclivity of the United States population to devise lawsuits for every contretemps, the harassment of foreign sovereigns by exposure to the jurisdiction of the United States courts would no doubt be considerable.'
41. 103 S Ct 1962 (1983).
42. *See* generally 90 Yale LJ 1861 (1981). But *see* Frolova *v.* USSR, 761 F2d 370 (7th Cir, 1985), to the effect that the Soviet Union was entitled to sovereign immunity in a suit for an injunction and damages when Soviet officials refused to permit plaintiff's husband to emigrate. Plaintiff had unsuccessfully contended that since the USSR was a party to the UN Charter (59 Stat 1031, TS No. 993) and the Helsinki Accords (73 Dept State Bull 323, 1975), the USSR had waived its sovereign immunity for violation of fundamental human rights.

    For a waiver of sovereign immunity, *see* Proyecfin de Venezuela, SA *v.* Banco Industrial de Venezuela, 760 F2d 390 (2nd Cir, 1985). The court here was not concerned that US courts 'will become the courts of choice for local disputes between foreign plaintiffs and foreign sovereign defendants' because 'the traditional doctrine of *forum non conveniens* . . . is still applicable in cases arising under the Foreign Sovereign Immunities Act.' Cf. DeSanchez *v.* Banco Central de Nicaragua, 770 F2d 1385 (5th Cir, 1985) upholding the sovereign immunity under the FSIA.
43. *Supra note* 41. In the Verlinden case the US Supreme Court observed that the FSIA 'does not appear to affect the traditional doctrine of *forum non conveniens*'. Indeed, Congress was particularly concerned that US courts were not 'turned into small international courts of claims . . . open . . . to all comers to litigate any dispute which any private party may have with a foreign state anywhere in the world.'
44. 647 F2d 320 (2nd Cir, 1981).
45. *See* 14 Seton Hall L Rev 598 (1984). In Kalamazoo Spice Extraction Co *v.* The Provisional Military Government of Socialist Ethiopia, —F Supp—(WD Mich, 1985) the defendant expropriated plaintiff's 80% interest in an Ethiopian corporation, and argued that US courts had no jurisdiction because the expropriated property had

no situs in the United States, and furthermore the defendant government was not engaged in 'commercial activity' in the United States. But the federal district court upheld subjectmatter jurisdiction under FSIA, Section 1605(a)(3), applying to cases 'in which rights in property taken in violation of international law are in issue and that property . . . is owned or operated by an agency or instrumentality of the foreign state . . . which was engaged in commercial activity in the United States.' The seizure of the controlling stock interest in the foreign corporation was deemed to be a taking of control of assets and profits of the corporation, and therefore fell within Section 1605(a)(3) of FSIA. Furthermore, the court found that the foreign corporation was an agency of the foreign state that owns the property at issue, and also that the foreign corporation was engaged in commercial activity in the US based upon its substantial sales and purchases in the US. The court rejected defendant's argument that the International Court of Justice was the exclusive forum for adjudication of expropriation claims. *See* earlier version of same case at 729 F2d 422 (6th Cir, 1984), holding that the Act of State doctrine was inapplicable.

46. 437 NYS2d 219 (1980).
47. 28 USC 1602 ff.
48. *See* 28 USC 1620(d).
49. 28 USC 1608.
50. *See* 28 USC 1609 to 1611.
51. *See* International Schools Service *v.* Iran, 505 F Supp 178 (D NJ, 1981); Harris Corp *v.* National Iranian Radio and Telephone, 691 F2d 1344 (11th Cir, 1982); Alberti *v.* Empresa Nicaraguense de la Carne, 705 F2d 250 (7th Cir, 1983); and Gray *v.* Permanent Mission, 443 F Supp 816 (SDNY 1978), aff 508 F2d 1044 (2nd Cir, 1978).
52. 104 S Ct 2755 (1984).
53. Section 3 herein.
54. 660 F2d 1136 (6th Cir, 1981).
55. 756 F2d 591 (7th Cir, 1985).
56. 71 S Ct 153 (1950).
57. *See* Trial Magazine (Sept. 1984) at pp. 60–70.
58. 364 A2d 43 (NJ, 1976).
59. 335 F Supp 1104 (SDNY, 1971).
60. 103 S Ct 1033 (1983).
61. Section 3 herein.
62. *Supra* note 4.
63. *See* generally 51 J Air Law & Commerce 1988 *et seq.* (1985).
64. 'Subject to the provisions of Chapter 171 of this Title, the district courts, together with the United States District Court for the District of the Canal Zone and the District Court of the Virgin Islands, shall have exclusive jurisdiction of civil actions on claims against the United States for money damages accruing on and after 1 January 1945, for injury or loss of property, or personal injury or death caused by negligent or wrongful acts or omissions of any employee of the Government while acting within the scope of his office or employment, under the circumstances where the United States, if a private person, would be liable to the claimant in accordance with the law of the place where the act or omission occurred.
    Section 2671 provides:
    'As used in this chapter and sections 1346(b) and 2401(b) of this title, the term "Federal Agency" includes the executive departments, the military departments, independent establishments of the United States, and corporations primarily acting as instrumentalities or agencies of the United States, but does not include any contractor with the United States.

"Employee of the Government" includes officers or employees of any federal agency, members of military or naval forces of the United States, members of the National Guard while engaged in training or duty under sections 316, 502, 503, 504 or 505 of title 32, and persons acting on behalf of a federal agency in an official capacity temporarily or permanently in the service of the United States, whether with or without compensation.

"Acting within the scope of his office or employment", in the case of a member of the military or naval forces of the United States or a member of the National Guard as defined in section 101(3) of title 32, means acting in the line of duty.'

65. 346 US 15 (1953) at p. 42.
66. 350 US 61 (1955) at p. 75.
67. 104 S Ct 2755 (1984) at p. 2768. According to the New York Times (8 May 1986) at p. A13, there could be no liability on the part of the US government for the deaths of 269 passengers aboard the Korean Airlines plane which was shot down by Soviet fighters when the plane strayed over Soviet territory. The federal district court in the District of Columbia ruled that neither the Federal Aviation Administration nor the US Defense Department had failed to perform any required duties in connection with the disastrous flight: 'Any duty the United States may have had toward plaintiffs' decedents would not extend to the unforeseeable, tragic consequences of the disaster . . . the Soviets' unnecessary act of aggression against KAL 007 was a superceding cause of harm insulating the United States from any liability.'
68. 751 F2d 303 (8th Cir, 1985).

68.1 816 F2d 1417 (10th Cir, 1978).

68.2 — F2d — (9th Cir, 22 June 1987).

69. 348 US 110 (1955).
70. *See* Feres *v.* US, 240 US 135 (1950).
71. *See* US *v.* Stanley, —US— (25 June 1987), wherein the federal government was 'shielded' from liability for secret experiments in the 1950s with LSD and other mind-boggling drugs.
72. *Id.*
73. 400 F2d 558 (9th Cir, 1968).
74. 749 F2d 1530 (11th Cir, 1985).
75. 779 F2d 1492 (11th Cir, 1986).
76. *See* Shearer *v.* US, 105 S Ct 3039 (1985).
77. 28 USC 2675(a).
78. *See* Rothman *v.* US, 434 F Supp 13 (Cal, 1977).
79. *See* United States *v.* Chatham, 415 F Supp 1214 (Ga, 1976).
80. 28 USC 2492.
81. *See* Richard *v.* US, 369 US 1 (1962).
82. 28 USC 2502.

Chapter 4. The Defense of 'Forum Non Conveniens'

Section 1. Forum Non Conveniens Doctrine

In spite of the increased ease and convenience with which people can travel and communicate today,[1] courts in the United States continue to apply the doctrine of *forum non conveniens*.[1.1] In essence, the doctrine means that a court with little relation to either the parties or the cause of action may decline jurisdiction of a case otherwise properly before it.[2] The doctrine presupposes that there are at least two or more forums in which the defendant is amenable to service of process or to whose jurisdiction defendant will consent.[3] At common law *forum non conveniens* allowed, in certain circumstances, dismissal of an action where there was a more convenient, alternate forum, either domestic or foreign.[4] Today in the federal area 28 USC 1404(a) allows a federal district court to transfer an action to another federal forum in which the action might have been brought. In 1983 the Eighth US Court of Appeals in Lehman *v.* Humphrey Cayman, Ltd[5] specifically held that the federal district court should have exercised jurisdiction over the case rather than dismissing the action on grounds of *forum non conveniens*.[6] Here plaintiff's husband was presumed dead after a sailing accident in November 1980 in the Caribbean, and suit for wrongful death was brought against the hotel in the Caribbean in the federal district court of Iowa where plaintiff and her husband resided. The defendant hotel was a corporation organized under the laws of the British West Indies. The appellate federal court reversed the dismissal by the lower court, pointing out that the trial court had abused its discretion,[7] on these grounds:

a. the trial court failed to weigh the relevance of either the plaintiff's residence or plaintiff's choice of forum;
b. defendant's burden of producing witnesses in Iowa was not exceptionally greater than the burden on the plaintiff;
c. defendant's inability to implead the sailboat owner-renter was not due such great importance nor weight; and
d. both the State of Iowa and the Cayman Islands, British West Indies, had a public interest in the products liability litigation.

The case In Re Air Crash Disaster Near Bombay, India,[8] involved an Air India aircraft which crashed into the sea shortly after takeoff from Bombay; all passengers, mostly India nationals, were killed, and suit was brought in the federal district court for the Western District of Washington, home of The Boeing

Company, manufacturer of the aircraft. Prior to suit all claims against Air India were settled, and so the lawsuit was based on allegations that malfunctioning component parts on the aircraft caused the crash. Defendants contended that the crash resulted from the crew's faulty operational control of the aircraft. Pointing out that evidence supporting defendants' contention was to be found in India, defendants moved for dismissal on *forum non conveniens* grounds. The court refused to dismiss, finding that plaintiffs had no alternative forum in which to litigate.[9]

Earlier in 1981 in Hodson *v.* A H Robins Co[10] the federal district court for the Eastern District of Virginia, the home base of the defendant product manufacturer, refused to dismiss the British plaintiffs' action on *forum non conveniens* grounds. The court stressed the 'balance of convenience' factors delineated by the US Supreme Court in Piper Aircraft Co *v.* Reyno[11] including the axiom that plaintiffs' choice of forum should not be disturbed, particularly when defendant cannot show an available, alternate forum. Here the foreign plaintiffs sustained injuries from defendant's Dalkon Shield IUD product which had been inserted in their persons by British physicians in England. But the court emphasized that all decisions and planning, marketing and testing of the products and the actual assembling of the IUDs had occurred not in England but in the Commonwealth of Virginia: 'The place of injury is not the sole test of where the claim arises'.[12] It should be noted that the Reyno case[13] was an action in which there were alternate courts, both federal, State and foreign,[14] and the alternate federal forum was deemed to be more convenient; the court dismissed in favor of Scotland, the most convenient forum.[15]

The federal transfer statute, 28 USC 1404(a), was adopted by Congress in 1948 with much the same purpose as the common law doctrine of *forum non conveniens*. The language of Section 1404(a) sets as the test not only the convenience of the parties and witnesses, but also the interests of justice. It would thus appear that the discretion to transfer a case to another federal court under Section 1404(a) is much broader than under the *forum non conveniens* doctrine. Indeed, Section 1404(a) was not intended to replace the common law doctrine of *forum non conveniens*.[16] But the US Supreme Court in 1955 in Norwood *v* Kirkpatrick[17] did declare: 'When Congress adopted Section 1404(a) it intended to do more than just codify the existing law on *forum non conveniens*. Congress . . . was revising as well as codifying. The harshest result of the application of the old doctrine of *forum non conveniens*, dismissal of the action, was eliminated . . .'[18] The federal district court for the Southern District of New York in 1950 reasoned differently: 'Section 1404(a) has not limited the application of *forum non conveniens* to cases which are capable of being transferred from one federal district to another. Otherwise, it would be a denial of a federal court's inherent power to refuse jurisdiction in cases which should not have been brought in the United States, but rather in the courts of a foreign jurisdiction.'[19] The US Supreme Court in Piper Aircraft Co *v.* Reyno[20] stated in 1981 that 'Section 1404(a) transfers are different than dismissals on the grounds of the common law doctrine of *forum non conveniens*'.[21] Whatever be the final disposition of the argument as to the relationship between the federal transfer statute and the doctrine of *forum non conveniens*, it should be clear that the former demonstrated the intent of Congress to alleviate in the latter the harshness of dismissal of a case, perhaps brought by a foreign plaintiff.

An interesting question arises as to the appealability of conditional orders of dismissal for *forum non conveniens*.[22] In Koke *v.* Phillips Petroleum[23] the plaintiffs were British subjects working under foreign contracts of employment; they were injured while working as divers aboard a vessel in the Norwegian sector of the North Sea. They sued their employers, the vessel owner and the vessel charterer and the federal district court entered a conditional order of dismissal for *forum non conveniens*. The Fifth US Court of Appeals questioned its jurisdiction to entertain an appeal from a conditional dismissal, but nevertheless held that the conditional dismissal was appealable as a final decision under 28 USC 1291 because the conditions were conditions subsequent, rather than conditions precedent, to dismissal. The district court's conditional order required all defendants to consent to jurisdiction in a single appropriate foreign forum, all defendants to waive any defense regarding the statute of limitations, and all defendants consenting to satisfy any judgment rendered in the selected foreign court.[24]

Non-appealability of the denial of a motion to dismiss on a claim of *forum non conveniens* was also affirmed in Carlenstolpe *v.* Merck & Co.[24.1] Here a Swedish citizen had alleged that the US manufacturer's hepatitis vaccine caused his arthritis; the defendant, sued in the federal district court for the Southern District of New York, moved under FRCP Rule 12(b)(3) to dismiss on the grounds of *forum non conveniens*, contending that Sweden was the proper forum because (a) the Swedish government had approved the vaccine; (b) the injury occurred in Sweden; and (c) the important witnesses all resided in Sweden. In denying defendant's motion to dismiss, the trial court pointed out that defendant had not shown that New York 'would be unreasonably inconvenient'. The Second US Court of Appeals in 1987 affirmed the ruling that interlocutory, non-final district court orders are not appealable unless the three criteria set forth by the US Supreme Court in Cohen *v.* Beneficial Industrial Loan Corp[24.2] are satisfied, to wit: (1) the trial court order must conclusively determine the disputed question; (2) the order must resolve an important issue compeletely separate from the merits of the action; and (3) the order must effectively be unreviewable on appeal from a final judgment. The federal appellate court opined that 'it is undisputed that Merck developed, produced, and tested the vaccine in New Jersey and Pennsylvania', thereby making it probable that any evidence relating to defects in manufacturing or in design of the drug product would be located in those States, not in Sweden! The court emphasized that 'the public interest in having a US court decide issues concerning possible tortious conduct occurring in this country' makes New York the convenient forum for all the parties to the litigation.

The purpose of the 'final decision' rule is simply to prevent piecemeal litigation and to respect the autonomy of the lower courts. In Firestone Tire & Rubber Co *v.* Risjord[25] the US Supreme Court stated that the finality requirement—

'[e]mphasizes the deference that appellate courts owe to the trial judge as the individual initially called upon to decide the many questions of law and fact that occur in the course of a trial. Permitting piecemeal appeals would undermine the independence of the district judge, as well as the special role that individual plays in our judicial system. In addition, the rule is in accordance with the sensible policy of "avoid[ing] the obstruction to just claims that would come from permitting the harrassment and cost of a succession of separate appeals from the various rulings to which a litigation may give rise, from its initiation to entry of judgment". (quoting Cobbledick *v.* United States, 309 US 323, 325 (1940).'

In balancing the competing considerations of the inconvenience of piecemeal review and the danger of denying justice by delay the highest court developed an exception to the finality rule, to wit: 'collateral order' doctrine, as articulated in Cohen *v.* Beneficial Loan Corp.[26] Appellate review of certain orders which do not ultimately terminate the litigation but which 'finally determine claims of right separable from the collateral to rights asserted in the action too important to be denied review and too independent of the cause itself to require that appellate considerations be deferred until the whole case is adjudicated' are permitted. For a court order to fall within the exception for 'collateral orders', it must completely determine a disputed question, resolve an important issue completely separate from the merits of the main action, and be effectively unreviewable on appeal from a final judgment. As the Fifth US Court of Appeals in 1962 in Rodriguez *v.* Pan American Life Insurance Co[27] observed:

'There is a clear distinction between the review of transfer orders [for *forum non conveniens*] under 28 USC § 1404(a), which are interlocutory, and, therefore, reviewable rarely, if at all, and orders of dismissal [for *forum non conveniens*] which being final, are appealable as of right.'

Undoubtedly, the landmark case on *forum non conveniens* is the 1981 decision of the US Supreme Court in Piper Aircraft Co *v.* Reyno.[28] An airplane crash in Scotland caused the death of the plaintiff whose estate sued the US corporation that had manufactured the aircraft and the propeller of the Scottish airline that owned the aircraft. Suit was brought in the federal district court in Pennsylvania where the aircraft manufacturer was located. In upholding dismissal upon *forum non conveniens* grounds, the court unfortunately went too far with its xenophobia or fear of strangers by asserting that a foreign plaintiff's choice of forum away from his or her home is entitled to much less weight by the court than a US plaintiff's choice of forum! The Reyno case has since then been interpreted as a means of excluding foreign plaintiffs from suing US defendants in US forums.[29] The highest US court spelled it out:

'When the home forum has been chosen, it is reasonable to assume that this choice is convenient. When the plaintiff is foreign, however, this assumption is much less reasonable. Because the central purpose of any *forum non conveniens* inquiry is to ensure that the trial is convenient, a foreign plaintiff's choice deserves less deference.'

It is well to note that there were no eyewitnesses to the plane crash, but subsequent investigation by Scottish authorities indicated that pilot error and improper maintenance were the probable causes of the crash. These resolved facts were said to justify the hearing in Scotland, although the Scottish airline and the pilot were not named as defendants in the US law suit. (A separate action against the pilot and Scottish airline had been commenced in Scotland.) The initial suit had been brought in a California state court by the secretary of the plaintiffs' counsel as representative of the victims of the crash, all victims being Scottish. The case was immediately removed to the federal court in California, and then transferred to the federal district court in Pennsylvania pursuant to 28 USC 1404(a) because the Pennsylvania manufacturer of the propeller was not subject to personal jurisdiction in California. The trial court, whose determination was upheld by the US Supreme Court, had contended that the plaintiffs' choice of forum was not entitled to the normal degree of deference because of the flagrant 'forum-shopping' by 'foreign citizens seeking to benefit from the more liberal tort rules provided for the protection of citizens and residents of the United States'. The Third US Court of Appeals[30] had reversed on the ground that dismissal of the action would have resulted in a change in the governing substantive law to the detriment of the plaintiffs who relied upon the doctrine of Strict Liability that was not available in Scotland. The appellate court determined that both California and Pennsylvania had paramount interests in the dispute as the situs of the manufacturers of both the aircraft and the propeller, and that 'public interest' weighed in favor of trial in the United States. But the US Supreme Court disagreed on many particulars, especially because 'Scotland has a very strong interest in this litigation' and 'the American interest in this accident is simply not sufficient to justify the enormous commitment of judicial time and resources that would inevitably be required if the case were to be tried here'. It is interesting to note that the US Supreme Court had granted *certiorari* to consider the following two questions, to wit:

1. 'whether, in an action in the federal district court brought by foreign plaintiffs against American defendants, the plaintiffs may defeat a motion to dismiss on the ground of *forum non conveniens* merely by showing that the substantive law that would be applied if the case were litigated in the district court is more favorable to them than the law that would be applied by the courts of their own nation'; and
2. 'whether a motion to dismiss on grounds of *forum non conveniens* should be denied whenever the law of the alternate forum is less favorable to recovery than that which would be applied by the district court'.

The highest court obviously answered both questions in the 'negative'. The federal district court in Pennsylvania had previously concluded that 'if the foreign law that ought to govern a case does not protect its citizens as fully as the law of the dismissing forum, that is a matter to be dealt with in the foreign forum'.

A survey of cases since the 1981 Reyno case shows that federal district courts have not applied the principles of the Reyno case, as illustrated by Fiacco *v.* United Technologies Corp,[31] where dismissal was denied because one plaintiff was from New York; In Re Aircrash Disaster Near Bombay, India, on 1 January 1978,[32] where dismissal was denied on grounds that the alternative forum of India was unlikely to hear plaintiffs' claim; and Canadian Overseas Ores, Ltd *v.* Compania de Acero del Pacifico,[33] where the dismissal was denied because Chile was not an adequate forum. Yet the language of the Reyno case still dominates the thinking of bench and bar: 'American interest in (such) accidents is simply not sufficient to justify the enormous commitment of judicial time and resources that would inevitably be required if the cases were to be tried here'.[34]

On the other hand, the Reyno decision did not even consider the jurisdictional provisions of various Friendship, Commerce and Navigation treaties of the United States, which treaties confer on foreign plaintiffs a jurisdictional footing equal to or identical with that of their domestic counterparts.[35] It is indeed difficult to comprehend the logic of the argument of US defendants who in making the motion to dismiss on *forum non conveniens* grounds contend that they are inconvenienced by the fact that suit is brought against them in the United States and not in the foreign country! As a defensive tactic the dismissal motion should be carefully examined by the court for its inherent bad faith, as the US defendant seeks to abandon US law in favor of the labyrinthal processes and procedures in the foreign jurisdiction generally more favorable to defendants.

It was Judge Timbers of the Second US Court of Appeals in Alcoa SS Co *v.* M/V Nordic Regent[36] who picturesquely delineated the elusive doctrine of *forum non conveniens*:

> 'The doctrine of *forum non conveniens* is not a neat divider, like a fence, which separates the cases where jurisdiction should be retained from those where it should not. Instead, it meanders, like a river; and as a river with time may change its course by the erosion and build-up of its banks, so too the judge-made doctrine of *forum non conveniens* develops new twists and bends, shrinking and growing as it confronts novel factual situations.'

There are defenses to the invocation of the doctrine of *forum non conveniens* such as the statute of limitations; some courts have held that the *forum non conveniens* doctrine will not apply if the alternative forum's statute of limitations would bar plaintiff's claim.[37] Other courts have held that plaintiff's failure to determine the proper forum and file suit there prior to the running of the statute of limitations does not require a court to entertain a suit which it would otherwise dismiss.[38] Defendant's consent to waive any statute of limitations issue would seem to end the argument then and there.[39] Of course, the court may condition the dismissal upon defendant's acceptance of the suit in the alternative forum.[40] In Kassapas *v.* Arkon Shipping Agency, Inc[40.1] the Louisiana appellate court in 1986 reversed the lower court's dismissal of a wrongful death action on grounds of *forum non conveniens*. The court ruled that *forum non conveniens* was procedural, and to sanction the motion would usurp the State legislature's authority, i.e., Article 123 of the Louisiana Code of Civil Procedure provides for *forum non conveniens* transfer from one district court to another but not to a foreign forum. Article 123 simply does not permit *forum non conveniens* dismissal.

Another defense against the motion to dismiss upon *forum non conveniens* grounds may involve the contingency fee system for plaintiffs' lawyers. Indeed, many courts may look upon the prohibition of contingency fees in the foreign forum as a factor favoring retention of the case in US courts. The impecunious foreign plaintiff must not forego his day in court, and so the US court retains jurisdiction as against dismissal under *forum non conveniens*. Lack of enforceability of a foreign judgment is also a defense against dismissal for *forum non conveniens*.

Where the foreign plaintiff sues in the United States, the question of enforceability of a favorable judgment is of considerable importance.[41] The foreign plaintiff's home forum may not have jurisdiction over the assets and property of the defendant and thus be unable to enforce a judgment obtained in the home forum. Accordingly, the enforcement of a judgment may well be a defense to the motion to dismiss based upon *forum non conveniens*, especially where defendant's assets and property are within the United States.

One of the many problems confronting the foreign plaintiff in US courts is the need to bring all possible defendants into court, including both domestic and foreign parties as well as witnesses and documents from abroad. In most cases the US court will not have the power of compulsory process over foreign parties, witnesses and documents; the foreign forum may similarly lack the power over parties, witnesses and documents.[42] However, the defendant or defendants may offer to produce all necessary parties, witnesses and documents for litigation in the foreign forum (where strict liability and high damages are inapplicable) in exchange for dismissal of the action on grounds of *forum non conveniens*. To the US court such an offer by defendant or defendants is attractive for it tends to conserve judicial resources and perhaps creates a single forum which will have jurisdiction over most, if not all, necessary parties, witnesses and documents. Thus, where a US court finds it desirable to look beyond products liability, its inability to obtain jurisdiction over all other possible parties, witnesses and documents will point toward a *forum non conveniens* dismissal.[43]

The unfavorable application of law should not preclude a court from exercising its discretion to dismiss on the basis of *forum non conveniens*, according to the US Supreme Court in Piper Aircraft Co *v.* Reyno.[44] Even drastic limitations of liability are not crucial, provided that the foreign forum is likely to treat the parties fairly and justly. In Phoenix Canada Oil Co *v.* Texaco, Inc,[45] the federal district court in Delaware retained jurisdiction because of its concern about Ecuador's ability to provide effective relief; and in Mobil Tankers Co *v.* Mene Grande Oil Co[46] the Third US Court of Appeals refused to relegate the case to a Venezuelan forum because of Venezuelan 'remedies are far less conducive to fair administration of justice than those available under our admiralty rules. The mode of trial, the lack of adequate pre-trial procedures, and the limitation on the manner in which expert testimony may be offered do not comport with our concepts of fairness.' On the other hand, US court should perhaps hesitate to impose their concepts of justice and fairness on foreign jurisdictions,[47] and should give respect to the principles of comity under which the foreign country prescribes its own remedy due to its strong interest in the litigation.[48] But it seems incongruous for a New York appellate court to affirm a dismissal on *forum non conveniens* grounds when, in truth, the trial court had found that the action involving foreign law and a foreign language would unduly burden the court![48.1] The trial court had opined that 'Italy would have a far greater interest in determining the dispute at bar. In addition, retention of the action, involving not only foreign law but a foreign language, would unduly burden this court, whereas plaintiff is fluent in Italian and had already retained Italian counsel'.

Section 2. The Forum-Selection Clause

There are always those fortunate situations for the foreign plaintiff where a forum-selection clause in the contract or perhaps in the advertising or labelling of the product actually dictates the forum in the United States. In The Breman *v.* Zapata Off-Shore Company[49] the US Supreme Court in 1972 ruled that a forum-selection clause setting suit in London, England, was '*prima facie* valid and should be enforced unless enforcement is shown by the resisting party to be "unreasonable" under the circumstances'. Here the forum-selection clause was included in a maritime towage contract, and was apparently in accord with Section 187 of Restatement (Second) of the Foreign Relations of the United States which applied the common law rule that in general 'the law of the state chosen by the parties to govern their . . . rights and duties will be applied.' Obviously here enforcement of the forum-selection clause would not be 'seriously inconvenient' nor would the resisting party be 'effectively deprived of its day in court.'[50] A forum-selection clause should not be set aside unless the clause was fraudulently inserted in the understanding between the parties or was imposed on an unsophisticated party to the litigation or was contrary to public policy. The court did, however, make a distinction between contracts of American parties that stipulate a remote foreign forum, and a contract or stipulation where at least one party is not an American citizen or subject; in the latter instance the court intimated that a neutral place might be chosen for good reasons. But circumvention of US law would be a reason for denying enforcement of the forum-selection clause, as illustrated by Bisso *v.* Inland Waterways Corp[51] where US law on a tow would be circumvented by foreign law and foreign court. In the instant case[52] a German corporation had agreed to tow the off-shore drilling rig of defendant, a US corporation, to the Adriatic Sea under a contract that provided that 'any dispute arising must be treated before the London Court of Justice'. The drilling rig was severely damaged in a storm and was towed instead to Miami, Florida, where defendant sued the German corporation, alleging negligent towage and breach of contract. The German corporation filed suit with the High Court of Justice in London, and then when the six-month period for filing a limitation-to-liability action was about to expire, filed in the same federal court in Miami, Florida, as did the defendant who refiled its initial claim. The federal district court for the Middle District of Florida denied the motion of the German corporation to stay the pending action pending determination of the London suit, and furthermore enjoined the German corporation from prosecuting the suit in London. The Fifth US Court of Appeals affirmed, but the US Supreme Court vacated that judgment as Chief Justice Burger declared that the forum-selection clause should be specifically enforced unless defendant could show that enforcement would be unreasonable and unjust or that the clause was invalid for such reasons as fraud or overreaching.

In General Engineering Corp *v.* Martin Marietta Alumina, Inc[53] the suit revolved about a construction contract in the US Virgin Islands, and the forum-selection clause identified the State of Maryland and Maryland law as applicable in event of a dispute. The contractor sued for additional costs in the Virgin Islands court where it was incorporated, and while the federal district court disregarded the forum-selection clause because the Virgin Islands was a more convenient place than the State of Maryland, the appellate court enforced the clause, pointing out that witness testimony from the Virgin Islands could be taken by deposition if the witnesses could not be present in Maryland for the trial: 'In sum . . . the forum-selection clause was freely bargained for and does not contravene an important public policy'.[54] The fact that the jury could not visit the work site was insufficient to defeat the forum-selection clause.[55]

The presence of a 'forum-selection clause' in a contract or bill of lading or on the label of the product obviates the necessity of 'forum-shopping', a practice frowned upon by many courts, despite the presumption in favor of a plaintiff's choice of forum.[56] In Panama Processes, SA *v.* Cities Service Co[57] the federal district court insisted that plaintiff's choice of forum should not be disturbed unless the balance of competing interests is decidedly in favor of the defendant. The California Court of Appeal in Holmes *v.* Syntex Laboratories Inc,[58] in ruling against dismissal of the suit under *forum non conveniens*, evidenced respect for plaintiffs' choice of US forum. Plaintiffs were a group of British women (and their spouses as well as representatives of other deceased women) who were severely injured or disabled or who received fatal injuries following ingestion of defendant's oral contraceptive product. Although the trial court dismissed the suit on *forum non conveniens* grounds, the California appellate court ruled that the trial court had 'abused its discretion', reasoning that British law was inadequate and that 'other relevant factors' bolstered the view of the court in favor of 'plaintiffs' choice of forum',[59] Indeed, the California appellate court opined that the rule of substantial deference to plaintiffs' choice of forum has much greater importance in California than in the federal courts.

The US Supreme Court in Keeton *v.* Hustler Magazine[60] in 1984 endorsed the art of 'forum-shopping': 'Plaintiff's successful search for a state with a lengthy statute of limitations is no different from the litigation strategy of countless plaintiffs who seek a forum with favorable substantive or procedural rules or sympathetic local populations'. And in Friends for All Children, Inc *v.* Lockheed

Aircraft Corp[61] the District of Columbia Court of Appeals upheld the forum choice of the plaintiffs, perhaps because the federal government was involved in a humanitarian endeavor. Here the President of the United States in 1975 commissioned a transport plane to fly Vietnamese orphans to the US for possible adoption; approximately fifteen minutes after takeoff from Saigon the aft ramp, pressure door and cargo door fell off, and ten minutes later the plane crashed into a rice paddy; miraculously 150 orphans survived. The plaintiff, a non-profit Colorado corporation responsible for the support of the orphaned children, brought suit against the airplane manufacturer, and the jury verdicts in favor of the survivors were very substantial; in 1982 the defendant settled for the sum of $13.5 million. But the settlement did not affect the 73 orphans adopted by foreign parents and who resided in foreign countries; to these law suits defendant moved to dismiss on *forum non conveniens* grounds. The federal district court denied the motion to dismiss, favoring plaintiffs' choice of forum, the familiarity of the US court with the claims, and the availability of witnesses in the US. Also the 'strong public interest' that the US had in the litigation was an important factor. The District of Columbia US Court of Appeals agreed, finding that the plaintiffs were really not 'foreign' and that there was no alternative forum; indeed, all the plaintiffs' claims had involved the same crash, the same class of injured persons, the same defendants, and the same evidence. To dismiss the action here would mean that only those orphans adopted by American parents would have recovered. A policy restricting access to US courts of resident aliens as opposed to citizens would be unconstitutional under the Fourteenth Amendment.[62]

It should be noted that the doctrine of *forum non conveniens* had been codified in California in 1971 in Section 410.30(a) of the California Civil Procedure Code: 'When a court upon motion of a party or its own motion finds that in the interest of substantial justice an action should be heard in a forum outside this State, the court shall stay or dismiss the action in whole or in part on any conditions that may be just.' The practical effect was to prevent 'forum-shopping' non-residents from filing suits in California courts simply because they stand to benefit from California law. The codified rule also protects non-resident defendants from harassment by 'forum-shopping' plaintiffs.

The residence of the plaintiff in the forum is no guarantee that the forum is the 'convenient' place for the litigation. A corporation, for example, may 'reside' in several forums, and therefore there is no reason to assume that its choice of forum is necessarily more 'convenient' than any other forum, including a foreign forum. Indeed, if the plaintiff corporation conducts extensive international business, it is probably capable of resolving legal problems stemming from those foreign operations in that foreign jurisdiction without undue burden.[63] A federal district court in Tennessee readily found personam jurisdiction against a West German equipment manufacturer because that West German company had for at least ten years exploited the US market; indeed, visits were made by representatives of the West German company to the Tennessee plaintiff's plant, and all sales of equipment were made direct to the Tennessee plaintiff's plant.[63.1]

In summary, the 'forum-selection' clause is readily enforcible by US courts, as attested to by the US Supreme Court, because

a. the transactions involved a freely negotiated private international agreement;
b. the parties sought to provide for a neutral forum for the resolution of any disputes that may arise from their contractual relationship;
c. 'the elimination of all uncertainties by agreeing in advance on a forum acceptable to both parties is an indispensable element in international trade, commerce and contracting';
d. the clause was an essential part of the agreement, to wit: 'there is strong evidence that the forum clause was a vital part of the agreement, and it would be unrealistic to think that the parties did not conduct their negotiations, including fixing the monetary terms, with the consequences of the forum clause figuring prominently in their calculations'.[64]

Limitations on the enforcement of the 'forum selection' clause include
a. fraud or coercion;[65]
b. the public policy of the forum;
c. adhesion contracts or contracts dictated without negotiation;[66] and
d. statutory restrictions that preclude judicial determinations.[67]

Forum-selection clauses are favored by The Hague Conference on Private International Law,[68] which in 1964 adopted Article 1 that provided that the parties may by agreement on the choice of court designate, for the purpose of deciding disputes which arise between them, either the courts of one of the contracting states or a court expressly named of one of the contracting states. Excluded from Article 1 of the Convention were matters concerning the status or capacity of persons or questions of family law, questions of succession, questions of bankruptcy, and rights in immovable property. Unfortunately this Convention has not yet been ratified, so that the rule remains but an approval of the effort to allow the parties to choose a forum of their own. One of the risks in forum-selection clauses is Prorogation or the conferring of jurisdiction on a court where no jurisdiction exists; obviously the parties cannot by contract or agreement create subjectmatter jurisdiction. Derogation is the barring of the action in certain forums, and most courts frown upon loss of jurisdiction where jurisdiction otherwise exists.

Section 3. The Bhopal, India, Catastrophe: A Crucible for 'Forum Non Conveniens'

Some 2,100 residents of Bhopal, India, lost their lives and perhaps as many as 200,000 persons were injured, when methyl isocyanate gas leaked from a Union Carbide Company plant on 3 December 1984 in Bhopal. The prime question from the onset of the lengthy litigation surrounding the catastrophe has been the forum where the cases would be tried. The attractiveness of US courts for the foreign plaintiffs was obvious when compared with the expected difficulties experienced by litigators in the courts of India. Indeed, the doctrine of *forum non conveniens*[69] is the crucible for the resolution of the issue as to where the cases will be tried, especially after all prior efforts to effect settlement went for naught as the India Government rejected a tentative offer by Union Carbide Company of $350 million along with lawyers representing many of the individual victims of the catastrophe.[70]

The doctrine of *forum non conveniens* as the crucible raises the insurmountable question as to whether US courts should retain jurisdiction and not dismiss the law suits because to do the latter might jeopardize success on part of the foreign plaintiffs who would be relegated to their inadequate home forum, which means that justice delayed may well be justice denied. Favoring US litigation are also such factors as social, political and economic justice available in US courts as a showcase for international comity, despite the financial burden of trial upon the US court and the financial burden of indigent India plaintiffs to come to the US for trial, and despite the liberality of the contingency fee system.

Among the factors favoring dismissal of the law suits under *forum non conveniens* are the following:

a. the place of the toxic tort is the foreign forum of India where the victims and all the parties are physically located; under India law the law suits can only be brought where the defendant is located, where the tort was committed, or where the defendant carries on its business;[71]
b. the immediate and operable decision to manufacture and market the pesticide methyl isocyanate was made by the India subsidiary under authority delegated to it by its US parent company and with the legal sanction of the local, State and national governments of India where the plant was located;
c. data as to the relevant operative facts of the specific catastrophe are available as evidence in India;
d. the paramount interest of the India governments is embodied in having its own citizens who died or suffered irreparable injury promptly and adequately compensated in India currency;
e. a short US statute of limitations may in fact bar the suits, while in India the courts can and have waived the applicable statute of limitations to achieve justice under the circumstances;[72]
f. India law is readily applied by India courts, in contrast to the normal reluctance of US courts to apply any foreign law;
g. the foreign judgment obtained in India will be recognized and enforced in the US, if necessary against the US parent company should the assets of the foreign subsidiary prove to be insufficient;
h. India courts would not encounter the problem encountered by US courts in acting against a foreign subsidiary; the US court might not be able to control nor supervise its activities due to the doctrine of extraterritoriality;
i. judgment and/or settlement of these cases in India would not seriously hamper or hinder the thousands of workers' compensation cases pending in India in contrast to judgment and/or settlement according to US living standards, should the US court handle the litigation; and
j. the contingency fee system is not available in India and therefore India procedure does not run the risk of outrageous exploitation of victims who receive a small percentage of monies recovered; it should be noted that the national government of India had agreed to waive all filing and other costs on behalf of the victims.[73]

The India judicial system is federal in nature, and the Supreme Court of India follows jurisdictionally the US Supreme Court in being the final resort for cases from the 22 states and 9 union territories or federal districts. Preliminary hearings in India commence in the Subjudges or Magistrates Courts, or in the District Courts if trial is necessary, or in the High Courts of the State, or even in the Supreme Court of India, should the Government of India be a party to the litigation as would be the case here. The Constitution of India provides under Part 3 for the protection of fundamental rights and human rights of all citizens, and such rights are readily enforcible in all the courts of India. Part 4 of the Constitution of India delineates 'directive principles of state policy' for society at large, in contrast to the individual rights enumerated in part 3, so that India governments at all levels must comply with mandates for public education, public health, protection of the environment, and similar protections for the individual's safety.[74]

The national government of India and the State of Madhya Pradesh (where the catastrophe occurred) recognize 'liability without fault' which legal principle promises well for the thousands of victims.[75] However, India jurisprudence encompasses many shortcomings affecting plaintiffs, as illustrated by the following:

a. tort actions generally abate with the death of the person, for there are no wrongful death statutes, although wives and children of the deceaseds may sue for loss of support and for loss of services;
b. there is no jury trial in personal injury cases;
c. a percentage of the claim may be paid as a filing fee, and therefore *ad damnum* is unusually small;
d. contributory negligence is a defense even where strict liability is applicable;
e. assumption of the risk is a valid defense to all causes of action; and
f. the statute of limitation is 2 years from the date of death under the Fatal Accidents Act.[76]

It should be observed that the national government of India and the state of Madhya Pradesh are potential defendants under Article 300 of the Constitution of India which expressly states that the Government of India 'may sue or be sued by the name of the Union of India' and the government of a State 'may sue and be sued by the name of the State'.[77] The prerequisite in each instance is that the tort committed must be a non-sovereign function for which immunity may not be claimed. But damages awarded by India courts, whether against governments or against private persons or companies, is incredibly low: 'The Indian law of torts follows the British, erring wherever possible on the side of meanness. The damages awarded for a loss of expectation of life hovers around Rs. 5000 (or roughly $400)'.[78]

On 12 May 1986 the federal district court for the Southern District of New York, in an opinion by Judge John F. Keenan, dismissed the action entitled In Re Union Carbide Corporation Gas Plant Disaster at Bhopal, India, in December 1984[79] upon *forum non conveniens* grounds. The 63-page opinion embraced five principal determinations, to wit:

1. no deference should be given to a plaintiff's choice of forum when the plaintiff is a foreigner and not a citizen nor resident of the United States;
2. a court should not give consideration to an unfavorable choice in the law for the plaintiff;
3. the alternative forum in India is available;
4. the defendant is amenable to service of process in India; and
5. India courts are adequate and can handle the complex litigation.

Judge Keenan pointed out that India courts have emerged from their colonial past, that court delays in India have been highly exaggerated, that court fees are irrelevant since they can be waived, that discovery limitations in India courts are not crucial, that the lack of impleader apparently does not worry the defendant, that no class action is available does not militate against the adequacy of the India forum, and that the lack of contingency fees for plaintiffs' attorneys is not decisive. However, Judge Keenan did condition the dismissal of the action upon three conditions:

1. defendant agrees to abide by the broad discovery rules as in US courts;
2. defendant agrees to be bound by the judgment or award of the India court; and
3. defendant agrees to waive the defense of the statute of limitations.

On or about 13 June 1986 it appeared that the defendant Union Carbide Corporation did agree to these conditions, although the defendant reserved the right to appeal those conditions.[80] Subsequently in 1987 the Second US Court of Appeals affirmed the transfer of the action to the India court.

It is self-evident that the doctrine of *forum non conveniens* allows a court to decline jurisdiction, even though jurisdiction is authorized by a general venue statute. Defendant's case rested upon the US Supreme Court's holdings in 1947 and in 1981 that dismissal of the suit by foreign plaintiffs was in the best interests of the United States and the US defendant.[81] Judge Keenan was apparently convinced that the India legal system was adequate to handle the Bhopal litigation; he noted that plaintiffs and the *amicus curiae* had rested their contention that the India legal system was inadequate upon the affidavit of a University of Wisconsin Law School professor who specialized in South Asian studies. Judge Keenan responded by pointing out that the learned US professor was not 'admitted to practice in India and the Court views his opinions concerning the Indian legal system, its judiciary and bar, as far less persuasive than those of N. A. Palkhivala and J. B. Dadachanji, each of whom has been admitted to practice in India for over 40 years, both being Senior Advocates before the Supreme Court of India.'[82] Furthermore, according to Judge Keenan,

> 'the Bhopal tragedy has already been approached with imagination in India. Demonstrating the creativity and flexibility of the Indian system, the Parliament of India has passed the Bhopal Act in order to deal with the cases . . . The Bhopal Act permits the case to be treated "speedily, effectively, equitably and to the best advantage of the claimants".'[83]

It might be noted that there was an option other than dismissal or retention of jurisdiction that the US court did not consider, to wit: a compromise position whereby the US court decides the issue of liability and the India court decides the issue of damages, assuming that the US court finds for the plaintiffs on the liability issue. This bifurcation is consonant with the purposes of the India Code of Civil Procedure[84] which facilitates the liability trial in the US by providing that questions of law may readily be referred to India High Courts or to commissions established to inquire into the pertinent questions of India law.[85] Should the US court find for the plaintiffs on the issue of liability, the India court, cognizant of India's standard of living and tradition of damage awards or judgments, can give monetary effect to that judgment. Section 601 of Restatement (Revised 1983) of the Foreign Relations Law of the United States states by way of analogy that there is a duty to make reparation in favor of the aggrieved party by the polluter within the framework of the polluter's legal system.

On 19 January 1987 the Indian government urged the Bhopal court in India to consider the 'multinational enterprise theory' of liability as applicable to Union Carbide, so that proof of negligence would be precluded. Apparently a special panel of the Indian Supreme Court had in December 1986 invoked the 'absolute and non delegeable' theory of liability in a decision against Shriram Food and Fertlizers Co whose storage tank containing a poisonous chemical collapsed in December 1985 causing the death of one person and hospitalizing 300 persons.[85.1]

Section 4. International Maritime Litigation and Forum non Conveniens

In 1972 the federal district court of the Southern District of New York, admittedly one of the nation's busiest courts, found 'no reason why this court with its heavy burdens and responsibilities should be burdened with cases like these which, from every point of view, should be tried in the courts of the nation where all the relevant events occurred and whose own citizens are primarily involved. Certainly this district . . . has no conceivable relation to this litigation except for the fact that the defendant happens to be doing business here.'[86] Unfortunately, congested dockets have prompted US admiralty courts to apply the doctrine of *forum non conveniens*[87] more frequently than ever before. However, in many international maritime collision cases involving foreign plaintiffs, US courts have strictly construed the *forum non conveniens* doctrine so as to deny dismissal of the claim, as illustrated by Poseidon Schiffahrt GmbH *v.* M/S Netuno.[88] But in general the swing is in favor of dismissal of the foreign plaintiff's claim because US courts refuse to impose what they deem to be burdens on court time and court resources.[89]

It can be argued that US admiralty courts should retain jurisdiction of foreign claimants' international maritime collision actions especially where the action of the foreign plaintiff coincides with the needs of US shipping interests, i.e., the maintenance of high navigational standards in US territorial waters and the promotion of international comity. Unfortunately for the foreign plaintiff US courts are beginning to respect the adequacy and even the convenience of the foreign forum as a suitable alternative forum, thereby favoring dismissal of the US action.[90] Yet international comity is strengthened by the broad jurisdiction and unlimited venue of US admiralty courts. Indeed, a dismissal of a suit by a foreign plaintiff suing in US court may preclude any semblance of uniformity on such vital issues as defenses, joint and several liability, contribution, indemnification and even imputation of fault or negligence. A collision claimant's choice of forum greatly affects his recovery, and a foreign forum, adequate as a alternative forum in other respects, may not give the foreign plaintiff a full opportunity to be heard, for example; US courts, particularly admiralty courts, are sophisticated and experienced in handling international maritime collision matters.[91]

It should be observed that effective 29 December 1982 amendments to the Jones Act have significantly reduced the foreign offshore worker's access to US courts. Section 688(b)(1) of Title 28 of USC bars suits under US law by foreign plaintiffs who are not citizens of the US or resident aliens, if the incident sued upon occurred during the 'exploration, development, or production of off-shore mineral or energy resources . . . in the territorial water or waters overlaying the continental shelf of a nation other than the United States, its territories or possessions.' The 1982 amendment allows a suit to be brought under US law only when no remedy is available 'under the laws of the nations asserting jurisdiction over the area in which the incident occurred, or under the laws of the nation in which at the time of the incident the person for whose injury or death a remedy is sought maintained citizenship or residency.'

Prior to 1936 when Congress enacted the Carriage of Goods By Sea Act, or COGSA,[92] the 'forum-selection' clause[93] in the ocean bill of lading determined what forum and what law would be applied to any cause of action arising out of that bill of lading. But COGSA, whose purpose, *inter alia*, was the acceptance of an international bill of lading, provided that the shipowner had the freedom to alter contractually the terms of the international bill of lading if the change did not decrease the shipowner's liability.[94] Thus, COGSA in effect supersedes 'forum-selection' clauses in ocean bills of lading, as shown in Union Insurance Society of Canton *v.* SS Elikon.[95] Here the foreign plaintiff brought an action in the federal district court as subrogee of a US corporation against the German owner of the defendant ship. The foreign plaintiff contended that suit in the federal court in Virginia was in accord with the 'forum-selection' clause in the bill of lading, and the court agreed with the foreign plaintiff. But the Fourth US Court of Appeals reversed, viewing the 'forum-selection' clause in the bill of lading as a contract of adhesion which should be eliminated by the enactment of COGSA. In another respect, in Carbon Black Export Co *v.* SS Monrosa,[96] the Fifth US Court of Appeals refused to accept the validity of the 'forum-selection' clause, pointing out that private parties to a contract lack the competence necessary to forum an agreement which would be binding on a court with proper jurisdiction.[97]

COGSA has frequently favored the foreign forum, as shown by Murillo Ltd *v.* The Bio Bio,[98] which held that the Swedish courts would apply COGSA and Swedish courts were more convenient for the parties. West German courts were favored in New York Underwriters Insurance Co *v.* M/S Wurtenberg[99] and

Japanese courts were favored in Takemura & Co *v* SS Tsuneshima Maru.[100]

The US Supreme Court in East River Steamship Corp *v.* Transamerica Delaval, Inc[101] posed the prime question by Mr Justice Blackmun in these words:

> 'In this admiralty case, we must decide whether a cause of action in tort is stated when a defective product purchased in a commercial transaction malfunctions, injuring only the product itself and causing purely economic loss. The case requires us to consider preliminarily whether admiralty law, which already recognizes a general theory of liability for negligence, also incorporates principles of products liability, including strict liability. Then, charting a course between products liability and contract law, we must determine whether injury to a product itself is the kind of harm that should be protected by products liability or left entirely to the law of contracts.'

And the highest court responded: 'We hold that a manufacturer in a commercial relationship has no duty under either a negligence or strict products liability theory to prevent a product from injuring itself . . . We do not reach the issue whether a tort cause of action can ever be stated in admiralty when the only damages sought are economic.'

Notes

1. *See generally* 7 BC Int & Comp L Rev (1984) at pp. 32 *et seq.*

1.1 *Forum non conveniens*, or 'the forum is not convenient', delineates the power of a court to decline to exercise jurisdiction under certain circumstances. It is a discretionary power that courts may utilize, giving deference to the interests of the parties to the litigation and to the competing demands of justice. Section 84 of Restatement (Second) of Conflict of Laws posits the rule that a court 'will not exercise jurisdiction if it is a seriously inconvenient forum'. The doctrine is said to reflect the requisite of any judicial system to protect both its legal machinery and court officers as well as the defendant or defendants from abuse or inconvenience or injustice by plaintiff or plaintiffs searching for the most advantageous forum in which to litigate the matter or matters.

Professor Barrett in 35 California L Rev 380 (1947) asserted that the earliest Scottish cases delineating *forum non competens*, in contrast to *forum non conveniens*, directed the doctrine to the question of jurisdiction or the power of the court to hear the case, even where the parties to the litigation were non-residents and even where trial in Scotland would have been inconvenient. Later the Scottish decisions embraced both the question of jurisdiction *and* the convenience of the parties to the litigation, and the plea of *forum non competens* was soon replaced by the plea of *forum non conveniens*, which centered about the issue of 'convenience' *after* the issue of jurisdiction had been settled. According to Professor Braucher in 60 Harvard L Rev 908 (1947), *forum non conveniens* was a defensive plea in Scottish law to prevent a plaintiff from forcing a defendant to litigate in a forum which technically had jurisdiction over the parties and over the subjectmatter, but in which the defense of the suit would be unfairly impractical or expensive.

It should be observed that the congestion of US court dockets today has compelled US courts to give serious consideration to motions for dismissal based on *forum non conveniens*. The court must critically evaluate the drain upon US court resources and whether an alternative foreign forum could equally serve the interests of justice. But courts must not overlook the fundamental principles of fairness and comity in ruling for or against motions for dismissal based on *forum non conveniens*.

The Latin words *forum non conveniens* appear to have no origins in either Roman law or early Continental civil law practice; *see* 35 Calif L Rev 380 (1947). Indeed, the earliest appearance of the words and the doctrine was in the late 1800's in a series of Scottish cases which set forth the established Scottish principle of permitting trial courts to refrain from hearing disputes when the purposes of justice would be better served by trial in another forum. *See* 5 Fordham Internat L J 533 (1982). In MacMaster *v.* MacMaster (Judgment of 7 June 1833, Sess, Scot, 11 Sess Cas, First Series 685) the Scottish court held that the presence of assets of the estate in the forum did not provide an appropriate basis for the suit against the absent foreign executor of the will. A subsequent decision in 1845, M'Morine *v.* Cowie (Judgment of 16 January 1845, Sess, Scot, & D Sess Cas 270) echoed the view that the forum was not 'proper' nor 'appropriate'. An 1884 Scottish decision, described in 5 Fordham Internat L J (*supra*, at page 536), declared that courts should not accept cases where 'it is not convenient nor fitting for the interests of the parties to entertain any individual case'.

In England it was not until 1875 that the doctrine of *forum non conveniens* appeared in an important decision; in Moystyn *v.* Fabrigas (1 CPD 161) the English court upheld its jurisdiction over an action between residents of the Spanish island of Minorca. Lord Mansfield summarily argued that 'it is impossible there could ever exist a doubt, but that a subject born in Minorca has as good a right to appeal to the King's courts of justice as one who is born within the sound of Bow Bell'. In the year 1906 in Logan *v.* Bank of Scotland (1 KB 141) Lord Barnes invoked the doctrine in these terms: 'The court should, on the one hand, see clearly that in stopping an action it does not do injustice, and, on the other hand, I think the court ought to interfere wherever there is such vexation and oppression that the defendant who objects to the exercise of the jurisdicton, would be subjected to such injustice that he ought not to be sued in the court in which the action is brought'. The English view is that the plea of *forum non conveniens* is not simply left to the discretion of the trial court, but must be grounded upon some factor such as 'vexation and oppression'. In 1978 in MacShannon *v.* Rockware Glass, Ltd (2 WLR 362) the House of Lords agreed that the English and the Scottish interpretations of the plea of *forum non conveniens* 'differ more in theoretical approach than in practical substance'. England today sanctions a 'stay practice' which permits the parties to go forward in perhaps another forum, the English version of *forum non conveniens*.

However, in 1984 the House of Lords in The Abidin Daver (1984, AC 398), followed by the English Court of Appeal in Metall und Rohstoff *v.* ACLI Metals (London) Ltd, (1984, 1 Lloyd's Rep 598), stated that 'judicial chauvinism has been replaced by judicial comity to an extent which . . . the time is now ripe to acknowledge, frankly is . . . indistinguisiable from the Scottish legal doctrine of *forum non conveniens*'. The decision of the House of Lords in The Abidin Daver (*supra*) arose out of an attempt by Cuban shipowners to bring admiralty proceedings in England following a collision between the Cuban vessel and a Turkish ship in Turkish territorial waters. The Turkish shipowners promptly commenced proceedings in the local Turkish court for damages for negligence. Three months later the Cuban shipowners 'arrested' a Turkish ship in England and commenced proceedings in England. The Turkish shipowners then applied to have the English court action stayed; the lower court agreed that the Turkish court was more convenient and a natural forum for the proceedings, but the Court of Appeals reversed, holding that no significance should be attached to the pending Turkish proceedings. (1983, 1 WLR 884). Lord Diplock, writing for the House of Lords reversed, taking the view that Turkey clearly had the closest connection to the controversy and that the Turkish local court was the natural forum for trial. He stated that it was not open to the English court to compare the quality of justice in other legal systems, and that where a party felt that he would not receive justice in another forum, it was necessary for him to say so in no uncertain terms, which plaintiff did not do here.

> 'Where a suit about a particular subject-matter between a plaintiff and a defendant is already pending in a foreign court which is a natural and appropriate forum for the resolution of the dispute between them, and the defendant in the foreign suit seeks to institute as plaintiff an action in England about the same matter to which the person who is plaintiff in the foreign suit is made defendant, then the additional inconvenience and expense which must result from allowing two sets of legal proceedings to be pursued concurrently in two different countries where the same facts will be in issue and the testimony of the same witnesses required, can only be justified if the would-be plaintiff can establish objectively by cogent evidence that there is some personal or judicial advantage that would be available to him only in the English action that is of such importance that it would cause injustice to him to deprive him of it.'

In the United States the doctrine of *forum non conveniens* was first discussed by a federal district court in Pennsylvania in the year 1801 in Willendson *v.* Forsoket (29 Fed Cas 1283). Here a Danish seaman sued his Danish captain for back wages after the Danish captain discharged him while the Danish vessel was docked in Philadelphia. The court declined to exercise jurisdiction, declaring that 'it has been my general rule not to take cognizance of disputes between masters and crews of foreign ships. I have commonly referred them to their own courts. In some very peculiar cases I have afforded the seamen assistance to protect them against oppression and injustice.' The court then concluded:

> 'Reciprocal policy, and the justice due from one friendly nation to another, calls for such conduct in the courts of either country. Whatever ill-humours or misconduct may have prevailed between the parties in this suit, the master now places the matter on a reasonable ground. He must give the sailor a certificate of forgiveness of past offenses, to avail him in his own country. If he takes the seaman on board, and there shall appear no deception in the present offer, I shall not further interfere, but dismiss the suit. If any difference should hereafter arise, it must be settled by a Danish tribunal.'

On the other hand, the US Supreme Court three years later in 1804 in Mason *v.* Ship Blaireau (6 US 240) took a more enlightened view by deciding to hear the case of a salvage claim filed in a federal district court in Maryland by the master of a British merchant ship against a French ship. Chief Justice Marshall stated:—

> '[U]pon principles of general policy, this court ought not to take cognisance of a case entirely between foreigners, [rather] than from any positive incapacity to do so. On weighing the considerations drawn from public convenience, those in favor of the jurisdiction appear much to overbalance those against it, and it is the opinion of this court, that, whatever doubts may exist in a case where the jurisdiction may be objected to, there ought to be none, where the parties assent to it.'

Undoubtedly, political considerations, called 'public convenience', weighed strongly in the court's decision to hear the case against the French ship.

The earliest discretionary dismissals by State courts involved suits between aliens for causes of action apparently unrelated to the forum, as illustrated by Gardner *v.* Thomas (14 Johns (NY) 133,1817), where the New York court refused to entertain a suit involving torts committed aboard a foreign vessel where both parties were non-resident aliens. A later New York case, Molony *v.* Dows (8 Abb Pr (NYCP) 316,1859), even went so far as to refuse to hear tort actions between citizens of another State. Even in 1848 a federal court declined to hear an admiralty suit between British subjects, stating that a US court should not be compelled to bestow its time and resources on litigation between parties 'owing no allegiance to its laws, and contributing in no way to its support', and at the same time causing delay in the processing of claims of US citizens. (One Hundred & Ninety-Four Shawls (18 F Cas 703, SDNY). On the other hand, the US Supreme Court in Hyde *v.* Stone (61 US 170) in 1857 ruled that federal courts 'are bound to proceed to judgment and to afford redress to suitors before them, in every case to which their jurisdiction extends. They cannot abdicate their authority or duty in any case in favor of another jurisdiction.' And this willingness on the part of US courts to hear suits between aliens on foreign causes of action (*see* Rea *v.* Hayden, 3 Mass 24,1807) was greatly encouraged by the dictum of Chief Justice Marshall in the 1821 decision of Cohens *v.* Virginia (19 US 264), when he stated that the judiciary had 'no more right to decline the exercise of jurisdiction which is given, than to usurp that which is not given'. Traditionally the alien, the foreigner, and the stranger were welcome in the United States to seek redress for grievances (*See* 9 Holdsworth, A History of English Law 97, 7th edn., 1956). Under Article III, Section 2, of the US Constitution 'the judicial power shall extend . . . to Controversies . . . between a State or the Citizens thereof . . . and foreign States, Citizens or Subjects'. But discretion to refuse jurisdiction of controversies between foreigners was approved in 1885 by the US Supreme Court in The Belgenland (114 US 355), an admiralty case arising from a collision of two foreign ships on the high seas; although it was finally determined that the federal district court here had properly taken jurisdiction, the highest court opined that 'circumstances often exist which render it inexpedient for the court to take jurisdiction of controversies between foreigners in cases not arising in the country of the forum'. And in 1932 in Canada Malting Co *v.* Paterson Steamships Ltd (285 US 413) Justice Brandeis stated that, as in admiralty, 'courts of equity and law (may) also occasionally decline, in the interests of justice, to exercise jurisdiction, where the suit is between aliens or non-residents or where for kindred reasons the litigation can more appropriately be conducted in a foreign tribunal'. Justice Frankfurter's dissenting opinion in Baltimore & Ohio Railroad Co *v.* Kepner (314 US 44,1941) referred to the 'familiar doctrine of *forum non conveniens*' as a manifestation of a civilized judicial system which was 'firmly imbedded in our law'.

2. *See* Section 84 of Restatement (Second) of Conflicts of Laws.
3. Note Schertenleib *v.* Traum, 589 F2d 1156 (2nd Cir, 1978).
4. *See* Koster *v.* Lumbermens Mutual Insurance Co, 330 US 518 (1947) at pp. 531–532.
5. 713 F2d 339 (8th Cir, 1983).
6. *See* 17 Creighton L Rev 1407 (1984).
7. *Supra* note 5 at pp. 340 and 341.
8. 531 F Supp 1175 (WD Wash, 1982) In Carlenstolpe *v.* Merck & Co,—F Supp—(SDNY, 12 Aug. 1986) a citizen and resident of Sweden suffered disabling arthritis which he attributed to two doses of hepatitis vaccine developed, tested and manufactured in the United States by the defendant. He was injected with the vaccine in Sweden. Defendant argued in favor of *forum non conveniens*, pointing out that Sweden had the paramount interest in determining product liability of drug products sold within Sweden. But the federal district court for the Southern District of New York rejected that argument: 'Where an allegedly defective drug has been developed, tested and manufactured in the United States, and is being distributed to and presumably used by American citizens, including citizens of the forum, the forum's interest in litigating the controversy is at least equal to that of the foreign citizen's home forum'. Indeed, the suit here did not challenge the acceptability of Sweden's decision to permit the use of the drug in Sweden, 'but rather challenges defendant's conduct in distributing the drug, both in Sweden and in America, allegedly without adequate testing and warning of its risks'.

   Similarly the New York court in Computer Graphic Laboratories, Inc *v.* SBP, SPA, decided 2 December 1986, ruled that the New York plaintiff was entitled to have New York courts and not Italian courts adjudicate the merits of a breach of contract claim. The *nexus* with New York delineated New York as the place where the agreements were negotiated and executed; the product was manufactured in New York, and the Italian defendant came to New York to operate the computer system; and New York law was chosen by the parties under the contract. Time was also of the essence, and Italian courts were simply too slow to schedule hearings!
9. *Supra* note 8 at pp. 1181 and 1182. Note that the court favored the application of India law:

   > 'I am persuaded by the reasoning of Bergeron [*v.* Koninklijke Luchtvaart Maatschappij, NV, 188 F Supp 594, (SDNY 1960), *appeal dismissed*, 299 F2d 78 (2d Cir 1962)] and conclude that I should choose, as between American law and Indian law, the one appropriate body of law to govern this litigation. A careful reading of the cases cited by plaintiffs demonstrates that these cases [McPherson *v.* Steamship South African Pioneer, 321 F Supp 42 (ED Va 1971); Noel *v.* Linea Aeropostal Venezolana, 260 F Supp 1002 (SDNY 1966), Fernandez *v.* Linea Aeropostal Venezolana, 156 F Supp 94 (SDNY 1957)] do not support the broad proposition that section 1 and section 4 (of Death on the High Seas Act, 46 USC 761 *et seq.*) provide cumulative remedies. Instead, each of the cases must be read somewhat more narrowly in the context of the particular circumstances it presents . . . India's paramount interest in this accident is evident. By any reasonable means of weighing and valuing the relevant points of contact, the *Lauritzen* analysis dictates the choice of Indian law in this case.'

10. 528 F Supp 809 (Ed Va, 1981).
11. 454 US235 (1981).
12. *Supra* note 10 at p. 815.
13. *Supra* note 11.
14. *Supra* note 11 at p. 240.
15. *Supra* note 11 at p. 261.
16. See Miskow *v*. The Boeing Co, 664 F2d 205 (9th Cir, 1981) at p. 719.
17. 349 US 29 (1955).
18. *Id*. at p. 32.
19. Latimer *v*. S/A Industrias Reunidas F. Motarazzo, 591 F Supp 469 (SDNY, 1985).
20. *Supra* note 11.
21. *Supra* note 11 at p. 261.
22. 9 Maritime Lawyer 297 (1984).
23. 730 F2d 211 (5th Cir, 1984).
24. *Id*. at p. 214.
24.1 —F Supp— (SDNY 1987), aff —F2d— (2nd Cir, 1987).
24.2 337 US 541 (1949).
25. 449 US 368 (1981).
26. 337 US 541 (1949).
27. 311 F2d 429 (5th Cir, 1962).
28. *Supra* note 11.

The 1947 landmark case on the doctrine of *forum non conveniens* was Gulf Oil Corp *v*. Gilbert (330 US 501), where the highest court recognized the power of courts to decline to exercise jurisdiction. A court may 'resist imposition upon its jurisdiction even when jurisdiction is authorized'.

The Gilbert case arose from an explosion and fire, allegedly the result of defendant's negligence, which destroyed plaintiff's warehouse in Virginia. Although plaintiff was a citizen of Virginia he sued the Pennsylvania defendant (doing business in Virginia) in the federal district court in New York. Plaintiff explained his choice of the New York forum on the grounds that the $400,000 sought in damages might 'stagger the imagination' of a Virginia jury. The federal district court in New York granted defendant's motion for dismissal on *forum non conveniens* grounds, pointing out that the events occurred in Virginia where the witnesses were also resident. (62 F Supp 291, 1945). But the Second US Court of Appeals reversed (153 F2d 833, 2nd Cir, 1946), and the US Supreme Court also reversed, reinstating the decision of the New York federal district court dismissing the case on *forum non conveniens* grounds. The highest court opined that the appropriate standard of review was abuse of discretion (which the trial court had not abused) by failure to consider both 'private interests' and 'public interests', the former embracing 'ease of access to sources of proof', 'availability of compulsory process' for unwilling witnesses, 'cost of obtaining attendance of witnesses', and 'all other practical problems that make trial of a case easy, expeditious and inexpensive', and the latter embracing the local interest in having localized controversies decided at home, avoidance of the burdens of jury duty and court calendar congestion in a community with no relation to the controversy, and the appropriateness of the governing law being interpreted and applied by a court familiar with that law. The court summed it all up in these two paragraphs:

> 'An interest to be considered, and the one likely to be most pressed, is the private interest of the litigant. Important considerations are the relative ease of access to sources of proof; availability of compulsory process for

> attendance of unwilling, and the cost of obtaining attendance of willing, witnesses possibility of view of premises, if view would be appropriate to the action, and all other practical problems that make trial of a case easy, expeditious and inexpensive. There may also be questions as to the enforcibility of a judgment if one is obtained. The court will weigh relative advantages and obstacles to fair trial. It is often said that the plaintiff may not, by choice of an inconvenient forum, 'vex,' harass,' or 'oppress' the defendant by inflicting upon him expense or trouble not necessary to his own right to pursue his remedy. But unless the balance is strongly in favor of the defendant, the plaintiff's choice of forum should rarely be disturbed.
>
> Factors of public interest also have a place in applying justice. Administrative difficulties follow the courts when litigation is piled up on congested centers instead of being handled at its origin. Jury duty is a burden that ought not to be imposed upon the people of a community which has no relation to the litigation. . . . There is a local interest in having localized controversies decided at home. There is an appropriateness in having the trial of a diversity case in a forum that is at home with the state law that must govern the case, rather than having a court in some other forum untangle problems in conflict of laws, and in law foreign to itself.'

It should be noted that the court felt that the restrictive view that *forum non conveniens* applied only in extreme cases of harassment and oppression (as held by the Second US Court of Appeals) was erroneous, although the court did state that 'a plaintiff may not, by choice of an inconvenient forum, "vex", "harass" or "oppress" the defendant by inflicting upon him expense or trouble not necessary to his own right to pursue a remedy'. This restrictive view was but one of the many 'private' and 'public' factors to be considered by the court alongside of 'the enforcibility of a judgment' and 'the relative advantages and obstacles to fair trial'. The court concluded that the doctrine of *forum non conveniens* should be applied only infrequently; and that unless the balance of factors is 'strongly in favor of the defendant, the plaintiff's choice of forum should rarely be disturbed'. In the companion case of Koster *v.* Lumbermens Mutual Casualty Co (330 US 123,1947) the court described the doctrine as an instrument of justice and the 'ultimate inquiry' is to determine where trial of the case will 'best serve the convenience of the parties and the ends of justice'.

The Gilbert decision clearly gave the federal courts and the State courts broad discretion in choosing the form that the doctrine of *forum non conveniens* would take in each jurisdiction. A federal district court or a State may simply have no interest in trying actions that have a minimal relationship to the federal district court or to the State. Note McGee *v.* International Life Insurance Co (355 US 220, 1957), in which the court accorded great importance to a State's 'manifest interest in providing effective means of redress for its residents'. But again the plaintiff's choice of forum rarely should be disturbed 'unless the balance is strongly in favor of the defendant'. And one factor must exist before a court can dismiss a case, i.e., grant the motion for dismissal based on *forum non conveniens*, and that factor is the availability of an alternative forum in which the case can be tried. Indeed, the availability and adequacy of the Alternative Forum is of paramount importance.

It is well to observe that the 'interests analysis' described by the US Supreme Court in the Gilbert case (*supra*) has resulted in a predominance of dismissals over 'retentions', as illustrated by Harrison *v.* Wyeth Laboratories (510 F Supp 1, CEDPA, 1980), holding that the United Kingdom had the paramount interest in regulating the distribution and labeling of pharmaceuticals in the United Kingdom; Mitchell *v.* General Motors Corp (439 F Supp 24, ND Ohio, 1977), stating that Canada had the greatest interest in the hearing of the claim brought by a Canadian resident against a US manufacturer of a defective automobile seat; and Noto *v.* Cia Secula di Armeanento (310 F Supp 639, SDNY 1970), declaring that New York and the federal courts had no interest in the dispute between Dutch and Italian parties that arose in an Iranian port. In 1983 the New York court in Islamic Republic of Iran *v.* Pahlavi (464 NYS2d 487) simply stated that New York had no interest in adjudicating the dispute between the people of Iran and the former Shah.

Subsequent to the US Supreme Court's 1947 decisions in Gilbert and Koster cases (supra), the court distinguished these cases from the situation in which a US plaintiff could be relegated to a foreign court. In Swift & Co Packers *v.* Compania Colombiana del Caribe (339 US 684, 1950), an admiralty suit by a US corporation against a foreign corporation, the trial court had dismissed the action on *forum non conveniens* grounds, and the highest court termed such conduct to be an abuse of discretion because a US plaintiff should not be deprived of the opportunity to seek justice in his own courts. Plaintiff's choice of forum carried much weight when the plaintiff was a US citizen or resident. Five years later in Burt *v.* Isthmus Development Co (218 F2d 353, 5th Cir, 1955; cert den 349 US 922, 1955) the Fifth US Court of Appeals heeded the counsel and reversed the dismissal on *forum non conveniens* grounds, holding that courts 'should require positive evidence of unusually extreme circumstances, and should be thoroughly convinced that material injustice is manifest before exercising . . . discretion to deny a citizen access to the courts of this country.' Furthermore, it would be 'inconsistent with the very purpose and function of the federal courts to hold that one may decline to hear a case and thereby in effect decree that a citizen must go to a foreign country to seek redress of an alleged wrong'. Here Mexican law would govern the cause of action and all defendants' witnesses were residents of Mexico; but the court determined that US courts were the proper forum. The Second US Court of Appeals in Olympic Corporation *v.* Societe Generale (462 F2d 376, 2nd Cir, 1972) summarized:

> 'In any situation, the balance must be very strongly in favor of the defendant, before the plaintiffs choice of forum should be disturbed . . . and the balance must be even stronger when the plaintiff is an American citizen and the alternative forum is a foreign one.'

29. *See* 6 Fordham Internat L J 577 (1983).
30. 630 F2d 149 (3rd Cir, 1980).
31. 524 F Supp 858 (SDNY, 1981).
32. 531 F Supp 1175 (Wash, 1982).
33. 528 F Supp 1337 (SDNY, 1982).
34. *Supra* note 11.
35. *See* Chapter 3, Section 1, herein.
36. 654 F2d 147 (2nd Cir, 1980).
37. *See* Schrieber *v.* Allis-Chalmers Corp, 448 F Supp 1079 (D Kan, 1978).
38. *See* Proctor & Schwartz, Inc *v.* Rollins, 634 F2d 738 (4th Cir, 1980), at p. 740.
39. *Supra* note 55 at p. 62.
40. *Id.*
40.1 485 Sond 565 (La Ct App., 1986).
41. *Supra* note 55 at p. 62.

42. *See* Hemmelgarn *v.* The Boeing Co, 106 Cal App3d 576 (1980) at p. 586.
43. Cf. Rule 12(b)(7) FRCP on dismissal for failure to join a party 'needed for just adjudication'.
44. 454 US 235 (1981).
45. 78 FRD 445 (D Del, 1978).
46. 363 F2d 611 (3rd Cir, 1966), cert den 385 US 945 (1966).
47. *See* Donahue *v.* Far Eastern Air Transport Co, 652 F2d 1032 (DC Cir, 1981) at p. 1038.
48. *See* Mannington Mills, Inc *v.* Congoleum Corp, 595 F2d 1287 (3rd Cir, 1979) at pp. 1297–1298, setting forth factors that a US court should weigh in resolving comity issues.
48.1 Troni *v.* Banco Popolare di Milano, —AD2d—, —NYS1d— (1st Dept., 16 April 1987).
49. 407 US 1 (1972).
50. *Id.*
51. 349 US 85 (1955).
52. *Supra* note 49.
53. 783 F2d 352 (3rd Cir, 1986).
54. *Id.*
55. Probably the earliest case to recognize the validity of 'forum selection' clauses was Mittenthal *v.* Mascagni, 66 NE 425, decided by the Massachusetts Supreme Judicial Court in 1903. Here an Italian symphony conductor had contracted to perform throughout the United States, Canada and Europe, and the 'forum selection' clause in the contract identified the courts of Florence, Italy, as the forum to hear any disputes arising out of the contract. In enforcing the clause the court observed that there was a need for certainty of a particular forum; furthermore, the 'forum selection' was deemed to be reasonable under the circumstances of the continuous travel necessitated by the terms of the contract. The test of 'reasonableness' was later attested to by the Second US Court of Appeals in Wm. H. Muller & Co *v.* Swedish American Line, 224 F2d 806 [1955], where a consignee of a shipment of goods from Sweden to the United States brought suit after the ship and the goods were lost at sea; the bill of lading contained a clause selecting the Swedish court as the proper forum. Although the plaintiff argued that such a clause violated his rights to full recovery for the lost cargo by the application of Swedish law, the court upheld the 'forum selection' clause as reasonable, especially since Sweden would be a more convenient forum for the ship's crew and the evidence concerning the ship's unseaworthiness, which were all in Sweden.

    On 3 July 1986 the New York Supreme Court, New York County, in National Union Fire Insurance Co *v.* Weir, —NYS2d—, upheld the forum-selection clause in the indemnification agreement signed by the defendant, to wit:

    > 'Any action or proceeding of any kind against the undersigned [referring to defendant] arising out of or by reason of the Indemnification and Pledge Agreement may be brought *in any State or Federal Court of competent jurisdiction in any County in the State of New York*, in addition to any other court in which such action may properly be brought' (emphasis supplied).'

    The court explained its ruling:

    > 'Forum-selection clauses are generally enforced unless the defendant can

show that enforcement would be unreasonable or unjust or that the clause is invalid for such reasons as fraud or overreaching (see Burger King Corp *v.* Rudzewich, —US—, 105 S Ct 2174 [1985]; Bremen *v.* Zapata Offshore Co, 407 US 1 [1972]; Bense *v.* Interstate Battery System of America, Inc, 683 F 2d 718 [2d Cir, 1982]; Supreme Merchandise Co, Inc, *v.* Iwahori Kinzoku Co, Ltd, —AD 2d—, NYLJ, 9 June 1986, p. 14, col. 5 [1st Dept]).

It appears that defendant is a "sophisticated investor" and that the indemnity agreement, including the forum clause was "freely negotiated". There is no showing that the forum-selection provision in the indemnity agreement is invalid because of fraud or overreaching and defendant has failed to demonstrate that trial in the contractual forum "will be so gravely difficult and inconvenient that he will for all practical purposes be deprived of his day in court" (see Bremen *v.* Zapata Offshore Co, *supra*, 407 US at 18).'

56. The Latin maxim *actor sequitur forum rei* requires that the suit be brought simply where the plaintiff finds the defendant, so that a presumption in favor of plaintiff's choice of forum was logical.
58. 500 F Supp 787 (SDNY, 1980).
59. 156 Cal App3d 372 (1984).
60. Note Great Northern Railway Co *v.* Superior Court, 12 Cal App3d 105 (1970), and Hemmelgarn *v.* Boeing Co, 106 Cal App3d 576 (1980) in which the court summarized 'factors' to be considered in ruling on a motion to dismiss:

'They include the amenability of the parties to personal jurisdiction in this state and in the alternative forum; the relative convenience to the parties and trial witnesses of the competing forums; the differences in the conflict of law rules applicable in the competing forums; the selection of a convenient, reasonable and fair place of trial; defendant's principal place of business; the extent to which the cause of action arose out of events related to this state; the extent to which any party will be substantially disadvantaged by a trial in either forum; the relative enforceability of judgments rendered in this state or the alternative forum; the relative inconvenience to witnesses and relative expense to parties of proceeding in this state or the alternative forum; the significance and necessity of a view by the trier of fact of physical evidence not conveniently movable from the alternative forum; the extent to which prosecution of the action in this state would place a burden upon this state's judicial resources equitably disproportionate to the relationship of the parties or cause of action to this state; the extent to which the relationship of the moving party to this state obligates him to participate in judicial proceedings here; this state's interest in providing a forum for some or all of the parties; this state's public interest in the litigation; the avoidance of multiplicity of actions and inconsistent adjudications; the relative ease of access to sources of proof; the availability of compulsory process for attendance of witnesses; the relative advantages and obstacles to a fair trial; the burden upon jurors, local court and taxpayers of a jurisdiction having a minimal relation to the subject of the litigation; the difficulties and inconveniences to defendant, the court and jurors incident to the presentation of evidence by deposition; and the availability of the suggested forum.'

61. 104 S Ct 1473 (1984).
62. 497 F Supp 313 (DC, 1980), aff 717 F2d 602 (DC Cir, 1983).
63. *See* Graham *v.* Richardson, 403 US 365 (1971).
63.1 S&S Screw Machine Co *v.* COSA Corp, 647 F Supp 600 (Tern, 1986).
64. *See* Generally 47 UNIV CHI Rev 373 (1980).
65. *Supra* note 49.
66. *See* Scherk *v.* Alberto-Culver Co, 417 US 506 (1974).
67. Note Section 80 of Restatement (Second) of Conflict of Law which states that a 'forum selection clause' will be disregarded if it is the result of over-reaching or the unfair use of unequal bargaining power.
68. *See* Krenger *v.* Pennsylvania Railroad Co, 174 F2d 556 (2nd Cir, 1949), cert den 338 US 866 (1949). *See* generally 61 Denver L J 4 (1984).
69. *See* Chapter 4, Section 2, herein.
70. *See* New York Times (23 Mar 1986) at pp. 1 *et seq.* It appears that the Government of India wanted 'nearly $1 billion in damages and would not subject itself to a rigorous accounting of how the money would be dispensed prompting concern by the attorneys that much of it would not reach the victims'.
71. *See* generally S Ramaswamy Iyer, The Law of Torts (India, 1950).
72. *Id.*
73. *See* New York Times (1 Dec 1985) at p. 18.
74. *See* 8 J of Bar Council of India 418 (1981).
75. *See* Ghosh *v.* Union of India, A I R 1983 Madhya Pradesh 138.
76. (AIR 1984 Madhya Pradesh 4, opinion by Judge Faizanuddin) the High Court of the State of Madhya Pradesh had occasion to point out that:

> 'tortious liability arises from the breach of duty primarily fixed by the law. Tortious duties exist by virtue of law itself and are not dependent upon any agreement or consent of the persons subjected to them. A person is under a duty not to assault another person, not to slander him, not to trespass on his land, because law required him not to do so and not because he has agreed or undertaken not to do so. Tortious liability is thus distinguishable for this reason from contractual and other liabilities. In other words, in tort the content of the duty is fixed by the law, while under contract all the contractual duties are fixed by the contract itself. Thus, the basic principle about rights and remedies is that if there is a right under law, there must be a remedy for its violation. But if the plaintiff cannot show any violation of legal right, he cannot succeed merely on the ground that he had sustained damages.'

77. *See* State of Punjab *v.* OGB Syndicate, AIR 1964, SC 669.
78. *See* 20 Texas Internat LJ 195 (1985) at p. 301:

> 'Beyond that, the law is chaotic. Compensation for the death of a wife is computed as the replacement price to hire a maid servant plus a small solatium. If a widower has remarried, the courts consider his bereavement as limited to the earning capacity of his wife. In one case, it was suggested that the presence of other sons could be used as a reason for devaluing the financial worth of a deceased child. High Courts have been known to cut down the size of meagre awards. Even where the evidence suggests that the family was poor, at least one court felt "there is nothing to suggest that the

family was in wants". Anxious to preserve the principle that the bereaved should not benefit from the dead, Indian courts have taken into account the amount that the plaintiffs stood to inherit from the deceased to virtually evaporate sound claims. Yet, the discretion of the courts is often wayward. Faced with a 78 year old lawyer politician of some social and political standing, the courts compensated relatively generously. Basically, Indian tort law is balanced in favor of the defendant. The amounts awarded are low. A very low premium is placed on injury and death. If the tort claims for personal injury and death have not been advanced in Indian courts, it is because it hardly seems worth it to fight for a sum of compensation which is roughly equal to—and, in most instances, lower than—the amount given to victims and their relatives as a result of governmental handouts.' (footnotes omitted)

79. MDL No. 626, Misc No 21–38 (JFK). (25 ILM 771 *et seq*)

UNITED STATES: DISTRICT COURT FOR THE SOUTHERN DISTRICT OF NEW YORK
OPINION *In Re: Union Carbide Corporation Gas Plant Disaster at Bhopal, India in December*, 1984
(*Forum Non Conveniens*; INDIAN LEGAL SYSTEM)
[12 MAY 1986]

UNITED STATES DISTRICT COURT
SOUTHERN DISTRICT OF NEW YORK

IN RE: UNION CARBIDE CORPORATION GAS PLANT DISASTER AT BHOPAL, INDIA IN DECEMBER 1984

MDL NO. 626, MISC NO 21–38 (JFK)
ALL CASES

Opinion and Order
Appearances:

For the Union of India:
ROBINS, ZELLE, LARSON & KAPLAN
Minneapolis, Minnesota
Of Counsel: Michael V. Ciresi, Esq
Bruce A. Finzen, Esq
Roberta B. Walburn Esq
BARRETT, SMITH, SCHAPIRO, SIMON & ARMSTRONG
New York, New York
Of Counsel: Gerald A. Novack, Esq

For Individual Plaintiffs:
WAITE, SCHNEIDER, BAYLESS & CHESLEY CO, LPA
Cincinnati, Ohio
Of Counsel: Stanely M. Chesley, Esq
Phillip B. Allen, Esq
Jan Levien, Esq

BAILEY & BRODER
New York, New York
Of Counsel: F. Lee Bailey, Esq
Michael C. Zwal, Esq
Liaison Counsel:
HOFFINGER FRIEDLAND DOBRISH BERNFELD & HASEN
New York, New York
Of Counsel: Jack S. Hoffinger, Esq

For Defendant:
KELLEY DRYE & WARREN
New York, New York
Of Counsel: Bud G. Holman, Esq
William A. Krohley, Esq

For *Amicus Curiae:*
CHRISTIC INSTITUTE
Washington, DC
Of Counsel: Rob Hager, Esq
Shelley D. Hayes, Esq

John F. Keenan, United States District Judge:

Factual Background

On the night of 2–3 December 1984 the most tragic industrial disaster in history occurred in the city of Bhopal, state of Madhya Pradesh, Union of India. Located there was a chemical plant owned and operated by Union Carbide India Limited ('UCIL'). The plant, situated in the northern sector of the city, had numerous hutments adjacent to it on its southern side which were occupied by impoverished squatters. UCIL manufactured the pesticides Sevin and Temik at the Bhopal plant at the request of, and with the approval of, the Government of India. (Affidavit of John MacDonald ('MacDonald Aff') at 2). UCIL was incorporated under Indian law in 1934. 50.9% of its stock is owned by the defendant, Union Carbide Corporation, a New York corporation. (MacDonald Aff at 1). Methyl Isocyanate (MIC), a highly toxic gas, is an ingredient in the production of both Sevin and Temik. On the night of the tragedy MIC leaked from the plant in substantial quantities for reasons not yet determined.

The prevailing winds on the early morning of 3 December 1984 were from Northwest to Southeast. They blew the deadly gas into the overpopulated hutments adjacent to the plant and into the most densely occupied parts of the city. The results were horrendous. Estimates of deaths directly attributable to the leak range as high as 2,100. No one is sure exactly how many perished. Over 200,000 people suffered injuries—some serious and permanent—some mild and temporary. Livestock were killed and crops damaged. Businesses were interrupted.

On 7 December 1984 the first lawsuit was filed by American lawyers in the United States on behalf of thousands of Indians. Dawni *et al v.* Union Carbide Corp, SD WVa. (84–2479). Since then 144 additional actions have been commenced in federal courts in the United States. The actions have all been joined and assigned by the

Judicial Panel on Multidistrict Litigation to the Southern District of New York by order of 6 February 1985.

The individual federal court complaints have been superseded by a consolidated complaint filed on 28 June 1985.

The Indian Government on 29 March 1985 enacted legislation, the Bhopal Gas Leak Disaster (Processing of Claims) Act (21 of 1985) ('Bhopal Act'), providing that the Government of India has the exclusive right to represent Indian plaintiffs in India and elsewhere in connection with the tragedy. Pursuant to the Bhopal Act, the Union of India, on 8 April 1985, filed a complaint with this Court setting forth claims for relief similar to those in the consolidated complaint of 28 June 1985.

By order of 25 April 1985 this Court established a Plaintiffs' Executive Committee, comprised of F. Lee Bailey and Stanley M. Chesley, Esqs, who represented individual plaintiffs and Michael V. Ciresi, Esq, whose firm represents the Union of India. Jack S. Hoffinger, Esq, who represents individual plaintiffs, was appointed liaison counsel for the Plaintiffs' Executive Committee.[1]

On 24 September 1985, pursuant to the Bhopal Act, the Central Government of India framed a 'scheme' for the Registration and Processing of Claims arising out of the disaster. According to the Union of India's counsel, over 487,000 claims have been filed in India pursuant to the 'scheme'.

There presently are 145 actions filed in the United States District Court for the Southern District of New York under the Judicial Panel for Multidistrict Litigation's order of 6 February 1985, involving approximately 200,000 plaintiffs.

Before this Court is a motion by the defendant Union Carbide Corporation ('Union Carbide') to dismiss the consolidated action on the grounds of *forum non conveniens*.

Discussion

The doctrine of *forum non conveniens* allows a court to decline jurisdiction, even when jurisdiction is authorized by a general venue statute. In support of its position that the consolidated action before the Court should be transferred to a more convenient forum within the Union of India pursuant to this doctrine, Union Carbide relies on the United States Supreme Court's decisions in Gulf Oil Corp *v.* Gilbert, 330 US 501 (1947) and Piper Aircraft Co *v.* Reyno, 454 US 235 (1981). The plaintiffs cite numerous other lower United States federal court cases in their briefs and seek to distinguish the Supreme Court's decisions from this case. Of course, Gilbert and Piper are the touchstones in sorting out and examining the contentions of both sides to this motion on the various factors bearing on convenience.

Piper teaches a straightforward formulation of the doctrine of *forum non conveniens*. A district court is advised to determine first whether the proposed

1. All counsel on the Plaintiffs' Executive Committee were most professional and helpful to the Court in this case. Mr Hoffinger agreed to proceed *pro bono* in this case, and waived any possible fee. The Court has been informed that neither Mr Hoffinger, nor anyone else on the Plaintiffs' Executive Committee, nor anyone in their law firms went to India on the days immediately following the tragedy to 'sign up' Indian plaintiffs. The behavior of many American lawyers who went to Bhopal, India during December 1984 and January 1985 is not before this Court on this motion. Suffice it to say that those members of the American bar who travelled the 8,200 miles to Bhopal in those months did little to better the American image in the Third World—or anywhere else. None of them were on the Plaintiffs' Executive Committee.

alternative forum is 'adequate'. This inquiry should proceed in the order followed below. Then, as a matter within its 'sound discretion', Piper at 257, the district court should consider relevant public and private interest factors, and reasonably balance those factors, in order to determine whether dismissal is favored. This Court will approach the various concerns in the same direct manner in which Piper and Gilbert set them out.

At this juncture, it would be appropriate to discuss the presumptions on a *forum non conveniens* motion. In Piper, the Court discussed its earlier finding in Koster *v.* Lumbermens Mutual Casualty Co, 330 US 518 (1947), which suggested that a plaintiff's choice of forum was entitled to great deference when the forum chosen was the home of the plaintiff. This presumption was based on the fact that the choice of the home forum indicated a reasonable assumption that the choice was convenient. Koster at 524. Conversely, the Piper Court found:

> When the plaintiff is foreign, however, this assumption is much less reasonable. Because the central purpose of any *forum non conveniens* inquiry is to ensure that the trial is convenient, a foreign plaintiff's choice deserves less deference.

Piper at 256 (footnote omitted).

In the case now before the Court, in which the plaintiffs, including the Union of India, are foreign, and share a home forum which is not the instant forum, the assumption that this forum is convenient is not completely reasonable. The foreign plaintiffs' choice of the United States forum 'deserves less deference' than would be accorded a United States citizen's choice. This Court will apply the presumption in favor of plaintiffs' choice of forum with 'less than maximum force'. Piper at 261. *See* note 23, *infra*.

1. Preliminary Considerations

'At the outset of any *forum non conveniens* inquiry, the court must determine whether there exists an alternative forum.' Piper at 254, n.22. The elements of that inquiry are set forth in Piper. First, the Court said, '[o]rdinarily, this requirement will be satisfied when the defendant is 'amenable to process' in the other jurisdiction'. Piper at 254, n.22, quoting Gilbert at 506–507. Gilbert states that the doctrine of *forum non conveniens* 'presupposes at least two forums in which the defendant is amenable to process'.

Extending the limited inquiry of Gilbert, the Piper Court delved into the relevance of the substantive and procedural differences in law which would be applied in the event a case was transferred on the grounds of *forum non conveniens*. The Piper Court determined that it was theoretically inconsistent with the underlying doctrine of *forum non conveniens*, as well as grossly impractical, to consider the impact of the putative transferee forum's law on the plaintiff in its decision on a *forum non conveniens* motion: '[I]f conclusive or substantial weight were given to the possibility of a change in law, the *forum non conveniens* doctrine would become virtually useless.' Piper at 250.[2]

2. The Court found a theoretical flaw in the opposite rule, as set forth by the Third Circuit. Noting that a plaintiff would choose the forum with the most favorable choice of law rules in the first instance, 'if the possibility of an unfavorable change in substantive law is given weight in the *forum non conveniens* inquiry, dismissal would rarely be proper'. Piper at 250.

The Court listed numerous practical considerations which led to its conclusion that an unfavorable change in law for plaintiff was not a relevant factor in the forum analysis. First, the Court observed that if the chance of a change in law were given substantial weight, choice of law questions would 'become extremely important'. Piper at 251. US courts would 'have to compare the rights, remedies, and procedures available' within the two proposed alternative forums, to determine whether a disadvantageous change in law would occur upon transfer. *Id*. Since '[t]he doctrine of *forum non conveniens*, however, is designed in part to help courts avoid conducting complex exercises in comparative law', the change in law analysis would subvert the doctrine itself. *Id*. Thus, a court engaged in the inquiry regarding the existence and adequacy of an alternative forum should not hinge its decision on an unfavorable change in law.[3]

Another practical concern relating to the 'change in law' inquiry was discussed by the Piper court. Based on the liberality of United States federal law as compared to much foreign law with respect to availability of strict liability for tort, malleable and diverse choice of law rules among the 50 states, availability of jury trials, contingent fee arrangements and extensive discovery provisions, the Court observed that a change of forum might frequently involve an unfavorable change of law for foreign plaintiffs suing American defendants. Piper at 252, n.18. Consequently, if the unfavorable change in law were a major factor in the analysis:

> [T]he American courts, which are already extremely attractive to foreign plaintiffs, would become even more attractive. The flow of litigation into the United States would increase and further congest already crowded courts.

Piper at 252 (footnotes omitted).

At the point, however, where the possible change in law would provide 'no remedy at all' to plaintiff, a court may conclude that no adequate alternative exists. As the Piper Court observed, it did not hold that:

> [T]he possibility of an unfavorable change in law should *never* be a relevant consideration in a *forum non conveniens* inquiry. Of course, if the remedy provided by the alternative forum is so clearly inadequate or unsatisfactory that it is no remedy at all, the unfavorable change in law may be given substantial weight; the district court may conclude that dismissal would not be in the interests of justice.

Piper at 254 (emphasis in original) (footnote omitted). Thus, while it is not a 'major factor' in the analysis, a court must at least consider the effect on plaintiffs of a change in law upon transfer.

To a great extent, the plaintiffs in this case argue that Indian courts do not offer an adequate forum for this litigation by virtue of the relative 'procedural and discovery deficiencies [which] would thwart the victims' quest for' justice. (Memorandum in Opposition by Plaintiffs' Executive Committee ('Memo in Opp') at 2). The defendant disputes this contention.

Plaintiffs' preliminary concern, regarding defendant's amenability to process in the alternative forum, is more that sufficiently met in the instant case. Union Carbide

3. Similarly, the Court determined that 'the possibility of a change in law favorable to defendant should not be considered'. Piper at 252, n. 19.

has unequivocally acknowledged that it is subject to the jurisdiction of the courts of India (Defendant's Memorandum in Reply filed 20 December 1985 ('Reply Memo') at 8); (oral argument 3 January 1986, transcript at 29, comment of Bud Holman, counsel for Union Carbide). Union Carbide is definitely amenable to process in India.

Beyond this initial test, plaintiffs and *amicus curiae*[4] argue that the Indian legal system is inadequate to handle the Bhopal litigation. In support of this position, plaintiffs have submitted the affidavit of Professor Marc S. Galanter of the University of Wisconsin Law School. Professor Galanter's credentials are impressive; he was a Fulbright Scholar at the Faculty of Law of Dehli University and specializes in South Asian Studies at the University of Wisconsin Law School. He is not, however, admitted to practice in India and the Court views his opinions concerning the Indian legal system, its judiciary and bar as far less persuasive than those of N. A. Palkhivala and J. B. Dadachanji, each of whom has been admitted to practice in India for over 40 years. Both are Senior Advocates before the Supreme Court of India. Mr Palkhivala served as Indian Ambassador to the United States from 1977 to 1979, and has represented the Indian government on three occasions before international tribunals.

Although the outcome of this analysis, given the rule of Piper regarding change in law, seems self-evident, the Court will review plaintiffs' argument on the inadequacy of the Indian forum out of deference to the plaintiffs.

A. Innovation in the Indian Judicial System

Professor Galanter describes the Indian common law legal system, inherited from the British, in terms of its similarity to that of other common law systems. He compares the system favorably to that of the United States or Great Britain in terms of the appellate structure, the rule of *stare decisis*, the role of the judiciary as 'guardian of [India's] democratic structure and protector of citizens' rights'. (Galanter Aff, at 6–12) before pointing to its ostensible deficiencies. According to Professor Galanter, India's legal system 'was imposed on it' during the period of colonial rule. (Galanter Aff at 11). Galanter argues that 'Indian legal institutions still reflect their colonial origins', (Galanter Aff at 12), in terms of the lack of broad-based legislative activity, inaccessibility of legal information and legal services, burdensome court filing fees and limited innovativeness with reference to legal practice and education. (Galanter Aff at 12).

On the question of innovativeness, Mr Palkhivala responds with numerous examples of novel treatment of complex legal issues by the Indian Judiciary.[5] In the words of the former ambassador of India to the United States, 'a legal system is not a structure of fossils but is a living organism which grows through the judicial process and statutory enactments'. (Palkhivala Aff at 3). The examples cited by defendant's experts suggest a developed and independent judiciary. Plaintiffs present no evidence to bolster their contention that the Indian legal system has not sufficiently emerged

4. Rob Hager, Esq for Citizens Commission on Bhopal, National Council of Churches, United Church of Christ Commission for Racial Justice, *et al.*
5. For example, Mr Palkhivala describes four cases in which the Indian Supreme Court crafted new and 'courageous' remedies in situations relating to abridgements of fundamental rights. (Palkhivala Aff at 6–7). Mr Dadachanji describes similar decisions in which he participated as an advocate, in his affidavit (Dadachanji Aff at 2–3). The Court recognizes the innovativeness of the Indian Courts, while refraining from an exhaustive survey of Indian case law.

from its colonial heritage to display the innovativeness which the Bhopal litigation would demand. Their claim in this regard is not compelling.

B. Endemic Delays in the Indian Legal System

Galanter discusses the problems of delay and backlog in Indian courts. Indeed, it appears that India has approximately one-tenth the number of judges, per citizen, as the United States,[6] and that postponements and high caseloads are widespread. Galanter urges that the backlog is a result of Indian procedural law, which allows for adjournments in mid-hearing, and for multiple interlocutory and final appeals. Numerous appeals and '[c]onsiderable delay [are] caused by the tendency of courts to avoid the decision of all the matters in issue in a suit, on the ground that the suit could be disposed of on a preliminary point'. (Galanter Aff at 17; 18–20, 21, quoting Indian Law Commission, 54th Report (1973) pp. 12–13).

This Court acknowledges that delays and backlog exist in Indian courts, but United States courts are subject to delays and backlog, too. *See* Remarks of Honorable Warren E. Burger, Chief Justice, Supreme Court of the United States, 100 FRD 499, 534 (1983).

However, as Mr Palkhivala states, while delays in the Indian legal system are a fact of judicial life in the proposed alternative forum, there is no reason to assume that the Bhopal litigation will be treated in ordinary fashion.

The Bhopal tragedy has already been approached with imagination in India. Demonstrating the creativity and flexibility of the Indian system, the Parliament of India has passed the Bhopal Act in order to deal with the cases arising from the sad events of 3 December 1984. The Bhopal Act permits the cases to be treated 'speedily, effectively, equitably and to the best advantage of the claimants'. (Palkhivala Aff at 11).

Mr Dadachanji refers to another Indian case which arose from a gas leak in New Dehli. The Chief Justice and another Justice of the Supreme Court of India ordered the presiding court to expedite adjudication of claims. MC Mehta *v.* Union of India. (Dadachanji Aff at 11 and Annexure A thereto). In another instance, the Indian Supreme Court directed the High Court to hear a given matter on a daily basis, and set a deadline for delivering judgment (Dadachanji Aff at 11 and Annexure B thereto). Other means of coping with delay are appointment of special tribunals by the Government of India (Dadachanji Aff at 12 and Annexure C thereto), and assignment of daily hearing duties to a single special judge, otherwise unburdened, to hear a special matter. (Dadachanji Aff at 11). This Court is persuaded, by the example of the Bhopal Act itself and other cases where special measures to expedite were taken by the Indian judiciary, that the most significant, urgent and extensive litigation ever to arise from a single event could be handled through special judicial accommodation in India, if required.

C. Procedural and Practical Capacity of Indian Courts

Plaintiffs contend that the Indian legal system lacks the wherewithal to allow it 'to

6. India allegedly has 10.5 judges per million population, as compared to 107 judges per million in the United States (Galanter Aff at 15).

deal effectively and expeditiously' with the issues raised in this lawsuit. (Memo in Opp p. 53).

Plaintiffs urge that Indian practitioners emphasize oral skills rather than written briefs. They allegedly lack specialization, practical investigative techniques and coordination into partnerships. These factors, it is argued, limit the Indian bar's ability to handle the Bhopal litigation. As Mr Dadachanji indicates, Indian lawyers have competently dealt with complex technology tranfers, suggesting capability within the technological and scientific areas of legal practice, if not 'specialization'. (Dadachanji Aff at 8). Moreover, Indian attorneys use experts, when necessary. As to investigative ability, Mr Dadachanji persuasively points out that the Central Bureau of Investigation ('CBI') of the Union of India is well equipped to handle factual inquiry, as is the Commission of Enquiry constituted by the state of Madhya Pradesh. (Dadachanji Aff at 8). While Indian attorneys may not customarily join into large law firms, and as Mr Palkhivala states, are limited by present Indian law to partnerships of no more than twenty, this alone or even in concert with other factors does not establish the inadequacy of the Indian legal system. (Palkhivala Aff at 8). There is no reason the Indian legislature could not provide for the expansion of law-firms, if such a choice is required. In any event, this Court is not convinced that the size of a law firm has that much to do with the quality of legal service provided. Many small firms in this country perform work at least on a par with the largest firms. Bigger is not necessarily better.

Moreover, since the Union of India purports to represent all the claimants, it is likely that if the case were transferred to India, the Attorney General or Solicitor General of India and the Advocate General of Madhya Pradesh, with attendant staffs would represent the claimants. The Indian bar appears more than capable of shouldering the litigation if it should be transferred to India. (Palkhivala Aff at 9).

Next plaintiffs and Professor Galanter argue that the substantive tort law of India is not sufficiently developed to accommodate the Bhopal claims. Plaintiffs trace the lack of sophistication in Indian tort law to the presence of court fees for litigants as inhibiting the filing of civil cuits. Though the filing fees may have had historical significance, they are irrelevant here. Professor Galanter acknowledges that court fees may be waived for 'poor parties or for specific classes of litigants'. (Galanter Aff at 28). In fact, filing fees have been waived for claimants in India in the Bhopal litigation already begun there.

Profession Galanter asserts that India lacks codified tort law, has little reported case law in the tort field to serve as precedent, and has no tort law relating to disputes arising out of complex product or design liability. (Galanter Aff at 30–36). As an illustration of the paucity of Indian tort law, Professor Galanter states that a search through the *All-India Reports* for the span from 1914 to 1965 revealed only 613 tort cases reported. (Galanter Aff at 32). Mr Dadachanji responds that tort law is sparsely reported in India due to frequent settlement of such cases, lack of appeal to higher courts, and the publication of tort cases in specialized journals other than the *All-India Reports*. (Dadachanji Aff at 16–17; Palkhivala Aff at 10). In addition, tort law has been codified in numerous Indian statutes. (Dadachanji Aff at 16–17).

As Professor Galanter himself states, 'the major categories of tort, their elements, the [theories] of liability, defenses, *respondeat superior*, the theories of damages—are all familiar'. (Galanter Aff at 37). Which is different, Galanter asserts, is the complete absence of tort law relating to high technology or complex manufacturing processes. This is of no moment with respect to the adequacy of the Indian courts. With the groundwork of tort doctrine adopted from the common law and the precedential weight awarded British cases, as well as Indian ones, it is obvious that a well-developed base of tort doctrine exists to provide a guide to Indian courts presiding over the Bhopal litigation. In any event, much tort law applied in American cases involving complex technology has its source in legal principles first enunciated in Victorian England. *See*, *eg*, Rylands *v*. Fletcher, 1868, LR 3 HL 330. As Mr Palkhivala stated in his affidavit:

> The plant itself was the product of highly complex technology, but complexity of the technology cannot be equated with complexity of legal issues. The principles of liability and damages involved in the Bhopal cases are all well established in India. The complexity is not in the nature of determination of legal issues but in the application of the law to the events which took place in Bhopal. Well settled law is to be applied to an unusual occurrence.

(Palkhivala Aff at 7).

Plaintiffs next assert that India lacks certain procedural devices which are essential to the adjudication of complex cases, the absence of which prevent India from providing an adequate alternative forum. They urge that Indian pre-trial discovery is inadequate and that therefore India is an inadequate alternative forum. Professor Galanter states that the only forms of discovery available in India are written interrogatories, inspection of documents, and requests for admissions. Parties alone are subject to discovery. Third-party witnesses need not submit to discovery. Discovery may be directed to admissible evidence only, not material likely to lead to relevant or admissible material, as in the courts of the United States. Parties are not compelled to provide what will be actual proof at trial as part of discovery.

These limits on discovery are adopted from the British system. Similar discovery tools are used in Great Britain today. This Court finds that their application would perhaps, however, limit the victims' access to sources of proof. Therefore, pursuant to its equitable powers, the Court directs that the defendant consent to submit to the broad discovery afforded by the United States Federal Rules of Civil Procedure if or when an Indian court sits in judgment or presides over pre-trial proceedings in the Bhopal litigation.[7] Any dismissal of action now before this Court is thus conditioned on defendant's consent to submit to discovery on the American model, even after transfer to another jurisdiction.

The ostensible lack of devices for third-party impleader or for organizing complex cases under the law of the state of Madhya Pradesh are two other procedural deficiencies which plaintiffs assert preclude a finding that India offers an adequate alternative forum. Assuming for the moment that, upon appropriate transfer, the Bhopal litigation would be adjudicated by the local district court in Bhopal, and that the law of Madhya Pradesh would be applied, this Court is still not moved by plaintiffs' argument regarding impleader or complex litigation.

Although no specific provision in the Indian Code of Civil Procedure permits the impleading of third-parties from whom contribution is sought, other provisions in the Code do provide for impleader. As both parties to this motion state, Order 1, Rule

7. A federal court has the power to condition transfer under the doctrine of *forum non conveniens* upon 'the condition that defendant corporations agree to provide the records relevant to the plaintiff's claims'. Piper at 257, n. 25. While the Court feels that it would be fair to bind the plaintiffs to American discovery rules, too, it has no authority to do so.

10(2) of the Indian Code of Civil Procedure 'allows the court to add additional parties if the presence of those parties is "necessary in order to enable the Court effectively and completely to adjudicate upon and settle all questions involved in the suit"'. (Galanter Aff at 60; Dadachanji Aff at 18). Professor Galanter posits that a joint tortfeasor would not be considered a necessary party, and would not be joined. Defendant's expert, conversely, asserts that a party can be added to prevent multiplicity of suits and conflicts of decisions. Thus, Mr Dadachanji argues, defendants would be able to seek contribution from third-parties if joinder would prevent repetitive litigation or inconsistency. Moreover, the broad provision of inherent powers to aid the ends of justice, as codified at Section 151 of the Indian Code of Civil Procedure would prevent an ultimate miscarriage of justice in the area of impleader. (Dadachanji Aff at 19).[8]

The absence of procedures or mechanisms within the Indian judiciary to handle complex litigation is presented as support for plaintiffs' position regarding the non-existence of an adequate alternative forum. Professor Galanter asserts, for example, that Indian judges do not promote settlements. The point is wholly irrelevant to the question of whether an adequate alternative forum exists. In any event, this Court has labored hard and long to promote settlement between the parties for over a year, to no avail. It would appear that settlement, although desirable for many reasons, including conservation of attorneys' fees and costs of litigation, preservation of judicial resources, and speed of resolution, is unlikely regardless of the level of activism of the presiding judge.

Plaintiffs' next contention is that since no class action procedure exists in India expeditious litigation of the Bhopal suits would be impossible. As with all of plaintiffs' other arguments, this purported deficiency does not constitute 'no remedy' at all. Professor Galanter himself acknowledges that Order 1, Rule 8 of the Indian Code of Civil Procedure provides a mechanism for 'representative' suits, 'where there are numerous persons having the same interest in one suit'. (Galanter Aff at 54). Even if the current state of Indian law regarding 'representative' suits involves application of the mechanism to pre-existing groups such as religious sects or associations, there is no reason to conclude that the Indian legislature, capable of enacting the Bhopal Act, would not see its way to enacting a specific law for class actions. In addition, it does not appear on the face of Order 1, Rule 8 that the 'representative' suit is expressly limited to pre-existing groups. The Indian district court could adopt the rule for use in a newly created class of injured, whose members all have 'the same interest' in establishing the liability of the defendant. An Indian court has law available to create a representative class, or perhaps a few different representative classes. The 'scheme' for registration and processing of claims, *see supra*, at 4, could perform the task of evaluating the specific amounts of claims. Moreover, Mr Dadachanji gives at least three examples where Indian courts have consolidated suits pursuant to their inherent power under Section 151 of the Indian Code of Civil Procedure. In at least one case, such consolidation allegedly occurred without consent of the parties. (Dadachanji Aff at 9). The absence of a rule for class actions which is identical to the American rule does not lead to the conclusion that India is not an adequate alternative forum.

8. The Court observes that the alleged problem would appear to act to the detriment of defendant, not plaintiffs. It is Union Carbide which urges that third-party defendants are necessary. (Memo in Support at 27–28). Defendant discounts the supposed unavailability of third-party impleader, while the plaintiffs find its lack objectionable. These postures lead the Court to the conclusion that this argument is not compelling in either direction. The lack of specific third-party practice will not concern the Court if it does not concern Union Carbide.

Final points regarding the asserted inadequacies of Indian procedure involve unavailability of juries or contingent fee arrangements in India. Plaintiffs do not press these arguments, but Mr Palkhivala touches upon them. They are easily disposed of. The absence of juries in civil cases is a feature of many civil law jurisdictions, and of the United Kingdom. Piper at 252, n.18 and citations therein. Furthermore, contingency fees are not found in most foreign jurisdictions. Piper at 252, n.18. In any event, the lack of contingency fees is not an insurmountable barrier to filing claims in India, as demonstrated by the fact that more than 4,000 suits have been filed by victims of the Bhopal gas leak in India, already. According to Mr Palkhivala, moreover, well-known lawyers have been known to serve clients without charging any fees. (Palkhivala Aff at 8).

Plaintiffs' final contention as to the inadequacy of the Indian forum is that a judgment rendered by an Indian court cannot be enforced in the United States without resort to further extensive litigation. Conversely, plaintiffs assert, Indian law provides *res judicata* effect to foreign judgments, and precludes plaintiffs from bringing a suit on the same cause of action in India. (Galanter Aff at 63–65). Mr Dadachanji disputes this description of the Indian law of *res judicata*. He asserts that the pendency, or even final disposition, of an action in a foreign court does not prevent plaintiffs from suing in India upon the original cause of action. Plaintiffs would not be limited, Mr Dadachanji argues, to an Indian action to enforce the foreign judgment. (Dadachanji Aff at 19–20). In addition, he states that an Indian court, before ordering that a foreign judgment be given effect, would seek to establish whether the foreign court had failed to apply Indian law, or misapplied Indian law. (Dadachanji Aff at 20).

The possibility of non-enforcement of a foreign judgment by courts of either country leads this Court to conclude that the issue must be addressed at this time. Since it is defendant Union Carbide which, perhaps ironically, argues for the sophistication of the Indian legal system in seeking a dismissal on grounds of *forum non conveniens*, and plaintiffs, including the Indian Government, which state a strong preference for the American legal system, it would appear that both parties have indicated a willingness to abide by a judgment of the foreign nation whose forum each seeks to visit. Thus, this Court conditions the grant of a dismissal on *forum non conveniens* grounds on Union Carbide's agreement to be bound by the judgment of its preferred tribunal, located in India, and to satisfy any judgment rendered by the Indian court, and affirmed on appeal in India. Absent such consent to abide by and to 'make good' on a foreign judgment, without challenge except for concerns relating to minimal due process, the motion to dismiss now under consideration will not be granted. The preference of both parties to play ball on a distant field will be taken to its limit, with each party being ordered to be bound by the decision of the respective foreign referees.

To sum up the discussion to this point, the Court determines that the Indian legal system provides an adequate alternative forum for the Bhopal litigation. For from exhibiting a tendency to be so 'inadequate or unsatisfactory' as to provide 'no remedy at all', the courts of India appear to be well up to the task of handling this case. Any unfavorable change in law for plaintiffs which might be suffered upon transfer to the Indian courts, will, by the rule of Piper, not be given 'substantial weight'. Differences between the two legal systems, even if they inure to plaintiffs' detriment, do not suggest that India is not an adequate alternative forum. As Mr Palkhivala asserts with some dignity, '[w]hile it is true to say that the Indian system today is different in some respects from the American system, it is wholly untrue to say that it is deficient or inadequate. Difference is not to be equated with deficiency.' (Palkhivala Aff at 4).

Piper at 254. The inquiry now turns to a weighing of the public and private interest factors.

2. Private Interest Concerns

The Gilbert Court set forth a list of considerations which affect the interests of the specific litigants to an action, and which should be weighed in making a *forum non conveniens* determination. The so-called private interest factors, along with public interest factors discussed below, were not intended to be rigidly applied. As the Court stated in Piper,

> '([E]ach case turns on its facts.' If central emphasis were placed on any one factor, the *forum non conveniens* doctrine would lose much of the flexibility that makes it so valuable.

Piper at 249–50. Recognizing that '[p]articularly with respect to the question of relative ease of access to sources of proof', 'the private interests point in both directions', the Supreme Court nevertheless upheld a district court's decision to dismiss a case in favor of the relative convenience of a forum in Scotland. Piper at 257. By contrast, this Court finds that the private interests point strongly one way. As in Piper, it appears that the burdensome effect of a trial in this forum supports a finding that the private interest factors in this case weigh strongly in favor of dismissal.

A. Sources of Proof

The first example of a private interest consideration discussed in Gilbert is 'relative ease of access to sources of proof'. As stated, the analysis of this issue must hinge on the facts. Limited discovery on the issue of *forum non conveniens* has taken place, pursuant to the Court's order of 14 August 1985.[9] The Court can therefore proceed to discuss this question.

Union Carbide argues that virtually all of the evidence which will be relevant at a trial in this case is located in India. Union Carbide's position is that almost all records relating to liability, and without exception, all records relevant to damages, are to be found in and around Bhopal. On the liability question Union Carbide asserts that the Bhopal plant was managed and operated entirely by Indian nationals, who were employed by UCIL. (Affidavit of Warren J. Woomer, formerly Works Manager of the Bhopal plant ('Woomer Aff') at 2). Defendant asserts that the Bhopal plant is part of UCIL's Agricultural Products Division, which has been a separate division of UCIL for at least 15 years, and that the plant had 'limited contact' with UCIL's Bombay headquarters, and almost no contact with the United States. (Woomer Aff at 4, 32). Woomer claims to have been the last American employed by UCIL. He departed from Bhopal in 1982. (Woomer Aff at 2).

Woomer describes the structure and organization of the Bhopal facility at the time of the accident. The plant had seven operating units, each headed by a manager

9. Discovery was ably managed by Magistrate Michael H. Dolinger, of the Southern District of New York.

or department head, each an Indian national.[10] The managers or department heads each reported either directly to the plant's General Works Manager, or to one of three Assistant Works Managers. (Woomer Aff at 6). Each of these is also an Indian national. Three of the operating units which at this very early stage of inquiry into liability appear to have been potentially involved in the MIC leak are the Carbon Monoxide, MIC/Phosgene and Carbamoylation units. (Woomer Aff at 7–10). The Carbon Monoxide and MIC/Phosgene units together employed 63 employees, all Indian nationals. (Woomer Aff at 9). The Carbamoylation unit employed 99 Indian nationals. (Woomer Aff at 10). Mr Woomer states that an inquiry into the cause of the accident would require interviews with at least those employees who were on duty at the Bhopal facility 'immediately prior or after the accident'; Mr Woomer asserts that there are 193 employees, all Indians, who must be interviewed. (Woomer Aff at 58).[11]

In addition to the seven operating units, the Bhopal plant contained seven functional departments which serviced operations.[12] The seven heads of the units reported within the plant much as the department heads did.

The maintenance unit was apparently subdivided into departments including Instrumentation, Mechanical Maintenance, both part of the Agricultural Chemical Maintenance unit, which employed 171 people in total, and Plant Engineering and Formulation Maintenance, which employed 46 people. (Woomer Aff at 11–12). In addition, the Utilities and Electrical department employed 195 people. (Woomer Aff at 13). According to Mr Woomer, the various maintenance organizations performed repairs on equipment, provided engineering support, fabricated certain equipment, salvaged other portions, and controlled utilities, temperatures and pressures throughout the plant. (Woomer Aff at 11–14).

Moreover, according to Mr Woomer, these UCIL departments also kept daily, weekly and monthly records of plant operations, many of which were purportedly seized by the CBI and selected for copying by CBI immediately after the accident.[13] The records and reports of the various maintenance units would likely be relevant to the question of liability at trial.

Of the additional functional units, it is possible that Quality Control, with 54 employees, Purchasing, with 53, or Stores may have been directly involved in the disaster by virtue of their participation in analyzing plant output, procuring raw materials for the chemical processes of the plant, and maintaining spare parts and certain chemicals. (Woomer Aff at 14–19). Thus, the records and reports of these three departments may be necessary to an investigation of liability. While examination of members of the Works Office department and Industrial Relations department would likely be less directly useful, information regarding plant budgets and employee

10. The seven operating units included Carbon Monoxide, MIC/Phosgene, Carbamoylation, Alpha Napthol, Aldicarb, Utilities and Formulations.
11. Mr Woomer states that a post-accident technical team sought to interview these 193 employees. According to Mr Woomer, the Indian CBI, which had stepped into the plant following the tragedy, advised the technical team that interviews could be conducted only of the General Works Manager and MIC Production Manager, neither of whom was present at the time of the leak. (Woomer Aff at 57–58).
12. The seven functional units were Maintenance, Quality Control, Stores, Purchasing, Safety/Medical, Industrial Relations and Works Office. (Woomer Aff at 6).
13. Mr Bud Holman, Counsel for Union Carbide, states in his second affidavit that over 36,000 of the 78,000 pages of documents seized by the CBI represent plant operation records. (Holman Aff 2 at 5). He asserts that 1,700 pages deal with maintenance work performed in 1983 and 1984. (Holman Aff 2 at 8).

histories might be of relevance. Of great important are the records and reports of the Safety/Medical department, which was responsible for daily auditing of safety performance in all departments, training and testing on safety rules, maintaining safety statistics and planning and implementing safety drills. (Woomer Aff at 22–23). The 31 Indian employees of this department worked with the Central Safety Committee of the plant, whose members were drawn from plant management, and the Departmental Safety Committees. Operating units were required to monitor plant safety mechanisms weekly, and to keep monthly checklists. (Holman Aff 2 at 9). The Central Safety Committee met monthly, as did the Departmental Safety Committees. (Woomer Aff at 39). The MIC Unit held monthly safety committee meetings, for example, and issued monthly reports. (Woomer Aff at 41). Quarterly 'Measures of Performance' reviews also covered safety issues, and were required of each operating unit. (Woomer Aff at 40). Certainly, interviews of the plant personnel involved in safety reports and audits would be particularly relevant to the investigation of the disaster.

Plaintiffs refer to three occasions upon which Union Carbide, not UCIL, employees conducted safety audits at the Bhopal plant. As defendant correctly argues, these three events constitute a very small fraction of the thousands of safety audits conducted at the Bhopal facility. The three audits, moreover, were conducted in 1979, the fall of 1980 and in May of 1982, many years prior to the accident which is the subject of this lawsuit. (Plaintiffs' Memo in Opp at 25).[14]

Two accidents which occurred previously at the Bhopal plant might also be of relevance to the liability inquiry in this litigation. On 24 December 1981, a phosgene gas leak killed a UCIL maintenance worker. Reports of the fatality were sent to Union Carbide management in the United States. (Woomer Deposition, Exs 30 and 31). Plaintiffs assert that the accident report called for increased training in Bhopal by United States employees of Union Carbide's Institute, West Virginia, plant. Defendant states that the responsibility for remedying problems in the Bhopal plant rested with the plant itself, and that Union Carbide did not make any recommendations, and was involved only to the extent of receiving a copy of the report which called for its involvement in further training. (Woomer Aff at 41).

The second accident at Bhopal prior to the disaster of December 1984 took place on 9 February 1982, when a pump seal, perhaps improperly used, failed. (Memo in Opp at 24; Woomer Aff at 41). Many employees were injured, and at least 25 were hospitalized. Plaintiffs discuss the fact that Robert Oldford, president of Union Carbide Agricultural Products Company ('UCAPC') a wholly-owned subsidiary of Union Carbide headquartered in the United States, was in Bhopal at the time of the February 1982 leak. (Memo in Opp at 24). Union Carbide asserts that Mr Oldford was visiting UCIL's Research and Development Centre, located several miles from the Bhopal plant for an unrelated purpose, and was only coincidentally in Bhopal when the leak occurred. To the extent that this presence in India in 1982 has any

14. The 1982 'Operational Safety Survey' was apparently fairly extensive. It was conducted by three United States employees of Union Carbide, and led to a report which discussed 'major' concerns and possibility of 'serious personnel exposure'. (Memo in Opp at 25). Mr Woomer asserts, and plaintiffs do not refute, that this Survey was not intended to 'serve a policing function', but was performed at the specific request of UCIL. In addition, follow-up responsibility 'rested exclusively with UCIL plant management.' (Woomer Aff at 37–38).
Moreover, Union Carbide states that the Union of India, itself, conducted similar safety audits and made recommendations. (Affidavit of Ranjit K. Dutta, Business Manager of Union Carbide Agricultural Products Company ('Dutta Aff') at 58–64).

significance, Mr Oldford, and any other United States employees of Union Carbide who conducted safety audits in Bhopal or were present when accidents occurred there, may be flown to Bhopal for testimony or discovery.

In addition to safety data, two other types of proof may be relevant to a trial of this case on the merits. Information regarding plant design, commissioning and start-up may bear upon the liability question. Information pertinent to employee training should also have significance.

Leaving aside the question of whether the Government of India or UCIL chose the site and product of the Bhopal plant, the Court will evaluate the facts which bear on the issue of relevant records. The findings below concern the location of proof only, and bear solely upon the *forum non conveniens* motion. The Court expressly declines to make findings as to actual liability at this stage of the litigation.

Plaintiffs and defendant agree that in 1973 Union Carbide entered into two agreements with UCIL which were entitled 'Design Transfer Agreement' and 'Technical Service Agreement'. According to plaintiffs, Union Carbide, pursuant to the Design Transfer Agreement provided a process design to UCIL, the 'detailing [of which] was undertaken in India'. (Memo in Opp at 17). The process design package consisted of the basic plan of the factory, which was to be fleshed out in the detailing phase. Plaintiffs state that at least nine Union Carbide technicians travelled to India to monitor the progress of the project. Union Carbide also allegedly assigned a 'key engineer', John Couvaras, to serve as UCIL Bhopal project manager. Mr Couvaras allegedly 'assumed responsibility for virtually every aspect of the detailing of the process design', and approved detail reports of 'not only UCIL but also independent contractors, including Humphreys & Glasgow Consultants Private Ltd and Power Gas Limited' of Bombay, India. (Memo in Opp at 17–20).[15]

Plaintiffs also claim that '[n]o change of any substance was made from Union Carbide's design during the detailing phase'. Plaintiffs note that only 'one portion' of the process design work provided to UCIL by Union Carbide was not used. (Memo in Opp at 20). In effect, plaintiffs seek to establish that Union Carbide was the creator of the design used in the Bhopal plant, and directed UCIL's relatively minor detailing program. They urge that for the most part relevant proof on this point is located in the United States.

Defendant seeks to refute this contention, with notable success. Turning first to the affidavit of Robert C. Brown, who describes himself as 'chief negotiator for Union Carbide Corporation in connection with the two agreements it entered into with . . . UCIL in November, 1983', the Court is struck by the assertion that the two agreements were negotiated at 'arms-length' pursuant to Union Carbide corporate policy, and that the Union of India mandated that the Government retain 'specific control over the terms of any agreement UCIL made with foreign companies such as Union Carbide Corporation'. (Brown Aff at 3–4).[16]

15. Plaintiffs assert that Mr Couvaras exemplifies Union Carbide's 'international employee' whose mobility throughout the Union Carbide affiliates causes '[a]ny notion of discrete corporate identities [to] blur[ ]'. (Memo in Opp at 18–19).
16. As support, Mr Brown points to the Union Carbide Corporate Policy Manual, Section 1.10 wich states:

> The 'arms-length principle' is a central consideration in transfer and pricing of all technology transactions with affiliates.

'Arms length' is defined as: →

Mr Brown alleges that the Letter of Intent issued by the Union of India in March 1972, pursuant to which construction and design of the plant were allowed to ensue provided, *inter alia*, that:

> (2) [F]oreign collaboration and import of equipment be settled to the satisfaction of the Government.

Mr Brown claims, on personal information, that UCIL told him that Union Carbide would not be allowed to be involved in the Bhopal project beyond the provision of process design packages. (Brown Aff at 5). The Design Transfer Agreement indicates that Union Carbide's duty under the Agreement was to provide process design packages, and that UCIL, not Union Carbide, would be responsible to 'detail design, erect and commission the plant'. (Defendant's Ex. 4, § 4.1). Union Carbide, accordingly, issued limiting warranties with respect to the design packages, detailing of which it would not be involved with. (Brown Aff at 7, Ex 4, §§ 4.1, 12.3).

The nature of UCIL's detail design work is discussed in the affidavit of Ranjit K. Dutta, who has held various positions at UCIL and UCAPC. From 1973 through 1976, Mr Dutta was employed as General Manager of the Agricultural Products Division of UCIL. (Dutta Aff at 2).

Mr Dutta asserts that the Bhopal facility was built by UCIL over the eight years from 1972 to 1980. (Dutta Aff at 8). He asserts that Union Carbide's role in the project was 'narrow', and limited to providing 'certain process design packages for certain parts of the plant'. (Dutta Aff at 9). He continues, stating:

> Once it did that, it had no further design or engineering role,

and that:

> [T]he process design packages which Union Carbide Corporation provided are nothing more than summary design starting points . . . They set forth only the general parameters . . . A plant cannot be constructed from a process design package. The detail design comprises approximately 80 percent of the sum of the man hours involved in the design of any project and transposes the general process design parameters into an actual design which can be used for purchasing equipment and actual construction.

(Dutta Aff at 9–12). (emphasis omitted).

According to Mr Dutta, during the five years between the date upon which Union Carbide submitted process designs, and the date upon which the plant started-up, there were only four visits to Bhopal by Union Carbide process design engineers. (Dutta Aff at 14). In contrast, he asserts that ten to fifteen UCIL engineers, working primarily out of Bombay, were involved in design detailing. (Dutta Aff at 16). These UCIL engineers oversaw the 55 to 60 Indian engineers employed by the Bombay

← The principle whereby inter-company transactions between Union Carbide and its affiliates, or between affiliates, will reflect the cost to unrelated parties of the same or similar technology under similar circumstances.

(Plaintiffs' Exhibit 3). Thus, Mr Brown argues that Union Carbide related with UCIL much as it would have with an unaffiliated, or even competing company.

engineering firm which performed the detail design work. This firm, Humphreys and Glasgow, submitted designs and drawings to the UCIL engineers for approval. Corrected drawings were returned by UCIL to Humphreys and Glasgow for changes, and sent back to UCIL for final approval. (Dutta Aff at 19–24).[17] Mr Dutta alleges that 'at no time were Union Carbide Corporation engineering personnel from the United States involved in approving the detail design or drawings prepared upon which construction was based. Nor did they receive notices of changes made.' (Dutta Aff at 24).

Mr Dutta expressly states that the MIC storage tank and monitoring instrumentation were fabricated or supplied by two named Indian sub-contractors. The vent gas scrubber is alleged to have been fabricated in the Bhopal plant shop. (Dutta Aff at 25).

Of the 12,000 pages of documents purportedly seized by the CBI regarding design and construction of the Bhopal plant, an asserted 2,000 are design reports of Humphreys and Glasgow, UCIL or other contractors. Defendant claims that blueprints and calculations comprise another 1,700 pages of documents held by the CBI. Five thousand pages of contractors' files, including specifications and contracts are asserted to be in India. In addition, Union Carbide claims that blueprints and diagrams may not reflect final design changes as incorporated into the actual plant, and that the detail design engineers' testimony will be needed to determine the configuration of the actual plant.[18] (Holman Aff 2 at 15–16).

One final point bearing on the information regarding liability is contained in the affidavit of Edward Munoz, at a relevant time the General Manager of UCIL's Agricultural Products Division. He later acted as Managing Director of UCIL. Mr

17. Humphreys and Glasgow were allegedly responsible for the following:

> Among other things, developing final equipment and unit layouts and plot plans, including equipment layout drawings, detailed piping arrangement drawings, layout of electrical equipment; the steel structure, including detail design and working drawings for the buildings and foundation; mechanical equipment design including specification of all proprietary and fabricated equipment; review and certification of vendor's drawings and documents, preparation of orthographic piping drawings for all portions of the plant, preparation of isometric piping drawings, preparation of preliminary and final bills of materials for pipes, valves, gaskets, instrument associated hardware, electrical conduit; electrical engineering work, instrument engineering, including drawings on instrument hook ups, lists of instruments, review of instrument specification and data sheets; definition of material and make calculation to size insulation, preparation of insulation lists, preparation of material take off and inquiry specification packages, procurement assistance including assisting in evaluation of bids and selection of vendors, inspection of certain equipment and materials to ensure proper workmanship and compliance with specifications and codes, and coordinating where Indian law required inspection or certification by governmental inspections; preparation of a project schedule, project reports and costs control reports at least once per month, construction supervision including supervision of mechanical testing of installed equipment, assistance in commissioning.

(Dutta Aff at 19–20).

18. Mr Couvaras, whom plaintiffs assert was a 'key engineer' for the project, and enjoyed mobility between Union Carbide and UCIL, is described by Mr Dutta as primarily a UCIL employee. The 'international employee' status he carried is explained as a pension accounting mechanism. (Dutta Aff at 27).

Munoz has submitted an affidavit in which he states that Union Carbide decided to store MIC in large quantities at the Bhopal plant, despite Mr Munoz' warnings that MIC should be stored only in small amounts because of safety. (Memo in Opp at 15–16; Munoz Aff). Mr Dutta, for defendant, asserts that there was never any issue of token storage of MIC at Bhopal, as Mr Munzo states, and that there is no truth to Mr Munoz' assertion that he was involved in the storage issue. (Dutta Aff at 30).[19] The Court cannot make any determination as to the conflicting affidavits before it. This question, which involves credibility concerns, is left for later in the litigation. To the extent that this particular matter bears upon the relative ease of access to sources of proof, Mr Munoz and Mr Dutta both may be called to testify at trial or discovery. Mr Dutta's home is in Bhopal. (Dutta Aff at 1). The Court is not aware of the whereabouts of Mr Munoz at this time. Either of the two could travel to either alternative forum.

In addition to design and safety records, material regarding training of Bhopal personnel is likely to be relevant to the question of liability. Plaintiffs state that Warren Woomer supervised the training of UCIL personnel at Union Carbide's Institute, West Virginia plant. According to plaintiffs, 40 UCIL employees were transported to Institute's MIC facility for lengthy training. (Memo in Opp at 22). Mr Woomer states in reply that the 40 employees thus trained represented a fraction of the over 1,000 employees who were trained exclusively in Bhopal. (Woomer Aff at 43). In addition, Mr Woomer asserts that the training at Institute was pursuant to an arms-length agreement, that UCIL selected the parties to be trained, and that UCIL paid Union Carbide for the training. (Woomer Aff at 43). Moreover, Mr Woomer's description of the training provided at Bhopal suggests that each of the plant's employees had lengthy cumulative training, of which the Institute training was but a very small portion. (Woomer Aff at 46). Personnel records, in any event, are located in Bhopal. (Holman Aff 2 at 4).

The briefs and affidavits contain considerable discussion on the matter of commissioning and start-up of the Bhopal plant. The Court need not resolve the question of who was responsible for these aspects of plant operation. However, the Court determines that the manual regarding start-up was prepared by Indian nationals employed by UCIL. (Woomer Aff at 48).

In the aggregate, it appears to the Court that most of the documentary evidence concerning design, training, safety and start-up, in other words, matters bearing on liability, is to be found in India. Much of the material may be held by the Indian CBI. Material located in this country, such as process design packages and training records of the 40 UCIL employees trained at Institute, constitutes a smaller portion of the bulk of the pertinent data than that found in India. Moreover, while records in this country are in English, a language understood in the courts of India, certain of the records in India are in Hindi or other Indian languages, as well as in English. (Holman Aff 2 at 12). The Indian language documents would have to be translated to be of use in the United States. The reverse is not true. It is evident to the Court that records concerning the design, manufacture and operation of the Bhopal plant are relatively more accessible in India than in the United States, and that fewer translation

19. Mr Dutta asserts that Mr Munoz was a paid consultant to a member of Plaintiffs' Executive Committee at the time the affidavit was made. No documentary proof of this assertion has been submitted. (Dutta Aff at 31; Holman Aff 2 at 18). Moreover, two affidavits submitted on behalf of defendant state that Mr Munoz was removed from his position as Union Carbide Corporation Division President in 1978, and is 'extremely bitter as a result of the removal'. (Dutta Aff at 31; Holman Aff 2 at 18).

problems would face an Indian court than an American court. Since Union Carbide has been directed to submit to discovery in India pursuant to the liberal grant of the American Federal Rules of Civil Procedure, and this opinion is conditioned upon such submission, any records sought by plaintiffs must be made available to them in India. The private interest factor of relative ease of access to sources of proof bearing on liability favors dismissal of the consolidated case.[20] The Indian Government is asserted to have been involved in safety, licensing and other matters relating to liability. Records relating thereto are located in India, as are the records seized by the CBI. Although plantiffs state that all such records could and would be made available to this Court, it would be easier to review them in India. Transmittal and translation problems would thereby be avoided.

B. Access to Witnesses

Gilbert teaches a second important consideration under the heading of private interests, the 'availability of compulsory process for attendance of willing, and the cost of obtaining attendance of unwilling, witnesses'. Gilbert at 508. As discussed in detail above, most witnesses whose testimony would relate to questions of causation and liability are in India. Engineers from UCIL and Humphreys and Glasgow and other sub-contractors, of whom there are hundreds, are located in India. Shift employees from the possibly malfunctioning units, safety monitoring personnel, those responsible for training, safety auditing, procurement, compliance with regulations and other operations might be required to testify. More than likely, many of these potential witnesses do not speak English, and would require translators. Many of the witnesses are not parties to this litigation. Therefore, as the Court of Appeals for the Second Circuit has stated in the context of a *forum non conveniens* motion:

> In fact, the plaintiffs' cases on liability will depend in large measure upon the knowledge and activities of such witnesses as the employees of [companies] who are not parties to this litigation, but who directly participated in the events which gave rise to it. The United States District Court in New York, however, has no power to subpoena any of these witnesses. It is unlikely that many would be willing to travel to New York to testify; and the cost, in any event, would be prohibitively great.

Fitzgerald *v.* Texaco, (521 F2d 448, 451–52 (2d Cir. 1975), *cert denied*, 423 US 1052

20. Union Carbide asserts throughout its briefs and affidavits that evidence relevant to the question of damages is located in India, as well. Certainly the victims themselves, and, for the most part, their medical records, are found in or near Bhopal. However, as plaintiffs argue, a 'head count' of witnesses is not dispositive of a *forum non conveniens* motion. (Memo in Opp at 74–79). Not all of the victims would need to be transported to the United States to describe their injuries. The Bhopal 'scheme' provides a mechanism for evaluating each individual's claim. Only representative plaintiffs need testify as to damages. This Court would not countenance the impractical and time-consuming process of calling each of the approximately 200,000 victims at a trial in this country. Evidence on damages, as well as liability, is found in India, but not to the overwhelming extent contended by defendant. Moreover, the Court is concerned with the policy effect of allowing the number of foreign victims to affect directly the *forum non conveniens* determination. If carried to the extreme, this 'head count' doctrine would mean that the more people hurt, the less likely a suit in this country would be.

(1976) (footnote omitted). In contrast, the relatively few witnesses who reside in the United States are primarily employed by Union Carbide. As employees of a party they would probably be subject to the subpoena power of Indian courts. Transportation costs would also be lower, since fewer people would have to make the journey to testify.

The presence of the Indian Government in this action is also of critical importance on this motion. Plaintiffs assert that 'all necessary officials and employees of the Central Government will voluntarily comply with requests to attend trial'. (Memo in Opp at 70; Answer to No 124 of Defendant's First Requests for Admission Exhibit 55). This statement does not provide for attendance by officials of Madhya Pradesh or the Bhopal municipality, whom Union Carbide indicates might be impleaded as third-party defendants. As witnesses only, these officials would not be subject to this Court's subpoena power. As third-party defendants, they might be immune from suit in the United States by the terms of the Foreign Sovereign Immunities Act, 28 USC § 1602 *et seq*. State and city officials might also lack sufficient contacts with this district to allow this Court to exercise personal jurisdiction over them.

While Union Carbide might be deprived of testimony of witnesses or even potential third-parties if this action were to proceed in this forum, no such problem would exist if litigation went forward in India.

The unavailability of compulsory process for Indian non-party witnesses, of whom there are many, such as would ensure their presence at a trial in this country, the high cost of transporting the large number of Indian nationals to the United States, as well as the need to translate their testimony should they appear, all support the argument favoring dismissal of this action on *forum non conveniens* grounds. The private interest concerns regarding witnesses emphasize the logic of defendant's position. Relatively fewer witnesses reside in the United States than in India. Almost all of the witnesses located in this country are employees of defendant, and would be subject to compulsory process in India as a result. Transportation costs for the relative few would not compare to the alternate costs of transporting hundreds of Indian witnesses. Since English is widely spoken in India, less translation would be required for foreign witnesses in India than in the converse situation. Should this case be tried in India, fewer obstacles to calling state and local officials as witnesses or parties would face the defendant. The Court determines that this private interest factor weighs in favor of dismissal.

C. Possibility of View

The third private interest factor articulated in Gilbert is the ease of arranging for a view of the premises around which the litigation centers. Plaintiffs assert that the notion that a jury view of the plant and environs is necessary is 'simply preposterous'. (Memo in Opp at 71). Plaintiffs note that a viewing of the premises is rarely conducted in products liability cases, since videotapes, pictures, diagrams, schematics and models are more instructive than an actual view. (Memo in Opp at 71). A viewing of the plant and hutments would probably not be of the utmost importance in determining liability, and this consideration is not afforded great weight on this motion.

However, the instant case is not identical to the product design defect case cited by plaintiffs, in which a district court judge determined that 'the present appearance of the defendants' facilities may or may not be relevant to production which occurred' in the period in which the allegedly violative manufacture occurred. Hodson *v.* A. H. Robins Co, Inc, 528 F Supp 809, 822 (ED Va 1981), *aff'd* 715 F2d 142 (4th Cir 1983). In the instant case, the site of the accident was sealed after the leak, and the present condition of the plant might be relevant to a finding of liability. A viewing may not be necessary, but conceivably could be called for later in the litigation. An Indian court is in a far better position than this Court to direct and supervise such a viewing should one ever be required. This consideration, though minor, also weighs in favor of dismissal.

In summary, then, the private interest factors weigh greatly in favor of dismissal on grounds of *forum non conveniens*. Since the 'balance is strongly in favor of the defendant' the foreigh plaintiffs' choice of a foreign forum is given less than maximum deference, the Court determines that dismissal is favored at this point in the inquiry. Gilbert at 508.

3. Public Interest Concerns

The Gilbert Court articulated certain factors which affected the interests of non-parties to a litigation to be considered in the context of the doctrine of *forum non conveniens*. These public interest concerns were held to be relevant to a court's determination of whether to dismiss on these grounds. The Supreme Court expressly identified a few factors:

> Administrative difficulties follow for courts when litigation is piled up in congested centers instead of being handled at its origin. Jury duty is a burden that ought not to be imposed upon the people of a community which has no relation to the litigation. In cases which touch the affairs of many persons, there is reason for holding the trial in their view and reach rather than in remote parts of the country where they can learn of it by report only. There is a local interest in having localized controversies decided at home. There is an appropriateness, too, in having the trial of a diversity case in a forum that is at home with the state law that must govern the case, rather than having a court in some other forum untangle problems in conflict of laws, and in law foreign to itself.

Gilbert at 508–9. The Court will consider these various factors in turn, as well as others discussed by the parties and *amicus curiae*.

A. Administrative Difficulties

As is evident from the discussion thus far, the mere size of the Bhopal case, with its multitude of witnesses and documents to be transported and translated, obviously creates administrative problems.

There can be no doubt that the Bhopal litigation will take its toll on any court which sits in judgment on it. This Court sits in one of the busiest districts in the country, and finds, as a matter within its experience, that this is a 'congested center' of litigation as described in Gilbert at 508. The burden which would be imposed should litigation continue here was aptly described by the Court of Appeals for the Second Circuit in Schertenlieb *v.* Traum, 589 F2d 1156 (2d Cir 1978). Reviewing a district judge's ruling for dismissal on the grounds of *forum non conveniens*, the Second Circuit observed that 'were it not for the somewhat unusual fact that it is the forum resident who seeks dismissal, we would have to say very little regarding the exercise of Judge Metzner's discretion in dismissing this case'. Schertenlieb at 1164. In affirming the ruling for dismissal, the Court of Appeals asked the rhetorical question:

> If litigation is in a clearly inconvenient forum, why should defendant and the court be burdened with its continuing there, if an alternative forum now exists so that plaintiff will not be without a remedy?

Schertenlieb at 1163.

This Court has already determined that because of the location of the preponderance of the evidence in India, and the difficulty of transporting documents and witnesses to this forum, this district is clearly an inconvenient forum for the litigation. An alternative forum is seen to exist in India. This Court feels that the answer to the Schertenlieb question is clear.

A district judge in this district, in Domingo *v.* States Marine Lines, 340 F Supp 811 (SDNY 1972) evaluated the administrative concerns of the Southern District of New York, relevant to this Court today, a full fourteen years later. The Domingo court stated:

> It is scarcely necessary to dwell on the fact that this Court is the most heavily burdened Federal District Court in the country. The Civil Calendar grows more congested all the time. The priority now properly given to the disposition of criminal cases tends to increase this congestion. I see no reason why this Court, with its heavy burdens and responsibilities, should be burdened with cases like these which, from every point of view, should be tried in the courts of the nation where all the relevant events occurred and whose citizens are primarily involved. Certainly, this district and the Metropolitan area in which it is situated have no conceivable relation to this litigation except for the fact that the defendant happens to be doing business here.

Domingo at 816.

The defendant in this case, involved as it appears to have been in the process design phase of the plant's construction, may have a slightly less tenuous connection to this forum than a corporation which is merely doing business here. Certain business conducted in New York, or in corporate headquarters in Danbury, Connecticut, may have been directly related to development or operation of the UCIL facility in Bhopal. However, almost 'all the relevant events' leading to and following from the accident occurred in India. Indian citizens are primarily involved in the case, both as witnesses and claimants. The substantial administrative weight of the case should be centered on a court with the most significant contacts with the event. Thus, a court in Bhopal, rather than New York, should bear the load.

In addition to the burden on the court system, continuation of this litigation in this forum would tax the time and resources of citizens directly. Trial in this case will no doubt be lengthy. An assigned jury would be compelled to sit for many months of proof. Because of the large number of Indian language-speaking witnesses, the jurors would be required to endure continual translations which would double the length of trial. The burden on the jurors themselves, and on their families, employers and communities would be considerable. The need for translation would be avoided if trial were to be held in Bhopal.

Clearly, the administrative costs of this litigation are astounding and significant. Despite its deep concern for the victims of the tragedy, this Court is persuaded by a recent relevant decision of the New York State Court of Appeals. In the opinion in Islamic Republic of Iran *v.* Pahlavi, 62 NY2d 474 (1984), *cert denied*, 105 SCt 783 (1985), with reference to a decision discussing actions brought in New York by the Iranian Government against the Shah and his wife, the Court of Appeals stated that:

> [T]he taxpayers of this State should not be compelled to assume the heavy financial burden attributable to the cost of administering the litigation contemplated when their interest in the suit and the connection of its subject matter . . . is so ephemeral.

Islamic Republic at 483 (citations omitted). Administrative concerns weigh against retention of this case.

B. The Interests of India and the United States

Plaintiffs, and especially *amicus curiae* emphasize this point of argument in opposition to the motion to dismiss. Concerned with the asserted possibility of developing a 'double-standard' of liability for multinational corporations, plaintiffs urge that American courts should administer justice to the victims of the Bhopal disaster as they would to potential American victims of industrial accidents. The public interest is served, plaintiffs and *amicus* argue, when United States corporations assume responsibility for accidents occurring on foreign soil. 'To abandon that responsibility,' *amicus* asserts, 'would both injure our standing in the world community and betray the spirit of fairness inherent in the American character.' (*Amicus* Brief at 4). The specific American interests allegedly to be served by this Court's retention of the case include the opportunity of creating precedent which will 'bind all American multinationals henceforward', (*Amicus* Brief at 20); promotion of 'international cooperation', (*Amicus* Brief at 22–23); avoidance of an asserted 'double standard' of liability, and the prevention of 'economic blackmail of hazardous industries which would extract concessions on health and environmental standards as the price of continuing operations in the United States'. (*Amicus* Brief at 20). An additional American public interest ostensibly to be served by retention of the litigation in this forum is advanced by plaintiffs themselves. They assert that the deterrent effect of this case can be distinguished from the situation in Piper, where the Court rejected the argument that 'American citizens have an interest in ensuring that American manufacturers are deterred from producing defective products, and that additional deterrence might be obtained if Piper and [its co-defendant] were tried in the United States, where they could be sued on the basis of both negligence and strict liability'. Piper at 260. The Court stated that:

> [T]the incremental deterrence that would be gained if this trial were held in an American court is likely to be insignificant. The American interest in this accident is simply not sufficient to justify the enormous commitment of judicial time and resources that would inevitably be required if the case were to be tried here.

Piper at 260–211. According to plaintiffs, the potential for greater deterrence in this case is 'self-evident'.

The opposing interest of India is argued to be ill-served by sending this litigation to India. Pointing to the fact that the Union of India chose this forum, plaintiffs state that there can be 'no question as to the public interest of India'. (Memo in Opp at 91). Union Carbide's statements regarding the interests of India in this litigation are summarily dismissed by the plaintiffs, who state that 'Union Carbide, whose actions caused the suffering of an entire city, has not standing to assert this belated concern for the welfare of the Indian populace'. (Memo in Opp at 91).

Union Carbide, not surprisingly, argues that the public interest of the United States in this litigation is very slight, and that India's interest is great. In the main, the Court agrees with the defendant.

As noted, Robert C. Brown states in his affidavit on behalf of Union Carbide that the Indian Government preserved the right to approve foreign collaboration and import of equipment to be used in connection with the plant. *See supra* at 32. In addition, Mr Brown quoted experts from the 1972 Letter of Intent entered into by the Union of India and UCIL, one term of which required that 'the purchase of only such design and consultancy services from abroad as are not available within the country' would be allowed. (Brown Aff at 6). Ranjit K. Dutta states that the Indian Government, in a process of 'Indianization', restricted the amount of foreign materials and foreign consultants' time which could be contributed to the project, and mandated the use of Indian materials and experts whenever possible. (Dutta Aff at 35). In an alleged ongoing attempt to minimize foreign exchange losses through imports, the Union of India insisted on approving equipment to be purchased abroad, through the mecahnism of a 'capital goods license'. (Dutta Aff at 48–50).

The Indian Government, through its Ministry of Petroleum and Chemicals, allegedly required information from UCIL regarding all aspects of the Bhopal facility during construction in 1972 and 1973, including 'information on toxicity' of chemicals. (Dutta Aff at 44). The Ministry required progress reports throughout the course of the construction project. These reports were required by the Secretariat for Industrial Approvals, the Director General of Technical Development and the Director of Industries of Madhya Pradesh. (Dutta Aff at 45). Moreover, UCIL was ultimately required to obtain numerous licenses during development, construction and operation of the facility. (Dutta Aff at 46). The list of licenses obtained fills five pages.[21]

The Indian Government regulated the Bhopal plant indirectly under a series of environmental laws, enforced by numerous agencies, much as the Occupational Safety and Health Administration, the Environmental Protection Agency and state and local agencies regulate the chemical industry in the United States. (Dutta Aff at 53–56). Emissions from the facility were monitored by a state water pollution board, for example. (Dutta Aff at 64). In addition, state officials periodically inspected the fully-constructed plant.[22] (Dutta Aff at 56). A detailed inquiry into the plant's operations was conducted by the Indian Government in the aftermath of the December 1981 fatality at the MIC unit and the February 1982 incident involving a

21. Indian federal and municipal officials also allegedly conducted on-site inspections resulting in approvals for portions of the construction, including approvals for the flare tower, MIC layout and storage, unit refrigeration and MIC/Phosgene structure. (Dutta Aff at 46–47; Exs 102–104).
22. One such regular inspection appears to have taken place approximately two weeks before the MIC disaster. (Dutta Aff at 56; Ex 116).

pump seal. (Dutta Aff at 58–62). Numerous federal, state and local commissions obviously, investigated the most tragic incident of all, the MIV leak of December 1984.

The recital above demonstrates the immense interest various Indian governmental agencies in the creation, operation, licensing and regulation, and investigation of the plant. Thus, regardless of the extent of Union Carbide's own involvement in the UCIL plant in Bhopal, or even of its asserted 'control' over the plant, the facility was within the sphere of regulation of Indian laws and agencies, at all levels. The comments of the Court of Appeals for the Sixth Circuit with respect to its decision to dismiss a products liability action on *forum non conveniens* grounds seem particularly apposite. In in re Richardson-Merrell, Inc., 545 F Supp 1130 (SD Ohio 1982), *modified sub nom* Dowling *v.* Richardson-Merrell Inc, 727 F2d 608 (6th Cir 1984), the court reviewed a dismissal involving an action brought by a number of plaintiffs, all of whom were citizens of Great Britain.[23] Defendant in the action was a drug company which had developed and tested a drug in the United States which was manufactured and marketed in England. The suit was brought against the American parent, not the British subsidiary, for injuries allegedly resulting from ingestion of the offending drug in England and Scotland. The district court, in dismissing the case, stated that:

> This action involves the safety of drugs manufactured in the United Kingdom and sold to its citizens pursuant to licenses issued by that government. The interest of the United Kingdom is overwhelmingly apparent. New York, and Ohio [the United States forums] for that matter, have a minimal interest in the safety of products which are manufactured, regulated and sold abroad by foreign entities, even though development or testing occurred in this country.

In re Richardson-Merrell, Inc, 545 F Supp at 1135 (footnote omitted). The Sixth Circuit confirmed this view of the public interests, stating:

> The interest of the United Kingdom in this litigation is great. The drug was manufactured under a British license by British companies and was marketed, and prescribed in the United Kingdom. The alleged injuries took place in England and Scotland and the plaintiffs are citizens and residents of those countires. When a regulated industry, such as pharmaceuticals in this case and passenger aircraft operations in Piper Aircraft, is involved, the country where the injury occurs has a particularly strong interest in product liability litigation . . . Though no single factor should be determinative in ruling on a *forum non conveniens* motion, the nature of the product and its status as regulated or not must be considered.

23. Only a small number of plaintiffs in the Bhopal litigation are United States citizens. of the 200,000 plaintiffs, approximately nine are American. They have filed the complaints numbered 85 Civ 0447, 85 Civ 1096 and 85 Civ 2098. This is of relative insignificance on this motion to dismiss. 'The federal courts have not felt constrained to retain jurisdiction over predominantly foreign cases involving American plaintiffs where an examination of the Gilbert factors demonstrated that the action is more appropriately brought in a foreign forum . . . [T]he presence of a handful of American plaintiffs does not preclude such dismissal.' Nai-Chao *v.* Boeing Co, 555 F Supp 9, 21 (ND Ca 1982), Aff'd sub nom Cheng *v.* Boeing Co, 708 F2d 1406 (9th Cir 1983).

Dowling, 727 F2d at 616.

The Indian government, which regulated the Bhopal facility, has an extensive and deep interest in ensuring that its standards for safety are complied with. As regulators, the Indian government and individual citizens even have an interest in knowing whether extant regulations are adequate. This Court, sitting in a foreign country, has considered the extent of regulation by Indian agencies of the Bhopal plant. It finds that this is not the appropriate tribunal to determine whether the Indian regulations were breached, or whether the laws themselves were sufficient to protect Indian citizens from harm. It would be sadly paternalistic, if not misguided, of this Court to attempt to evaluate the regulations and standards imposed in a foreign country. As another district court stated in the context of a drug product liability action brought by foreign plaintiffs in this country,

> Each government must weigh the merits of permitting the drug's use . . . Each makes its own determination as to the standards of degree of safety and duty of care . . . This balancing of the overall benefits to be derived from a product's use with the risk of harm associated with that use is peculiarly suited to a forum of the country in which the product is to be used . . . The United States should not impose its own view of safety, warning, and duty of care required of drugs sold in the United States upon a foreign country when those same drugs are sold in that country.

Harrison *v.* Wyeth Laboratories, 510 F Supp 1, 4 (ED Pa 1980), *aff'd mem*, 676 F2d 685 (3d Cir 1982). India no doubt evaluated its need for a pesticide plant against the risks inherent in such development. Its conclusions regarding '[q]uestions as to the safety of [products] marketed' or manufactured in India were 'properly the concern of that country'. Harrison at 4 (emphasis omitted). This is particularly true where, as here, the interests of the regulators were possibly drastically different from concerns of American regulators. The Court is well aware of the moral danger of creating the 'double-standard' feared by plaintiffs and *amicus curiae*. However, when an industry is as regulated as the chemical industry is in India, the failure to acknowledge inherent differences in the aims and concerns of Indian, as compared to American citizens would be naive, and unfair to the defendant. The district court in Harrison considered the hypothetical instance in which a products liability action arising out of an Indian accident would be brought in the United States. The court speculated as follows:

> The impropriety of [applying American standards of product safety and care] would be even more clearly seen if the foreign country involved was, for example, India, a country with a vastly different standard of living, wealth, resources, level of health care and services, values, morals and beliefs than our own. Most significantly, our two societies must deal with entirely different and highly complex problems of population growth and control. Faced with different needs, problems and resources in our example India may, in balancing the pros and cons . . . give different weight to various factors than would our society . . . Should we impose our standards upon them in spite of such differences? We think not.

Harrison at 4–5. This Court, too, thinks that it should avoid imposing characteristically American values on Indian concerns.

The Indian interest in creating standards of care, enforcing them or even extending them, and of protecting its citizens from ill-use is significantly stronger than the local interest in deterring multinationals from exporting allegedly dangerous technology. The supposed 'blackmail' effect of dismissal by which plaintiffs are troubled is not a significant interest of the American population, either. Surely, there will be no relaxing of regulatory standards by the responsible legislators of the United States as a response to lower standards abroad.[24] Other concerns than bald fear of potential liability, such as convenience or tax benefits, bear on decisions regarding where to locate a plant. Moreover, the purported public interest of seizing this chance to create new law is no real interest at all. This Court would exceed its authority were it to rule otherwise when restraint was in order.

The Court concludes that the public interest of India in this litigation far outweighs the public interest of the United States. This litigation offers a developing nation the opportunity to vindicate the suffering of its own people within the framework of a legitimate legal system. This interest is of paramount importance.[25]

C. The Applicable Law

Gilbert and Piper explicitly acknowledge that the need of an American court to apply foreign law is an appropriate concern on a *forum non conveniens* motion, and can in fact point toward dismissal. Gilbert at 509; Piper at 260. Especially when, as here, all other factors favor dismissal, the need to apply foreign law is a significant consideration on this type of motion. Piper at 260, n. 29. A federal court is bound to apply the choice of law rules of the state in which an action was originally brought; even upon transfer to a different district, 'the transferee district court must be obligated to apply the state law that would have been applied if there had been no change of venue'. Van Dusen *v.* Barrack, 376 US 612, 639 (1964). Thus, this Court, sitting over a multidistrict litigation, must apply the various choice of law rules of the states in which the actions now consolidated before it were brought.[26] Rather than undertake the task of evaluating the choice of law rules of each state separately, the Court will treat the choice of law doctrine *in toto*. The 'governmental interest' analysis, employed by many jurisdictions, requires a court to look to the question of which state has the most compelling interest in the outcome of the case. India's interest in the outcome of the litigation exceeds America's, *see supra* at 44–58. The *lex loci delicti* analysis used in other jurisdictions indicates that the law of the state where the tort occurred should be applied. The place in which the tort occurred was, to a very great extent, India. Other states apply the 'most significant relationship' test, or 'weight of contacts' test, which evaluate in which state most of the events constituting the tort

24. In any event, plaintiffs' 'deterrence' and 'blackmail' arguments presuppose that Union Carbide would be held more accountable by an American than by an Indian tribunal. Certainly, there is a real possibility of a substantial Indian judgment against defendant, which would serve an identical deterrent function, and prevent a rush of multinationals to foreign locations.

25. While the accident is more than a 'local controversy', given the interests of the Indian populace, it is certainly a national controversy which should be 'decided at home'. Gilbert at 508–9. No doubt Indian citizens, many of whom barely are acquainted with their American lawyers, will find the case more accessible if it is tried 'in their view' in India.

26. Upon a cursory review of the individual complaints comprising this action, the Court notes that suits were brought in California, Connecticut, the District of Columbia, Florida, Illinois, Louisiana, Maryland, New Jersey, New York, Pennsylvania, Tennessee, Texas and West Virginia, at a minimum.

occurred. The contacts with India with respect to all phases of plant construction, operation, malfunction and subsequent injuries are greater in number than those with the United States. Thus, under any one of these three doctrines, it is likely that Indian law will emerge as the operative law. An Indian court, therefore, would be better able to apply the controlling law than would this United States Court, or a jury working with it. This public interest factor also weighs in favor of dismissal on the grounds of *forum non conveniens*.

Conclusion

It is difficult to imagine how a greater tragedy could occur to a peacetime population than the deadly gas leak in Bhopal on the night of 2–3 December 1984. The survivors of the dead victims, the injured and others who suffered, or may in the future suffer due to the disaster, are entitled to compensation. This Court is firmly convinced that the Indian legal system is in a far better position than the American courts to determine the cause of the tragic event and thereby fix liability. Further, the Indian courts have greater access to all the information needed to arrive at the amount of the compensation to be awarded the victims.

The presence in India of the overwhelming majority of the witnesses and evidence, both documentary and real, would by itself suggest that India is the most convenient forum for this consolidated case. The additional presence in India of all but the less than handful of claimants underscores the convenience of holding trial in India. All of the private interest factors described in Piper and Gilbert weigh heavily toward dismissal of this case on the grounds of *forum non conveniens*.

The public interest factors set forth in Piper and Gilbert also favor dismissal. The administrative burden of this immense litigation would unfairly tax this or any American tribunal. The cost to American taxpayers of supporting the litigation in the United States would be excessive. When another, adequate and more convenient forum so clearly exists, there is no reason to press the United States judiciary to the limits of its capacity. No American interest in the outcome of this litigation outweighs the interest of India in applying Indian law and Indian values to the task of resolving this case.

The Bhopal plant was regulated by Indian agencies. The Union of India has a very strong interest in the aftermath of the accident which affected its citizens on its own soil. Perhaps Indian regulations were ignored or contravened. India may wish to determine whether the regulations imposed on the chemical industry within its boundaries were sufficiently stringent. The Indian interests far outweigh the interests of citizens of the United States in the litigation.

Plaintiffs, including the Union of India, have argued that the courts of India are not up to the task of conducting the Bhopal litigation. They assert that the Indian judiciary has yet to reach full maturity due to the restraints placed upon it by British colonial rulers who shaped the Indian legal system to meet their own ends. Plaintiffs allege that the Indian justice system has not yet cast off the burden of colonialism to meet the emerging needs of a democratic people.

The Court thus finds itself faced with a paradox. In the Court's view, to retain the litigation in this forum, as plaintiffs request, would be yet another example of imperialism, another situation in which an established sovereign inflicted its rules, its standards and values on a developing nation. This Court declines to play such a role. The Union of India is a world power in 1986, and its courts have the proven capacity to mete out fair and equal justice. To deprive the Indian judiciary of this opportunity to stand tall before the world and to pass judgment on behalf of its own people would be to revive a history of subservience and subjugation from which India has emerged. India and its people can and must vindicate their claims before the independent and legitimate judiciary created there since the Independence of 1947.

This Court defers to the adequacy and ability of the courts of India. Their interest in the sad events of 2–3 December 1984 at the UCL plant in the City of Bhopal, State of Madhya Pradesh, Union of India, is not subject to question or challenge. The availability of the probative, relevant, material and necessary evidence to Indian courts is obvious and has been demonstrated in this opinion.

Therefore, the consolidated case is dismissed on the grounds of *forum non conveniens* under the following conditions:

1. Union Carbide shall consent to submit to the jurisdiction of the courts of India, and shall continue to waive defenses based upon the statute of limitations;

2. Union Carbide shall agree to satisfy any judgment rendered by an Indian court, and if applicable, upheld by an appellate court in that country, where such judgment and affirmance comports with the minimal requirements of due process;

3. Union Carbide shall be subject to discovery under the model of the United States Federal Rules of Civil Procedure after appropriate demand by plaintiffs.

SO ORDERED.

Dated: New York, New York
12 May 1986

(Signed)
John F. Keenan
USDJ

80. *See* New York Times (13 June 1986) at P. D3:

> 'The Union Carbide statement raised several questions: What are the company's intentions and how does it plan to abide by the judge's decisions? Will the case be in the awkward position of getting under way in the Indian courts while under appeal in the United States? And how will Judge Keenan—who in the past has shown impatience with the pace of the proceedings—respond to Union Carbide's announcement?'

Subsequently Union Carbide filed an appeal on 10 July 1986, limiting its opposition to the court's ruling that only Union Carbide was subject to US discovery. (New York Times 11 July 1986, at p. D3). On 5 September 1986 the Indian Government filed a civil suit in Bhopal against Union Carbide representing 518,000 claimants. (New York Times 6 Sept 1986 at p. 35). The *ad damnum* was $3 billion.

81. *See* the decisions of the US Supreme Court in Gulf Oil Corp *v.* Gilbert, 330 US 501 (1947) and in Piper Aircraft Co *v.* Reyno, 454 US 235 (1981).
82. *Supra* note 79.
83. *Id.* The New York Times (23 December 1985) in an editorial described how India salutes American justice:

> 'India, suing in America for the victims of the Bhopal disaster, has told the

court its citizens cannot get justice in India. That's a breathtaking statement, however necessary to maintain the lawsuit against Union Carbide in the United States. The chemical company has moved to dismiss India's suit and may prevail if courts here are persuaded that India's own courts can do the job.

Civil justice in America has many weaknesses but India's legal brief is a rare tribute to its strengths. Some of the tribute, surely, is tactical. India prefers the District Court in New York in large part because its Federal judges and juries are more generous than India's in their damages awards. Suing in the United States gives the Indian plaintiffs surer access to the parent multinational company—and its assets; a judgment won in India might limit recompense to the assets of the chemical plant subsidiary.

The contrasts in systems, however, also go to the quality of our justice and they are worth noting. India discourages civil suits with high fees, payable in advance, and with rules that forbid lawyers from working for a contingency fee. In America, plaintiffs too poor to buy admittance to court can often hire a lawyer who collects a fee only if victorious.

That encourages litigation and clogs courts, but India's high barriers do not save its courts from huge back-logs; job and property disputes requiring no fees or only small fees have left it with 10 million pending cases, some rivaling the Charles Dickens 'Bleak House' lawsuit in age and complexity.

India produces literate civil servants but not judges that match America's. Its law of wrongful death and other compensation for injury is relatively undeveloped, often leaving the injured without redress. India's pleading in the current case pointedly admits that its system is ill equipped to settle liability and damages for more than 2,000 deaths and thousands of severe injuries.

Equally important to India is the American system of gathering evidence, which permits lawyers to demand key documents from the other party, no matter how damaging. These civil 'discovery' mechanisms are often abused by American lawyers to wear down opponents with excessive demands. But when used properly the process can speed justice by giving both sides an early, realistic assessment of their prospects at trial.

Perhaps this tribute to American procedures can compensate for the damage done to our reputation by the American lawyers who raced to India and scoured the Bhopal disaster area to sign up plaintiffs. However the courts decide the jurisdictional issue, India's pleadings gave them a well-deserved compliment.'

84. First Schedule, Order XXVI, Sections 19–22.
85. First Schedule, Order XLVI.
    85.1 New York Times (20 Jan. 1987) at p. D5.
86. *See* Domingo *v.* States Marine Lines, Inc, 1972 Am Mar. Cas 937.
87. *See* Chapter 4, Section 2, herein.
88. 335 F Supp 684 (D Ga, 1973).
89. *See* Paper Operations Consultants International, Ltd *v.* Hong Kong Amber, 513 F2d 667 (9th Cir, 1975).
90. *See* Anglo-American Grain Co *v.* S/T Mina D'Amico, 169 F Supp. 908 (D Va, 1979).
91. *See generally* 16 Cornell Internat L J 121 (1983).

92. 49 Stat 1207.
93. *See* Chapter 4, Section 1, herein.
94. *See* 46 USC 1303 (8).
95. 642 F2d 721 (4th Cir, 1981).
96. 254 F2d 297 (5th Cir, 1958).
97. *See generally* 6 Suffolk Transnat L J 1 (1982).
98. 127 F Supp 12 (SDNY, 1955).
99. 235 F Supp 909 (SDNY, 1964).
100. 197 F Supp 909 (SDNY, 1961).
101. 80 L Ed 865 (1986).

Chapter 5. International Products Liability in Brief

Section 1. International Products Liability Today

(For a thorough and up-to-date analysis of international products liability today, see the author's treatise, 'International Products Liability', 2 vol, published by Kluwer Law Books, 1987).

In July 1985 the European Community, an advanced, international political order with a well-developed legal system, took a solemn step forward in the liberalization of European products liability law when its Council of Ministers, after more than eight years of talks, adopted the EC Directive on Product Liability.[1] The action was hailed as a victory for consumers as Strict Liability in Tort became the order of the day, although the seven of ten EC member States (which still rely on the traditional negligence system) have until 1988 to pass conforming legislation in compliance with the EC Directive. Unfortunately, even then uniformity of law will not be possible for variations in national law are permitted during a 10-year transitional period; for example, some EC member states do not hold manufacturers liable for 'development risks', that is, the defects in the product which were not discoverable during manufacturing operations in light of then current scientific, medical and technical knowledge. The State of the Art defense for product manufacturers is simply not recognized in every EC member state, and so the lack of uniformity in law persists even today.

The foreign plaintiff suing in the United States, while sanguine about the future of products liability success in European courts, must prefer the many current advantages of suit in US courts. The European Community is decidedly concerned with the individual, and even the European Court of Justice entertains suits by individuals under Article 173 of the EEC Treaty: 'Any natural or legal person may, under the same conditions, institute proceedings against a decision addressed to that person ...',[2] But the European Community itself simply cannot achieve uniformity of law, due to the following factors: member States are unwilling to surrender part or all of their sovereignty; EC requires unanimous vote instead of majority vote; member States may still exercise veto powers; the powers of the European Parliament are severely limited; and nearly every treaty or international agreement contains a reservation in behalf of member States who dictate when and when not they will comply with EC rules, regulations, and products liability laws.

In sharp contrast thereto US courts have made great strides in achieving a certain uniformity of products liability law, despite the prevalence of more than fifty distinct jurisdictions. Of particular note is the recognition of a private cause of action in statutes such as the Consumer Product Safety Act;[3] in Swenson *v.* Emerson[4] the Minnesota Supreme Court held that a private cause of action existed for violation of the statute, which private action could be brought in federal or state courts. Accordingly, the foreign plaintiff suing in the US and faced with a product where the manufacturer has violated any rule of the CPSA such as failing to report prior incidents, can now have an additional cause of action under CPSA which provides for jurisdiction in the federal courts if the federal courts are believed to be the most favorable forum, or in the state courts as an additional claim. Jurisdiction is had in the federal courts[5] provided damages exceed $10,000, and diversity of citizenship is not required. One of the fringe benefits of bringing the action under CPSA is that the court may award plaintiff's attorney reasonable counsel fees and expert witness fees which are ordinarily not available in typical products liability litigation.[6]

Products liability in the US today is still highly mobile in the sense that foreign plaintiffs may find that movement into another state jurisdiction may give more favorable substantive law than first realized.[7] A 1986 example is the decision of the First US Court of Appeals in Laperi *v.* Sears, Roebuck & Co[8] applying the law of the Commonwealth of Massachusetts. Here several actions were brought by the plaintiff as administrator of the estates of his three teenage sons who perished in a fire in their home when a smoke detector sold by one defendant failed to detect smoke since it was disabled by an electrical fire induced by a commonplace short circuit. The basis of the claim was a failure to warn consumers that the smoke detector would become inoperative if fire interrupted electrical power. The diversity action against the manufacturer and the distributor of the allegedly defective product resulted in a jury verdict of $350,000 in each of the three actions and $750,000 for injuries to the wife, for a total of $1.8 million. The court in affirming the jury verdict, pointed out: 'The defendants failed to warn purchasers that a short circuit which causes an electrical fire may also render the smoke detector useless in the very situation in which it is expected to provide protection: in the early stages of a fire . . . We reject defendants' argument that the risk that an electrical fire could incapacitate an AC-powered smoke detector is so obvious that the average consumer would not benefit from a warning.' It should be noted that the plaintiff father was an electrical handyman who is supposed not to have known of the danger of a fire-related short circuit disabling the smoke alarm. (The appellate court rejected the $750,000 award to the wife as excessive.)

Another apt example of the unpredictability of substantive and procedural law in both federal and state courts is American Special Risk Insurance Co *v.* Delta America Re Insurance Co,[9] decided by the federal district court for the Southern District of New York in 1986. A motion to dismiss on *forum non conveniens* grounds was refused, as the court rejected arguments that the need for accessibility to English witnesses and English documents mandated dismissal. Such arguments, according to the court, were undercut by 'the ease of modern jet travel and telecommunications'. Furthermore, the fact that English law would likely govern interpretation of the contracts involved in the litigation is not persuasive because English law is 'easily comprehended by counsel and the court'.

Does a state court have jurisdiction to hear a case brought against a foreign company whose products were used as components by another foreign manufacturer and sold in the state? The California Supreme Court in Asahi Metal Industry Co, Ltd *v.* Superior Court[10] answered 'yes'. In essence, the plaintiff was also a foreign manufacturer and the defendant was a foreign supplier of component parts, as the story of the litigation unfolded, to wit: Cheng Shin was sued several years ago by a California resident after one person was killed and another was injured in a motorcycle accident in California. The case was settled for a large sum of money, after plaintiff asserted that there was a defect in the motorcycle tube. Thereupon, the defendant Cheng Shin of Taiwan countersued for indemnification from the Japanese manufacturer of the tube's metal air valve assembly, Asahi Metal. Asahi Metal, as the foreign plaintiff, challenged the jurisdiction of the California court on the ground that Asahi Metal never marketed any product in California or in the United States. Furthermore, Asahi Metal asserted that it had no knowledge that its component part would be used in products marketed in the United States. But the California Superior Court disagreed, and pointed out that Asahi Metal 'is aware that a substantial number of its products will be sold in the forum state'. The California appellate court in 1984 agreed, however, with Asahi Metal, but the California Supreme Court reversed: 'The forum state does not exceed its powers under the Due Process Clause if it asserts personal jurisdiction over a corporation that delivers its products into the stream of commerce with the expectation that they will be purchased by consumers in the forum state', quoting from World-Wide Volkswagen Corp *v.* Woodson,[11] decided by the US Supreme Court in 1980. The California Supreme Court emphasized that 'the stream of commerce theory approved in World-Wide Volkswagen has also been applied to component part manufacturers':

> 'Although Asahi did not design or control the system of distribution that carried its valve assemblies into California, Asahi was aware of the distribution system's operation, and it knew that it would benefit economically from the sale in California of products incorporating its components. . . . Thus, Asahi's contacts with the state are sufficient to permit California, consistent with the requirements of due process, to exercise jurisdiction over Asahi in an action arising from those contacts.'

The highest California court concluded:

> 'Asahi introduced its products into the stream of commerce with the expectation that they would be sold in California. This conduct satisfies the constitutional requirement of minimum contacts with the forum state. Moreover, jurisdiction in California is fair and reasonable given

> California's interest in protecting its consumers, and the interests of California and Cheng Shin in avoiding inconsistent results and a multiplicity of litigation. Accordingly, the trial court's order denying Asahi's motion to quash service of summons was proper. The petition for writ of mandate is denied and the alternative writ is discharged.'

Certiorari was granted to the US Supreme Court, and hearings began in October 1986. The highest court reversed, holding that State courts could not entertain jurisdiction over cases involving people and companies from different foreign countries. Apparently, the court was cognizant of the argument that a ruling in favor of State courts might increase the costs and the uncertainties of international law, for another State court might render a decision to the contrary. In short, State court jurisdiction would be an 'unreasonable' assertion of jurisdiction.[12.1] Jurisdiction, according to the court, cannot be asserted under the Due Process clause simply because 'the defendant was aware of its product's entry into the forum State through the stream of commerce; jurisdiction requires 'an action of the defendant purposefully directed toward the forum State'. The court also observed that 'the unique burdens placed upon one who must defend oneself in a foreign legal system should have significant weight in assessing the reasonableness of stretching the long arm of personal jurisdiction over national borders'.[12.2]

Section 2. International Aviation and the Foreign Plaintiff

The foreign plaintiff is frequently a victim of international aircraft crashes, and therefore is a prime candidate for suit against the tortfeasor or tortfeasors in the US courts. Suits against the federal government are frequent, especially where there is evidence of fault on the part of a federal agency;[13] but the US Supreme Court, as exemplified in United States *v.* Varig Airlines,[14] has protected the federal government from liability by applying under the FTCA the 'discretionary function exception': 'The basic inquiry concerning the application of the discretionary function exception is whether the challenged acts of a Government employee—whatever his or her rank—are of the nature and quality that Congress intended to shield from tort liability. Second, whatever else the discretionary function exception may include, it plainly was intended to encompass the discretionary acts of the Government acting in its role as a regulator of the conduct of private individuals . . .'[15]

Carriage by air, if international, is governed by international conventions, agreements and protocols; international carriage by air is applicable where the places of departure and destination are situated in different countries, or where the air carriage starts and ends at the same place or in the same country but a stopover is made in a foreign country. The stopover must be 'commercial', i.e., at a place where the air carrier is permitted to embark or disembark passengers or cargo. A carriage by air between places situated within the same country but separated by high seas or by the territory of another state or country, may be deemed 'international carriage by air'.[16] The basic international convention governing international carriage by air is the Warsaw Convention (1929) or the 'Convention for the Unification of Certain Rules Relating to International Carriage by Air'.[17] This Magna Carta of international aviation liability has been so universally accepted that of the six or more amending protocols or conventions, only The Hague Protocol of 1955 is still in force[18] with the original Warsaw Convention. (The 1955 protocol reformulated the conditions of unlimited liability and increased the designated limits of liability.) The Warsaw Convention[19] avoids the difficult problem of choice of law by providing for uniform solutions, no matter where any of the elements of jurisdiction may point, such as the place of registration of the aircraft, the place of the accident, the nationality of the passengers or of the shipper of the cargo, the residence of the claimants, etc etc. The purpose of the Warsaw Convention was to spread the risk of loss by pre-determining the level of compensation to be paid to victims. The special compensatory scheme precludes the parties from agreeing upon the exclusion of a carrier's liability in case of a passenger's contributory negligence, for example; nor can the parties agree on limits of liability lower than those established by the Convention. And the grossly inadequate damages limitation of $8,300 and the restrictive venue requirements of the Warsaw Convention have produced increasing litigation over the past fifty-seven years.[20] But suits by foreign plaintiffs in US courts have been encouraged, as illustrated by Benjamins *v.* British European Airways[21] where the Second US Court of Appeals held that a Dutch citizen suing a British airline for injuries sustained in a plane crash in England was entitled to bring suit in the federal district court, even though both parties were aliens because the suit 'arose under the Warsaw Convention . . . (and the federal court) must recognize an internationally binding body of uniform air law'.[22]

The US Supreme Court in its 1984 decision in Franklin Mint Corp *v.* TWA, Inc[23] ruled that the monetary limitations on air carrier liability set forth in Article 22 of the Warsaw Convention[24] are as valid today as when the treaty was drafted in 1929. The use of the last official price of gold as a conversion factor was consistent with the Convention's original purpose of perpetuating a very low and static ceiling on recovery for passenger death and cargo loss.[25] Here plaintiff sued the airline for the loss of four packages of coins weighting 714 pounds, delivered to TWA for transportation from Philadelphia to London. The parties stipulated that TWA was at fault for the loss,[26] but disagreed on the amount of TWA's liability.

The Warsaw Convention is in one sense a no-fault statute for victims of an airplane accident involving international carriage by air, where the cause of the accident is unknown, and they are entitled to compensation without proof of the cause of the accident. Today it is scientifically possible to pinpoint the cause of an accident, so the rationale of the 1929 Warsaw Convention does not hold good. But to surmount the low liability limitations of the Warsaw Convention the victims of air crashes sue the aircraft manufacturer, the maintenance service company, the air traffic controller, the weather station, and countless other defendants exclusive of the air carrier; to remove the case from the chains of the Warsaw Convention the victims of air crashes must prove willful misconduct on the part of the air carrier.[27]

It would appear that in international aviation cases the doctrine of *forum non conveniens*[28] is not applicable, even if the defendant is an American airline. In Macedo *v.* The Boeing Co[29] the plaintiffs were Portuguese citizens suing on behalf of Portuguese citizens killed in a crash of the aircraft on the island of Madeira, Portugal. The American defendants moved to dismiss on *forum non conveniens* grounds, arguing that Portugal was a more convenient forum, but the Seventh US Court of Appeals reversed because the federal district court failed to consider the unavailability of contingency fees in Portugal, the taxation of losing parties in Portugal, and the restrictive discovery procedures in Portugal.[30]

The thrust of the Warsaw Convention was also to achieve some degree of uniformity of law. As the Fifth US Court of Appeals in Block *v.* Air France[31] stated: 'The court has an obligation to keep interpretation as uniform as possible. To fulfill that obligation and follow the consensus as to construction, the court should resort to legislative history and relevant extrinsic aids.'[32] Even the English Court of Appeals in Corocraft *v.* Pan American[33] overruled a lower English court for refusing to follow certain US decisions construing the Warsaw Convention. But international uniformity may not be achievable nor practicable.[34] Indeed, the Warsaw Convention has been blamed for greatly deterring international commercial accident litigation.[35] By creating limits of liability, originally to protect the fledgling industry, the Convention has been effective in producing settlements.

Wrongful death actions arising under the Warsaw Convention may be brought in State courts solely under State law, according to Rhymes *v.* Arrow Air, Inc.[35.1] The plane crash in Newfoundland brought death to 248 soldiers, and suit was begun in a Florida court. Efforts of the carrier to remove the case to the federal district court went for null, as the court ruled in 1986 that the wording of the Warsaw Convention, 'any action for damages, however founded, can only be brought subject to the conditions and limits set out in this Convention', meant that State courts could entertain jurisdiction. The Convention pre-empts State law only to the extent that damages exceed the Convention limits.

Section 3. The Renvoi Problem

In the international products liability situation the spectre of Renvoi can rear its ugly head despite its age and lack of frequent application. Renvoi is a choice of law rule that depends upon what the forum court and the foreign tribunal, if any, regards as the appropriate choice of law to be applied in the given situation before the forum court. Renvoi may refer to either a state's 'internal law', i.e., the law to be applied in purely domestic situtions, or a state's 'whole law', i.e., the law that state would apply to the multistate situation by reference to its own choice of law rules. If the forum state refuses to consider the choice of law rules of the state to which it refers, the forum state is said to reject the renvoi; if the forum state finds in the foreign choice of law rule a reference back to the law of the forum and applies its own 'internal law', then it is said that the forum state accepts the renvoi.[36]

In Re Schneider's Estate[37] the deceased, a naturalized American citizen of Swiss birth, died domiciled in New York, leaving as an asset of his estate certain real property located in Switzerland. In his will he attempted to dispose of his Swiss property in a manner which was contrary to Swiss law, i.e., he sought to deprive certain heirs of a guaranteed fraction of the property. Since the administratrix has already sold the Swiss property the New York surrogate was called upon to approve or disapprove of the transaction. At the outset the surrogate was confronted by what is the meaning of the law of the situs of the Swiss property, that is, whether Swiss internal law or Swiss whole law should be applied. The surrogate favored Swiss whole law, but admitted that 'if the forum must look to the whole law of the situs, and that law refers the matter to the law of the domicile, this latter reference must be considered to be the whole law of the latter country also, which would refer the matter back to the law of the situs, which process would continue without end.' Nevertheless, the surrogate decided that 'a reference to the law of the situs necessarily entails a reference to the whole law of that country, including its conflict of laws rules'. After extensive research and opinion the surrogate concluded that 'the Swiss law would refer a matter such as this to the New York internal law, under which law the will is a valid disposition of the testator's property. The testamentary power of this decedent would not be curtailed . . .'

This much ado about nothing principle has been severely criticized by legal scholars as presenting difficulty of ever discovering the substantive law to be applied.[38] Obviously renvoi cannot achieve uniformity if it is applied in the same way to both the forum state and by the foreign state.[39] Also there are such practical obstacles as requiring the forum state to inform itself not only of the foreign state's conflict of laws rules but also of the foreign rules on renvoi. Indeed the New York surrogate was subsequently criticized by Professor Falconbridge:[40] 'Both under the treaty and apart from the treaty the New York court was wrong in applying domestic New York law. Under the treaty the court should have given effect to the reference to the domestic law of the situs. Having wrongly disposed of the treaty as being a statement of existing conflict rules, the court was then confronted with the problem of renvoi . . . The New York court misconstrued the relevant conflict rule of Swiss law (finding a reference by that rule to the law of the domicile, when there was no such reference in the circumstances of the case) and failed completely to consider whether in any event Swiss law would have accepted a reference back to Swiss law, and in the result applied domestic New York law although a Swiss court would have applied domestic Swiss law.'[41]

In 1962 the US Supreme Court in Richards *v.* US[42] noted that the Federal Tort Claims Act which subjects the federal government to tort liability 'under circumstances where the United States, if a private person, would be liable to the claimant in accordance with the law of the place where the act or omission occurred'. The court declared that this referred to the 'whole law' of the place where the defendant acted; to apply the 'internal law' of that place would often result in treating the Government unlike a private person similarly situated, because the usual choice of law rule looks to the place of injury and because state courts increasingly depart from the traditional rules.

Section 4. Settlement: Model Agreement for Product Liability Claim Resolution

The foreign plaintiff suing in the US might, in order to avoid the unfavorable complexities surrounding *forum non conveniens* dismissal, consider the possibility of settling or resolving the claim through a non-binding process, described in the CPR Model Agreement for Product Liability Claim Resolution, developed by the Center for Public Resources, 680 Fifth Avenue, New York, NY10019. This process is prompt, reasonable and likely to result in settlement of the claim, provided that the defendant is also amenable to the process. A qualified 'neutral' selected by the parties actually makes the reasoned determination as to the settlement value of the case, based upon

a. disclosure by both parties of essential information, and
b. presentation by each party of its case in a highly abbreviated form. While the decision of the 'neutral' is non-binding on the parties, the determination by the 'neutral' provides a realistic basis for settlement negotiations.

Normally discovery is limited to that information for which the party has a substantial need, so that the issues may be promptly defined.

The proceedings are essentially non-institutional in the sense that the parties by agreement have selected the 'neutral' and conduct the hearing apart from the Center for Public Resources or any other institution or court. The 'neutral', after selection by the parties, designates the time and place for the hearing, generally within seventy days of his appointment.

The CPR Model Agreement for Product Liability Claim Resolution, published by the Center for Public Resources, in February 1986, reads as follows:

'CPR Model Agreement for Product Liability Claim Resolution

This model agreement is intended for use by parties to a personal injury product liability controversy who wish to resolve their controversy promptly on the basis of a non-binding, reasoned, oral determination by an experienced neutral of the settlement value of their case. The neutral is chosen by mutual agreement, if need be with the assistance of a 'selector'. The parties exchange essential information and present their case before the neutral in highly abbreviated form. The parties are free to modify the model agreement. With minor changes the model also may be used for non product liability tort claims.

Agreement made , 19 between
of
represented by
('Plaintiff'); and
of

represented by
('Defendant').
Whereas, Plaintiff has made a claim against Defendant as the result of an incident alleged to have occurred on , 19
in
which is alleged to have involved a product of the Defendant known as

(the 'incident'); and
Whereas, the parties wish to attempt to resolve their controversy through a non-binding process, as described in this agreement.
Now, Therefore, the parties agree as follows:
1. NEUTRAL
1.1. *Number*. The proceeding shall be conducted before one neutral.
1.2. *Selection*. The neutral shall be

who has agreed to serve and whose compensation has been agreed to between the parties and the neutral.

Alternate:

1.2. *Selection*. The parties will attempt to agree on the selection of the neutral. If within 10 days from the date of this agreement the parties shall not have agreed on a neutral and determined his or her willingness to serve, either or both parties may request (the 'selector')* to nominate candidates having the qualifications set forth in paragraph 1.3. Within 10 days the selector shall submit to the parties the names of not fewer than three nominees, together with a brief statement of each nominee's qualifications and the per diem or hourly rates charged by such nominee. Each party shall strike from the list the names of any persons who are unacceptable to it and shall number the remaining names to indicate an order of preference. Each party shall mail the list to the selector within seven days of having received it. The selector will designate the neutral from the panel members acceptable to all parties, in accordance with the designated order of mutual preference. If a party does not return the list of nominees within seven days, the selector will assume that all of the nominees are acceptable to that party. If no nominee is acceptable to both parties, the selector will schedule and hold a meeting with the parties to agree on a neutral. If a neutral is not designated within seven days of said meeting, the proceeding shall be deemed terminated.

1.3. *Qualifications of Neutral*. Unless the parties otherwise agree, the selector named in paragraph 1.2 shall nominate candidates who shall have served as a judge in a court of general jurisdiction, or who are attorneys who have practiced law for at least ten years and who have extensive experience in litigation. Unless the parties otherwise agree, if Plaintiff's claim is in litigation, the neutral shall reside or have an office in the state in which such litigation is pending; and if no such litigation is pending, in the state in which Plaintiff resides or the state in which the incident occurred.

1.4. *Conflict of Interest.* Each party shall promptly disclose to the other party any circumstances known to it which would cause reasonable doubt regarding the impartiality of an individual under consideration or appointed as a neutral. Any such individual shall promptly disclose any such circumstances to the parties. If any such circumstances have been disclosed, before or after the individual's appointment, the individual shall not serve, unless the parties agree in writing.

1.5. *Communication with Neutral.* Unless the parties otherwise agree, neither party, nor anyone acting on its behalf, shall unilaterally communicate with the neutral, except as specifically provided for herein.

1.6. *Compensation.* The neutral's per diem or hourly charges will be established at the time of appointment.

1.7. *Hold Harmless.* The neutral shall not be liable for any act or omission in connection with his or her role as neutral in this proceeding.

2. Disclosure of Information

2.1. *Plaintiff's Statement.* Plaintiff's attorney will deliver to Defendant's attorney and to the neutral, within twenty days of the date of this agreement, but not before the selection of a neutral, unless otherwise agreed:

- a description of the time, place and incident out of which the claim arises, including a particularized description of the product allegedly involved;
- the amount of the demand, with itemization of special damages and economic losses;
- a particularized statement of the nature of the defect, and any test results and written expert's report on which Plaintiff intends to rely at the hearing;
- copies of all medical and hospital records arising out of the incident, and all other documents on which Plaintiff intends to rely at the hearing.

Plaintiff's attorney also shall make available to Defendant's attorney at that time for non-destructive study and testing the Defendant's product alleged to be involved in the incident. If Defendant's attorney so requests, Plaintiff's attorney shall make the Plaintiff available for examination at a mutually agreed time and place by a physician selected by Defendant's attorney.

2.2. *Defendant's Statement.* Within twenty days (unless otherwise agreed) after receiving Plaintiff's Statement Defendant's attorney will deliver to Plaintiffs attorney and to the neutral a statement of Defendant's position with respect to the claim, including a particularization of Defendant's defenses and the bases therefor, as well as relevant documents and test results on which Defendant intends to rely at the hearing. Defendant's attorney shall furnish to Plaintiff's attorney as soon as they become available copies of any written expert records on which Defendant intends to rely at the hearing.

2.3. *Discovery.* No discovery shall take place in this proceeding, except as the parties otherwise agree. Any discovery in this proceeding shall be expeditious and aimed at determining essential facts, without prejudice to the parties' right to conduct further discovery if this proceeding should fail to result in a resolution of the case. If litigation between the parties with respect to Plaintiff's claim is pending, any discovery previously taken in such litigation may be used in this proceeding. Discovery taken in this proceeding may be used in litigation between the parties with respect to the incident.

3. Statements and Exhibits

3.1. Not less than 10 days before the hearing, each party shall deliver to the other, and to the neutral, a concise statement, not exceeding ten $8\frac{1}{2}'' \times 11''$ double spaced pages, setting forth its factual and legal position on the issues of the case, as well as all documents and other exhibits on which the party intends to rely at the hearing.

4. The Hearing

4.1. *Purpose.* The hearing (the 'hearing') is intended to present each party's best case to the other party and the neutral in highly abbreviated form. The hearing is not a trial.

4.2. *Place and Time.* Unless the parties otherwise agree, the neutral shall designate by not less than 30 days' written notice to the parties' attorneys the place and time of the hearing; provided that the hearing shall commence not less than 30 days, and not more than 60 days, from the date on which Defendant's Statement is submitted, in accordance with paragraph 2.2. The neutral may postpone the hearing date for reasons he or she finds compelling.

4.3. *Neutral to Preside.* The neutral shall preside at the hearing and shall make rulings on procedure at the hearing to the extent not set forth in this agreement.

4.4. *Presentations.* Plaintiff shall have 60 minutes to present its case-in-chief. Following such presentation, Defendant shall have 90 minutes to present its case-in-chief and to rebut Plaintiff. Thereupon, Plaintiff shall have an additional 30 minutes for rebuttal. Each attorney may use the time allotted in any manner he or she sees fit. Question and answer testimony by witnesses will not be taken. The presentation by counsel, however, can be combined, at counsel's discretion, with oral statements by expert and fact witnesses, as well as any form of documentary or visual evidence. Cross-examination is not permitted. The neutral may ask questions for clarification at any time.

4.5. *Rules of Evidence.* No rules of evidence, including rules of relevance, will apply, except that the rules pertaining to privileged communications and attorney work product will apply.

4.6. *Attendance of Parties.* Plaintiff and an employee or other representative of Defendant authorized to settle the case (other than outside counsel in the case) shall attend the hearing, unless the parties otherwise agree.

4.7. *Record.* The hearing shall not be recorded by any means.

5. Determination

5.1. *Nature and Announcement of Determination.* The neutral shall make a determination as to the settlement value of the case, in accordance with the law which he or she believes governs. The neutral shall orally communicate such determination, and the reasons underlying the same, to the parties in person, preferably on the day of the hearing, and at the latest on the day following the hearing. Such determination shall not be binding on either party.

5.2. *Settlement Negotiations.* If the neutral's determination should not be acceptable to either or both parties, they will engage in settlement negotiations immediately following the announcement of the neutral's determination. The neutral shall be available to mediate such negotiations.

6. Court Proceedings

6.1. *Commencement of Litigation and Extention of Limitations Period.* Neither party may commence litigation with respect to the subject matter of the proceeding until the proceeding shall have terminated in accordance with Section 9 hereof. Execution of this agreement shall extend all applicable statutes of limitation by a period equal to the duration of the proceeding, from the date of this agreement until the proceeding is terminated in accordance with Section 9. The parties will take such other action, if any, required to effectuate such extension or waiver of the governing statutory periods.

Alternate (if litigation is pending):

6.1. *Stay of Litigation.* The parties will promptly present a joint motion to the Court in which litigation between the parties is pending to request a stay of all proceedings pending conclusion of this proceeding; provided, however, that the grant of such stay shall not be a condition to the continuation of this proceeding.

7. Confidentiality

7.1. *Compromise Negotiation.* The entire process is a compromise negotiation. The parties will maintain in confidence all offers, promises, conduct and statements, whether oral or written, made in the course of the proceeding by any of the parties, their agents, employees, experts and attorneys, and by the neutral for the purpose of these compromise negotiations. Such offers, promises, conduct and statements shall be treated as if subject to Rule 408 of the Federal Rules of Evidence and are inadmissible and not discoverable for any purpose, including impeachment, in litigation between the parties. Evidence which is otherwise admissible or discoverable shall not be rendered inadmissible or non-discoverable as a result of its presentation or use in this proceeding. Depositions taken in this proceeding may be used in litigation between the parties.

7.2. *Neutral as Witness.* The neutral will be disqualified as a trial witness, consultant, or expert for any party, and his or her oral and written determination and opinions will be inadmissible for all purposes in this or any other dispute involving either or both of the parties hereto or in any subsequent proceeding of any kind.

8. Costs

8.1. *Division of Costs.* The fees and expenses of the neutral and the selector, and all other expenses of the proceeding, will be borne equally by the parties, unless the parties otherwise agree. Each party shall bear its own costs of the proceeding.

9. Termination

9.1. Neither party may terminate the proceeding unilaterally; provided that if the proceeding shall not have been terminated in accordance with the subsequent sentence within 180 days of the date of this agreement, either party may terminate the proceeding at any time thereafter by written notice to the other party and the neutral. The proceeding shall be deemed terminated when (a) a neutral is not selected by the end of the seven day period referred to in the last sentence of Alternate paragraph 1.2 hereof; or (b) the neutral's determination is made; or (c) the parties enter into a settlement agreement; or (d) the parties agree in writing to discontinue the proceeding; whichever event first occurs.

10. Code of Professional Responsibility

10.1. Counsel for the parties expressly acknowledge their obligation under the applicable code of professional responsibility and agree to pursue this process in accordance therewith. Without limiting the foregoing, counsel agree that all written and oral statements made by them will be based upon a good faith belief in their truth and accuracy.
In Witness Whereof, the parties by their attorneys have executed this Agreement as of the date first above written.

Plaintiff
by
Plaintiff's Attorney
Defendant
by
Defendant's Attorney'

Notes

1. *See* The Wall Street Journal (26 July 1985) at p. 25.
2. *See* generally 17 Cornell Internat L J 61 (1984).
3. 15 USC 2051 *et seq.*
4. 374 NW2d 690 (Minn, 1985).
5. 15 USC 2072 (a).
6. 15 USC 2060 (f).
7. *See* Chapter 4, Section 1, herein.
8. 787 F2d 726 (1st Cir, 1986).
9. —F Supp—(SDNY, 1986).
10. 39 Cal 3rd 35, 702 P 2d 543 (1985).
11. 444 US 786 (1980).
12. The dissent of Justice Lucas is tersely stated:

> 'I respectfully dissent. The Supreme Court of the United States has authoritatively stated that a foreign corporation's knowledge or foreseeability that its product will be used in another state is not sufficient to subject it to *in personam* jurisdiction. The corporation must purposefully avail itself of the privilege of conducting activities in the forum state. . . . The net result of the majority's decision is that a Taiwanese corporation can litigate in California against a Japanese corporation that has absolutely no connection with California in a case in which the California plaintiffs have declared themselves made whole. Surely our overburdened courts should be concerned with disputes that more directly involve California.'

12.1.—US—(1987); *see* New York Times (16 March 1987) at p. D2.

12.2 ABAJ (1 April 1987) at pp. 45 *et seq.*

13. *See* Clemente *v.* US, 567 F2d 1140 (1st Cir, 1977), reversing 426 F Supp 1 (D PR, 1976), cert den 435 US 1006 (1977) where the great baseball star, Roberto Clemente, was killed when a plane he had chartered to fly relief supplies to earthquake victims in Nicaragua crashed shortly after take-off from Puerto Rico. The plaintiffs sued the Federal Aviation Administration, or FAA, claiming that FAA employees had negligently failed to warn the passengers that the aircraft was overweight and lacked a proper flight crew. The federal district court found 'a duty on the part of the FAA to inspect aircraft and to warn plaintiffs' decedents of any irregularities'. But the First US Court of Appeals reversed and thereby insulated the federal government from liability for its acknowledged failure to comply with one of its own directives! According to the Court, the FAA Act did not create any duty 'to provide a particular class of passengers particular protective measures'. The Court recognized that while the FAA director had the legal power to issue the order and require employees to perform the duties, his action was 'entirely gratuitous'. The employees' duty was only to his superior and 'is totally distinguishable from a duty owed by the government to the public on which liability could be based'. The fact that the employee could be subject to disciplinary measures for his failure to follow directions was not 'the kind of a breach cognizable by tort law'. In short, the FAA directive which was designed to protect the public was emasculated by the Court, as members of the public were denied the very protection that the FAA directive intended.
14. —US—(1984).

15. According to the court,

> 'The Government, on the other hand, urges that the basic responsibility for satisfying FAA air safety standards rests with the manufacturer, not with the FAA. The role of the FAA, the Government says, is merely to police the conduct of private individuals by monitoring their compliance with FAA regulations. According to the Government, the FAA accomplishes its monitoring function by means of a 'spot-check' program designed to encourage manufacturers and operators to comply fully with minimum safety requirements. Such regulatory activity, the Government argues, is the sort of governmental conduct protected by the discretionary function exception of the Act. We agree that the discretionary function exception precludes a tort action based upon the conduct of the FAA in certificating these aircraft for use in commercial aviation.'

16. *See generally* Mankiewicz, The Liability Regime of the International Air Carrier (1981).
17. 49 Stat 3000.
18. Amending Article 32 of the Warsaw Convention, 49 Stat 3000, TIAS No 876.
19. *Id.*
20. *See generally* The Forum (1978) at pp. 542 to 558.
21. 572 F2d 913 (2nd Cir, 1977).
22. *See In Re* Air Crash in Bali, Indonesia, 684 F2d 1301 (9th Cir, 1982), where the plaintiffs had claimed that the airline was guilty of 'willful misconduct' and that consequently it did not have the benefit of the Warsaw Convention's limitation of liability. But the jury found no willful misconduct, and the trial court, following the verdict, ruled that under California law a decedent could not by contract compromise his survivor's right to wrongful death recovery. The Court therefore ruled that the contractual limitations imposed by the Warsaw Convention and subsequent agreements were ineffective, and the airline appealed. The United States Court of Appeals for the Ninth Circuit first drew attention to the anachronistic limitation imposed by the Warsaw Convention and all but demanded that it be abandoned. The Court stated: 'Whatever its benefits in 1934, the district court noted that the low limitation on liability cannot be justified today by the conditions that existed in 1934'. The Court observed that the airline industry is no longer in its infancy: '(t)he pioneering conditions and the lack of technical advancement and passenger safeguards which faced the industry when Warsaw was adopted have been supplanted by a technologically and commercially mature industry'. The court then expressed its regret at being unable to reject the treaty simply because it no longer served the purpose for which it was designed. The Court said:

> 'Unfortunately, we know of no doctrine that would allow us to examine congressional enactments to see if they still serve the purpose for which they were designed. If the Warsaw Convention was intended to preempt state law in the area of liability for wrongful death on international flights, we may not avoid preemption by substituting our judgment for that of Congress to hold that the Convention has outlived its usefulness. Furthermore, Congress has had ample opportunity to reconsider the wisdom of the Convention, but it has yet to effect any changes.'

The Court found that the application of California law was in conflict with the Warsaw Convention and was preempted by it. It therefore reversed the District Court's decision that wrongful death beneficiaries, in California, were not limited by the Convention.

23. 104 S Ct 1776 (1984).
24. The Article reads in relevant part:

> 'In the transportation of checked baggage and of goods, the liability of the carrier shall be limited to a sum of 250 francs per kilogram . . . The sums mentioned above shall be deemed to refer to the French franc consisting of $65\frac{1}{2}$ milligrams of gold at the standard fineness of nine hundred thousandths.'

It was a simple matter to calculate the value of the French gold franc specified in Article 22 while there was an official price of gold in the United States. However, when the United States Congress repealed the US gold standard on 1 April 1978, Article 22 calculations of liability raised difficult issues of treaty interpretation.

25. *See generally* 17 Internat Law & Pol 323 (1985).
26. *See* Martin *v.* Pan American World Airways, Inc, 563 F Supp 135 (DC, 1985) upholding liability under the Warsaw Convention, despite plaintiff's effort to negate the application of the Warsaw Convention because defendant's baggage handler had failed to attach a baggage tag to the luggage and record the weight of the baggage on the baggage claim ticket. See also ALR Fed 513.
27. *See* Pekelis *v.* TWA, Inc, 187 F2d 122 (2nd Cir, 1981), cert den 341 US 951 (1932). *See* Trial Magazine (May 1983) at pp. 20–21:

> 'Let us stop for a moment to consider what the effect of the elimination of this willful misconduct exception to limited liability means. Two cases immediately come to mind. Recently a Japanese aircraft crashed with loss of life because the pilot, who had been drinking and had a history of psychiatric problems, deliberately flew the plane into the ground. Were this flight subject to the Warsaw Convention the conduct clearly would have constituted willful misconduct, and any limitation on recovery would have been set aside. Under the protocols, however, even such a gross example of negligence would have been protected—that is, the limitation would not be broken under any circumstances. Another example is the fiery crash last 19 July of a Pan American World Airways 727 in New Orleans, which took the lives of all 146 passengers, some of whom, 18 Americans included, were flying on international tickets. Had such an accident occurred under the proposed treaties, surviving families of those victims flying on domestic tickets could have received compensation commensurate with their loss—while families of victims holding international tickets would have been limited to settlements of $109,000 or less from the airline, even though pilot error may have contributed to the crash. These cases demonstrate the absurdity of probable outcomes had these treaties been ratified.'

Pre-judgment interest and costs authorized under New York law may be added to an award in the maximum amount allowed for property damages by the Warsaw Convention, according to Aerolineas Argentinas *v.* Servair, Inc, decided by the New York Civil Court, New York County, on 10 December 1986:

'Article 28 of the Warsaw Convention may be interpreted to allow the law of the forum on pre-judgment interest . . . The airline's liability is known upon the date of the loss; interest is earned by the airline on that amount from that date until judgment. Were pre-judgement interest disallowed, the money paid would, in essence, be less than the limitation imposed by the Convention. It would be the present value of a future payment, a discounted amount. And the limit would not be uniformly fixed worldwide because it would vary according to the degree of congestion in each forum's courts, procedural delays and the tactics of the parties.'

28. *See* Chapter 4, Section 2, herein.
29. 693 F2d 683 (7th Cir, 1982).
30. 'We have already indicated the substantial fees which a Plaintiff in Portugal must pay in advance. Portuguese attorneys are not permitted to accept a case on a contingent fee arrangement. Plaintiffs will be presenting a very considerable amount of documentary proof, and will be required to obtain translations. *Expense alone might well deprive them, in reality, of an alternative forum in Portugal.* In addition, the Plaintiffs presented considerable material tending to substantiate their claim that several manufacturer Defendants were aware that the data in use concerning the required stopping distance of the 727 aircraft understated the additional requirement for wet runways. They argue persuasively that this demonstrates their special need for discovery under federal rules in order to make an adequate presentation of their claims. The claims of financial hardship and need for discovery were not dealt with in the decision of the Court.' [Emphasis added] (p. 690).
31. 386 F2d 323 (5th Cir, 1967), cert den 392 US 905 (1968).
32. *See also* Maximov *v.* US, 299 F2d 565 (2nd Cir, 1962).
33. (1968) 2 All ER 871.
34. *See* 'The Vienna Convention on the Law of Treaties', UN Doc A/Conf 39/27, dated 23 May 1969; note the following articles:

'Article 46
Provisions of international law regarding competence to conclude treaties

1. A State may not invoke the fact that its consent to be bound by a treaty has been expressed in violation of a provision of its internal law regarding competence to conclude treaties as invalidating its consent unless that violation was manifest and concerned a rule of its internal law of fundamental importance.

2. A violation is manifest if it would be objectively evident to any State conducting itself in the matter in accordance with normal practice and in good faith.

Article 47
Specific restrictions on authority to express the consent of a State

If the authority of a representative to express the consent of a State to be bound by a particular treaty has been made subject to a specific restriction, his omission to observe that restriction may not be invoked as invalidating the consent expressed by him unless the restriction was notified to the other negotiating States prior to his expressing such consent.

Article 48
Error

1. A State may invoke an error in a treaty as invalidating its consent to be bound by the treaty if the error relates to a fact or situation which was assumed by that State to exist at the time when the treaty was concluded and formed an essential basis of its consent to be bound by the treaty.

2. Paragraph 1 shall not apply if the State in question contributed by its own conduct to the error or if the circumstances were such as to put that State on notice of a possible error.

3. An error relating only to the wording of the text of a treaty does not affect its validity; article 79 then applies.

Article 49
Fraud

If a State has been induced to conclude a treaty by the fraudulent conduct of another negotiating State, the State may invoke the fraud as invalidating its consent to be bound by the treaty.

Article 50
Corruption of a representative of a State

If the expression of a State's consent to be bound by a treaty has been procured through the corruption of its representative directly or indirectly by another negotiating State, the State may invoke such corruption as invalidating its consent to be bound by the treaty.

Article 51
Coercion of a representative of a State

The expression of a State's consent to be bound by a treaty which has been procured by the coercion of its representative through acts or threats directed against him shall be without any legal effect.

Article 52
Coercion of a State by the threat or use of force

A treaty is void if its conclusion has been procured by the threat or use of force in violation of the principles of international law embodied in the Charter of the United Nations.'

35. *See* 7 BC Internat and Comp L Rev (1984) at pp. 36 *et seq*.
    35.1 636 F Supp 737 (SD Fla, 1986).
36. *See generally* 51 Harv L Rev 1165 (1938).
37. 96 NYS2d 652 (1950).
38. *See* 1 Beale, Conflict of Laws (1935) at pp. 55–58.
39. *See* 51 Harv L Rev 1310 (1938).
40. 6 Vand L Rev 708 (1953) at pp. 730–731.
41. *Id*.
42. 369 US 1(1962).

Chapter 6. Pre-Trial Preparation for the Foreign Plaintiff in US Courts

Section 1. Discovery In General

The foreign plaintiff in a US court need hardly be told that discovery procedures are sufficiently liberal that pre-trial preparation is adequately assured. In theory, discovery procedures are designed to make lawsuits a genuine search for truth and to eliminate surprise at trial; but broad discovery can also turn pre-trial preparation into an Inquisition unless supervised by the court and moderated by the opposing party. There are essentially at least five discovery devices which are used in state and federal courts, to wit: Interrogatories, Production of Documents, Depositions, Physical and Mental Examinations, and Demand for Admissions. Except for privileged information such as communications between an attorney and client, husband and wife, doctor and patient, and clergyman and penitent, and perhaps the work product of an attorney, all information about the litigated matter is available by way of such discovery devices. Interrogatories are written questions submitted by one party to another party seeking disclosure of relevant information; answers are supplied under oath; but interrogatories are not fruitful generally because the person answering the questions is not the party but his attorney. Production of Documents is achieved by the service of a Notice to Produce, which device compels the party served to produce for inspection relevant documents and perhaps tangible property provided both are properly identified and provided both are in the hands, care, custody or control of the party. Depositions may be written or oral: a deposition upon written questions may be submitted to the party by a court reporter who reads the questions and records the answers of the deponent in a transcript; or an oral deposition which most closely resembles the trial, for the party is deposed under oath with respect to questions posed by the opposing attorney, and all answers and questions are transcribed for production at trial. A deposition can be simply obtained by sending a Notice of Deposition to the party or to his attorney, and that person or another person with personal knowledge of the particular subjectmatter must appear at a designated time and place for the deposition. The Demand for Admissions is a short-cut device designed to require the party to admit the genuineness of a document, for example, as well as the truth of the contents of the document. Notice to Produce a party for a physical or mental examination frequently requires a court order since a professional person is required to assess the merits of the examination.

Cooperation among the nations in the field of pre-trial discovery leaves much to be desired.[1] Almost all countries that are signatories to The Hague Evidence Convention[2] have declared that they will not accept letters of request issued for the purpose of obtaining pre-trial discovery of documents. The foreign plaintiff is undoubtedly aware of this lack of international cooperation and perhaps has premised his case upon documentary evidence already in the United States. There is no corollary in the civil law systems of foreign countries to the US practice of unsupervised pre-trial discovery at the sole initiative of the parties; civil law countries consider all such proceedings as part of trial, and all evidence obtained must be taken by the judge as part of the record of the case. English courts regard pre-trial discovery as 'fishing expeditions' and have refused to participate in such proceedings.[3] Depositions of foreign witnesses are barred in England,[4] although on occasion discovery of documents has been permitted provided that the request is specific and detailed to describe the document. The question has therefore naturally arisen as to whether a federal court might order a foreign person or foreign company over which the federal court has personal jurisdiction to comply with US rules on pre-trial discovery without reference to the procedures of its home country or the procedures of The Hague Evidence Convention; In Societe Nationale *v.* US District Court[5] the Eighth US Court of Appeals answered 'yes'. Here plaintiff sued a French airplane manufacturer in connection with a plane crash. Unfortunately, the US court gave no explanation for its determination that the court has extraterritorial powers where personal jurisdiction is relevant.

US governmental agencies frequently are involved in discovery proceedings for Congress has delegated the duty to investigate all major air accidents, for example, to the Civil Aeronautics Board[6] which has today been supplanted by the National Transportation Safety Board.[7] The foreign plaintiff who is a victim of an air crash in the US may therefore avail himself of the air accident investigation reports as part of his own discovery procedures. But in Cippollone *v.* Liggett Group, Inc[8] the plaintiffs had been prohibited from disseminating or publicizing material concerning the tobacco industry's knowledge of the adverse effects of smoking and the industry's efforts to conceal that knowledge, until the court saw the light and modified the magistrate's order so as to cover only confidential information.[9]

Discovery abuse is perhaps best illustrated in United States *v.* American Telephone & Telegraph Co[10] where defendant had asked for 500,000 documents from Litton Industries, although this discovery request was later pared down to 35,000 documents; the court commented that 'frivolous resistance to legitimate discovery requests must be curtailed if justice is to be done', and then amazingly held that the discovery request was legitimate, must be complied with, and Litton Industries must bear the expense of such discovery. In Penthouse International Ltd *v.* Playboy Enterprises, Inc[11] the willful misconduct of the plaintiff in failing to comply with the discovery process prompted the court to dismiss the complaint.

Section 2. Obtaining Evidence Abroad

Often the foreign plaintiff suing in US courts has need, like the US plaintiff, for obtaining evidence abroad. Since each nation normally has exclusive sovereign rights over its own territory, courts of one country generally cannot perform acts, nor can individual parties, in another nation's territory.[12] US courts have need, like the US plaintiff, for obtaining evidence abroad. Since each nation normally has exclusive sovereign rights over its own territory, courts of one country generally cannot perform acts, nor can individual parties, in another nation's territory. However, custom has opened some doors, and the usual process for obtaining evidence in one country for use in litigation in another is by means of Letters Rogatory.[13] In Volkswagenwerk Aktiengesellschaft *v.* Superior Court[14] the California court defined Letters Rogatory in these terms: 'Letters Rogatory are the medium, in effect, whereby one country, speaking through one of its courts, requests another country, acting through its own courts and by methods of court procedure peculiar thereto and entirely within the latter's control, to assist the administration of justice in the former country; such request being made, and being usually granted, by means of comity existing between nations in ordinary peaceful times.'[15] But the intricacies and administrative obstacles resulted in limited use of that discovery device for obtaining evidence abroad.

The United States in 1964 joined The Hague Conference on Private International Law,[16] which the following year drafted The Hague Convention on the Service Abroad of Judicial and Extrajudicial Documents in Civil or Commercial Matters.[17] The United States became a party to this Convention in 1969. The following year The Hague Convention on the Taking of Evidence Abroad in Civil or Commercial Matters[18] was completed and came into force in 1972 in the United States. In 1980 the United States signed both the Inter-American Convention on Letters Rogatory[19] and the Additional Protocol thereto.[20] In December 1980 the United States acceded[21] to The Hague Convention Abolishing the Requirement of Legalization for Foreign Public Documents,[22] but it was not until 1981 that this latter Convention entered into force for the United States.[23] Thus, the United States, despite its late start in 1964, has entered into several multilateral conventions on international judicial recognition that should pave the way for the successful foreign plaintiff suing in US courts.[24]

The foreign plaintiff suing in US courts is immeasurably aided by Rule 45(e)(2) of the Federal Rules of Civil Procedure which authorizes witnesses located in foreign countries to be subpoenaed if the witnesses are nationals or residents of the United States.[25] The subpoena may require the production of documents and the personal appearance of the witness before the US court or before some person designed by that court.[26] But a subpoena cannot be issued to a witness abroad unless the US court finds both that the subpoena is necessary in the interests of justice and that it is impossible to obtain testimony or documents in any other manner.[27] The validity of this procedure was upheld by the US Supreme Court in Blackmer *v.* US,[28] a case involving a US citizen who was served with a subpoena in France and who was held in contempt for refusing to comply: 'As his attendance is needed in court, it is appropriate that the Congress should authorize the court to direct the notice to be given and that it should be in the customary form of a subpoena. ... The question of the validity of the provision for actual service of the subpoena in a foreign country is one that arises solely between the Government of the United States and the citizen. The mere giving of such a notice to the citizen in the foreign country of the requirement of his government that he shall return is in no sense an invasion of any right of the foreign government; and the citizen has no standing to invoke any such supposed right. . . .'[29] It should be observed that under The Hague Evidence Convention[30] US diplomatic officers, consular agents and commissioners involved in serving the subpoena may not use compulsion to serve the subpoena, nor to take the evidence of any witness, unless application is made to the local foreign authorities for the use of compulsion and the application is granted.[31]

Section 39(1) of Restatement (Second) of the Foreign Relations Law of the United States states: 'A state having jurisdiction to prescribe or enforce a rule of law is not precluded from exercising its jurisdiction solely because such exercise requires a person to engage in conduct subjecting him to liability under the law of another state having jurisdiction with respect to that conduct'. However, Section 40 requires that a court moderate exercise of its jurisdiction in light of five factors, to wit: vital national interests of each of the states; the extent and nature of the hardship that inconsistent enforcement actions would impose upon the person; the extent to which the required conduct is to take place in the territory of the other state; the nationality of the person; and the extent to which enforcement by action of either state can reasonably be expected to achieve compliance with the rule prescribed by that state.[32] These Restatement sections are significant in the issuance of subpoenas for foreign financial records from jurisdictions adhering to rigid bank secrecy laws. US courts have generally favored enforcement of subpoenas; in United States *v.* Davis[33] the court stressed that 'the United States has a strong national interest in the effective enforcement of its criminal laws'.[34] In Garpeg Ltd *v.* US[35] the court observed that 'the interest of Hong Kong in maintaining its bank secrecy doctrine, a commercial concern, does not directly involve an express statutory concern vital to the government itself'. On the other hand, a Texas district court in In Re Grand Jury Investigation, John Doe,[36] refused to compel consent to disclosure of records held by foreign banks on Fifth Amendment grounds; the court refused to compel waiver of secrecy rights because the depositor was neither a defendant nor an investigation's target: 'No court has ever compelled a foreign citizen or corporation to waive rights conferred upon it by foreign law.[37]

In civil law countries testimony is generally taken down verbatim but is summarized and rephrased by the foreign judge who conducts the proceedings. While some US courts may not allow the narrative summary of testimony to be admitted into evidence, Rule 28(b) of FRCP does permit the summary to be admitted in federal courts. The Hague Evidence Convention[38] authorizing such summaries is a treaty of the United States, and is therefore binding on state and federal courts alike as the supreme law of the land.[39]

Serving notice on parties located in foreign countries is covered generally under Rule 4(e) of FRCP which provides that service upon a party not an inhabitant of, or found within, the state shall be made pursuant to the terms set forth in any applicable statute of the United States or order of the court.[40] If no statute is applicable or the court has not issued an order, Rule 4(e) provides that service may be made in any manner set forth in other provisions of Rule 4. Dissatisfied with the general vagueness of Rule 4(e) the US Supreme Court in 1963 approved a new paragraph known as Rule 4(i), entitled 'Alternative Provisions for Service in a Foreign Country'.[41] Rule 4(i) prescribes five methods of service in addition to the methods delineated in Rule 4(e), to wit:

1. in such manner as prescribed by the law of the foreign country in which service of the notice is to be made;
2. as directed by a foreign authority in response to a letter rogatory;
3. by making personal service;
4. by any form of mail requiring a signed receipt which has been sent by the clerk of the court in which the suit is proceeding; and
5. as directed by the court.[42]

Interestingly, The Hague Convention on the Service Abroad of Judicial and Extrajudicial Documents in Civil or Commercial Matters[43] provided for various methods of service of documents including service by mail,[44] although at least 14 of the 23 countries signatory to the Convention have indicated that their ratification did not extend to service by mail. In Vorhees *v.* Fischer & Krecke[45] the Fourth US Court of Appeals held that service by mail in West Germany would have been proper under Rule 4(i) but for the Convention which superseded the 1963 Rule, concluding that as between the United States and West Germany the Convention had to be interpreted in accord with West Germany's reservation in Article 10, the court found that the attempt to serve the defendant by mail was ineffective because it was contrary to West Germany's reservation. But in 1983 new Rule 4(c)(2)(ii) provided that the primary method of serving process is by sending, via first class mail, a copy of the summons and the complaint to the defendant abroad; the summons and complaint are to be accompanied by a notice of receipt of summons, an acknowledgement form, and a return envelope. If the defendant does not respond to the summons and complaint by signing and returning the acknowledgement form within 20 days of receipt, the serving party must then effect personal service.[46] A federal district court in Delaware in Akzona Inc *v.* duPont[47] faced the situation where the defendant sought to bring a counterclaim against the Dutch plaintiffs; defendant made service by serving plaintiffs' registered agent in Delaware, by serving the Delaware Secretary of State and by mailing process pursuant to Rule 4 (c)(2)(C)(ii). The court approved the service as being consonant with Delaware law and ignored any reference to the FRCP, although it intimated that the federal rule was designed to provide a manner of service and had no effect on the question whether a particular party was amenable to service. In essence, the court ruled that state law controls as to a party's amenability to service to service.

It should be noted that discovery abroad, according to In Re Societe Nationale Industrielle Aerospatiale,[48] must proceed according to the Federal Rules of Civil Procedure for documents and evidence in defendant's possession, even though documents and evidence are located abroad. The defendant had countered with the argument that failure to follow The Hague Convention would lead to defendant's criminal liability under a 'French blocking statute'. In Daimler-Bens Akt *v.* US District Court[49] the court ordered in 1986 the defendant to answer interrogatories and produce documents, and a petition for *mandamus* was brought by defendant to recall the court order. The Tenth US Court of Appeals ruled that The Hague Convention did not apply to the production of evidence by a party subject to the jurisdiction of US courts.[50]

The Asian-African Legal Consultative Committee in February 1986 promulgated a Model of Bilateral Arrangements on Mutual Assistance for the Service of Process and the Taking of Evidence Abroad in Civil or Commercial Matters.[51] This document represents a step in the direction of bilateral arrangements between interested governments rather than any regional or international effort at obtaining evidence abroad.

Section 3. Marine Insurance Generally

It has been said that marine insurance runs the gamut of things that can go wrong with a ship from its building to its operation and the cargo that it is carrying. Marine insurance is also complex for it is seldom clear whether admiralty law or federal or even state law applies to a given situation. Hull insurance is the policy issued to cover damage or loss to the vessel; protection and indemnity insurance policies are for protection against liability, and their coverages are generally restrictive and often result in litigation. In Wilburn Boat Co. *v.* Fireman's Fund Insurance Co[52] a small houseboat was carrying passengers on a Texas lake when the boat caught fire; the insurance carrier defended on a breach of warranties in that the houseboat owner had warranted that the vessel would be used only for private pleasure and not for hire. Under Texas law that breach of warranty would not have voided the risk because it did not contribute to the loss. The US Supreme Court in reversing the Fifth US Court of Appeals held that federal law or federal rules would not apply to breach of warranty in a houseboat policy but that the state law of Texas would be applicable. Thus, the marine insurance policy was not within the general maritime law, according to the court. Yet six years later in Kossick *v.* United Fruit Co.[53] the same court held that an oral contract by a shipowner was enforceable in maritime law and New York law which required a writing was not applicable.

Marine insurance is a sensitive instrument in the sense that mere misrepresentation or concealment readily voids the policy; the highest degree of good faith is imposed upon the insured.[54] In the US an insured is deemed responsible for the unseaworthiness of a vessel under theories of lack of good faith or neglect.[55] A contract to procure marine insurance on a vessel has been held not to be a maritime proceeding in Warner *v.* The Bear;[56] but a suit for failure to procure insurance on a ship was held to be a maritime proceeding in Isbrandtsen *v.* US.[57]

State law or federal maritime law were the alternatives posed by the court, and it appears that the choice is not uniformly accepted. In Granite State Minerals, Inc *v*. American Insurance Co,[58] for example, a suit brought to recover under an insurance contract as the result of the vessel's grounding, the defense of lack of timely notice was accepted by the federal district court in Massachusetts applying Massachusetts law because 'The policy was made, issued and delivered in Massachusetts and therefore is a Massachusetts contract'. There apparently was no federal maritime law involving late notice. In Kalmbach, Inc *v*. Insurance Company of the Commonwealth of Pennsylvania[59] the Ninth US Court of Appeals applied Alaskan law over federal admiralty law so that a 'held covered' clause was deemed to have overriden conditions in the policy which required an approval for the voyage and a favorable long-range weather forecast.

Marine insurance policies were at the core of a dispute between an American and a French insurance company in US Aviation Underwriters, Inc *v*. Preservatrice-Fonciere Compagnies D'Assurance,[60] decided in March 1986 by the federal district court for the Southern District of New York. Here both companies successfully defended lawsuits brought by the next-of-kin of passengers killed in the crash of a jet aircraft; but the cost of defense exceeded $300,000, and a dispute arose as to which insurance carrier would have to shoulder all or part of that expense. The court labeled the American carrier the 'primary' carrier and the French carrier the 'excess' carrier, and ruled that the 'primary' carrier would have to bear the entire expense because its policy pre-dated the policy issued by the French insurer. Furthermore, there was no basis on which the French insurer could be compelled to contribute toward the successful defense: its coverage was to take effect 'only after the exhausting of the insurance previously taken out'.[61] The court refused to apply French law here under which the renewal of an insurance contract could be treated as a new contract, thereby negativing the court's determination that the American insurer's policy pre-dated the policy of the French insurer.

In Luria Brothers *v*. Alliance Assurance Co, Ltd[62] the Second US Court of Appeals examined a complex fact situation in which the insured ship charterer, having paid the victims of its negligence a princely sum of money and after having incurred substantial legal fees in the unsuccessful defense of the actions, sought indemnification from the marine insurers. Among the items of contention was a $900,000 *ex gratia* payment by the insurers to the ship charterer; but the court ruled that the issue of restitution as demanded by the insurers was not before the court since the insurers had not requested restitution in the pleadings. Similarly the court ruled that the insurers had not raised a nondisclosure defence (i.e., the ship was not seaworthy) and therefore this defense was deemed to have been waived. Since the marine insurers had declined coverage for the ship charterer, the court declared that an insured may settle rather than proceed to trial where there is a fair chance of being held liable.[63] Also the insured would be reimbursed for legal expenses without the insurers' approval once the insurers had disclaimed all liability as the insurers had done so here. Thus, the ship charterer was to be indemnified and allowed to recover its legal expenditures. Interestingly, the fault of the ship charterer was abundantly clear from the very beginning, although the foreign plaintiffs had also sued the shipowner, the agent, the US Government and

Lloyds, the US government for improper inspection of the ship (despite the preclusion under United States *v.* S A Empresa *et al*[64]) and Lloyds for wrongly certifying the vessel as seaworthy.

Notes

1. *See generally* 19 Houston L Rev 361 (1982). In South Carolina Insurance Co *v.* Assurantie Provincien, (CA, 1985) 3 WLR 739, the English court, where the English plaintiffs sued the American defendant, was asked by the English plaintiffs to halt the pre-trial discovery of documents permitted by a US court where the defendant had commenced another action just prior to service of process in the English court. The English Court of Appeals dismissed defendant's appeal, pointing out that once the parties have submitted to the jurisdiction of the English court, that court's inherent power to control the litigation before it, encompassed the power to order the American defendant to desist from further proceedings in the US court.

   And in Remington Products, Inc *v.* North American Philips Corp, 107 FRD 642 (Conn, 1985) the federal district court in Connecticut found that the Dutch defendant's refusal to provide discovery data was made in bad faith, although the Dutch defendant argued that a Dutch nondisclosure or 'blocking' statute precluded such discovery. Subsequently the Dutch defendant did comply, but was still held liable for sanctions in the amount of $178,162.37 for reasonable costs and attorney's fees.
2. The Hague Convention on the Taking of Evidence Abroad in Civil or Commercial Matters, 23 UST 2555, TIAS No 7444 (28 USC 1781).
3. *See In Re* Westinghouse Electric Corporation Uranium Contracts Litigation (1978), 2 WLR 81 (HL, 1977).

   In *In Re* Anschuetz & Co, GmbH, 754 F2d 602 (5th Cir, 1985) the Fifth US Court of Appeals directed its anger at the West German corporation:

   > 'Anschuetz' interpretation of the treaty, taken to its logical conclusion, would give foreign litigants an extraordinary advantage in United States courts. Insofar as Anschuetz seeks discovery it would be permitted the full range of free discovery provided by the Federal Rules. But when a United States adversary sought discovery, this discovery would be limited to the cumbersome procedures and narrow range authorized by the Convention.'
4. *See* Aboujdid *v.* Gulf Aviation Co, 437 NYS2d 219 (1980).

   Note that under the Federal Rules of Civil Procedure and most state rules, a party can compel another party to appear for deposition by simply filing a notice of deposition. *See* Wright & Miller, Federal Practice and Procedure, Section 2107 (1970). In Schultz *v.* KLM, 21 FRD 20 (ED NY, 1957) the federal district court ordered the defendant Dutch airline to bring its employees from The Netherlands to New York for depositions in a case involving a KLM aircraft crash in Ireland.
5. —F2d—(8th Cir, 1986).

6. Pub L 85–726m 72 Stat 781 (1958) and Pub L 87–810, 76 Stat 921 (1962).
7. 49 USC 1441, 1903(a)(1)(A).
8. 106 FRD 573 (D NJ, 1985).
9. Note Seattle Times Co *v.* Rhinehart, 467 US 20 (1984) where Mr Justice Powell, writing for an unanimous US Supreme Court, stated:

> 'The critical question that this case presents is whether a litigant's freedom comprehends the right to disseminate information that he has obtained pursuant to a court order that both granted him access to that information and placed restraints on the way in which the information might be used. In addressing that question it is necessary to consider whether the "practice in question [furthers] an important or substantial governmental interest unrelated to the suppression of expression" and whether "the limitation of First Amendment freedoms [is] no greater than is necessary or essential to the protection of the particular governmental interest involved".'

10. 86 FRD 603 (D DC, 1979) at p. 656.
11. 86 FRD 396 (SDNY 1980), aff 663 F2d 371 (2nd Cir, 1981). In Fjelstad *v.* American Honda Motor Co, Inc, 762 F2d 1334 (9th Cir, 1985) the defendant, a wholly owned subsidiary of the Japanese automobile manufacturer objected to discovery requests on the ground that the Japanese parent company had the requested data. The trial court granted partial summary judgment against the defendant for this discovery abuse, but the Ninth US Court of Appeals reversed, holding that the sanction was too severe!
12. *See* Section 20 of Restatement (Second) of the Foreign Relations Law of the United States, Comment b thereof.
13. *Supra* note 1 at p. 367.
14. 33 Cal App3d 503 (1973).
15. *Id.* at p. 507.
16. 22 USC 269g; *also see* generally 11 Harv Internat L J 476 (1970).
17. 20 UST 361, TIAS No 6638, 658 UNTS 163; *also see* Rule 4(i) of FRCP at 28 USC 98.
18. 23 UST 2555, TIAS No 7444; *also see* 28 USC 1781.
19. 14 ILM 339 (1975).
20. 18 ILM 1238 (1979).
21. 20 ILM 790 (1981).
22. 527 UNTS 189, and Rule 44 of FRCP at 28 USC 80.
23. 20 ILM 790 (1981).
24. *Supra* note 1 at p. 369.
25. 28 USC 1783(a).
26. *Id.*
27. *Id.*
28. 284 US 421 (1932), upholding the validity of 28 USC 711 to 718.
29. *Supra* note 28 at pp. 438–439.
30. *Supra* note 18.
31. *See* Federal Trade Commission *v.* Compagnie de Saint-Gobain-Pont-a-Mousson, 636 F2d 1300 (DC Cir, 1980).
    A striking illustration of the complexity of obtaining foreign evidence is seen in Falzon *v.* Volkswagenwerk, 417 Mich 889 (1983). In 1974 plaintiffs were severely injured in their Volkswagen bus when it suddenly swerved sharply and crashed into a bridge, leaving the parents paraplegic and seriously injuring three children. Suit was

brought in 1977, and during the course of discovery plaintiffs issued notices to take in West Germany the depositions of thirteen employees of the West German defendant, and defendant moved to quash on grounds of The Hague Evidence Convention. Three years later in 1980 the lower Michigan court ordered the depositions to go forward at the US Consulate in West Germany if the parties did not agree to take the depositions at defendant's factory in West Germany. The defendant applied to the US Supreme Court for a stay of discovery, and it was granted in 1982. But the Michigan Supreme Court then denied defendant's application for leave to appeal, and plaintiffs again filed notices of depositions to take place at defendant's factory in West Germany. Again, the US Supreme Court granted a stay of the discovery (461 US 1303) in 1983, stating that 'there was a substantial chance that the applicant would prevail, and that the injury resulting from a denial of the stay would be irreparable'. Again, the Michigan Supreme Court denied the application for leave to appeal, and when the US Government advised the court that depositions would *not* be taken by consular officials in West Germany, the US Supreme Court dismissed the appeal by the defendant. (104 S Ct 1260) in 1984. Where this leaves the parties is anybody's guess!

In Re Anschuetz & Co, 754 F2d 602 (5th Cir, 1985) the federal appellate court held that The Hague Evidence Convention did not supplant the FRCP where the US court has jurisdiction over the foreign resident under a State's long arm statute. It was argued by the foreign resident of West Germany that ordering depositions in West Germany without proceeding under The Hague Evidence Convention constituted a violation of German judicial sovereignty and international law. But the court opined that 'none of the cases . . . indicate . . . that the purpose of the Convention was to restrict the exercise of *in personam* jurisdiction by the United States courts over foreign nationals properly before it'. Indeed, The Hague Evidence Convention does not purport to limit the jurisdiction of any nation, although the thrust of many US decisions is that the US party should first attempt to seek discovery under the Convention. *See* General Electric Co *v.* North Star International, 39 Fed R Serv2d 207 (ND Ill, 1984).

32. *See* United States *v.* First National City Bank, 398 F2d 897 (2nd Cir, 1968) at p. 902.
33. 767 F2d 1025 (2nd Cir, 1985).
34. *Id.* at p. 1035.
35. 583 F Supp 789 (SDNY, 1984) at p. 796.
36. 599 F Supp 746 (SD Tex, 1984).
37. *Id.* at p. 748.
38. *Supra* note 18.

In Japan judges gather evidence, but there is apparently no Japanese statute or decision that precludes Japanese nationals from testifying by oral disposition in Japan. Note that Japan is not a signatory to The Hague Evidence Convention. *See* Trial magazine (August 1986) at p. 20. Indeed, parties from foreign states that are signatories to the Convention are bound by the FRCP in most instances, as illustrated by Slauenwhite *v.* Bekum Maschinenfabriken, 104 FRD 616 (Mass, 1985).

39. *See* Asakura *v.* City of Seattle, 265 US 332 (1924) at p. 341.
40. Rule 4(e) states:

> 'Whenever a statute of the United States or an order of court thereunder provides for service of a summons, or of a notice, or of an order in lieu of summons upon a party not an inhabitant of or found within the state in which the district court is held, service may be made under the circumstances

and in the manner prescribed by the statute or order, or, if there is no provision therein prescribing the manner of service, in a manner stated in this rule. Whenever a statute or rule of court of the state in which the district court is held provides (1) for service of a summons, or of a notice, or of an order in lieu of summons upon a party not an inhabitant of or found within the state, or (2) for service upon or notice to him to appear and respond or defend in an action by reason of the attachment or garnishment or similar seizure of his property located within the state, service may in either case be made under the circumstances and in the manner prescribed in statute or rule.'

41. Rule 4(i) provides:

'(1) Manner. When the federal or state law referred to in subdivision (e) of this rule authorizes service upon a party not an inhabitant of or found within the state in which the district court is held, the service is to be effected upon the party in a foreign country, it is also sufficient if service of the summons and complaint is made:(A) in the manner prescribed by the law of the foreign country for service in that country in an action in any of its courts of general jurisdiction; or (B) as directed by the foreign authority in response to a letter rogatory, when service in either case is reasonably calculated to give actual notice; or (C) upon an individual, by delivery to him personally, and upon a corporation or partnership or association, by delivery to an officer, a managing or general agent; or (D) by any form of mail, requiring a signed receipt, to be addressed and dispatched by the clerk of the court to the party to be served; or (E) as directed by order of the court. Service under (C) or (E) above may be made by any person who is not a party and is not less than eighteen years of age or who is designated by order of the district court or by the foreign court. On request, the clerk shall deliver the summons to the plaintiff for transmission to the person or the foreign court or officer who will make the service.

'(2) Return. Proof of service may be made as prescribed by subdivision (g) of this rule, or by the law of the foreign country, or by order of the court. When service is made pursuant to subparagraph (1)(D) of this subdivision, proof of service shall include a receipt signed by the addressee or other evidence of delivery to the addressee satisfactory to the court.'

42. Prior to 1983 in Zurini *v.* US, 189 F2d 722 (8th Cir, 1951) a court had approved service by mail.
43. 20 UST 361, TIAS No 6638; as of 1985 the following countries have become members of the Convention: France, West Germany, Italy, Japan, United Kingdom, Barbados, Belgium, Botswana, Czechoslovakia, Denmark, Egypt, Finland, Greece, Israel, Luxembourg, Malawi, the Netherlands, Norway, Portugal, Seychelles, Sweden, Turkey and the United States.
44. Article 10 thereof.
45. 697 F2d 574 (4th Cir, 1983).
46. Personal services must be made pursuant to Rule 4(d)(1) or 4(d)(3), which respectively state:

'(1) Upon an individual other than an infant or an incompetent person, by delivering a copy of the summons and of the complaint to him personally or by leaving copies thereof at his dwelling house or usual place of abode with some person of suitable age and discretion then residing therein or by delivering a copy of the summons and of the complaint to an agent authorized by appointment or by law to receive service of process.

'(3) Upon a domestic or foreign corporation or upon a partnership or other unincorporated association which is subject to suit under a common name, by delivering a copy of the summons and of the complaint to an officer, a managing or general agent, or to any other agent authorized by appointment or by law to receive service of process and, if the agent is one authorized by statute to receive service and the statute so requires, by also mailing a copy to the defendant.' See further FDIC *v.* Sims, 100 FRD 792, 794 (ND Ala 1984).

47. 607 F Supp 227 (D Del, 1984).
48. 782 F2d 120 (8th Cir, 1986), cert den 90 L Ed2d 976 (1986).
49. 805 F2d 340 (10th Cir, 1986).
50. *See* NYLJ (6 Feb 1987 at p. 1, 'How Evidence Is Obtained Abroad'.
51. *See* 25 ILM 920 *et seq.* (1986):

'Asian-African Legal Consultative Committee: Model Text for Bilateral Agreements on the Taking of Evidence

Model for Bilateral Arrangements on Mutual Assistance for the Service of Process and the Taking of Evidence Abroad in Civil or Commercial Matters

Preamble

The States Parties to the present Arrangements, Desirous of bringing about closer co-operation in the matter of mutual assistance for service process, taking of evidence and other related functions in aid of judicial proceedings relating to civil or commercial matters,

Have agreed as follows:

CHAPTER I. GENERAL PROVISIONS

Article 1
Use of terms

For the purposes of these Arrangements:

(a) *Process:* means any notice, writ, summons or any other type of document, which is required to be served on a party or witness in judicial proceedings relating to civil or commercial matters;
(b) *Requesting State:* means the State which requests the service of process in the territory of another State or the State from which a request to take evidence, obtain information or perform some other judicial act emanates;
(c) *Requested State:* means the State in which the service is to be effected or the State in which the request is to be executed for taking of evidence, or performing some other judicial act or obtaining information;
(d) *Central Agency:* means the authority which is empowered:
(i) to transmit to a Central Agency of the other Contracting State requests or letters

of request for the purpose of service of process or for taking of evidence, or performing some other judicial act, or obtaining of information, emanating from a competent authority of its own State; and

(ii) to receive and to take action on requests or letters of request transmitted by a Central Agency of the other Contracting State.

Article 2
Scope of the Arrangements

1. The Contracting States undertake to afford each other, in accordance with and subject to the provisions of these Arrangements, mutual assistance with regard to service of process, taking of evidence or performing some other judicial act, or obtaining of information, by means of requests or letters of request issued for the purpose, addressed by a competent authority in one State Party to a competent authority of the other State in civil or commercial proceedings.
2. Letters of request shall not be used for taking of evidence which is not intended for use in judicial proceedings.
3. The expression 'other judicial act' does not cover the issuance of any process by which judgments or orders are executed or enforced, or orders for provisional or protective measures.

Article 3
Execution of request or letter of request noncommitment to recognition of the judgment

Execution of the request or the letter of request shall not imply ultimate recognition of the jurisdiction of the authority issuing it or a commitment to recognize the validity of the judgment it may render or to enforce it.

Article 4
Central Agency

1. Each Contracting State shall designate or establish a Central Agency through which requests or letters of request to the other Contracting State shall be transmitted. Requests or letters of request from the other Contracting State shall be received by the Central Agency which shall forward them to the competent authorities in its own State for taking action.
Note: Federal States shall be free to designate or establish more than one Central Agency and this paragraph would need to be adapted accordingly.
2. Each Contracting State shall inform the other Contracting State the name and address of the Central Agency (or Agencies) designated or established in accordance with the provisions of this Article.

Article 5
Legalisation

The request or the letter of request shall be presumed to be duly legalised in the requesting State when the same is signed and bears the seal or stamp of a Central Agency.

Article 6
Language

1. The request or the letter of request and the appended documentation shall be drawn up in the   language(s) or be accompanied by a translation into that language/those languages.
2. The reply shall be prepared and transmitted in the language(s) specified in paragraph 1 or be accompanied by a translation.
3. Any translation accompanying a request or a letter of request shall be certified as correct, by a person qualified for this purpose under the law of either State.

Article 7
Time-limits

The competent authority issuing the request may indicate a time-limit for the service of process or taking of evidence, obtaining of information or performing some other judicial act in the requested State. The competent authority shall briefly state the reasons for establishing such time-limit. The Central Agency of the requested State shall communicate with the Central Agency of the requesting State if any difficulty is experienced in adhering to the time-limit. The competent authority of the requesting State shall have the option to indicate a further period of time for taking action on the request.

Article 8
Compliance with the Arrangements

If the Central Agency of the requested State considers that the request or the letter of request does not comply with the provisions of the present Arrangements it shall promptly inform the requesting Central Agency and specify its objections.

Article 9
Grounds for non-compliance with the request or the letter of request

1. The execution of a request or of a letter of request may be refused if the requested State considers that its sovereignty, security, public policy or other essential interests (ordre public) would be prejudiced thereby.
2. The execution of a letter of request may also be refused if:
(a) the execution of the letter of request does not fall within the functions of the judiciary or any other competent organ of the requested State; or
(b) the requested State considers that the execution of the letter of request might prejudice the fundamental rights of any person; or that the letter of request concerns information held in confidence the disclosure of which is prohibited by law;

(c) [the letter of request seeks to obtain
   (i) a statement from any person of the documents relevant to the proceedings to which the request relates which are or have been in his possession, custody or power; or
   (ii) the production of any documents other than particular documents specified in the request as being documents appearing to the competent authority in the requesting State initiating the request to be, or to be likely to be, in his possession, custody or power.]* or

(d) [the letter of request relates to taking of evidence prior to judicial proceedings or in 'pre-trial discovery of documents' as known in the common law system.]*

3. [Execution of a request or of a letter of request may not be refused solely on the ground that under its internal law the requested State claims exclusive jurisdiction over the subject-matter of the proceedings or that its internal law would not permit the bringing of the proceedings to which the request or letter of request relates.]

4. In any case in which the execution of a request or a letter of request is refused, the Central Agency of the requested State shall promptly inform the requesting Central Agency and state the grounds for such refusal.

CHAPTER II. SERVICE OF PROCESS

Article 10
Form of Request

1. The authority competent under the law of the requesting State shall forward a request for the service of process to its own Central Agency for transmission to the requested State.

2. The request for the service of process shall be drawn up in accordance with form 'A' appended to the present Arrangements and the document to be served or a copy thereof shall be annexed to it. The request and the document shall both be provided in duplicate.

Article 11
Execution of request for service

1. The authorities of the requested State shall effect service of the process on the person to be served by any method prescribed or permitted by its internal law.

2. Where the competent authority of the requesting State has indicated any particular method of service, an endeavour shall be made to comply with such request provided that the same is not inconsistent with the laws of the requested State.

3. A summary of the document to be served, drawn up in accordance with form 'C' appended to the present Arrangements, shall be served together with the document.

* In negotiating these Arrangements Governments may choose to include either sub-paragraph (c) or (d). These sub-paragraphs cover the same ground i.e. they allow the refusal of letters of request, issued in the context of a pre-trial discovery of documents, which seek to obtain testimony on, or production of, unspecified documents ('fishing expeditions').

Article 12
Certificate of the executing authority for service of process

The Central Agency of the requested State or any authority which it may have designated for that purpose, shall complete a certificate in form 'B' appended to the present Arrangements.

Article 13
Costs

The requested State shall be entitled to be reimbursed by the requesting State:
(a) the fees or charges paid for effecting service as authorised under the law of the requested State; and
(b) the costs occasioned by the use of a special procedure requested by the competent authority of the requesting State.

Article 14
Service of process by diplomatic or consular officers

A diplomatic or consular officer of a Contracting State may, in the territory of the other Contracting State and within the area where he exercises his functions, effect service of judicial documents upon his own nationals provided no measures of compulsion be applied.

Article 15
Service of process by post and other modes

Subject to any objection on the part of a Contracting State:
(a) each Contracting State may send judicial documents by postal channels, directly to persons in the other Contracting State;
(b) the judicial personnel, officials or other competent persons in a Contracting State may effect service of judicial documents directly through the judicial personnel, officials or other competent persons in the other Contracting State; and
(c) any person interested in a judicial proceeding may effect service of judicial documents directly through the judicial personnel, officials [legal practitioners] or other competent persons in the other Contracting State.

Chapter III. Taking of Evidence

Article 16
Form of Request

1. The authority or judicial officer competent under the law of the requesting State shall forward to its own Central Agency a letter of request for taking of evidence or performing some other judicial act of an analogous nature with the request to transmit

it to the Central Agency of the requested State. The letter of request shall be drawn up in form 'D' appended to the present Arrangements.
2. The relevant authorities in the requesting State shall ensure that its formalities and procedures prescribed by its laws for the admissibility or validity of the requests made in the letter of request are fully complied with before taking any action under this article.

Article 17
Execution of letters of request

1. The authority responsible for the execution of letters of request shall apply its internal law as to the methods and procedures to be followed.
2. However, it shall follow any special method or procedure specified in the letter of request unless that procedure conflicts with the internal law of the requested State or is impossible of performance by reason of its internal practice and procedure or by reason of practical difficulties.
[3. If the requesting State desires witnesses or experts to give evidence on oath, it shall expressly so state, and the requested State shall comply with the request if its internal law does not prohibit the same.]
4. In the execution of the letter of request, the authorities of the requested State shall not require any person to give evidence in respect of any matter where he has a privilege or duty to refuse to give such evidence under the law of the requested State or of the requesting State.
5. The requested State may transmit original or certified copies of records or documents requested.

Article 18
Notice to the requesting authority regarding time and place of the execution of the request

1. On the express request of the requesting authority the requested State shall inform that authority of the time when, and the place where, the proceedings will take place. The requested State shall endeavour to send such information directly to the parties when the authority of the requesting State so desires.
2. The officials designated by the requesting State and parties concerned may be present or be represented at the proceedings, if the same is not inconsistent with the internal law.

Article 19
Application of the measures of compulsion by the authority
[In the execution of the letter of request, the requested authority shall apply appropriate measures of compulsion in the instances and to the same extent as are provided for by its internal law.]

Article 20
Costs

1. The requested State shall be entitled to be reimbursed by the requesting State:
(a) the fees or charges paid to experts, witnesses, interpreters or any other person as authorised under the law of the requested State; and
(b) the costs occasioned by the use of a special procedure requested by the competent authority of the requesting State.

[2. The requested State whose law obliges the parties themselves to secure evidence may, after having obtained the consent of the requesting Central Agency, appoint a suitable person to execute the letter of request. When seeking such consent the requested Central Agency shall indicate the approximate costs which would result from following of this procedure. If the requesting Central Agency gives its consent the requesting State shall reimburse the costs incurred; without such consent the requesting State shall not be liable for the costs.]

Article 21
Taking of evidence by diplomatic or consular officers

1. A diplomatic or consular officer of a Contracting State may, in the territory of the other Contracting State and within the area where he exercises his functions, take the evidence of nationals of his home State in aid of proceedings commenced in the courts of that State, without application of any compulsion.
2. If an attempt to obtain evidence in the manner provided for in paragraph 1 of this Article fails, it shall not prevent a letter of request being subsequently sent to the Central Agency of the requested State in accordance with Article 16 of these Arrangements.

Article 22
Taking of evidence by commissioner

The Commissioner appointed by a judicial authority in a Contracting State to record the evidence of a witness or expert, for the purposes of proceedings pending before it, may take such evidence in the other Contracting State, provided a competent authority of that State has given its endorsement or authorisation on the warrant of commission and subject to such terms and conditions as may be specified in the endorsement or authorisation.

Chapter IV. Request for Information and Documents

Article 23
Request for information on laws and regulations

The Contracting States agree to furnish each other with information on their laws and regulations relating to civil or commercial matters, both substantive and procedural, whenever a request is made by a Contracting State.

Article 24
Requests for judicial records

1. Upon the request made by a judicial authority of the requesting State transmitted through the Central Agency, extracts from and information relating to judicial records shall be made available to the same extent and in like manner as these are available as between the judicial authorities in the requested State.
2. The requesting authority shall specify the purpose for which the extract or information referred to in paragraph 1 is required and may not use such extract or information for any other purpose.
3. If compliance with any request made under this Article involves expense for the requested State, it may obtain reimbursement of such expense from the requesting State.

Chapter V. Final Provisions

Article 25
Entry into force of the Arrangements

[1. The present Arrangements shall be subject to ratification.]
[2. The Arrangements shall enter into effect days after the date of exchange of instruments of ratification and shall remain in force for a period of years.]

Article 26
Other international agreements, practices or arrangements

Except as may be specified herein, nothing in these Arrangements shall affect existing or future bilateral or multilateral agreements, practices or other arrangements between the Contracting States which relate to matters dealt with in these Arrangements.
Note: If certain existing bilateral or multilateral agreements, practices or arrangements are to be replaced or superseded, in whole or in part, and those agreements or arrangements so permit, this should be specified in a second paragraph to this Article.

Article 27
Difficulties arising in operation of the Arrangements to be settled through negotiation

Any difficulties which may arise between Contracting States in regard to the interpretation or application of these Arrangements shall be settled through negotiation.

Article 28
Revision of the Arrangements

At the request of any Contracting State, the State Parties shall enter into negotiations with a view to examine the provisions of these Arrangements and to consider the advisability of a revision or of an enlargement of the scope of these Arrangements.

Article 29
Denunciation of the Arrangements

Either Contracting State may denounce these Arrangements by means of a notification communicated to the other State Party. Denunciation shall take effect six months after the date of receipt of such instrument of denunciation.'
'*Note:* the Committee decided that the provisions in regard to which some differences of view had been expressed should be placed within square brackets [ ] so that the governments may give special consideration to those articles whilst negotiating agreements.'

The official Explanatory Notes on Chapters III and IV are set forth hereinafter:

'CHAPTER III. TAKING OF EVIDENCE

Articles 16 to 22 in Chapter III of these Arrangements contain provisions concerning the taking of evidence abroad. The primary mode contemplated is by means of transmission of letters of request through the Central Agency but other channels such as taking of evidence by diplomatic and consular personnel or by a Commissioner are also provided for in Articles 21 and 22.

Article 16

Article 16 stipulates that the letter of request is to be sent by the authority, competent under the law of the requesting State, i.e. a Court or judicial officer to its own Central Agency as provided under Article 4 paragraph 1, with the request to transmit it to the Central Agency of the requested State.

The letter of request has to be drawn up in a manner provided for in Form 'D' appended to the Arrangements. This is with a view to evolve some kind of uniformity and to ensure that all necessary particulars and information requested for the purpose of recording of evidence are duly communicated to the requested State.

A suggestion made by the delegate of Singapore which was generally acceptable in principle required a provisions to be made in the text that the relevant authorities in the requesting State shall ensure that all formalities and procedures prescribed by its laws for issue of the letter of request had been complied with. There was however a difference of view whether the provision should be made in Article 16 itself or in Form D.

Article 17

This Article regulates the modes and procedures to be followed by the competent authority responsible for the execution of letters of request.

Paragraph 1 contains the general rule that the evidence shall be recorded according to the internal laws and procedures applicable in the requesting State.

Paragraph 2 provides for a situation where the requested State makes a request to the requested State to follow a special method or procedure for taking of evidence. The requested State may, however, decline such request if, (i) the procedure is in conflict with its internal laws; (ii) it is impossible of performance by reason of its internal practice and procedures; or (iii) there are practical difficulties. The reason for incorporation of the provision in paragraph 2 is that the requested State should assist to the extent possible in making available the recorded evidence in the manner commonly used in the proceedings before the courts and tribunals of the requesting State.

There can be numerous instances where the requested State might find it difficult or impossible to have the evidence taken in the particular manner required. This primarily arises on account of wide divergence in the procedures applied in various systems. For example, in some countries it is the normal practice to follow the adversary procedure where the witness is examined by counsel and cross-examined on his evidence before a Judge, but in some other countries it is the Judge alone who records the evidence and himself puts questions to the witness. Then again, in the practice of some States evidence is recorded verbatim in the question-answer form whilst in others the evidence would be recorded in the narrative or summary form as dictated by the Judge. Besides, some systems permit the court to appoint a Commissioner to record the evidence in order to save the time of the Court but in other systems this would clearly not be permissible.

Paragraph 3 provides that if the evidence of witnesses or experts is to be taken on oath, it should be expressly so stated by the requesting State. The requested State has to honour such request unless the same conflicts with its internal laws. As there were some differences of views on this paragraph, it has been put within square brackets.

Paragraph 4 recognises the right of the individual to refuse to testify in respect of a matter which he cannot be compelled to disclose by reason of the privilege enjoined under the law of the requesting State or of the requested State. Such matters would often include disclosure of any fact or information which might be of a self-incriminating nature or matters which have been disclosed to him in confidence, such as, in the case of doctors, lawyers, journalists etc. The provision of this paragraph further contemplates that no evidence should be requested in regard to any matter where the witness has a duty to refuse to give evidence, such as the information in his possession on official matters covered by the Official Secrets Act. It is presumed that when the witness has a privilege or duty to refuse to give evidence, he will claim such privilege or invoke the provisions of law under which he has a duty to refuse to give evidence at the time when the evidence is recorded.

Paragraph 5 gives an option to the requested State to transmit either the original or certified copies of records or documents taken as evidence.

Article 18

Paragraph 1 deals with the matter of notice to be given regarding the time and place of recording of evidence to the requesting State and also to the parties to the proceedings in aid of which the evidence is required. It is recognised that no such notice would be necessary unless the requesting State so desires. The procedure for communication of the notice would naturally vary from country to country. Whilst some countries may prefer to channelise such communications through the Central Agency, others could well agree to such notice being sent by the concerned judicial authority directly to a designated official of the requesting State and/or the parties to the proceedings.

Paragraph 2 contemplates that any official or officials designated by the requesting State as also the parties to the proceedings should be enabled to be present at the time when the evidence is recorded. This, however, is subject to any prohibition contained in the internal law of the requested State.

Article 19

Article 19 deals with the question of application of the measures of compulsion by the authority recording the evidence in execution of the letter of request. Since there were certain differences of views, the provisions of this Article have been retained within square brackets. The objective behind this Article is that judicial assistance in the matter of recording of evidence should not be frustrated by the refusal of the witness to appear to give evidence or his refusal to answer questions and also to produce documents or other tangible objects. It is therefore contemplated that the requested State should assist in the matter by employing the same degree of compulsion as it would under its internal laws in regard to domestic proceedings of the same nature.

Article 20

The provisions of this Article deal with the question of reimbursement of costs incurred by the requested State in the execution of the letter of request in the various circumstances and subject to conditions specified in this Article. It was stated in the course of discussions at the Working Group that the reimbursement of the costs should be done by the requesting State but it would be open to that State to recoup the costs from the party for whose benefit the evidence was obtained.

Article 21

This Article recognises the competence of the diplomatic or consular officer to take evidence of nationals of his home State in aid of proceedings commenced in the courts of that State. It may however be clarified that the power of the diplomatic or consular officer to take such evidence would be governed by the laws of the State which he represents. What this Article contemplates is that if the diplomatic or consular officer is authorised under the laws of his home State to take the evidence, the other State will permit him to exercise such functions. This is subject to the condition that the diplomatic or consular officer shall not apply any method of compulsion whilst recording evidence.

Although these Arrangements contemplate recording of evidence through issue of letters of request transmitted through the Central Agency as being the principal mode, the use of diplomatic or consular channels is also permitted. In some cases it may be simpler to apply that procedure, such as in cases where evidence by means of a sworn affidavit would be sufficient or the witness is ready and willing to give evidence without the need of any compulsion. There was some difference of view as to whether this provision was suitable.

The provisions of paragraph 1 clarify the powers and functions of a diplomatic or consular officer in the matter, namely (i) he may act only in the area in which he exercises his functions; (ii) he may take evidence subject to the willingness of the witness, that is, without compulsion; (iii) he may take evidence only with respect to the proceedings which are pending in the courts of a State which he represents; (iv) he may take the evidence only of nationals of his home State.

Paragraph 2 of this Article is intended to clarify that if an attempt to obtain evidence through the diplomatic or consular channels fails, it would not prejudice any subsequent effort to obtain evidence through employing the mode of the issue of a letter of request through the Central Agency. Such cases may happen where the witness may refuse to respond to a notice sent by the diplomatic or consular officer or where it may appear that the evidence could not be obtained without some measure of compulsion.

Article 22

Article 22 recognises an alternative method for recording of evidence which has often been used among neighbouring countries or countries having the same system of law and procedures. Although the Arrangements contemplate the principal mode for recording of evidence as being the one through the issue of letters of request channelised through the Central Agency, it was felt that the system of taking of evidence by a Commissioner should also be retained since this could be speedy and more attuned to the proceedings in aid of which the evidence is required. Nevertheless, it is to be appreciated that many countries of the Asian-African region may not be familiar with this type of procedure which had been in vogue in common law system principally among the countries of the British Empire. The provisions of this Article specify the circumstances and the conditions subject to which the Commissioner may take evidence, namely (a) the Commissioner shall be appointed by a judicial authority to record the evidence of a witness or expert for the purpose of proceedings pending before that judicial authority; (b) the State in which the evidence is to be recorded shall give its endorsement or authorisation to the Commissioner to record such evidence; and (c) the authorisation shall be subject to such terms and conditions as may be specified.

52. 348 US 310 (1955).
53. 365 US 731 (1961).
54. *See* Thebes Shipping, Inc *v.* Assicurazioni Ausonia, SPA, 599 F Supp 405 (SDNY, 1984), for example.
55. *See* New York New Haven & Hartford Railroad Co *v.* Gray, 240 F2d 460 (2nd Cir, 1957), cert den 353 US 966 (1957).
56. 126 F Supp 529, (D Alas, 1955).
57. 233 F2d 184 (2nd Cir, 1956).
58. 435 F Supp 159 (D Mass, 1977).
59. 529 F2d 552 (9th Cir, 1976).
60. —F Supp— (SDNY, 1986).
61. *Id.*
62. 780 F2d 1082 (2nd Cir, 1986).
63. *See* Bunge Corp *v.* London and Overseas Insurance Co, 394 F2d 496 (2nd Cir, 1968), cert den 393 US 952 (1968).
64. 104 S Ct 2755 (1984), holding that the US was not liable for issuing type certification of aircraft under the 'discretionary function' exception under the Federal Tort Claims Act.

Chapter 7. Trial Preparation for the Foreign Plaintiff in US Courts

Section 1. Keeping All Defendants in the Lawsuit

Since the US courts appear as El Dorado to the foreign plaintiff unaccustomed to high verdicts and/or judgments, it is well to note that the more defendants named, served and retained in the lawsuit the more probable is the likelihood of achieving that success. The 1986 decision of the New York Appellate Division, First Dept, in Carrao *v*. Heitler and Haber[1] illustrated how the court responded to plaintiff's initial difficulty in failing to identify the product by retaining all the defendants in the lawsuit. Here the plaintiff, when she was nine months old in 1970, was given an injection of measles vaccine; the infant plaintiff began to experience seizure episodes together with a fever and rash, and subsequently was found to be suffering from epilepsy and to be mentally retarded. In 1975 the infant plaintiff, institutionalized in a permanent home for severely retarded persons, by her father and natural guardian, commenced the lawsuit against the two pediatricians and the manufacturer of the vaccine Dow Chemical; in 1979 a second action was brought against Eli Lilly & Co, Merck Sharp & Dohme, and Philips Roxane Laboratories, all of whom could have manufactured the particular vaccine. In 1982 after the two actions were consolidated, motions were made by Merck and Roxanne to dismiss based upon lack of product identification; two courts granted and then reversed the dismissal, and finally 'on the eve of trial, on about March 1985, all four defendants moved again to dismiss claiming that 'the evidence leads to the conclusion that none of them manufactured the measles vaccine used on the infant plantiff'. Defendants Merck and Roxanne were dropped, and the New York appellate court reversed that order on the basis that 'there are many triable issues of fact as to whether either of these defendants manufactured the offending vaccine. . . . The instant case presents a classic illustration of the difficulties in identifying the particular product used, when there are a number of different manufacturers and the administering physicians' records are not precise. It is just not possible at this time to come to a conclusion that any of the above named defendants, as a matter of law, was not the manufacturer of the vaccine used to immunize the infant plaintiff. Accordingly, same should be left for the jury to decide.'

The thrust of the above New York case is a comfort to the foreign plaintiff suing in US courts for not only was it not necessary to identify the product with particularity but the court was willing to keep all defendants in the law suit pending trial of the action.

Section 2. Defense of the Statute of Limitations and/or Repose

Traditionally the US conflicts of law doctrine construed the question of whether the statute of limitations or the statute of repose was applicable to the law of the forum state as a remedy and not as a right.[2] This meant that the forum state made the determination as to whether the action was time-barred under its own procedural rules. Although many European courts still follow that practice, there have been in recent years exceptions to the practice in order to insure respect for uniformity of law and to preclude forum-shopping.[3] Some states havc adopted 'borrowing statutes', i.e., statutes authorizing the forum state to borrow the statute of limitations or the statute of repose applicable in the state where the cause of action arose. Obviously, 'borrowing statutes' do not necessarily aid the foreign plaintiff suing in US courts if the net result is to apply a shorter statute of limitations or shorter statute of repose from the home forum of the foreign plaintiff. One illustration is found in Heavener *v.* Uniroyal Inc[4] where one defendant was a tire manufacturer with headquarters in New Jersey, the forum state, and the other defendant was a Delaware retailer of trucks using those tires. Plaintiffs were residents of North Carolina who had purchased the truck in North Carolina where the accident occurred, causing personal injury and property damage. The reason why the North Carolina plaintiffs chose to bring their action in New Jersey was due to the fact that the North Carolina statute of limitations had expired, while the New Jersey statute had not yet expired; furthermore, New Jersey had no 'borrowing statute' which would have compelled the New Jersey court to apply the expired statute of limitations of North Carolina. But the New Jersey court determined that New Jersey had no substantial interest in the law suit between North Carolina plaintiffs and the defendants, and ruled that North Carolina law was applicable; therefore, the suit in New Jersey was time-barred. In essence, the New Jersey court simply frowned upon forum-shopping.[5]

Statutes of repose run not from the date of the accrual of the action, as does the statute of limitations, but from the date of the manufacture of the product or from the date of the first sale of the product. The time framework may be ten, or twenty, or even thirty years, and nearly every state has a statute of repose in force.[6]

A cause of action may accrue at different periods of time, depending upon the particular jurisdiction, as illustrated by Miller *v.* A. H. Robins Co, Inc[7] and by Kesinger *v.* Abbott Laboratories.[8] In the former case, applying Indiana law, the issue presented was whether or not a physician's comment to the plaintiff that the IUD she was using was a possible cause of her pelvic inflammation marked the commencement of the statute of limitations; Indiana's statute of limitations begins to run 'from the date the plaintiff knew or should have discovered that she suffered an injury or an impingement, and

that it was caused by the product or act of another'.[9]
The Seventh US Court of Appeals ruled that the plaintiff was aware of her injury when she was hospitalized and when her physician made the above comment to her, and therefore her action was time-barred. On the other hand, in the latter case,[10] the California court observed that in 1974 plaintiff had been informed that her cancer was caused by her mother's ingestion of diethylstilbestrol, manufactured by the defendant, although it was not until 1977 that plaintiff learned the identity of the probable manufacturer of that drug product; in 1980 plaintiff learned of the allegations that these DES manufacturers failed to test adequately the product and to warn of its risks. The California court targeted the year 1980 as the date when the statute of limitations should begin to run, and therefore plaintiff's action was not time-barred.[11] The conflict between state jurisdictions points up the sovereignty of the states jealous of their prerogative to decide upon such questions as the defense of the action.

The plaintiffs were passengers on a cruise ship when they were injured as the ship grounded near Greece; their tickets stated that any claim against the vessel for bodily injury must be brought within one year in accordance with a federal statute that prohibits a shorter statute of limitations. Plaintiffs commenced suit in the New York court after the expiration of the one year period, but the court refused to dismiss contending that the type-size requirement of the ticket under New York law was not met. The New York appellate court reversed, pointing out that the New York statute had been pre-empted by the federal maritime law. The New York Court of Appeals on 26 December 1985, in Lerner *v.* Karageorgis Lines, Inc[12] agreed: 'The Federal Judiciary Act, by virtue of its "saving to suitors" clause[13] vests original jurisdiction of all admiralty and maritime cases concurrently in the federal district and state courts. In maritime cases, state courts must apply federal law "to secure a single and uniform body of maritime law". A state court may not limit a party's substantive rights by applying its own procedural rules if those rules would "significantly affect the result of the litigation, i.e., would be outcome determinative". Thus, New York CPLR 4544 which is a rule of evidence, may not be employed to nullify a contractual limitation enforceable under federal maritime law.'

The filing of an exclusive federal action in a state court does not toll the time bar, according to the Third US Court of Appeals in Bailey *v.* Carnival Cruise Lines, Inc.[14] To hold otherwise, according to the court, would encourage frivolous claims in state courts, waste state judicial resources, and create a methodology for increasing the overall costs of litigation for defendants.

Section 3. Admission of Foreign Public Records

In preparation for trial the foreign plaintiff suing in US courts will be concerned about the admission of foreign public records and reports, as delineated in Rule 803(8)(C) of the Federal Rule of Evidence. This Rule lists hearsay evidence which is admissible even though the declarant is available as a witness:

'Records, reports, statements, or data compilations, in any form, of public offices or agencies, setting forth (A) the activities of the office or agency, or (B) matters observed pursuant to duty imposed by law as to which matters there was a duty to report . . . (C) in civil actions and proceedings . . . factual findings resulting from an investigation made pursuant to authority granted by law, unless the sources of information or other circumstances indicate lack of trustworthiness.'[15]

This Rule obviates the necessity and inconvenience of forcing public officials to appear in court merely to lay a foundation for a public record admissibility, which public record is presumed to be valid and trustworthy. Prior to 1975 when Rule 803(8)(C) and the Federal Rules of Evidence were adopted[16] public records from abroad were admitted under the 'business records' exception to the hearsay rule.[17] In 1977 in Melville *v.* American Home Assurance Co[18] the court ruled that investigative reports containing factual findings in the form of evaluative conclusions were admissible into evidence, unless 'sources of information or the circumstances indicate lack of trustworthiness'. Indeed, courts have analyzed this concept of 'trustworthiness' in terms of possible motiviation,[19] the special skill or experience of the foreign official,[20] and whether a hearing was held and the level at which it was conducted.[21] In Lloyd *v.* American Export Lines, Inc[22] the Third US Court of Appeals was confronted with an evidentiary question concerning a US Coast Guard report which it upheld as admissible: 'The Coast Guard proceeding was a rather elaborate hearing conducted before a professional hearing examiner. In addition to documentary evidence, testimony was received under oath, subject to direct and cross examination. . . . The Coast Guard's findings . . . are highly relevant and clearly admissible'. But 'a formal hearing is not a *sine qua non* of admissibility under Rule 803 (8)(C) when other indicia of trustworthiness are present'.[23] In Wetherill *v.* University of Chicago[24] the plaintiff attempted to introduce a report on various safety aspects of diethylstilbestrol, which report was prepared by a Ralph Nader organization indirectly associated with several DES-affected mothers, the mother of the plaintiff herein, and a witness for the plaintiff in another DES action. The court in denying admission of the report discerned possible motivational problems and inequalities which rendered the report untrustworthy.

Foreign public records generally are admissible under Rule 803 (8)(C) as shown in Federal Aviation Administration *v.* Landy[25] where the Second US Court of Appeals admitted into evidence a telex sent by the German Government through the US State Department to the plaintiff federal agency; the telex was authenticated by the FAA inspector to whom it was sent.[26] But in Bokkelen *v.* Gruman Aerospace Corp[27] the federal district court considered the admissibility of a letter from a Brazilian official to the defendant, and denied its admissibility because it was not clear that the letter met the requirements of Rule 803 (8)(C); subsequently, after the letter was certified as to authenticity by a stipulation of all the parties, the letter was admitted into evidence. Uncertified weather reports, however, were admitted in Insurance Company of North America *v.* S/S Italica[28] because the court found that the reports possessed sufficient indicia of reliability when the party introducing them 'made diligent efforts to obtain a final certification and the opposing party had reasonable opportunity to investigate the authenticity and accuracy of the documents which had been made available over a year before trial'.[29]

In the English decision Rio Tinto Zinc Corp *v.* Westinghouse Electric Corp,[29.1] it was pointed out that the rights of discovery against non-parties are very restricted; only in personal injury cases is the disclosure of documents in the hands of non-parties who are not under the control of a party possible, provided that the documents are sought for trial.

Section 4. Application of Foreign Law in US Courts

In the earliest US decisions like Talbot *v.* Seeman[30] in the year 1801 the US Supreme Court had held that foreign law had to be proved as a fact and could not be judicially noticed. At common law the issue of foreign law was a question of fact and not a question of law.[31] As a result, when foreign law was misapplied, it was an error of fact and could not be reviewed upon appeal, perhaps giving rise even to an unjust enrichment claim.[32] But in 1962, at least in the federal courts, the Uniform Interstate and International Procedure Act,[33] under Section 4.03 thereof, declared that a court's determination of foreign law is one of law and not of fact and is subject to judicial review on appeal. In 1966 Rule 44.1 of the Federal Rules of Civil Procedure, modeled after that Uniform Act, as amended in 1975, provided that 'a party who intends to raise an issue concerning the law of a foreign country shall give notice in his pleadings or other reasonable written notice. The court, in determining foreign law, may consider any relevant material or source, including testimony, whether or not submitted by a party or admissible, under the Federal Rules of Evidence. The court's determination shall be treated as a ruling on a question of law.' As an aid to that determination of foreign law Rule 44.1 prescribed minimum notice requirements of reliance on foreign law, permits the court to carry out its own independent research into that foreign law, and even suspends the application of the Federal Rules of Evidence on the question of admissibility of evidence of foreign law.[34] The notice requirement is not met when the issue of foreign law was not raised until the appellate level, as in Ruff *v.* St Paul Mercury Insurance Co.[35] Mention of foreign law in a brief was deemed sufficient notice by the Fifth US Court of Appeals in First National City Bank *v.* Compania de Aguaceros SA.[36] Nevertheless, foreign law requires notice to the adversary or at least identification in the pleadings or some other form of notice to withstand a motion to dismiss for failure to state a claim upon which relief can be granted under Rule 12(b)(6) of FRCP.[37]

In Manos *v.* Trans World Airlines[38] the federal district court in Illinois faced the issue of a manufacturer's liability to third parties for manufacturing defective products. The foreign law applicable were certain tort provisions of the Italian Civil Code, and the court entertained the testimony of two expert witnesses on Italian law, reviewed the only treatise available on Italian tort law, and finally adopted the test of causation set forth in Boeing Airplane Co *v.* Brown[39] because one of the experts on Italian law had identified that US case as setting forth a test of causation analogous to that in Italian law!

Before foreign law can be noticed or pleaded, as delineated above, the choice of foreign law must be made by the court. In Morgan Guaranty Trust Co *v.* Garrett[40] the federal district court for the Southern District of New York resolved the question of the choice of law applicable to a fatal airplane crash in New York involving Connecticut and North Carolina decedents. The court opted for the application of New York law because New York law alone implemented 'tort policy goals of deterrence, effective loss distribution over a large segment of society, and rapid compensation of the plaintiffs'.[41] On the other hand, the New York Court of Appeals about the same time in Schultz *v.* Boy Scouts of America, Inc[42] favored the application of New Jersey law because New York had abolished charitable immunity rules and the loss allocation rules in New Jersey favored the parties who were domiciliaries of New Jersey; furthermore, application of 'foreign law'. i.e., New Jersey law here, reduced the opportunity for forum-shopping, rebutted charges of bias on the part of the forum court in favor of its own laws, and brought predictability and consistency to the law.[43]

The Sixth US Court of Appeal in Bennett *v.* Enstrom Helicopter Corp,[44] which involved a fatal helicopter crash in New Zealand, a Michigan helicopter manufacturer, and foreign plaintiffs, applied the foreign law of New Zealand as the exclusive remedy. In the federal district court in Michigan the plaintiffs sought damages under the Michigan Wrongful Death Statute.[45] The court applied the principle that in a diversity case the federal court is required to apply the conflict of laws doctrine of the forum state,[46] and therefore the *lex loci delicti* rule was applicable unless it would be contrary to an announced Michigan public policy; the trial court concluded that the mere fact of manufacture of the helicopter in Michigan was insufficient reason to apply Michigan law. Since the *lex loci delicti* rule was to govern the case the court established the substantive law of New Zealand, and relied upon an affidavit of a former Prime Minister of New Zealand in delineating plaintiffs' exclusive remedy.

In maritime or admiralty tort cases choice of law is an important factor under the doctrine of *forum non conveniens*.[47] Choice of law decisions are subject to *de novo* review under the factors set forth in Lauritzen *v.* Larsen[48] and Hellenic Lines *v.* Rhoditis[49] in which cases the US Supreme Court articulated these factors as influencing choice of law decisions, to wit: the place of the tortious act, the law of the flag, the allegiance or domicile of the injured persons, the allegiance of the vessel owner, the place of the employment contract, the inaccessibility of a foreign forum, the law of the forum, the shipowner's base of operations. But courts have not given full attention to these identified factors, as shown in Chiazor *v.* Transworld Drilling Co[50] where the Fifth US Court of Appeals took a different tack: 'While certain of the eight factors may be substantial in one context, they may be of lesser or importance in another . . . here we are faced with a "vessel" (a submersible drilling rig) that has been permanently stationed off the coast of Nigeria . . . such factors as place of wrongful act, allegiance or domicile of the injured, and place of contract, which may be less substantial in the shipping context, tend to take on added significance under the present circumstances.'[51] The same court the following year in Zekic *v.* Reading & Bates Drilling Co[52] refused to apply US law to a suit by a foreign seaman who was injured aboard a drilling rig in Italian waters while working for a US corporation. Choice of law was a paramount issue in Koke *v.* Phillips Petroleum Co,[53] also decided by the Fifth US Court of Appeals in 1984. Here plaintiffs were British subjects working under foreign contracts of employment who were injured while working as divers aboard a semi-submersible vessel during oil field service operations in the Norwegian sector of the North Sea. Their employers were Swiss and British, respectively, and they sued in the federal district court in Texas under the Jones Act[54] which as of 29 December 1982, barred suits under US law by foreign plaintiffs who are not citizens of the US or resident aliens, if the accident occurred during the 'exploration, development, or production of off-shore mineral or energy resources . . . in the territorial water or waters overlaying the continental shelf of a nation other than the US, its territories or possessions.'[55] This restriction did not apply to the instant plaintiffs because the incidents occurred before the date of the amendment, but the court was undoubtedly mindful of the amendment when it determined that US law did not apply to plaintiffs' claims and entered a conditional order of dismissal on *forum non conveniens* grounds.[56] The district court's order was conditioned on all defendants consenting to jurisdiction in a single appropriate foreign forum, all defendants waiving any defense regarding the statute of limitations, and all defendants consenting to satisfy any judgment rendered in the selected foreign forum. While the federal appellate court affirmed, it did so upon the basis that the conditional dismissal was appealable as a 'final decision' under Section 1291 of Title 28 of US Code.[57]

It should be observed, however, that US courts in general are reluctant to apply foreign law, and indeed the need for a US court to apply foreign law is an appropriate concern on a *forum non conveniens* motion.[58] In the 1986 New York case of National Bank and Trust Co of North America *v.* Banco de Vizcaya, S.A.[58.1] the court observed that

> 'the center of gravity for these transactions was Spain and a New York court would be obligated to apply Spanish law which would govern those claims based on acts and representations which took place in Spain and involved transactions between the Spanish offices of two banks. . . . While not an insurmountable burden for the court, deciphering the applicable Spanish law has hardly been an easy task for these litigants. . . . There is no reason to conclude that the Spanish courts would not entertain this civil suit and that the ultimate relief (would) . . . not (be) obtainable in Spain. Should the Spanish courts reject civil jurisdiction over this matter, the parties may apply to the New York court for appropriate relief.'

Federal District Court Judge John F Keenan in *In Re* Union Carbide Corporation Gas Plant Disaster at Bhopal, India, in December 1984[59] agreed:

'A federal court is bound to apply the choice of law rules of the state in which an action was originally brought ... The "governmental interest" analysis, employed by many jurisdictions, requires a court to look to the question of which state has the most compelling interest in the outcome of the case. India's interest in the outcome of this litigation exceeds America's ... Thus, ... it is likely that Indian law will emerge as the operative law. An Indian court, therefore, would be better able to apply controlling law than would this United States Court, or jury working with it.'[60]

It is evident that choice of law, and in particular the application of foreign law by US courts is a problem unto itself. The federal district court in California in *In Re* Paris Air Crash[61] remarked with tongue in cheek:

'the law on Choice of Law in the various states and in the federal courts is a veritable jungle which if the law can be found out, leads not to a Rule of Action but a reign of chaos dominated in each case by the judge's Informed Guess as to what some other state than the one in which he sits would hold its law to be.'

The action here arose out of a crash in France of a Douglas DC-10 passenger airplane manufactured in California and owned and operated by Turkish Airlines. There were at least five choices of law:
1. the law of California where the alleged acts of negligence in the aircraft manufacture occurred;
2. the law of the domicile of the decedents;
3. the law of the domicile of the surviving claimants;
4. the law of France where the crash occurred; or
5. the law of Japan which was the domicile of a survivor.

The California federal court observed that California specifically takes the 'governmental interests' approach, the objective of which is to determine the law that most appropriately applies to the issues involved and to consider the interests of all the litigants and all the states involved. The court found that California had no interest in the distribution of proceeds to foreign decedents, claimants or survivors, but California was definitely interested in (1) deterring tortious conduct by California defendants; (2) avoiding the imposition of excess financial burdens on California.[62] California law therefore was applicable.

The State of Arizona also flexed its muscle in Weldelken *v.* Superior Court[63] and readily applied Arizona law despite the fact that Mexico was clearly the place of the negligence and the place of the injury of the Arizona-resident plaintiff. The Arizona court held that plaintiff was entitled to be compensated for his injury under Arizona law and not under-compensated under Mexican law. Plaintiff was a widower and resident of Scottsdale, Arizona, and a member of a local organization of which the defendant was also a member; defendant resided in Tucson, Arizona but had a vacation home in Sonora, Mexico. Prior to October 1979 the membership organization invited club members to spend a vacation at defendant's Mexico home; and with two friends plaintiff arrived, only to discover that the Mexican government had shut off all electricity on defendant's property. In the darkness plaintiff fell and suffered a broken hip. He was treated at a local Mexican clinic and then transferred by helicopter to the Tucson, Arizona, hospital for surgery. Plaintiff sued defendant in Arizona seeking US compensation for his injuries, medical expenses and lost earnings. The court found support for its determination to apply *Lex Fori* in Section 145 of Restatement (Second) of Conflicts of Law, which provides that 'the rights and liabilities of the parties with respect to an issue in tort are determined by the local law of the state which, with respect to that issue, has the most significant relationship to the occurrence and the parties . . .' Subsection (2) lists contacts which determine this relationship, as follows: place of injury, place of conduct, domicile, nationality, place of incorporation, place of business of the parties, and the place where the relationship of the parties is centered. The Arizona court then examined the 'most significant relationship' and the issues in question: of the four contacts listed in Section 145(2) above, two clearly attached to Mexico and two obviously attached to Arizona, where both litigants are domiciled, both are American nationals, and defendant had advertised the weekend party in Arizona via an Arizona organization of which both litigants were members, the solicitation to come to Mexico reaching the plaintiff and being accepted by him in Arizona. In short, the 'relationship between the parties' centered in Arizona, according to the court. It should be noted that in Mexico accident victims are allowed to recover under a compensatory system indexed to the prevailing low wages set by Mexican labor law, and therefore accident victims who are not Mexican citizens seek to have any other law applied. In holding that there was little reason to apply the Mexican measure of damages, the Arizona court was buttressed by the Texas decision of Gutierrez *v.* Collins,[64] where the Texas court refused to use the Mexican damages law in an action by one Texas resident against another for injuries in Mexico. Also see Hurtado *v.* Superior Court[65] where two California residents collided in Mexico causing the death of a passenger who was a Mexican citizen. The California court held that defendant, as a non-domiciliary of Mexico, had no basis for invoking the Mexican law on damages because Mexico had no interest in denying full recovery to its residents injured by non-Mexican defendants.

The Arizona court in the Weldelken case (*supra*) stressed the fact that the dispute was a purely private matter between two Arizona residents; neither public accommodations nor public transportation facilities were used; Mexican tourism was not involved; the accident did not occur at a Mexican hotel; and the trip to Mexico was sponsored not by the Mexican government but by a private American citizen from Arizona. While Mexico had a degree of interest in the premises liability imposed upon defendant, based upon his possessory interest in Mexican land, the interest on balance should yield to the superior interests of Arizona, the common domicile of both litigants. Mexico's socialized system of health care with its low wages and low payments simply did not fit into the Arizona relationship between two Arizona residents; the financial accountability of the defendant must be judged by Arizona standards and not by Mexican standards. Defendant 'cannot claim that the imposition of Arizona negligence or damage standards is an unfair surprise. He has offered no indication that he relied in any way on the Mexican limited liability scheme. Rather, he concedes that he purchased liability insurance on his Puerto Penasco property through an Arizona insurance carrier in the amount of $300,000 and obviously relied on the expectation that Arizona insurance would cover any liability resulting from his interest in Mexican land. . . . Having considered fully the relevant factors and interests of both states, we conclude that Arizona has the most significant relationship to this occurrence and these parties.'

Consonant with both *Lex Loci Delicti* and *Lex Fori* rules is the 'interest analysis' approach to the choice of law, and it is the 'interest analysis' approach that has been adopted today by most US courts. In Re Air Crash Disaster at Mannheim, Germany[66] the federal court in Pennsylvania in 1983 observed that 34 foreigners and 12 US citizens (the crew and passengers of the helicopter that crashed) had filed separate suits against the Pennsylvanian helicopter manufacturer, and that therefore varying rules of Choice of Law would undoubtedly apply to these several cases. Accordingly, the court granted defendant's motion to consolidate the cases, and an 'interests analysis' approach determined that Pennsylvania law would govern both the liability issue and the damages issues. (It was no coincidence that compensatory damages were greater under Pennsylvania law than under West German law.)

It should be observed that, ever since Erie Railroad Co *v.* Tompkins,[67] all questions of substantive law must be decided according to State law when the case is in the federal courts. Indeed, federal courts frequently refer questions of State law back to the respective State courts when the State law on the point is unclear. In New York for example, according to Rule 500.17,[68] whenever it appears to the US Supreme Court, to any US Court of Appeals, or to a court of last resort of another State that determinative questions of New York law are involved in a matter pending before it for which there is no controlling precedent of the New York Court of Appeals, such a court may certify the dispositive questions of law to the New York Court of Appeals. In Indiana a certification procedure occurred in Eli Lilly & Co *v.* Home Insurance Co[69] as the District of Columbia Court of Appeals obtained answers on Indiana law from the Indiana Supreme Court.

Section 5. Admiralty Law and the Foreign Plaintiff

The foreign plaintiff like other plaintiffs who suffered damages from a maritime tortfeasor have access to the admiralty jurisdiction of the federal courts as stated in the US Constitution.[70] Torts committed on the high seas, in US maritime waters, or on vessels and aircraft belonging in whole or in part to US citizens, properly belong within the admiralty side of the federal courts.[71] A maritime tort committed within foreign waters means that concurrent jurisdiction with courts of that foreign country whose waters was the scene of the maritime tort will result.[72]

The maritime tort, whether adjudicated in the admiralty side of the federal court or the appropriate state court, involves such defenses as comparative negligence[73] but includes no assumption of the risk,[74] *inter alia*. The standard of care owed to passengers aboard a vessel is that of reasonable care, as illustrated by Rainey *v*. Paquet Cruises, Inc[75] where the Second US Court of Appeals ruled in favor of 'reasonable care under the circumstances' as applicable in passenger cases. The extent to which the circumstances surrounding maritime travel are different from those encountered in daily life and involve more danger to the passenger, will determine how high a degree of care is reasonable in each case.'[76] On the other hand, in Alpert *v*. Zim Lines, Inc,[77] the same court seventeen years earlier favored a 'high degree' of care for passengers injured aboard a vessel. And in 1985 the same court in Blanco *v*. US[78] disappointed the plaintiffs (a Honduran wife and children of the US decedent); the decedent died on the high seas and a negligence claim was asserted against the United States which would ordinarily be liable for injuries suffered by a civilian crew on a bare-boat chartered vessel managed by a civilian shipping company for the United States. But the court found that the vessel was a public vessel[79] so that the reciprocity clause of the Public Vessel Act applied and denied the alien claimants the right to sue the United States since the claimant's country cannot be sued by a US plaintiff. Furthermore, the US treaty with Honduras granting citizens of each country similar rights to sue does not overcome the reciprocity clause.

Punitive damages has long been associated with admiralty cases; it was in the year 1818 in The Amiable Nancy case[80] that the admiralty court first awarded punitive damages in a suit for marine trespass resulting from an act of piracy when armed men from a US brig boarded the ship and helped themselves to her gear, cargo and even the possessions of her crew. Although the US Supreme Court in that case refused to impose punitive damages on the shipowners, it stated that if the suit had been brought against those persons who actually boarded and plundered the ship, punitive damages would have been available under general maritime law.[81] However, it was not until 1966 in Phillip *v*. United States Lines Co[82] that punitive damages in admiralty became a reality. The case of In Re Angela Briley, Inc,[83] decided in 1985 by the federal district court for the Western District of Louisiana resulted in a jury award of $10 million in punitive damages against one tortfeasor and an award of $1 million in punitive damages against the other tortfeasor. In 1962 the US Supreme Court in Vaughan *v*. Atkinson[84] had sanctioned an award of attorneys' fees as an element of punitive damages where the shipowner had refused to provide maintenance and cure, conduct which the court delineated as callous, willful and persistent. But the Second US Court of Appeals in Thyssen, Inc *v*. S S Fortune Star, *et al*[85] in 1985 reversed an award of punitive damages to a shipper against a carrier for an unreasonable deviation from a contract of carriage; punitive damages were not recoverable for a breach of contract unless the conduct constituting the breach was also a tort for which punitive damages are recoverable, as set forth in Section 355 of Restatement (Second) of Contracts. Furthermore, according to the court, the case did not fit within one of the exceptions to the general rule prohibiting an award of punitive damages in actions for breach of contract, to wit: 'conduct reflecting vindictiveness and individual humiliation'.[86]

The federal district court case of Laker Airways, Ltd *v.* Pan American World Airways, Inc[87] involved the right of foreign citizens to petition their government for redress of grievances. Here the British airline filed suit against four US airlines and eight foreign airlines including two British airlines, alleging violations of US antitrust laws and a conspiracy to monopolize air travel between New York and Great Britain as well as to drive the foreign plaintiff out of business. Plaintiff also sought to restrain the two British defendants from petitioning the British government for legislation prohibiting plaintiff from pursuing this law suit. The court denied plaintiff's motion, holding that, although it had the authority to enjoin the defendants from petitioning the British government in order to protect the US jurisdiction, the court should refrain from exercising that power in light of the significant interest of Great Britain in the political rights of its subjects. It should be noted that the two British defendants had earlier succeeded in obtaining an injunction from the British High Court of justice prohibiting plaintiff from taking any further steps to prosecute its claim against them in US courts.[88] The federal district court, however, did grant the request of the foreign plaintiff to enjoin the remaining defendants from taking any action 'in a foreign court or otherwise' that would interfere with the foreign plaintiff's prosecution of its claims or the court's jurisdiction to adjudicate those claims.[89] In the meantime the British Court of Appeal issued a permanent injunction prohibiting plaintiff from filing papers with the US federal district court and ordering plaintiff to dismiss the action against the British defendants;[90] but the English House of Lords[91] dissolved the injunction. The federal district court, insofar as the British defendants were concerned, agreed with the British defendants that 'a United States tribunal is (not) compelled by the First Amendment to protect an alien's desire to speak in a foreign country or to petition the governmental authorities of a foreign nation'.[92] But in Huang *v.* Sentinel Government Securities[92.1] the Second US Court of Appeals in 1987 rejected attempts to obtain jurisdiction over an English corporation based upon several transatlantic telephone calls and upon a visit by the English company's chief financial officer to New York! The court expressly found that the English company did not 'purposefully avail itself of the privilege of conducting activities within the forum.'

It is obvious that products liability has had an impact on admiralty law, and vice versa.[93] Where state courts have not provided plaintiffs with the benefits of Strict Liability, Comparative Negligence, and similar liberal doctrines, some plaintiffs resort to the device of seeking to apply maritime law to their product liability situation. It was not until 1972 in Executive Jet Aviation, Inc *v.* Cleveland[94] that the US Supreme Court added the requirement of another *nexus* (besides the existing *situs* test), to wit: the tort must 'bear a significant relationship to traditional maritime activity'.[95] Yet in Foremost Insurance Co *v.* Richardson[96] in 1982 the same court opined that pleasure craft are not automatically excluded from an admiralty action. Indeed, this *nexus* of a traditional maritime activity involves an evaluation of the functions and roles of the parties, the types of vehicles and instrumentalities involved, the causation and type of injury, as recognition of the traditional concepts of the thrust of admiralty law.[97] In Sperry Rand Corp *v*. Radio Corporation of America[98] plaintiff sought recovery from the component manufacturer of a gyro in a ship's autopilot system; when the gyro failed due to a defect in the product, the ship left the channel and ran aground, causing property damages and personal injuries. The court found the necessary *nexus* to invoke admiralty, to wit: the defective component manufactured by the defendant was in the ship's navigation system, and the result of the tort was a traditional maritime casualty. It was in Oman *v*. Johns-Manville Corp[99] that the Fifth US Court of Appeals spelled out the traditional maritime activity *nexus:* 'When a collision occurs of a ship founders at sea, the law of admiralty looks to those rules to determine fault, liability, and all other questions that may arise from such a catastrophe. Through long experience the law of the sea knows how to determine whether a particular ship is seaworthy. . . .'

The US Supreme Court in two 1986 decisions spelled out answers to such questions as to whether a plaintiff may win and admiralty suit for products liability based solely on harm to the defective product and whether a State tort law may be applied to an accident that occurs on the high seas. In both instances the answer was 'no'. In the former instance, East River Steamship Co *v*. Transamerican Delavel Co[100] the highest court stated that admiralty law does embrace strict liability, but a case involving only economic injury to the product itself rather than injury to a person or to other property, falls within the realm of contract and warranty and not tort law. In the latter instance, Offshore Logistics Co *v*. Tallentire[101] the widows of two oil platform workers sued a transport company after one of the company's helicopters crashed into the sea while on its way to an oil-drilling platform 35 miles off the coast of Louisiana. Under the Death on the High Seas Act[102] the widows were entitled to recover for economic losses; but they also sued under Louisiana law for loss of consortium and other non-economic damages; the court simply stated that federal law pre-empts application of state law beyond the state's own territorial waters.

Invoking admiralty jurisdiction in a products liability situation generally works to the advantage of the plaintiff consumer for a variety of reasons, to wit: applicability of comparative negligence in a jurisdiction which does not follow comparative negligence; the all-encompassing maritime lien; and the doctrine of laches, *inter alia*. But the product claim must bear a significant relationship to traditional maritime activity, as delineated in Harville *v*. Johns-Manville Products Corp,[103] where the court stated that admiralty jurisdiction will not exist where land-based trades were applied on a ship and the plaintiff was injured by a product of such land-based trades. The point is that these trades were not unique to maritime service or the traditional work done by seamen.

Notes

1. —AD2d—(20 May 1986).
2. *See* generally Leflar, American Conflicts Law, Par 85.
3. *See* Chapter 4, Section 1, herein.
4. 63 NJ 130, 305 A2d 412 (1973).
5. *See* Henry *v.* Richardson-Merrell, Inc, 508 F2d 28 (3rd Cir, 1975).
6. *See* Thornton *v.* Mono Mfg Co, 99 Ill App3d 722, 425 NE2d 522 (1981) and Dague *v.* Piper Aircraft Corp, 418 NE2d 207 (Ind, 1981). In Costello *v.* Unarco Industries, Inc, 490 NE2d 675 (Ill, 1986) the Illinois Supreme Court ruled that a cause of action that is discovered after the enactment of a statute of repose but is based on occurrences sufficiently predating enactment so as to render the claim extinguished under the terms of the statute, will *not* be terminated on the effective date of the statute of repose but will continue until the party has had a reasonable period of time within which to preserve his claim by filing suit. The case involved asbestos products which allegedly caused the wrongful death from mesothelioma.
7. 766 F2d 1102 (7th Cir, 1985).
8. —Cal App3d—(1985).
9. *Supra* note 7.
10. *Supra* note 8.
11. Note Anthony *v.* Abbott Laboratories, 489 A2d 43 (RI, 1985) where the Rhode Island court held that the statute of limitations begins to run in a drug liability case when a plaintiff discovers or with reasonable diligence should have discovered, the wrongful conduct of the product manufacturer.
12. 485 NYS2d 532 (1985).
13. 28 USC 1331 (1).
14. 774 F2d 1577 (3rd Cir, 1985).
15. *See* T'Kach *v.* US, 242 F2d 937 (5th Cir, 1957).
16. *See* Pub L 93–595, 88 Stat 1926 (1975).
17. *See* Northwestern Mutual Life Insurance Co *v.* Linard, 57 FRD 552 (SDNY, 1972) which admitted into evidence a maritime accident investigation report prepared by a Liberian official following an official proceeding under authority of Liberian law.
18. 443 F Supp 1064 (EDPa, 1977).
19. *See* Palmer *v.* Hoffman, 318 US 109, 63 S Ct 477 (1943).
20. *See* generally 42 Iowa L Rev 363 (1957).
21. *See* Franklin *v.* Skelly Oil Co, 141 F2d 568 (10th Cir, 1944).
22. 580 F2d 1179 (3rd Cir, 1978).
23. *See* Baker *v.* Elcona Homes Corp, 588 F2d 551 (6th Cir, 1978).
24. 518 F Supp 1387 (ND Ill, 1981).
25. 705 F2d 624 (2nd Cir, 1983), cert den 104 S Ct 243 (1984).
26. *Supra* note 25 at p. 633.
27. 432 F Supp 329 (SDNY, 1977).
28. 567 F Supp 59 (SDNY, 1983).
29. *Id*, at pp. 61 and 62. Note Rule 44(a)(2) of FRCP which reads:

   '*Proof of Official Record*
   (a) *Authentication*
   (2) *Foreign.* A foreign official record, or an entry therein, when

admissible for any purpose, may be evidenced by an official publication thereof; or a copy thereof, attested by a person authorized to make the attestation, and accompanied by a final certification as to the genuineness of the signature and official position (i) of the attesting person, or (ii) of any foreign official whose certification of genuineness of signature and official position relates to the attestation or is in a chain of certificates of genuineness of signature and official position relating to the attestation. A final certification may be made by a secretary of embassy or legation, consul general, consul, vice consul, or consular agent of the United States, or a diplomatic or consular official of the foreign country assigned or accredited to the United States. If reasonable opportunity has been given to all parties to investigate the authenticity and accuracy of the documents, the court may, for good cause shown, (i) admit an attested copy without final certification or (ii) permit the foreign official record to be evidenced by an attested summary with or without a final certification.'

29.1 2 WLR 81 HL (1978).
30. 5 US (1 Cranch) 1, 38 (1801).
31. *See* 7 Hastings Internat and Com P (1983) at pp. 137 *et seq*.
32. Section 46(c) of Restatement of Restitution.
33. 3 ULA 459 (1980).
34. *See* 20 Am J Comp L 470 (1978).
35. 393 F2d 500 (2nd Cir, 1968) at p. 502.
36. 398 F2d 779 (5th Cir, 1968).
37. *Cf.* Grice *v.* A/S J Ludwig Mowinckels, 477 F Supp 365 (SD Ala, 1979).
38. 324 F Supp 470 (ND Ill, 1971).
39. 291 F2d 310 (9th Cir, 1961).
40. 625 F Supp 752 (SDNY, 1986).
41. *Id.* at p. 755.
42. 65 NY2d 189 (1985).
43. *Supra* note 40 at pp. 758–759.
44. 679 F2d 630 (6th Cir, 1982).
45. Mich Com P Laws Ann Section 600 2922 (1982).
46. *See* Klaxon *v.* Stentor Electric Manufacturing Co.
47. *See* Chapter 4, Section 2, herein.
48. 345 US 571 (1953).
49. 398 US 306 (1970).
50. 648 F2d 1015 (5th Cir, 1981, cert den 455 US 1019 (1982).
51. *Id.* at pp. 1018–1019.
52. 680 F2d 1107 (5th Cir, 1982).
53. 730 F2d 211 (5th Cir, 1984).
54. 46 USC 688.
55. In essence the 1982 amendment allows suit to be brought under US law only where no remedy is available 'under the laws of the nation asserting jurisdiction over the area in which the incident occurred, or under the laws of the nation in which, at the time of the incident, the person for whose injury or death a remedy is sought maintained citizenship or residency.
56. *See* Chapter 4, Section 2, herein.
57. 28 USC § 1291 (1982) provides:

'The courts of appeals . . . shall have jurisdiction of appeals from all final decisions of the district courts of the United States, the United States District Court for the District of the Canal Zone, the District Court of Guam, and the District Court of the Virgin Islands, except where direct review may be had in the Supreme Court. The jurisdiction of the United States Court of Appeals for the Federal Circuit shall be limited to the jurisdiction described in sections 1292(c) and (d) and 1295 of this title.'

58. *See* Gulf Oil Corp *v*. Gilbert, 330 US 501 (1947) and Piper Aircraft Co *v*. Reyno, 454 US 235 (1981).
58.1 —NYSnd— (3 Oct 1986).
59. MDL No 626, SDNY, 12 May 1986.
60. *See also* Van Dusen *v*. Banack, 376 US 612 (1964) at p. 639.
61. 399 F Supp 732 (1975).
62. Note Section 6 of Restatement (Second) of Conflict of Laws delineates 'Choice of Law Principles' in these terms:—

'1. A court, subject to constitutional restrictions, will follow a statutory directive of its own state on choice of law.
2. When there is no such directive, the factors relevant to the choice of the applicable rule of law include:
(a) the needs of the interstate and international systems;
(b) the relevant policies of the forum;
(c) the relevant policies of other interested states and the relative interests of those states in the determination of the particular issue;
(d) the protection of justified expectations;
(e) the basic policies underlying the particular field of law;
(f) certainty, predictability, and uniformity of result; and
(g) ease in the determination and application of the law to be applied.'

And Section 145 sets forth the general principles:—

'1. The rights and liabilities of the parties with respect to an issue in tort are determined by the local law of the state which, with respect to that issue, has the most significant relationship to the occurrence and the parties under the principles stated in Section 6;
2. contacts to be taken into account in applying the principles of Section 6 to determine the law applicable to an issue includes:
(a) the place where the injury occurred;
(b) the place where the conduct causing the injury occurred;
(c) the relevant policies of other interested states and the relative interests of those states in the determination of the particular issue;
(d) the protection of justified expectations;
(e) the basic policies underlying the particular field of law;
(f) certainty, predictability, and uniformity of result; and
(g) ease in the determination and application of the law to be applied'.

63. 671 P2d 896 (Ariz, 1983).
64. 583 SW2d 312 (Texas 1979).
65. 522 P2d 666 (Cal, 1974).
66. 575 F Supp 521 (Pa, 1980).

67. 304 US 64 (1938).
68. Effective 1 January 1986; 1985 amendment to Section 3 of Article VI of the New York State Constitution; *see* 22 NYCRR §500.17.
69. 764 F2d 876 (DC Cir, 1985).
70. *See* 18 USC 7 with respect to maritime crimes.
71. *Id.*
72. For maritime crimes generally, *see* United States *v.* Flores, 289 US 137 (1933).
73. *See* Pope & Talbot *v.* Hawn, 346 US 406 (1953).
74. *See* Movible Offshore Co *v.* Ousley, 346 F2d 870.
75. 709 F2d 169 (2nd Cir, 1983).
76. *Id.*
77. 370 F2d 115 (2nd Cir, 1966).
78. 775 F2d 53 (2nd Cir, 1985).
79. *See* Barrie *v.* US, 615 F2d 829 (9th Cir, 1980).
80. 16 US (3 Wheat) 546 (1818).
81. *See generally* Trial Magazine (Feb 1986) at pp. 22 *et seq.*
82. 355 F2d 25 (3rd Cir, 1966).
83. —F Supp—(WD La, 1985).
84. 82 S Ct 997 (1962).
85. —F2d—(2nd Cir, 1985); for lower court, *see* 596 F Supp 865 (SDNY, 1985).
86. *Id.*
87. 604 F Supp 280 (DC, 1984).
88. *See* 79 Am J Internat L (1985) at pp. 1069 *et seq.*
89. *Supra* note 18 at p. 288.
90. British Airways Board *v.* Laker Airways, Ltd, 3 WLR 544 (CA).
91. 3 WLR 413 (HL).
92. *Supra* note 87 at p. 287. In Arkon Shipping Agency Inc *v.* Kassapas, 485 So2d 565 (La, 1986) plaintiffs were the survivors of two Greek crew members who died in an accident in a Soviet harbor aboard a Greek ship owned by a Liberian corporation. It was in New York that the ship agency negotiated the charters for the ship owner and maintained the owner's bank account. The suit was brought in the federal district court in New York, but was dismissed on the basis of *forum non conveniens;* the court cited the nationality of the foreign ship owners and the foreign locale of the accident as well as the fact that the ship owners' contacts with New York were 'far too insubstantial'. While the appeal was pending, the ship itself on the Mississippi River was attached under Louisiana law; a motion for dismissal was granted under *forum non conveniens*, but later reversed by the Fifth US Court of Appeals which held that *forum non conveniens* was merely procedural and Louisiana was not bound by that doctrine. See —F2d—(5th Cir, 1986).

92.1 —F2d— (2nd Cir, 1987).

93. *See* For The Defense Magazine (June 1986) at pp. 10 *et seq.*
94. 409 US 249 (1972).
95. *Id.* at p. 268.
96. 457 US 668 (1982).
97. *See* Kelly *v.* Smith, 485 F2d 520 (5th Cir, 1973).
98. 618 F2d 319 (5th Cir, 1980).
99. 764 F2d 27 (5th Cir, 1985).
100. —US—(1986).
101. —US—(1986); for lower court opinion, *see* F2d/274 (5th Cir, 1985).
102. 46 USC 761 *et seq.*
103. 731 F2d 775 (11th Cir, 1984).

Chapter 8. Recognition and Enforcement of Foreign Judgments in US Courts

Section 1. Factors in US Court Recognition of Foreign Judgments

To the best interests of the foreign plaintiff, US courts will generally recognize foreign judgments based upon international comity, upon decisional law and statutes, and upon treaties and other international agreements. Some of the relevant factors for recognition of foreign judgments include the following: (a) absence of fraud;[1] (b) not in violation of US policy;[2] (c) not in violation of treaty or international agreement;[3] (d) full reciprocity with the foreign country;[4] (e) not *res judicata* nor collateral estoppel;[5] (f) adequacy of notice to the adverse party;[6] and (g) finality of the judgment.[7]

The fraud which defeats recognition of the foreign judgment must be more than 'intrinsic' such as fraud in the transaction or in the trial itself. The fraud must be 'extrinsic' by depriving the losing party of the opportunity to present his claim or his defense. Extrinsic fraud must be shown by clear and convincing evidence if US courts are to deny recognition to the foreign judgment.[8]

Foreign judgments that violate US policy are not enforceable in US courts.[9] Unfortunately, the definition of 'violation of US policy' is ambiguous; even the Uniform Foreign Money Judgments Recognition Act,[10] while recognizing the defense of 'public policy' does not delineate which 'public policies' will require a US court to refuse to recognize the foreign judgment.[11] In Somportex, Ltd *v.* Philadelphia Chewing Gum Corp[12] the Third US Court of Appeals stated that a foreign judgment must be injurious to public health, public morals, or public confidence or must undermine the public's sense of security for individual rights, before a US court will refuse to accord recognition to a foreign judgment.

Lack of reciprocity is another ground for refusal of US court to recognize foreign judgments. The US Supreme Court in Hilton *v.* Guyot[13] first adopted in the year 1895 the requirement of reciprocity, but the court did not state that lack of reciprocity would be dispositive of the issue; if the foreign judgment is based upon *in rem* or *quasi in rem* jurisdiction, or when the foreign judgment affects the status of persons, or when the foreign judgment is between citizens of foreign countries, or when the foreign judgment is in favor of a US citizen, the US court might recognize the foreign judgment.[14] The reasoning behind such an exception to lack of reciprocity is the keen desire even in US courts to terminate litigation and reduce the expense of the litigating parties.[15] On the other hand, some US courts have outright rejected the reciprocity defense;[16] in 1964 the US Supreme Court declined in Banco Nacional de Cuba *v.* Sabbatino[17] to require that the foreign state, whose judgment was up for recognition by the US court, extend to the United States standing to sue in its courts before the foreign plaintiff could sue in US courts. The Uniform Foreign Money Judgments Recognition Act[18] does not make reciprocity a precondition for recognition of foreign judgments. Lack of reciprocity is said to be consonant with a distrust of a foreign country's political and economic motives and this distrust is intensified between the developing countries and the developed countries, in part due to the history of exploitive colonial relationships and in part due to current poverty and economic disparities in the developing country; distrust extends readily to judicial proceedings.[19] The Calvo Clause in Venezuela[20] is but one example of that distrust: contracting parties in Venezuela are required to submit to local jurisdiction only and to waive all other judicial recourse in any court other than local Venezuelan courts.

The defenses of *res judicata* and collateral estoppel are based upon public policy discouraging repetitious litigation and bringing to a just end litigation generally. *Res judicata* is applicable when there is an identity of parties in both litigations; *res judicata* serves to preclude not only litigation of issues actually raised and determined in prior litigation, but also preclude issues that could have been raised but were nevertheless determined in the prior litigation. US courts have readily accepted the defense of *res judicata* to deny recognition to foreign judgments.[21] Similarly collateral estoppel precludes relitigation by holding that ultimate facts necessarily determined in a foreign judgment are dispositive of the issue.[22]

Recognition of a foreign judgment may have great impact upon the foreign relations of the United States in terms of rewarding friends and encouraging unfriendly countries to become more friendly. In Ackerman *v.* Levine[23] the Second US Court of Appeals ruled that the recognition and enforcement of the West German default judgment did not violate New York public policy to the 'extent that the judgment reflects an award of attorney's fees for which the attorney presented in the enforcement proceedings, at a minimum, evidence of client authorization and appropriate work product'. Service of process in the United States by registered mail satisfied The Hague Convention on Service Abroad of Judicial and Extrajudicial Documents in Civil or Commercial Matters.[24] The United States and the United Kingdom echoed their sentiments on recognition of judgments in a Convention on Recognition and Enforcement of Judgments signed by both countries on 26 October 1976, but the document itself is ambiguous and leaves much to be desired.[25]

Registration of foreign judgments in federal courts is provided by 28 USC 1963 which states: 'A judgment in an action for the recovery of money or property now or hereafter entered in any district court which has become final by appeal or expiration of time for appeal may be registered in any other district court by filing a certified copy of such judgment. A judgment so registered shall have the same effect as a judgment of the district court of the district where registered and may be enforced in like manner.' Section 1963A enacted in 1980 authorizes registration in US district courts of money or property judgments obtained in the Court of International Trade, in language almost identical to that of Section 1963.[26]

Sections 491 through 496 of the Restatement of Foreign Relations Law of the United States (Revised, 1983) delineate recognition and enforcement of foreign country judgments and arbitral awards.[26.1] The basic rule is found in Section 491(1): 'Except as provided in Section 492, a final judgment of a court of a foreign state granting or denying recovery of a sum of money, establishing or confirming the status of a person, or determining interests in property, is conclusive between the parties, and is entitled to recognition in the courts of the United States.' Comment b. to this Section defines recognition as arising 'in a context other than enforcement, for example, if the defendant seeks to rely on a prior adjudication of a controversy (*res judicata*),[26.2] or if either side seeks to rely on prior determination of an issue of fact or law relevant to an action pending in the forum.' Comment c. to this Section explains the significance of 'recognition', to wit:

> The authority and effectiveness of a foreign judgment entitled to recognition by courts in the United States is, generally, the same as that of a judgment of the courts of one State of the United States in the courts of another State. Normally the foreign judgment has no greater effectiveness in the state of recognition than it has in the state where the judgment was rendered. . . . However, no rule prevents a court in the recognizing state from giving greater preclusive effect to a judgment than would be given in the courts of the rendering state.

It would appear that the law of the country rendering the judgment determines the preclusive effect to be given to the foreign judgment in the courts of the US.[26.3] But many courts in the US take the opposite view, namely, that foreign country judgments should be accorded the same preclusive effects as domestic judgments,[26.4] and that the failure of the foreign country rendering the judgment to give the same preclusive effect is of no significance.[26.5] Still other courts in the US have applied American standards of preclusive effect without any reference to the 'choice of law' question.[26.6] The authors von Mehren and Trautman in a 1968 Harvard Law Review article[26.7] analyzed the problem of foreign judgment recognition as involving at least five policy bases, to wit:

> '[1] a desire to avoid the duplication of effort and consequent waste involved in reconsidering a matter that has already been litigated; [2] a related concern to protect the successful litigant, whether plaintiff or defendant, from harassing or evasive tactics on the part of his previously unsuccessful opponent; [3] a policy against making the availability of local enforcement the decisive element, as a practical matter, in the plaintiff's choice of forum; [4] an interest in fostering stability and unity in an international order in which many aspects of life are not confined to any single jurisdiction; and [5] in certain classes

of cases, a belief that the rendering jurisdiction is a more appropriate forum than the recognizing jurisdiction, either because the former was more convenient or because as the predominantly concerned jurisdiction or for some other reason its views as to the merits should prevail.[26.8]

Thus, the policy bases for recognition of foreign state judgments is unsettled, to say the least.

Section 2. Uniform Foreign Money Judgments Recognition Act

The Uniform Foreign Money Judgments Act (1962),[27] which is in force in many States including California, Colorado, New York, Illinois, Maryland, Alaska, Massachusettes, Michigan, Oklahoma, Oregon and Washington, is a boon to the foreign plaintiff suing in US courts since the Act applies to any foreign judgment that is final and conclusive and enforceable where rendered.[28] Section 1 of the Act defines both 'foreign judgment' and 'foreign state': 'foreign judgment' is 'any judgment of a foreign state granting or denying recovery of a sum of money, other than a judgment of taxes, a fine or other penalty, or a judgment for support in matrimonial or family matters'. 'Foreign state' refers to any state other than the United States, its territories or possessions; US judgments are accorded recognition under the Full Faith and Credit Clause of the US Constitution,[29] which does not apply to judgments rendered by foreign courts.[30] Section 2 of the Act requires, as indicated above,[31] that the foreign judgment be 'final and conclusive and enforceable where rendered even though an appeal therefrom is pending or is subject to appeal'; in Island Territory of Curacao *v.* Solitron Devices, Inc[32] the New York federal court opined that the judgment was final even though the Curacaon judgment was left open to either party to demand further arbitration and possibly to obtain further and more extensive damages. Section 4 of the Act delineates under subparagraph (a) that a foreign judgment is not conslusive if '(1) the judgment was rendered under a system which does not provide impartial tribunals or procedures compatible with the requirements of due process of law; (2) the foreign court did not have personal jurisdiction over the defendant; or (3) the foreign court did not have jurisdiction over the subjectmatter.' And Section 4, subparagraph (b) prescribes that a foreign judgment need not be recognized if

'1. the defendant in the proceedings in the foreign court did not receive notice of the proceedings in sufficient time to enable him to defend;
2. the judgment was obtained by fraud;
3. the cause of action or claim for relief on which the judgment is based is repugnant to the public policy of this state;
4. the judgment conflicts with another final and conclusive judgment;

5. the proceeding in the foreign court was contrary to an agreement between the parties under which the dispute in question was to be settled otherwise than by proceedings in that court; or
6. in the case of jurisdiction based only on personal service, the foreign court was a seriously inconvenient forum for the trial of the action.'

Under Section 6 of the Act the court may stay proceedings until an appeal has been determined 'or until the expiration of a period of time sufficient to enable the defendant to prosecute the appeal'. On pragmatic grounds foreign money judgments cannot be enforced in the US without first being translated from the foreign currency into US dollars; a court clerk simply cannot register the foreign judgment and translate it into domestic currency without statutory guidelines or an order of the court.

Section 3. Recognition and Enforcement of Foreign Judgments by the States

The US Constitution under Article IV, Section 1, requires each state to give full faith and credit to the public acts, records and judicial proceedings of every other state; but this constitutional mandate does not give any right, privilege or immunity to judgments of courts of foreign countries.[33] Some state courts have readily responded, however, by recognizing and enforcing the foreign judgment.[34] But it can be argued, as did the court in Zschernig *v.* Miller,[35] that state courts are improperly intruding into the field of foreign affairs but the basic requirements to be met by the state were set forth in the 1895 decision of the US Supreme Court in Hilton *v.* Guyot:[36] 'When an action is brought in a court of this country, by a citizen of a foreign country against one of our own citizens, to recover a sum of money adjudged by a court of that country to be due from the defendant to the plaintiff, and the foreign judgment appears to have been rendered by a competent court having jurisdiction of the cause and of the parties, and upon due allegations and proofs and opportunity to defend against them, and its proceedings are according to the course of a civilized jurisprudence, and are stated in a clear and formal record, the judgment is *prima facie* evidence, at least, of the truth of the matter adjudged . . .' State courts have risen to the occasion, and readily recognized and enforced foreign judgments.[37]

Comity is nothing more than respect for the determinations or decisions of another state or another country under their judicial system. Founded on convenience and utility Comity can render the forum appropriate or inappropriate.[38] Comity may suggest the dismissal of a case where vital national interests of a foreign sovereign, for example, are involved.[39] Other factors that state and federal courts consider in observing or not observing Comity were set forth in Grodinsky *v.* State:[40]

a. the degree of conflict of US state or federal law with the foreign law;
b. the nationality of the parties;

c. the relative importance of the alleged violation of conduct here compared to that abroad;
d. the availability of a remedy abroad and the pendency of litigation here;
e. the existence of intent to harm or adversely affect US trade or commerce, and the foreseeability of such intent;
f. the possible effects upon foreign relations if the court exercises jurisdiction and grants the relief requested;
g. whether the winning party will be forced to perform an act which is illegal in the foreign country or in conflict with public policy of the foreign country;
h. the ability of the court to make its order effective;
i. whether an order for relief would be acceptable in the US if made by a foreign nation under similar circumstances; and
j. whether a treaty with thc affected foreign country has addressed the issue.

Section 4. Denial of Enforcement of Foreign Country Injunction

The case of Pilkington Bros *v.* AFG Industries, Inc[41] involved a federal court in Delaware that was requested to issue a preliminary injunction duplicative of an *ex parte* interim injunction issued by a court of Great Britain.[42] The court applied Delaware law and the general principles of international comity, and denied the request. Plaintiff, a British company, had licensed the predecessor of the defendant Delaware corporation in technology involved in making 'float glass', a type of flat glass;[43] under the licensing agreements any disputes were to be arbitrated in London in accordance with English law. When plaintiff saw evidence that defendant was about to disclose the 'float glass' technology to a Portuguese company, plaintiff requested in England an interim injunction from the High Court of Justice, Queens Bench Division, Commercial Court, pursuant to England's Arbitration Act.[44] At a hearing defendant did not appear, although notified of the hearing, and the English court entered a detailed *ex parte* order restraining defendant from taking any action that could possibly lead to an exposure of 'float glass' technology covered by the license agreements. Shortly thereafter the British plaintiff sought a temporary restraining order from the federal district court in Delaware, but the US court held that plaintiff had failed to demonstrate irreparable injury and therefore was not entitled to issuance of a temporary restraining order. Plaintiff then requested the federal district court to 'duplicate a foreign interim injunction, without reference to the underlying dispute, where there are ongoing and continuous violations of that foreign injunction.' Again the federal district court denied plaintiff's request, basing its decision upon its belief that to do so would 'offend, rather than promote, principles of international comity'.[45] Issuance of a duplicative interim injunction would interfere unnecessarily with the English proceedings, and therefore the court granted summary judgment for the US defendant, preferring not to decide whether a lack of sufficient means of enforcement in a jurisdiction of a party's choice could entitle that party to a duplicative interim injunction in another jurisdiction.

It would appear that the federal district court exaggerated the danger of interfering with the English proceedings; the English injunction was a final judgment in the sense that it was 'not subject to additional proceedings in the rendering court other than execution'[46] and under Section 98 of Restatement (Second) of Conflict of Laws a 'valid judgment rendered in a foreign nation after a trial in a contested proceeding will be recognized in the United States so far as the immediate parties and the underlying cause of action are concerned.' Admittedly the English proceeding followed a default by the US defendant and lacked a trial connotation; but the clear trend in US decisions is an increased willingness of US courts to recognize and enforce foreign judgments, final or not final, absent evidence of collusion or extrinsic fraud, default judgments being given the same effect as judgments arrived at following plenary proceedings.[47]

Notes

1. *See* Section 4(b)(2) of the Uniform Act, *supra* note 27.
2. *See* Stern *v.* Siegal, 377 NYS2d 580 (1975) for discussion of the public policy of a State of the United States.
3. *See* Somportex, Ltd *v.* Philadelphia Chewing Gum Corp, 453 F2d (3rd Cir, 1971), cert den 405 US 1017 (1972).
4. *See* Hilton *v.* Guyot, 159 US 113 (1895).
5. *See* Leo Fiest, Inc *v.* Delmar Publishing Co, 232 F Supp 623 (ED Pa, 1964).
6. *See* the Due Process Clause of the US Constitution.
7. Section 1915 of the California Code of Civil Procedure, for example, allows recognition of foreign judgments if the judgment is indeed 'final', if it has been rendered by a tribunal of that state and if the foreign tribunal has jurisdiction over the parties according to its own laws.
8. *Supra* note 4.
9. *See* Zanzonico *v.* Neeld, 17 NJ 400, 111 A2d 772 (1955).
10. Section 2 herein.
11. Section 4 of the Uniform Act in Section 2 herein.
12. *Supra* note 3.
13. *Supra* note 4.
14. *See generally* 50 Columbia L Rev 791 (1950).
15. In the Somportex case, *supra* note 3, the court pointed out that the Comity of the US does not require it to give conclusive effect to the judgments of French courts; and that the ground for this determination is the lack of reciprocity on the part of France. The defendants offered to prove that the courts of France gave no force and no effect to judgments duly rendered by US courts. Accordingly, the court ruled that the French judgment was not recognizable and not enforceable due to lack of reciprocity.

16. Nicol *v*. Tanner, 256 NW2d 796, 801 (Minn 1976).
17. 376 US 398 (1964).
18. Section 2 herein.
19. *See generally* 11 Georgia J Internat & Comp L 638 (1891).
20. The Calvo Doctrine in essence requires an absolute waiver of foreign redress for aliens and alien corporations. See Friedman, 'The Changing Structure of International Arbitration Conventions; The Quandry of Non-Ratification', in 17 Harv Internat L J 131 (1976).
21. *See* Sangiovanni Hernandez *v*. Dominicana de Aviacion, 556 F2d 611 (1st Cir, 1977) and Cardy *v*. Cardy, 23 AD2d 117, 258 NYS2d 955 (1965).
22. *See* Bata *v*. Bata, 163 A2d 493 (Del, 1960), cert den 366 US 964 (1961).
23.—F2d—(2nd Cir, 1986).
24. 20 UST 361, TIAS No 6638.
25. The original draft had stated in Article 10 j that, in an action to recover damages for physical injuries or for damage to tangible property, the acts or omissions that occasioned the injury or damage must have substantially occurred, and the injury or damage must have been suffered, *within* the state in which the court of origin was exercising jurisdiction. Article 9 of the original draft stated that, except as permitted by the Convention, there should be no review of the judgment given by the court of origin, and recognition and enforcement should not be refused for the reason that the court of origin reached a different result from that which would have been reached by application of the law selected in accordance with the rules of international law applicable to the court addressed. The original draft proposed that the US judgment should be recognized and enforced without 'trial *de novo*' in English courts, although recognition of US judgments 'to the extent that they are for punitive or multiple damages' are denied. Article 4 delineates the many conditions necessary for recognition and enforcement of judgments, but amended Article 12 states that the court addressed shall not be bound by any conclusions of law reached by the court of origin. *See* 16 ILM 71 (1977).
26. The enforcement and recognition of foreign judgments is said to involve what is known as 'competence indirecte' or indirect jurisdiction, and it is this term which is the principal component of a decision to recognize and to enforce a foreign judgment, i.e., the determination that the foreign court had jurisdiction over the person of the defendant and the subject matter of the suit at the time of the commencement of the proceedings. On the other hand, it is the component, 'competence directe', which consists of the conditions under which courts will assume jurisdiction of cases which are brought before them for decision on the merits. *See generally* Delaume, American-French Private International Law 160 (2nd edn, 1961).

    But 'competence indirecte' need not be grounded necessarily on the elements of jurisdiction which would lead a court to take jurisdiction under its own national law to decide a similar case on the merits. There is also 'jurisdiction in the international sense'. [*See* von Mehren & Trautman, The Law of Multistate Problems 589 (1965)] which covers all situations in which a forum is prepared to entertain litigation involving non-national elements, even if other states will not recognize the judgment. The Hague Conference on Private International Law endeavored in a treaty to establish among different states common agreement on assuming jurisdiction over cases ('competence directe') in the absence of a choice of court agreement between the parties. Both of these conventions involved children, where in the interest of children a noble effort was made to reach agreement on the grounds of jurisdiction, the applicable law, and on recognition of judgments. What has been disappointing is the few states that have become signatories of these conventions on children. See, for example, Convention on Jurisdiction, Applicable Law and Recognition of Decrees Relating to Adoption, 15 November 1965, 2 Actes et Documents de la Dixieme Session de la Conference de la Haye de Droit International Prive 399 (1965).

26.1 *See generally* 70 Iowa L Rev 53 (1984).

26.2 *See* W. Freedman, Res Judicata and Collateral Estoppel (Quorum Books, 1987). *Note also* leading articles in 50 Columbia L Rev 783 (1950), 13 Houston L Rev 680 (1976); 24 Ohio St L J 291 (1963); 57 Oregon L Rev 377 (1978); and 72 Columbia L Rev 220 (1972).

26.3 *See* Bata *v.* Bata, 163 A2d 493 (Del Ch., 1960) and Schoenbrod *v.* Sieglar, 20 NY2d 403, 230 NE2d 638 (1967).

26.4 *See* Compagnie du Port de Rio de Janeiro *v.* Mead Morrison Manufacturing Co, 19 F2d 163 (Maine, 1927); Cannistraro *v.* Cannistraro, 223 NE2d 692 (Mass., 1967).

26.5 Note Carl Zeiss Stiftung *v.* VEB Carl Zeiss Jena, 293 F Supp 892 (SDNY, 1968), modif 433 F2d 686 (2nd Cir., 1970), cert den 403 US 905 (1971).

26.6 *See* Feuchter *v.* Bazurto, 528 P2df 178 (Ariz App., 1974) and Leo Feist, Inc *v.* Debmar Publishing Co, 232 F Supp 623 (ED Pa., 1964).

26.7 81 Harv L Rev 1601 (1968) at 1603–1604.

27. 13 ULA 270 (1980).
28. Section 2 thereof.
29. Article IV, Section 1; *see also* 28 USC 1738 (1976).
30. *See* Aetna Life Insurance Co *v.* Tremblay, 223 US 185 (1912).
31. *Supra* note 28.
32. 489 F2d 1313 (1st Cir, 1973), cert den 94 S Ct 2389 (1973).
33. *Supra* note 30; also Schoenbrod *v.* Sieglar, 20 NY2d 403, 230 NE2d 638 (1967).
34. *See* Atlantic Ship Supply, Inc *v.* M/V Lucy, 392 F Supp 183 (Md Fla, 1975), aff 55 F2d 1009 (5th Cir, 1977), where the court awarded a Costa Rican judgment full faith and credit.
35. 304 US 64 (1938) and also United States *v.* Belmont, 301 US 324 (1937).
36. *Supra* note 4.
37. *See* Hyde *v.* Hyde, 562 SW2d 194 (Tenn 1978); Nicol *v.* Tanner, 256 NW2d 796 (Minn 1976); Smith *v.* Smith, 72 Ohio App 203, 50 NE2d 889 (1943); and Svenska Handelsbanken *v.* Carlsen, 258 F Supp 448 (DC Mass 1966).
38. *See* Heerema Marine Contractors Co *v.* Santa Fe International Corp, 582 F Supp 445 (Cal, 1984).
39. *See* London Film Products, Ltd *v.* Intercontinental Communications, Inc, 580 F Supp 47 (SDNY, 1984).
40. 507 F Supp.
41. 581 F Supp 1039 (Del, 1984).
42. *See generally* 17 Conn L Rev 703 (1985).
43. *Supra* note 41 at p. 1041.
44. Secton 12(6)(h) thereof, 14 Geo 6, ch 27.
45. *Supra* note 41 at p. 1046.
46. Comment to Section 491 of Restatement of Foreign Relations Law of the United States (1983).
47. *See* Richie *v.* Margolies, 279 US 218 (1929) at p. 225, and Adamsen *v.* Adamsen, 151 Conn 172, 195 A2d 418 (1963).

    It should be observed that in the instant case England would recognize and enforce the interim injunction of a US court as a matter of common law, based upon the dictum in Acrow (Automation), Ltd, *v.* Rex Chainbelt, Inc, (1971) 1 WLR 1676.

Chapter 9. Arbitration and the Foreign Plaintiff in US Courts

Section 1. Enforcement of Arbitration Agreements Generally

The US Supreme Court has been emphatic concerning the 'liberal federal policy favoring arbitration agreements'[1] applicable in state as well as federal courts.[2] Indeed, the highest court has required that all courts 'rigorously enforce agreements to arbitrate even if the result is "piecemeal" legislation'.[3] Questions of arbitrability must be 'addressed with a healthy regard for the federal policy favoring arbitration' and 'any doubts concerning the scope of arbitral issues should be resolved in favor of arbitration'.[4] Thus, 'as with any other contract, the parties' intentions control, but those intentions are generously construed as to issues of arbitrability'.[5] It is no wonder that the foreign plaintiff suing in the US might well seek recognition and enforcement of an arbitration agreement or the arbitration clause in a commercial contract or pursuant to a prior-announced warning on the label of an allegedly unsafe product. In Flanagan *v.* Prudential-Bache Securities, Inc,[6] decided 10 June 1986 by the New York Court of Appeals, an arbitration clause in a contract of employment was recognized and enforced.

One of the most popular forums for arbitration is the London Court of International Arbitration, whose rules effective 1 January 1985, follow. A prime feature of the LCIA is that the parties have the maximum possible freedom to agree upon how the proceedings are to be conducted; if they fail to agree, the tribunal has the widest possible discretion to conduct the proceedings in a manner which it considers to be most efficient and effective in the particular circumstances of the case. There are weapons at the disposal of the parties and of the tribunal to neutralize dilatory tactics, for example. The place of arbitration under LCIA is wherever the parties agree, or if the parties fail to agree, then London is designated as the place of arbitration. Generally a sole arbitrator will handle the proceedings, although the parties may select three arbitrators. Willing parties can join the arbitration, and the parties are entitled as of right to an oral hearing. The fee of the arbitrator or arbitrators is computed on the basis of the time spent on the case rather than a proportion of the amount of dispute. The Rules are set forth hereinafter:—

'London Court of International Arbitration

Rules adopted to take effect from 1 January 1985

Where any agreement, submission or reference provides for arbitration under the Rules of the London Court of International Arbitration* (LCIA), the parties shall be taken to have agreed that the arbitration shall be conducted in accordance with the following Rules, or such amended Rules as the Court may have adopted to take effect before the commencement of the arbitration.

The Arbitration Court of the LCIA, in these Rules called 'The Court', has the function of ensuring the application of the Rules.

Article 1. Request for Arbitration

Any party wishing to commence an arbitration under these Rules ('the Claimant') shall send to the Registrar of the Court ('the Registrar') a written request for arbitration ('the Request') which shall include or be accompanied by:

(a) the names and addresses of the parties to the arbitration;
(b) copies of the contractual documents in which the arbitration clause is contained or under which the arbitration arises;
(c) a brief statement describing the nature and circumstances of the dispute, and specifying the relief claimed;
(d) a statement of any matters (such as the place or language of the arbitration, or the number of arbitrators, or their qualifications or identities) on which the parties have already agreed in relation to the conduct of the arbitration, or with respect to which the requesting party wishes to make a proposal;

Article 4. Communications between Parties and the Tribunal

4.1 Until the Tribunal is finally constituted and the Court determines that it would be appropriate for the parties and the Tribunal to communicate directly, all communications between parties and arbitrators shall be made through the Registrar. If and when the Court directs that communication shall take place directly between the Tribunal and the parties (with simultaneous copies to the Registrar) all further reference in these Rules to the Registrar shall thereafter be read as references to the Tribunal.

4.2 Where the Registrar, on behalf of the Tribunal, sends any communication to one party, he shall send a copy to each of the other parties.

4.3 Where any party sends any communication (including Statements under Article 6) to the Registrar, it shall include a copy for each arbitrator, and it

*Formerly called the London Court of Arbitration.

shall also send copies to all the other parties and confirm to the Registrar in writing that it has done so.

4.4 The addresses of the parties for the purpose of all communications during the proceedings shall be those set out in the Request, or as any party may at any time notify to the Registrar and to the other parties.

Article 5. Conduct of the Proceedings

5.1 The parties may agree on the arbitral procedure, and are encouraged to do so.

5.2 In the absence of procedural rules agreed by the parties or contained herein, the Tribunal shall have the widest discretion allowed under such law as may be applicable to ensure the just, expeditious, economical, and final determination of the dispute.

5.3 In the case of a three-member tribunal the Chairman may, after consulting the other arbitrators, make procedural rulings alone.

Article 6. Submission of Written Statements and Documents

6.1 Subject to any procedural rules agreed by the parties or determined by the Tribunal under Article 5, the written stage of the proceedings shall be as set out in this Article.

6.2 Within 30 days of receipt of notificaton from the Court of the appointment of the Tribunal, the Claimant shall send to the Registrar a Statement of Case setting out in sufficient detail the facts and any contentions of law on which it relies, and the relief claimed.

6.3 Within 40 days of receipt of the Statement of Case, the Respondent shall send to the Registrar a Statement of Defence stating in sufficient detail which of the facts and contentions of law in the Statement of Case it admits or denies, on what grounds, and on what other facts and contentions of law it relies. Any counterclaims shall be submitted with the Statement of Defence in the same manner as claims are set out in the Statement of Case.

6.4 Within 40 days of receipt of the Statement of Defence, the Claimant may send to the Registrar a Statement of Reply which, where there are counterclaims, shall include a Defence to Counterclaims.

6.5 If the Statement of Reply contains a Defence to Counterclaims, the Respondent has a further 40 days to send to the Registrar a Statement of Reply regarding Counterclaims.

6.6 All Statements referred to in this Article shall be accompanied by copies (or, if they are especially voluminous, lists) of all essential documents on which the party concerned relies and which have not previously been submitted by any party, and (where appropriate) by any relevant samples.

6.7 As soon as practicable following completion of the submission of the Statements specified in this Article, the Tribunal shall proceed in such manner as has been agreed by the parties, or pursuant to its authority under these Rules. If the Respondent fails to submit a Statement of Defence, or if at any point any party fails to avail itself of the opportunity to present its case in the manner directed by the Tribunal, the Tribunal may nevertheless proceed with the arbitration and make the award.

Article 7. Place of Arbitration

7.1 The parties may choose the place of arbitration. Failing such a choice, the place of arbitration shall be London, unless the Tribunal determines in view of all the circumstances of the case that another place is more appropriate.
7.2 The Tribunal may hold hearings and meetings anywhere convenient, subject to the provisions of Article 10.2, and provided that the award shall be made at the place of arbitration.

Article 8. Language of Arbitration

8.1 The language(s) of the arbitration shall be that of the document(s) containing the arbitration agreement, unless the parties have agreed otherwise.
8.2 If a document is drawn up in a language other than the language(s) of the arbitration, and no translation of such document is submitted by the party producing the document, the Tribunal, or if the Tribunal has not been appointed the Court, may order that party to submit a translation in a form to be determined by the Tribunal or the Court.

Article 9. Party Representatives

Any party may be represented by legal practitioners or any other representatives, subject to such proof of authority as the Tribunal may require.

Article 10. Hearings

10.1 Any party has the right to be heard before the Tribunal, unless the parties have agreed on documents-only arbitration.
10.2 The Tribunal shall fix the date, time and place of any meetings and hearings in the arbitration, and the Registrar shall give the parties reasonable notice thereof.
10.3 The Tribunal may in advance of hearings submit to the parties a list of questions which it wishes them to treat with special attention.
10.4 All meetings and hearings shall be in private unless the parties agree otherwise.

Article 11. Witnesses

11.1 Before any hearing, the Tribunal may require any party to give notice of the identity of witnesses it wishes to call, as well as the subject matter of their testimony and its relevance to the issues.

11.2 The Tribunal has discretion to allow, refuse, or limit the appearance of witnesses, whether witnesses of fact or expert witnesses.

11.3 Any witness who gives oral evidence may be questioned by each of the parties or their legal practitioners, under the control of the Tribunal. The Tribunal may put questions at any stage of the examination of the witnesses.

11.4 The testimony of witnesses may be presented in written form, either as signed statements or by duly sworn affidavits. Subject to Article 11.2 any party may request that such a witness should attend for oral examination at a hearing. If he fails to attend, the Tribunal may place such weight on the written testimony as it thinks fit, or exclude it altogether.

11.5 Subject to the mandatory provisions of any applicable law it shall be proper for any party or its legal practitioners to interview any witness or potential witness prior to his appearance at any hearing.

Article 12. Experts Appointed by the Tribunal

12.1 Unless otherwise agreed by the parties, the Tribunal:
- (a) may appoint one or more experts to report to the Tribunal on specific issues;
- (b) may require a party to give any such expert any relevant information or to produce, or to provide access to, any relevant documents, goods or property for inspection by the expert.

12.2 Unless otherwise agreed by the parties, if a party so requests or if the Tribunal considers it necessary, the expert shall, after delivery of his written or oral report, participate in a hearing at which the parties shall have the opportunity to question him, and to present expert witnesses in order to testify on the points at issue.

Article 13. Additional Powers of the Tribunal

13.1 Unless the parties at any time agree otherwise, and subject to any mandatory limitations of any applicable law, the Tribunal shall have the power, on the application of any party or of its own motion, but in either case only after giving the parties a proper opportunity to state their views, to:
- (a) determine what are the rules of law governing or applicable to any contract, or arbitration agreement or issue between the parties;
- (b) order the correction of any such contract or arbitration agreement, but

only to the extent required to rectify any mistake which he determines to be common to all the parties and then only if and to the extent to which the rules of law governing or applicable to the contract permit such correction;

(c) allow other parties to be joined in the arbitration with their express consent, and make a single final award determining all disputes between them;

(d) allow any party, upon such terms (as to costs and otherwise) as it shall determine, to amend claims or counterclaims;

(e) extend or abbreviate any time limits provided by these rules or by its directions;

(f) conduct such enquiries as may appear to the Tribunal to be necessary or expedient;

(g) order the parties to make any property or thing available for inspection, in their presence, by the Tribunal or any expert;

(h) order the preservation, storage, sale or other disposal of any property or thing under the control of any party;

(i) order any party to produce to the Tribunal, and to the other parties for inspection, and to supply copies of, any documents or classes of documents in their possession or power which the Tribunal determines to be relevant.

13.2 By agreeing to arbitration under these Rules the parties shall be taken to have agreed to apply only to the tribunal, and not to any court of law or other judicial authority, for an order under paragraphs (g), (h) or (i) of Article 13.1.

Article 14. Jurisdiction of the Tribunal

14.1 The Tribunal shall have the power to rule on its own jurisdiction, including any objections with respect to the existence or validity of the arbitration agreement. For that purpose, an arbitration clause which forms part of a contract shall be treated as an agreement independent of the other terms of the contract. A decision by the Tribunal that the contract is null and void shall not entail *ipso jure* the invalidity of the arbitration clause.

14.2 A plea that the Tribunal does not have jurisdiction shall be raised not later than in the Statement of Defence. A plea that the Tribunal is exceeding the scope of its authority shall be raised promptly after the Tribunal has indicated its intention to decide on the matter alleged to be beyond the scope of its authority. In either case the Tribunal may nevertheless admit a late plea under this paragraph if it considers the delay justified.

14.3 In addition to the jurisdiction to exercise the powers defined elsewhere in these Rules, the Tribunal shall have jurisdiction to determine any question of law arising in the arbitration; proceed in the arbitration notwithstanding the failure or refusal of any party to comply with these Rules or with the Tribunal's orders or directions, or to attend any meeting or hearing, but only after giving that party written notice that it intends to do so; and to receive and take into account such written or oral evidence as it shall determine to be relevant, whether or not strictly admissible in law.

Article 15. Deposits and Security

15.1 The Tribunal may direct the parties, in such proportions as it deems just, and subject to the confirmation of the Court that the amounts are in conformity with the Schedule of Costs, to make one or several interim or final payments on account of the costs of the arbitration. Such deposits shall be made to and held by the Court to the order of the Chairman of the Tribunal or sole arbitrator, and may be drawn from as required by the Tribunal. Interest on sums deposited, if any, shall be accumulated to the deposits.

15.2 The Tribunal shall have the power to order any party to provide security for the legal or other costs of any party by way of deposit or bank guarantee or in any other manner the Tribunal thinks fit.

15.3 By agreeing to arbitration under these Rules the parties shall be taken to have agreed to apply only to the Tribunal, and not to any court of law or other judicial authority, for an order under Article 15.1, or for an order for security for costs under Article 15.2.

15.4 Without prejudice to the right of any party to apply to a competent court for pre-award conservatory measures (except those referred to in Articles 15.1 and 15.2), the Tribunal shall also have the power to order any party to provide security for all or part of any amount in dispute in the arbitration.

15.5 In the event that orders under paragraphs 1, 2, and 4 of this Article are not complied with, the Tribunal may disregard claims or counterclaims by the non-complying party, although it may proceed to determine claims or counterclaims by complying parties.

Article 16. The Award

16.1 The Tribunal shall make its award in writing and, unless all the parties agree otherwise, shall state the reasons upon which its award is based. The award shall state its date and shall be signed by the arbitrator or arbitrators.

16.2 If any arbitrator refuses or fails to comply with the mandatory provisions of any applicable law relating to the making of the award, having been given a reasonable opportunity to do so, the remaining arbitrators shall proceed in his absence.

16.3 Where there is more than one arbitrator and they fail to agree on any issue, they shall decide by a majority. Failing a majority decision on any issue, the Chairman of the Tribunal shall make the award alone as if he were sole arbitrator. If an arbitrator refuses or fails to sign the award, the signatures of the majority shall be sufficient, provided that the reason for the omitted signature is stated.

16.4 The sole arbitrator or chairman shall be responsible for delivering the award to the Court, which shall transmit certified copies to the parties provided that the costs of the arbitration have been paid to the Court in accordance with Article 18.

16.5 Awards may be expressed in any currency, and the Tribunal may award that simple or compound interest shall be paid by any party on any sum which is the subject of the reference at such rates as the Tribunal determines to be appropriate, without being bound by legal rates of interest, in respect of any period which the Tribunal determines to be appropriate ending not later than the date upon which the award is complied with.

16.6 The Tribunal may make separate final awards on different issues at different times, which shall be subject to correction under the procedure specified in Article 17. Such awards shall be enforceable.

16.7 In the event of a settlement, the Tribunal may render an award recording the settlement if any party so requests. If the parties do not require a consent award, then on confirmation in writing by the parties to the Court that a settlement has been reached the Tribunal shall be discharged and the reference to arbitration concluded, subject to payment by the parties of any outstanding costs of the arbitration in accordance with Article 18.

16.8 By agreeing to arbitration under these Rules, the parties undertake to carry out award without delay, and waive their right to any form of appeal or recourse to a court of law or other judicial authority, insofar as such waiver may be validly made. The Awards shall be final and binding on the parties as from the date they are made.

Article 17. Correction of Awards and Additional Awards

17.1 Within thirty days of receipt of the award, unless another period of time has been agreed upon by the parties, a party may by notice to the Registrar request the Tribunal to correct in the award any errors in computation, any clerical or typographical errors or any errors of similar nature. If the Tribunal considers the request to be justified, it shall make the corrections within thirty days of receipt of the request. Any correction, which shall take the form of a separate memorandum, shall become part of the award.

17.2 The Tribunal may correct any error of the type referred to in Article 17.1 on its own initiative within thirty days of the date of the award.

17.3 Unless otherwise agreed by the parties, a party may request, within thirty days of receipt of the award, and with notice to the other party or parties, the Tribunal to make an additional award as to claims presented in the arbitral proceedings but not dealt with in the award. If the Tribunal considers the request to be justified, it shall make the additional award within sixty days.

17.4 The provisions of Article 16 shall apply *mutatis mutandis* to a correction of the award and to any additional award.

Article 18. Costs

18.1 The costs of the arbitration (other than the legal or other costs incurred by the parties themselves) shall be in accordance with the Schedule of Costs applicable to these Rules as of the date of the Request for Arbitration.

18.2 The Tribunal shall specify in the award the total amount of the costs of the arbitration, subject to the confirmation of the Court that the amount is in conformity of the Schedule of Costs. Unless the parties shall agree otherwise, the Tribunal shall determine the proportions in which the parties shall pay all or part of them to the Court. If the Tribunal has determined that all or any part of the costs of the arbitration shall be paid by any party other than a party which has already paid them to the Court, the latter shall have the right to recover the appropriate amount from the former.

18.3 The Tribunal shall have the authority to order in its award that all or a part of the legal or other costs of a party (apart from the costs of the arbitration) be paid by another party.

18.4 If the arbitration is abandoned, suspended or concluded, by agreement or otherwise, before the final award is made, the parties shall be jointly and severally liable to pay to the Court the costs of the arbitration as determined by the Tribunal, subject to the confirmation by the Court that the amount is in conformity with the Schedule of Costs. In the event that the costs so determined are less than the deposits made, there shall be a refund in such proportions as the parties may agree, or, failing agreement, in the same proportions as the deposits were made.

Article 19. Exclusion of Liability

19.1 Neither the Court nor any arbitrator shall be liable to any party for any act or omission in connection with any arbitration conducted under these Rules, save that arbitrators (but not the Court) may be liable for the consequences of conscious and deliberate wrongdoing.

19.2 After the award has been made and the possibilities of correction and additional awards referred to in Article 17 have lapsed or been exhausted, neither the Court nor any arbitrator shall be under any obligation to make any statement to any person about any matter concerning the arbitration, nor shall any party seek to make any arbitrator or any officer of the Court a witness in any legal proceedings arising out of the arbitration.

Article 20. General Rules

20.1 A party who knows that any provision of, or requirement under, these Rules has not been complied with and yet proceeds with the arbitration without promptly stating its objection to such non-compliance, shall be deemed to have waived its right to object.

20.2 In all matters not expressly provided for in these Rules, the Court and the Tribunal shall act in the spirit of these Rules and shall make every reasonable effort to ensure that the award is legally enforceable.'

In the United States the Federal Arbitration Act[6.1] and the UN Convention on the Recognition and Enforcement of Foreign Arbitral Awards[6.2] are popularly accepted as the vehicles for international arbitration, along with voluntary contractual and non-contractual efforts of the parties. The Act guides enforcement of arbitration agreements so as 'to ensure judicial enforcement of privately made agreements to arbitrate'.[6.3] Domestic case law has interpreted the Act as favoring arbitration even at the risk of bifurcated proceedings or piecemeal resolution of litigation.[6.4] The US Supreme Court's 1985 pronouncement in Mitsubishi Motors Corp *v.* Soler Chrysler-Plymouth[6.5] made it abundantly clear that statutory claims may be within the purview of an arbitration agreement even though the agreement did not specifically provide for resolution through arbitration. Indeed, in Metallgesellschaft AG *v.* M/V Capitan Constante[6.6] the Second US Court of Appeals approved the federal district court's confirmation of a *partial* final arbitration award for unpaid freight in a maritime action under the Federal Arbitration Act. Where a foreign state is party to the proceedings, the Foreign Sovereign Immunities Act[6.7] plays a surprising role in the commercial transaction being arbitrated, although courts in the US have barred the arbitrability of certain types or kinds of disputes on public policy grounds, federal securities law violations, antitrust claims, and anti-racketeering claims.[6.8]

In 1986 the State of Florida became the first state in the US to adopt a statute specifically designed for international arbitration, to wit: the Florida International Arbitration Act.[6.9] The Florida statute was designed to overcome the limitations of the Federal Arbitration Act which by its terms applies only to arbitrations that arise out of transactions involving the foreign, interstate or maritime commerce of the US. Similarly, the UN Convention applies only to awards that emanate from foreign countries that are parties to the Convention.

Section 2. Recognition and Enforcement of Foreign Arbitral Awards

A Japanese automobile manufacturer brought suit in the federal district court against a Puerto Rican automobile dealer for the purpose of obtaining a court order compelling arbitration of certain disputes arising out of a sales agreement between the parties. The clause in their sales agreement provided that 'all disputes, controversies or differences which may arise between (the parties) . . . out of or in relation to . . . this Agreement or for the breach thereof, shall be finally settled by arbitration in Japan in accordance with the rules and regulations of the Japan Commercial Arbitration Association.' Defendant in opposing the compulsory arbitration, argued that its antitrust counterclaims under the Sherman Act[7] could not be subject to arbitration. The federal district court in Puerto Rico ordered arbitration of most of the issues between the parties, relying upon the US Supreme Court decision in Scherk *v.* Alberto-Culver Co[8] which held that the international character of the transaction required enforcement of the arbitration agreement even as to antitrust claims. The First US Court of Appeals affirmed in part, but ruled that defendant's antitrust claims were not appropriate for arbitration.[9] The celebrated case, Mitsubishi Motor Corp *v.* Soler Chrysler-Plymouth, Inc,[10] reached the US Supreme Court, and in July 1985 that court affirmed that a US court should enforce an arbitration agreement even with respect to antitrust claims arising from an international commercial transaction: 'Concerns of international comity, respect for the capacities of foreign and transnational tribunals, and sensitivity to the need of the international commercial system for predictability in the resolution of disputes require (enforcement) of the parties' agreement, even assuming that a contrary result would be forthcoming in a domestic context.'[11] The highest court found that the Federal Arbitration Act[12] 'did not bar arbitration of the antitrust claims'; there was 'a strong presumption in favor of enforcement of freely negotiated contractual choice-of-forum provisions',[13] as evidenced by US accession to the New York Convention on the Recognition and Enforcement of Foreign Arbitral Awards.[14] The court, in essence rejected the views of the Second US Court of Appeals in American Safety Equipment Corp *v.* J. P. McGuire & Co,[15] favoring judicial and not arbitrational resolution of antitrust claims.[16] A dissenting opinion by Mr Justice Stevens focused upon his view that the arbitration agreement did not include nor encompass antitrust claims; furthermore, according to Justice Stevens, Congress did not intend the Federal Arbitration Act[17] nor the New York Convention[18] to apply to antitrust claims.

In the aftermath of the famed Mitsubishi Motors case[19] a federal district court in New York has held that claims of violation of the Racketeer Influenced and Corrupt Organizations Act, or RICO,[20] are arbitrable in an international case, Development Bank of the Philippines *v.* Chemtex Fibers, Inc.[21] Here the plaintiff foreign bank, as guarantor of notes given by a third party to defendant sued defendant for alleged overpayments made to defendant on behalf of the third party. Plaintiff alleged that defendant had submitted false accounts of disbursements. The court stayed the action brought by the foreign plantiff and ordered the parties to arbitration pursuant to the arbitration agreement between them. The court refused to follow a 1983 decision in Mineracao da Trinidade-Samitri *v.* Utah International, Inc,[22] which decision had been affirmed by the Second US Court of Appeals: 'Mineracao da Trinidade-Samitri is substantially weakened by the recent decision of the Supreme Court in Mitsubishi Motors . . . in which the Supreme Court rejected the rule in American Safety Equipment Corp where the antitrust claims sought to be litigated arose in an international commercial setting. . . . This case, like Mitsubishi Motors, arises in the context of international commerce; the desire for certainty and predictability in international commercial transactions is as compelling here as it was for the Supreme Court in Mitsubishi Motors; the interest of the domestic community in the enforcement of the federal anti-racketeering statute in these circumstances is certainly no stronger than the interest in the enforcement of American antitrust principles found wanting in Mitsubishi Motors, and is indeed arguably a great deal less strong.'[23] And in Sedima SPRL *v.* Imrex Co, Inc[24] the US Supreme Court eliminated judicially created requirements of prior criminal convictions and 'racketeering injury' from the elements of a civil cause of action under RICO.

In Dean Witter Reynolds, Inc *v.* Byrd[25] the highest court ruled that the policy favoring arbitration and the legislative mandate of the US Federal Arbitration Act[26] requires that the agreement of the parties to arbitrate prevail, and that arbitration is to proceed without delay when a party to a valid arbitration agreement seeks to compel the resistant party to arbitrate. Federal securities claims are arbitrable, as illustrated by Finkle & Ross *v.* A. G. Becker Paribas, Inc.[27] Even 'the issue of the scope of an arbitration clause is an appropriate matter for arbitration', according to the Second US Court of Appeals in Societe Generale de la Surveillance, SA *v.* Raytheon European Management and Systems Co.[28]

There is no federal policy excluding punitive damages claims from arbitration, according to Duggal International, Inc *v.* Sallmetall, BV [28.1], where the federal court denied a motion to strike a claim for punitive damages. The court rejected the argument that New York decisional law did not give the arbitrators the power to award punitive damages.

Section 3. Provisional Remedies in Aid of Arbitration

Chapter 1 of the US Arbitration Act[29] consists of two chapters, and Chapter 1 provides three kinds of pre-arbitration remedies or provisional remedies in aid of arbitration, to wit:

1. Section 3 states that a party to a federal court proceeding may apply to 'stay the trial of the action' until the conclusion of the arbitration;
2. if a party refuses to arbitrate, the aggrieved party may under Section 4 petition for 'an order directing that such arbitration proceed in the manner provided for in the arbitration agreement'; and
3. Section 8 provides that where a federal court has jurisdiction of 'a cause of action otherwise justiciable in admiralty', a party may commence a proceeding 'by libel and seizure of the vessel or other property of the other party according to the usual course of admiralty proceedings. . . . The court shall then have jurisdiction to direct the parties to proceed with arbitration and shall retain jurisdiction to enter its decree upon the award.'

Pre-award attachments and injunctions as provisional remedies in aid of arbitration are sanctioned in international and domestic commercial transactions,[30] especially when a defendant in a plenary action seeks a stay of the proceeding and an order pursuant to Section 3 of the US Arbitration Act directing the parties to arbitration.[31] On the other hand, Section 2 of the Act appears to preclude pre-award attachment, as shown in Metropolitan World Tanker Corp *v.* P. N. Pertambangan Minjakdangas Bumi Nasional,[32] where the federal district court in New York stated: 'To allow a resort to attachment before arbitral proceedings would seem to put an unnecessary and counterproductive pressure on a situation which could otherwise be settled expeditiously and knowledgeably in an arbitration context'. But a federal district court in California in Carolina Power & Light Co *v.* Uranex[33] concluded that a pre-award attachment, to the extent available under chapter 1 of the Act, would not conflict with 'the test or the apparent policies of the Convention'.[34] Indeed, 'the availability of provisional remedies encourages rather than obstructs the use of agreements to arbitrate'.[35] And in Cooper *v.* Ateliers de la Motobecane, SA[36] the New York Court of Appeals in 1982 vacated an attachment because it was not necessary 'in the arbitration context' nor was it necessary to subject the parties to 'foreign laws with which they are unfamiliar'.[37] The New York Legislature on 1 January 1986 amended Section 702 of the CPLR by expressly providing for the granting of pre-judgment attachments and injunctions in arbitration.[38] In essence, the New York statute permits preliminary injunctions and orders of attachment in connection with arbitrations if the moving party can demonstrate that any award which it might receive might become a nullity if the attachment or injunction is not granted. The moving party in New York no longer has to prove the existence of certain prerequisites set forth in Section 6201 of the CPLR.[39] Similarly, a plaintiff does not have to prove, in order to obtain a preliminary injunction, the existence of certain conditions under Section 6301 of the CPLR.[40]

In the federal courts the guiding spirit favoring arbitration since 1974 has been McCreary Tire & Rubber Co *v.* CEAT[41] which found that the terms of the New York Convention, or the UN Convention on the Recognition and Enforcement of Foreign Arbitral Awards, precluded court interference in international arbitration, except to refer the parties to arbitration. The federal district court for the Southern District of New York in Construction Exporting Enterprises, UNECA *v.* Nikki Maritime, Ltd[42] took a bold position that the UN Convention did not specifically address the subject of pre-award attachment and therefore it must have authorized pre-award attachment.[43] In 1984 in Rogers, Burgun, Shahine & Deschler, Inc *v.* Dongsam Construction Co[44] the same court pointed out that the existence of an arbitration does not preclude the court's authority to grant provisional remedies in aid of arbitration. And in Spyer, Van Der Vijver & Zwanenburg BV *v.* W & T Spyer, Inc[45] the same federal district court in 1985 denied a motion to stay an action pending arbitration in The Netherlands. Suit was brought by a Dutch produce company to recover $104,000 for goods sold and delivered, to which the US defendant had counterclaimed for 'several million dollars' alleging breach of contract and tortious interference with the contract. Judge Knapp observed that under the US Federal Arbitration Act[46] 'we may grant a stay only if satisfied that the issue before is is arbitrable under the terms of an "agreement" and that plaintiff is not in default in proceeding with the arbitration'. Judge Knapp found that the defendant was in default in proceeding with the arbitration in The Netherlands.

The UN Convention on the Recognition and Enforcement of Foreign Arbitrable Awards[47] was the subject examined by the New York Appellate Division, First Dept, in Intermar Overseas, Inc *v.* Argocean, SA,[48] dated 19 June 1986. Here the plaintiff and defendant, foreign nationals, entered into an agreement for leasing plaintiff's vessel for a term of five years. The lease agreement contained an arbitration clause. When defendants defaulted in making payments the plaintiff terminated the charterhire and obtained an *ex parte* attachment order against the defendants for the monies due. Plaintiff moved to confirm the attachments, but the trial court granted an order staying the attachment pending arbitration. But the appellate court reversed:

> 'So far as appears, there is nothing in the UN convention which precludes attachment, although it requires that nations which are signatories provide for enforcement of arbitration awards by the respective countries. The rationale . . . is that signatory nations will appropriately provide for such enforcement, without prejudgment attachment. Whatever the effect of those provisions, they cannot be binding in this case. If Intermar (plaintiff) is successful, it will have to sue to enforce the arbitration award against the defendants in Argentina, a non-signatory state. Intermar will not have the benefit of the Convention's enforcement provisions.'

The 'New York Convention' [48.1], cited above, unfortunately did not really provide for implementation or effective machinery for enforcement of agreements to arbitration *in futuro*. Therefore, a regional convention like the Inter-American Convention on International Commercial Arbitration [48.2], or IACICA, has become popular, and on 9 October 1986 the US Senate gave its advice and consent to ratification of this 1958 document, which, in essence, constitutes a timely regional arbitration initiative creating a framework of law and practice for the use of commercial arbitration in the Western Hemisphere. [48.3] the IACICA generally follows the arbitration rules of UNCITRAL [48.4]: Article 1 negates any law or doctrine that future disputes arbitration agreements are void, or, that to be enforceable, a valid arbitraton agreement requires another agreement of the parties defining the dispute after the dispute has arisen. Article 4 states that a final arbitral award shall have the status of a final judicial judgment, national or foreign. And Article 5 sets forth the various defences that may be utilized to resist enforcement of an arbitral award. [48.5]

Section 4. Arbitrability of International Disputes Under US Bankruptcy Code

In Matter of Hart Ski Manufacturing Co[49] involving the debtor's reorganization under Chapter 11 of the Bankruptcy Code, Maschinenfabrik Hennecke GmbH filed a proof of claim as an unsecured creditor for a sum of $175,000 based on an alleged sum due for certain equipment purchased by the debtor in 1977, three years before the 1980 bankruptcy proceeding. The debtor responded by asserting a counterclaim of $13 million alleging misrepresentation, breach of contract, breach of warranties and negligence. The creditor then filed a motion to dismiss the counterclaim and to stay the proceedings pending arbitration of issues by the International Chamber of Commerce[49.1] in accordance with the arbitration clause in the agreement between the parties. The Bankruptcy Court granted the creditor's motion; and upon appeal to the federal district court, it was found that the creditor had not waived its rights to arbitration by filing a proof of claim: 'The desirability of an arbitration clause in interntional transactions of this type is well recognized and must be respected.'[50] The Eighth US Court of Appeals affirmed, observing that any economic disadvantage or inconvenience to the debtor in having a determination of the dispute through international arbitration does not justify denial of the creditor's contractual right to arbitration.[51]

Section 5. UNCITRAL and Arbitration

On 21 June 1985 the United Nations Commission on International Trade Law, or UNCITRAL, adopted a model law on international commercial arbitration.[52] The law is designed to serve as a model of domestic arbitration legislation, making more uniform the practice and procedure of international commercial arbitration while freeing international arbitration from the parochial law of any given adopting state. Yet the underlying theme is the wide scope of party autonomy, the freedom of the parties to tailor the arbitration agreement to their respective needs. The parties may specify the international nature of the arbitrable subjectmatter under Article 1(3)(c); choose institutionalized arbitration and rules under Article 2(d); determine the number of arbiters under Article 10(1); and even agree to oral hearings under Article 24(1), *inter alia*.[53] Article 1(3) provides that an arbitration is deemed 'international', if the places of business of the parties are in different countries, if the arbitration or principal place of contract performance is a country other than that of the places of business of the parties, or if the parties expressly agree that the subjectmatter of the arbitration relates to more than one country.

One of the key provisions is that of limited and clearly defined instances of court intervention into the arbitration process; courts assist the arbitration process and do not interfere with the arbitral process. Article 5 expressly limits court intervention and assistance to specific instances such as the granting of provisional remedies in aid of arbitration under Article 9, assisting the arbitral tribunal in taking of evidence under Article 27, granting recourse against an award under certain conditions under Article 34, and enforcing an award under Article 35 or refusing enforcement under Article 36. The arbiters under the Model Law are given expansive powers subject only to the contrary agreement of the parties.

The UNCITRAL Model Law is divided into eight chapters and 36 articles, and contains many new and fascinating ideas. Under Article 3 written communications are deemed received if delivered on the day delivery was made; an enacting country may under Article 6 name a special court or courts to perform the functions of courts in the arbitral process; Article 8 delineates what is meant by a 'flawed' arbitration agreement that will not be recognized and enforced by the courts; Article 9 states that provisional remedies are not inconsistent with the arbitration process, and there is no waiver of the right to arbitration by seeking such interim relief from a court; Article 6(4) encourages the parties to appoint arbiters of 'a nationality other than the nationalities of the parties'; under Article 16 the arbiters are authorized to determine their own jurisdiction; failure to prosecute or failure to defend one's position at the hearings, if duly notified, amounts to a default under Article 25; in the absence of choice of law by the parties the law applicable shall be determined by the arbitral tribunal itself based upon the conflict of laws rules which it deems applicable, according to Article 28; and Article 34 provides a three-month limit for actions to set aside the award once validly made.

A comparison of the rules and procedures of the three major regimes for international arbitration, to wit: the International Chamber of Commerce Court of Arbitration (ICC), the International Centre for Settlement of Investment Disputes (ICSID), and the Arbitral Rules of the UN Commission on International Trade Law (UNCITRAL), resulted in the following *model* arbitration clause:[54]

> The arbitration shall be heard and determined by three arbitrators. In selecting the presiding arbitrator the party-appointed arbitrators of the appointing authority shall not select a person who is of the same nationality as either party or of the same nationality of either party-appointed arbitrators.
>
> The English language shall be used in the arbitral proceedings.
>
> All notices to be given in connection with the arbitration shall be in writing. All notices shall be sent by registered air mail, return receipt requested.
>
> The arbitrators shall determine the matters in dispute in accordance with the law of (place).
>
> The parties agree that the award of the arbitral tribunal will be the sole and exclusive remedy between them regarding any and all claims and counterclaims presented to the tribunal.
>
> The award shall be made and shall be payable in US dollars free of any tax or any other deduction.
>
> The award shall include interest from the date of any breach or other violation of this contract. The arbitrators shall also fix an appropriate rate of interest from the date of the breach of other violation to the date when the award is paid in full.

Notes

1. Moses H. Cone Memorial Hospital *v.* Mercury Construction Corp, 460 US 1 (1985) at p. 24.
2. *See* Southland Corp *v.* Keating, 465 US 120 (1985) at pp. 12 and 15.
3. Dean Witter Reynolds, Inc *v.* Byrd, 105 S Ct 1238 (1985) At p. 1243.
4. *Supra* note 1 at pp. 24 and 25.
5. Mitsubishi Motors Corp *v.* Soler Chrysler-Plymouth, Inc, 105 S Ct 3346 (1985) at p. 3354.
   US courts generally refer matters to arbitrators where there is a broad arbitration clause in the contract between the parties, although certain types of disputes have been barred from arbitration on public policy grounds, i.e., federal securities laws violations (McMahon *v.* Shearson/American Express, Inc, 788 F2d 94 (2nd Cir, 1986). On the other hand, no such restraints appear in international arbitration because of the strong federal policy in favor of arbitrating international disputes. (*See* Scherk *v.* Alberto-Culver Co, 417 US 506 (1974). In Mitsubishi Motors Corp *v.* Solar Chrysler-Plymouth, Inc, 105 S Ct 3346 (1985) the highest court observed that 'sensitivity to the need of the international commercial system for predictability in the resolution of disputes' does outweigh the consideration of courts being in control of private damage remedies.
6. —NY2d—(1986).

6.1 9 USC 1 *et seq.*

6.2 21 UST 2517, TIAS No. 6997.

6.3 *See* Dean Witter Reynolds, Inc *v.* Byrd, 105 S Ct 1238 (1985) and *generally* 21 Internat Lawyer 873 (Summer 1987).

6.4 *See* Moses H. Cone Memorial Hospital *v.* Mercury Construction Co, 460 US 1 (1983).

6.5 105 S Ct 3346 (1985). This important decision is printed in full hereinafter:

SUPREME COURT OF THE UNITED STATES

NOS. 83–1569 AND 83–1733

MITSUBISHI MOTORS CORPORATION, PETITIONER 83–1569 *v.* SOLER CHRYSLER-PLYMOUTH, INC.

SOLER CHRYSLER-PLYMOUTH, INC., PETITIONER 83–1733 *v.* MITSUBISHI MOTORS CORPORATION

ON WRITS OF CERTIORARI TO THE UNITED STATES COURT OF APPEALS FOR THE FIRST CIRCUIT

[July 2, 1985]

JUSTICE BLACKMUN delivered the opinion of the Court.

The principal question presented by these cases is the arbitrability, pursuant to the federal Arbitration Act, 9 USC §1 *et seq.*, and the Convention on the Recognition and Enforcement of Foreign Arbitral Awards (Convention), 21 UST 2517, TIAS No.

6997, of claims arising under the Sherman Act, 15 USC §1 *et seq*., and encompassed within a valid arbitration clause in an agreement embodying an international commercial transaction.

I

Petitioner-cross-respondent Mitsubishi Motors Corporation (Mitsubishi) is a Japanese corporation which manufactures automobiles and has its principal place of business in Tokyo, Japan. Mitsubishi is the product of a joint venture between, on the one hand, Chrysler International, SA ('CISA'), a Swiss corporation registered in Geneva and wholly owned by Chrysler Corporation, and, on the other, Mitsubishi Heavy Industries, Inc, a Japanese corporation. The aim of the joint venture was the distribution through Chrysler dealers outside the continental United States of vehicles manufactured by Mitsubishi and bearing Chrysler and Mitsubishi trademarks. Respondent-cross-petitioner Soler Chrysler-Plymouth, Inc (Soler), is a Puerto Rico corporation with its principal place of business in Pueblo Viejo, Guaynabo, Puerto Rico.

On October 31, 1979, Soler entered into a Distributor Agreement with CISA which provided for the sale by Soler of Mitsubishi-manufactured vehicles within a designated area, including metropolitan San Juan. App. 18. On the same date, CISA, Soler, and Mitsubishi entered into a Sales Procedure Agreement (Sales Agreement) which, referring to the Distributor Agreement, provided for the direct sale of Mitsubishi products to Soler and governed the terms and conditions of such sales. *Id*., at 42. Paragraph VI of the Sales Agreement, labeled 'Arbitration of Certain Matters', provides:

> 'All disputes, controversies or differences which may arise between [Mitsubishi] and [Soler] out of or in relation to Articles I–B through V of this Agreement or for the breach thereof, shall be finally settled by arbitration in Japan in accordance with the rules and regulations of the Japan Commercial Arbitration Association.' *Id*., at 52–53.

Initially, Soler did a brisk business in Mitsubishi-manufactured vehicles. As a result of its strong performance, its minimum sales volume, specified by Mitsubishi and CISA, and agreed to by Soler, for the 1981 model year was substantially increased. *Id*., at 179. In early 1981, however, the new-car market slackened. Soler ran into serious difficulties in meeting the expected sales volume, and by the spring of 1981 it felt itself compelled to request that Mitsubishi delay or cancel shipment of several orders. I Record 181, 183. About the same time, Soler attempted to arrange for the transshipment of a quantity of its vehicles for sale in the continental United States and Latin America. Mitsubishi and CISA, however, refused permission for any such diversion, citing a variety of reasons,[1] and no vehicles were transshipped. Attempts to

1. The reasons advanced included concerns that such diversion would interfere with the Japanese trade policy of voluntarily limiting imports to the United States, App. 143, 177–178; that the Soler-ordered vehicles would be unsuitable for use in certain proposed destinations because of their manufacture, with use in Puerto Rico in mind, without heaters and defoggers, *id*., at 182; that the vehicles would be unsuitable for use in Latin America because of the unavailability there of the unleaded, high-octane fuel they required, *id*., at 177, 181–182; that adequate warranty service could not be ensured, *id*., at 176, 182; and that diversion to the mainland would violate contractual obligations between CISA and Mitsubishi, *id*., at 144, 183.

work out these difficulties failed. Mitsubishi eventually withheld shipment of 966 vehicles, apparently representing orders placed for May, June, and July 1981 production, responsibility for which Soler disclaimed in February 1982. App. 131.

The following month, Mitsubishi brought an action against Soler in the United States District Court for the District of Puerto Rico under the federal Arbitration Act and the Convention.[2] Mitsubishi sought an order, pursuant to 9 USC §§4 and 201,[3] to compel arbitration in accord with ¶VI of the Sales Agreement. App. 15.[4] Shortly after filing the complaint, Mitsubishi filed a request for arbitration before the Japan Commercial Arbitration Association. *Id.*, at 70.

Soler denied the allegations and counterclaimed against both Mitsubishi and CISA. It alleged numerous breaches by Mitsubishi of the Sales Agreement,[5] raised a pair of defamation claims,[6] and asserted causes of action under the Sherman Act, 15 USC §1 *et seq.*; the federal Automobile Dealers' Day in Court Act, 70 Stat. 1125, as amended, 15 USC §1221 *et seq.*; the Puerto Rico competition statute, PR Laws Ann.,

2. The complaint alleged that Soler had failed to pay for 966 ordered vehicles; that it had failed to pay contractual 'distress unit penalties', intended to reimburse Mitsubishi for storage costs and interest charges incurred because of Soler's failure to take shipment of ordered vehicles; that Soler's failure to fulfill warranty obligations threatened Mitsubishi's reputation and good will; that Soler had failed to obtain required financing; and that the Distributor and Sales Agreements had expired by their terms or, alternatively, that Soler had surrendered its rights under the Sales Agreement. *Id.*, at 11–14.
3. Section 4 provides in pertinent part;

   'A party aggrieved by the alleged failure, neglect, or refusal of another to arbitrate under a written agreement for arbitration may petition any United States district court which, save for such agreement, would have jurisdiction under title 28, in a civil action or in admiralty of the subject matter of a suit arising out of the controversy between the parties, for an order directing that such arbitration proceed in the manner provided for in such agreement. . . . The court shall hear the parties, and upon being satisfied that the making of the agreement for arbitration or the failure to comply therewith is not in issue, the court shall make an order directing the parties to proceed to arbitration in accordance with the terms of the agreement.'

   Section 201 provides: 'The Convention on the Recognition and Enforcement of Foreign Arbitral Awards of June 10, 1958, shall be enforced in United States courts in accordance with this chapter'. Article II of the Convention, in turn, provides:

   '1. Each Contracting State shall recognize an agreement in writing under which the parties undertake to submit to arbitration all or any differences which have arisen or which may arise between them in respect of a defined legal relationship, whether contractual or not, concerning a subject matter capable of settlement by arbitration.

   '3. The court of a Contracting State, when seized of an action in a matter in respect of which the parties have made an agreement within the meaning of this article, shall, at the request of one of the parties, refer the parties to arbitration, unless it finds that the said agreement is null and void, unoperative or incapable of being performed.' 21 UST, at 2519. Title 9 USC, §203 confers jurisdiction on the district courts of the United States over an action falling under the Convention.
4. Mitsubishi also sought an order against threatened litigation. App. 15–16.
5. The alleged breaches included wrongful refusal to ship ordered vehicles and necessary parts, failure to make payment for warranty work and authorized rebates, and bad faith in establishing minimum-sales volumes. *Id.*, at 97–101.
6. The fourth counterclaim alleged that Mitsubishi had made statements that defamed Soler's good name and business reputation to a company with which Soler was then negotiating the sale of its plant and distributorship. *Id.*, at 96. The sixth counterclaim alleged that Mitsubishi had made a willfully false and malicious statement in an affidavit submitted in support of its application for a temporary restraining order, and that Mitsubishi had wrongfully advised Soler's customers and the public in its market area that they should no longer do business with Soler. *Id.*, at 98–99.

Tit. 10, §257 *et seq.* (1978); and the Puerto Rico Dealers' Contracts Act, PR Laws Ann., Tit. 10, §278 *et seq.* (1978 and Supp. 1983). In the counterclaim premised on the Sherman Act, Soler alleged that Mitsubishi and CISA had conspired to divide markets in restraint of trade. To effectuate the plan, according to Soler, Mitsubishi had refused to permit Soler to resell to buyers in North, Central, or South America vehicles it had obligated itself to purchase from Mitsubishi; had refused to ship ordered vehicles or the parts, such as heaters and defoggers, that would be necessary to permit Soler to make its vehicles suitable for resale outside Puerto Rico; and had coercively attempted to replace Soler and its other Puerto Rico distributors with a wholly owned subsidiary which would serve as the exclusive Mitsubishi distributor in Puerto Rico. App. 91–96.

After a hearing, the District Court ordered Mitsubishi and Soler to arbitrate each of the issues raised in the complaint and in all the counterclaims save two and a portion of a third.[7] With regard to the federal antitrust issues, it recognized that the Courts of Appeals, following *American Safety Equipment Corp.* v. *J. P. McGuire & Co.*, 391 F2d 821 (CA2 1968), uniformly had held that the rights conferred by the antitrust laws were '"of a character inappropriate for enforcement by arbitration."' App. to Pet. for Cert. in No. 83–1569, p. B9, quoting *Wilko* v. *Swan*, 201 F2d, 439, 444 (CA2 1953), rev'd, 346 US 427 (1953). The District Court held, however, that the international character of the Mitsubishi-Soler undertaking required enforcement of the agreement to arbitrate even as to the antitrust claims. It relied on *Scherk* v. *Alberto-Culver Co.*, 417 US 506, 515–520 (1974), in which this Court ordered arbitration, pursuant to a provision embodied in an international agreement, of a claim arising under the Securities Exchange Act of 1934 notwithstanding its assumption *arguendo* that *Wilko, supra*, which held nonarbitrable claims arising under the Securities Act of 1933, also would bar arbitration of a 1934 Act claim arising in a domestic context.

The United States Court of Appeals for the First Circuit affirmed in part and reversed in part. 723 F2d 155 (1983). It first rejected Soler's argument that Puerto Rico law precluded enforcement of an agreement obligating a local dealer to arbitrate controversies outside Puerto Rico.[8] It also rejected Soler's suggestion that it could not have intended to arbitrate statutory claims not mentioned in the arbitration agreement. Assessing arbitrability 'on an allegation-by-allegation basis', *id.*, at 159,

7. The District Court found that the arbitration clause did not cover the fourth and sixth counterclaims, which sought damages for defamation, see n. 6, *supra*, or the allegations in the seventh counterclaim concerning discriminatory treatment and the establishment of minimum-sales volumes. App. to Pet. for Cert. in No. 83–1569, pp. B10–B11. Accordingly, it retained jurisdiction over those portions of the litigation. In addition, because no arbitration agreement between Soler and CISA existed, the court retained jurisdiction, insofar as they sought relief from CISA, over the first, second, third, and ninth counterclaims, which raised claims under the Puerto Rico Dealers' Contracts Act; the federal Automobile Dealers' Day in Court Act; the Sherman Act; and the Puerto Rico competition statute, respectively. App. to Pet. for Cert. B12. These aspects of the District Court's ruling were not appealed and are not before this Court.
8. Soler relied on P. R. Laws Ann., Tit. 10, §278b–2 (Supp. 1983), which purports to render null and void '[a]ny stipulation that obligates a dealer to adjust, arbitrate or litigate any controversy that comes up regarding his dealer's contract outside of Puerto Rico, or under foreign law or rule of law'. See *Walborg Corp.* v. *Superior Court*, 104 DPR 184 (1975). The Court of Appeals held this provision pre-empted by 9 USC §2, which declares arbitration agreements valid and enforceable 'save upon such grounds as exist at law or in equity for the revocation of any contract'. 723 F2d, at 158. See *Southland Corp.* v. *Keating*, — US — (1984). See also *Ledee* v. *Ceramiche Ragno*, 684 F2d 184 (CA1 1982). Soler does not challenge this holding in its cross-petition here.

the court then read the arbitration clause to encompass virtually all the claims arising under the Sherman Act.[9]

Finally, after endorsing the doctrine of *American Safety*, precluding arbitration of antitrust claims, the Court of Appeals concluded that neither this Court's decision in *Scherk* nor the Convention required abandonment of that doctrine in the face of an international transaction. 723 F2d, at 164–168. Accordingly, it reversed the judgment of the Ditrict Court insofar as it had ordered submission of 'Soler's antitrust claims' to arbitration.[10] Affirming the remainder of the judgment,[11] the court directed the

9. As the Court of Appeals saw it, '[t]he question . . . is not whether the arbitration clause mentions antitrust or any other particular cause of action, but whether the factual allegations underlying Soler's counterclaims—and Mitsubishi's bona fide defenses to those counterclaims—are within the scope of the arbitration clause, whatever the legal labels attached to those allegations'. 723 F2d, at 159. Because Soler's counterclaim under the Puerto Rico Dealers' Contracts Act focused on Mitsubishi's alleged failure to comply with the provisions of the Sales Agreement governing delivery of automobiles, and those provisions were found in that portion of Article I of the Agreement subject to arbitration clause. 723 F2d, at 159–160.

    The court read the Sherman Act counterclaim to raise issues of wrongful termination of Soler's distributorship, wrongful failure to ship ordered parts and vehicles, and wrongful refusal to permit transshipment of stock to the United States and Latin America. Because the existence of just cause for termination turned on Mitsubishi's allegations that Soler had breached the Sales Agreement by, for example, failing to pay for ordered vehicles, the wrongful termination claim implicated t least three provisions within the arbitration clause: Article I–D(1), which rendered a dealer's order 'firm'; Article I–E, which provided for 'distress unit penalties' where the dealer prevented timely shipment; and Article I–F, specifying payment obligations and procedures. The court therefore held the arbitration clause to cover this dispute. Because the nonshipment claim implicated Soler's obligation under Article I–F to proffer acceptable credit, the court found this dispute covered as well. And because the transshipment claim prompted Mitsubishi defenses concerning the suitability of vehicles manufactured to Soler's specifications for use in different locales and Soler's inability to provide warranty service to transshiped products, it implicated Soler's obligation under Article IV, another covered provision, to make use of Mitsubishi's trademarks in a manner that would not dilute Mitsubishi's reputation and good will or damage its name and reputation. The court therefore found the arbitration agreement also to include this dispute, noting that such trademark concerns 'are relevant to the legality of territorially based restricted distribution arrangements of the sort at issue here'. 723 F2d, at 160–161, citing *Continental T. V., Inc.* v. *GTE Sylvania Inc.*, 433 US 36 (1977).

    The Court of Appeals read the federal Automobile Dealers' Day in Court Act claim to raise issues as to Mitsubishi's good faith in establishing minimum-sales volumes and Mitsubishi's alleged attempt to coerce Soler into accepting replacement by a Mitsubishi subsidiary. It agreed with the District Court's conclusion, in which Mitsubishi acquiesced, that the arbitration clause did not reach the first issue; it found the second, arising from Soler's payment problems, to restate claims already found to be covered. 723 F2d, at 161.

    Finally, the Court of Appeals found the antitrust claims under Puerto Rico law entirely to reiterate claims elsewhere stated; accordingly, it held them arbitrable to the same extent as their counterparts. *Ibid.*

10. Soler suggests that the court thereby declared antitrust claims arising under Puerto Rico law nonarbitrable as well. We read the Court of Appeals' opinion to have held only the federal antitrust claims nonarbitrable. See *id.*, at 157 ('principal issue on this appeal is whether arbitration of federal antitrust claims may be compelled under the Federal Arbitration Act'); *id.*, at 161 ('major question in this appeal is whether the antitrust issues raised by Soler's third counterclaim [grounded on Sherman Act] are subject to arbitration'). In any event, any contention that the local antitrust claims are nonarbitrable would be foreclosed by this Court's decision in *Southland Corp.* v. *Keating*, — US —, — (1984) (slip op. 7), where we held that the Federal Arbitration Act 'withdrew the power of the States to require a judicial forum for the resolution of claims which the contracting parties agreed to resolve by arbitration'. →

District Court to consider in the first instance how the parallel judicial and arbitral proceedings should go forward.[12]

We granted certiorari primarily to consider whether an American court should enforce an agreement to resolve antitrust claims by arbitration when that agreement arises from an international transaction. —US— (1984).

II

At the outset, we address the contention raised in Soler's cross-petition that the arbitration clause at issue may not be read to encompass the statutory counterclaims stated in its answer to the complaint. In making this argument, Soler does not question the Court of Appeals' application of ¶VI of the Sales Agreement to the disputes involved here as a matter of standard contract interpretation.[13] Instead, it argues that as a matter of law a court may not construe an arbitration agreement to encompass claims arising out of statutes designed to protect a class to which the party resisting arbitration belongs 'unless [that party] has expressly agreed' to arbitrate those claims, see Cross-Pet. for Cert. 8, i, by which Soler presumably means that the arbitration clause must specifically mention the statute giving rise to the claims that a party to the clause seeks to arbitrate. See 723 F2d, at 159. Soler reasons that, because it falls within the class for whose benefit the federal and local antitrust laws and dealers' acts were passed, but the arbitration clause at issue does not mention these statutes or statutes in general, the clause cannot be read to contemplate arbitration of these statutory claims.

We do not agree, for we find no warrant in the Arbitration Act for implying in every contract within its ken a presumption against arbitration of statutory claims.

→ 11. In this Court, Soler suggests for the first time that Congress intended that claims under the federal Automobile Dealers' Day in Court Act be nonarbitrable. Brief for Respondent and Cross-Petitioner 21, n. 12. Because Soler did not raise this question in the Court of Appeals or present it in its cross-petition, we do not address it here.

12. Following entry of the District Court's judgment, both it and the Court of Appeals denied motions by Soler for a stay pending appeal. The parties accordingly commenced preparation for the arbitration in Japan. Upon remand from the Court of Appeals, however, Soler withdrew the antitrust claims from the arbitration tribunal and sought a stay of arbitration pending the completion of the judicial proceedings on the ground that the antitrust claims permeated the claims that remained before that tribunal. The District Court denied the motion, instead staying its own proceedings pending the arbitration in Japan. The arbitation recommenced, but apparently came to a halt once again in September 1984 upon the filing by Soler of a petition for reorganization under Chapter 11 of the Bankruptcy Code, 11 USC §1101 *et seq.*

13. We therefore have no reason to review the Court of Appeals' construction of the scope of the arbitration clause in the light of the allegations of Soler's counterclaims. See n. 9, *supra*; *Southland Corp.* v. *Keating*, — US, at —, n. 7 (slip op. 12, n. 7).

Soler does suggest that, because the title of the clause referred only to 'certain matters', App. 52, and the clause itself specifically referred only to 'Articles I–B through V', *ibid.*, it should be read narrowly to exclude the statutory claims. Soler ignores the inclusion within those 'certain matters' of '[a]ll disputes, controversies or differences which may arise between [Mitsubishi] and [Soler] out of or in relation to [the specified provisions] or for the breach thereof'. Contrary to Soler's suggestion, the exclusion of some areas of possible dispute from the scope of an arbitration clause does not serve to restrict the reach of an otherwise broad clause in the areas in which it was intended to operate. Thus, insofar as the allegations underlying the statutory claims touch matters covered by the enumerated articles, the Court of Appeals properly resolved any doubts in favor of arbitrability. See 723 F2d, at 159.

The Act's centerpiece provision makes a written agreement to arbitrate 'in any maritime transaction or a contract evidencing a transaction involving commerce . . . valid, irrevocable, and enforceable, save upon such grounds as exist at law or in equity for the revocation of any contract.' 9 USC §2. The 'liberal federal policy favoring arbitration agreements', *Moses H. Cone Memorial Hospital* v. *Mercury Construction Corp.*, 460 US 1, 24 (1983), manifested by this provision and the Act as a whole, is at bottom a policy guaranteeing the enforcement of private contractual arrangements: the Act simply 'creates a body of federal substantive law establishing and regulating the duty to honor an agreement to arbitrate'. *Id.*, at 25, n. 32.[14] As this Court recently observed, '[t]he preeminent concern of Congress in passing the Act was to enforce private agreements into which parties had entered', a concern which 'requires that we rigorously enforce agreements to arbitrate'. *Dean Witter Reynolds Inc.* v. *Byrd*, —US—, — (1985) (slip op. 8).

Accordingly, the first task of a court asked to compel arbitration of a dispute is to determine whether the parties agreed to arbitrate that dispute. The court is to make this determination by applying the 'federal substantive law of arbitrability, applicable to any arbitration agreement within the coverage of the Act'. *Moses H. Cone Memorial Hospital*, 460 US, at 24. See *Prima Paint Corp.* v. *Flood & Conklin Mfg. Corp.*, 388 US 395, 400–404 (1967); *Southland Corp.* v. *Keating*, —US—, — — — (1984) (slip op. 9–10). And that body of law counsels

> 'that questions of arbitrability must be addressed with a healthy regard for the federal policy favoring arbitration. . . . The Arbitration Act establishes that, as a matter of federal law, any doubts concerning the scope of arbitrable issues should be resolved in favor of arbitration, whether the problem at hand is the construction of the contract language itself or an allegation of waiver, delay, or a like defense to arbitrability.' *Moses H. Cone Memorial Hospital*, *supra*, at 24–25.

See, *e.g.*, *Steelworkers* v. *Warrior & Gulf Navigation Co.*, 363 US 574, 582–583 (1960). Thus, as with any other contract, the parties' intentions control, but those intentions are generously construed as to issues of arbitrability.

There is no reason to depart from these guidelines where a party bound by an arbitration agreement raises claims founded on statutory rights. Some time ago this Court expressed 'hope for [the Act's] usefulness both in controversies based on statutes or on standards otherwise created'. *Wilko* v. *Swan*, 346 US 427, 432 (1953) (footnote omitted), see *Merrill Lynch, Pierce, Fenner & Smith, Inc.* v. *Ware*, 414 US 117, 135, n. 15 (1973), and we are well past the time when judicial suspicion of the desirability of arbitration and of the competence of arbitral tribunals inhibited the development of arbitration as an alternative means of dispute resolution. Just last Term in *Southland Corp.*, *supra*, where we held that §2 of the Act declared a national policy applicable equally in state as well as federal courts, we construed an arbitration clause to encompass the disputes at issue without pausing at the source in a state statute of the rights asserted by the parties resisting arbitration. —US, at —, and n. 7

14. The Court previously has explained that the Act was designed to overcome an anachronistic judicial hostility to agreements to arbitrate, which American courts had borrowed from English common law. See *Dean Witter Reynolds Inc.* v. *Byrd*, — US —, — — —, and n. 6 (1985) (slip op. 6–8, and n. 6); *Scherk* v. *Alberto-Culver Co.*, 417 US 506, 510, and n. 4 (1974).

(slip op. 12, and n. 7).[15] Of course, courts should remain attuned to well-supported claims that the agreement to arbitrate resulted from the sort of fraud or overwhelming economic power that would provide grounds 'for the revocation of any contract'. 9 USC §2; see *Southland Corp.*, — US, at —, n. 11 (slip op. 14, n. 11); *The Bremen* v. *Zapata Off-Shore Co.*, 407 US 1, 15 (1972). But, absent such compelling considerations, the Act itself provides no basis for disfavoring agreements to arbitrate statutory claims by skewing the otherwise hospitable inquiry into arbitrability.

That is not to say that all controversies implicating statutory rights are suitable for arbitration. There is no reason to distort the process of contract interpretation, however, in order to ferret out the inappropriate. Just as it is the congressional policy manifested in the federal Arbitration Act that requires courts liberally to construe the scope of arbitration agreements covered by that Act, it is the congressional intention expressed in some other statute on which the courts must rely to identify any category of claims as to which agreements to arbitrate will be held unenforceable. See *Wilko* v. *Swan*, 346 US, at 434–435; *Southland Corp.*, — US, at — (slip op. 13, n. 11); *Dean Witter Reynolds Inc.*, — US, at — (concurring opinion) (slip op. 1–2). For that reason, Soler's concern for statutorily protected classes provides no reason to color the lens through which the arbitration clause is read. By agreeing to arbitrate a statutory claim, a party does not forego the substantive rights afforded by the statute; it only submits to their resolution in an arbitral, rather than a judicial, forum. It trades the procedures and opportunity for review of the courtroom for the simplicity, informality, and expedition of arbitration. We must assume that if Congress intended the substantive protection afforded by a given statute to include protection against waiver of the right to a judicial forum, that intention will be deducible from text or legislative history. See *Wilko* v. *Swan*, *supra*. Having made the bargain to arbitrate, the party should be held to it unless Congress itself has evinced an intention to preclude a waiver of judicial remedies for the statutory rights at issue. Nothing, in the meantime, prevents a party from excluding statutory claims from the scope of an agreement to arbitrate. See *Prima Paint Corp.*, 388 US, at 406.

In sum, the Court of Appeals correctly conducted a two-step inquiry, first determining whether the parties' agreement to arbitrate reached the statutory issues, and then, upon finding it did, considering whether legal constraints external to the parties' agreement foreclosed the arbitration of those claims. We endorse its rejection of Soler's proposed rule of arbitration-clause construction.

III

We now turn to consider whether Soler's antitrust claims are nonarbitrable even though it has agreed to arbitrate them. In holding that they are not, the Court of Appeals followed the decision of the Second Circuit in *American Safety Equipment Corp.* v. *J. P. McGuire & Co.*, 391 F2d 821 (1968). Notwithstanding the absence of any explicit support for such an exception in either the Sherman Act or the federal Arbitration Act, the Second Circuit there reasoned that 'the pervasive public interest in enforcement of the antitrust laws, and the nature of the claims that arise in such

15. The claims whose arbitrability was at issue in *Southland Corp.* arose under the disclosure requirements of the California Franchise Investment Law, Cal. Corp. Code Ann. §31000 *et seq.* (West 1977). While the dissent in *Southland Corp.* disputed the applicability of the Act to proceedings in the state courts, it did not object to the Courts reading of the arbitration clause under examination.

cases, combine to make . . . antitrust claims . . . inappropriate for arbitration'. *Id.*, at 827–828. We find it unnecessary to assess the legitimacy of the *American Safety* doctrine as applied to agreements to arbitrate arising from domestic transactions. As in *Scherk* v. *Alberto-Culver Co.*, 417 US 506 (1974), we conclude that concerns of international comity, respect for the capacities of foreign and transnational tribunals, and sensitivity to the need of the international commercial system for predictability in the resolution of disputes require that we enforce the parties' agreement, even assuming that a contrary result would be forthcoming in a domestic context.

Even before *Scherk*, this Court had recognized the utility of forum-selection clauses in international transactions. In *The Bremen*, *supra*, an American oil company, seeking to evade a contractual choice of an English forum and, by implication, English law, filed a suit in admiralty in a United States District Court against the German corporation which had contracted to tow its rig to a location in the Adriatic Sea. Notwithstanding the possibility that the English court would enforce provisions in the towage contract exculpating the German party which an American court would refuse to enforce, this Court gave effect to the choice-of-forum clause. It observed:

> 'The expansion of American business and industry will hardly be encouraged if, notwithstanding solemn contracts, we insist on a parochial concept that all disputes must be resolved under our laws and in our courts. . . . We cannot have trade and commerce in world markets and international waters exclusively on our terms, governed by our laws, and resolved in our courts.' 407 US, at 9.

Recognizing that 'agreeing in advance on a forum acceptable to both parties is an indispensable element in international trade, commerce, and contracting', *id.*, at 13–14, the decision in *The Bremen* clearly eschewed a provincial solicitude for the jurisdiction of domestic fora.

Identical considerations governed the Court's decision in *Scherk*, which categorized '[a]n agreement to arbitrate before a specified tribunal [as], in effect, specialized kind of forum-selection clause that posits not only the situs of suit but also the procedure to be used in resolving the dispute'. 417 US, at 519. In *Scherk*, the American company Alberto-Culver purchased several interrelated business enterprises, organized under the laws of Germany and Liechtenstein, as well as the rights held by those enterprises in certain trademarks, from a German citizen who at the time of trial resided in Switzerland. Although the contract of sale contained a clause providing for arbitration before the International Chamber of Commerce in Paris of 'any controversy or claim [arising] out of this agreement or the breach thereof', Alberto-Culver subsequently brought suit against Scherk in a Federal District Court in Illinois, alleging that Scherk had violated §10(b) of the Securities Exchange Act of 1934 by fraudulently misrepresenting the status of the trademarks as unencumbered. The District Court denied a motion to stay the proceedings before it and enjoined the parties from going forward before the arbitral tribunal in Paris. The Court of Appeals for the Seventh Circuit affirmed, relying on this Court's holding in *Wilko* v. *Swan*, 346 US 427 (1953), that agreements to arbitrate disputes arising under the Securities Act of 1933 are nonarbitrable. This Court reversed, enforcing the arbitration agreement even while assuming for purposes of the decision that the controversy would be nonarbitrable under the holding of *Wilko* had it arisen out of a domestic transaction. Again, the Court emphasized:

'A contractual provision specifying in advance the forum in which disputes shall be litigated and the law to be applied is . . . an almost indispensable precondition to achievement of the orderliness and predictability essential to any international business transaction. . . .

'A parochial refusal by the courts of one country to enforce an international arbitration agreement would not only frustrate these purposes, but would invite unseemly and mutually destructive jockeying by the parties to secure tactical litigation advantages. . . . [It would] damage the fabric of international commerce and trade, and imperil the willingness and ability of businessmen to enter into international commercial agreements.' 417 US, at 516–517.

Accordingly, the Court held Albert-Culver to its bargain, sending it to the international arbitral tribunal bcfore which it had agreed to seek its remedies.

The Bremen and *Scherk* establish a strong presumption in favor of enforcement of freely negotiated contractual choice-of-forum provisions. Here, as in *Scherk*, that presumption is reinforced by the emphatic federal policy in favor of arbitral dispute resolution. And at least since this Nation's accession in 1970 to the Convention, see 21 UST 2517, TIAS 6997, and the implementation of the Convention in the same year by amendment of the federal Arbitration Act,[16] that federal policy applies with special force in the field of international commerce. Thus, we must weight the concerns of *American Safety* against a strong belief in the efficacy of arbitral procedures for the resolution of international commercial disputes and an equal commitment to the enforcement of freely negotiated choice-of-forum clauses.

At the outset, we confess to some skepticism of certain aspects of the *American Safety* doctrine. As distilled by the First Circuit, 723 F2d, at 162, the doctrine comprises four ingredients. First, private parties play a pivotal role in aiding governmental enforcement of the antitrust laws by means of the private action for treble damages. Second, 'the strong possibility that contracts which generate antitrust disputes may be contracts of adhesion militates against automatic forum determination by contract'. Third, antitrust issues, prone to complication, require sophisticated legal and economic analysis, and thus are 'ill-adapted to strengths of the arbitral process, *i.e.*, expedition, minimal requirements of written rationale, simplicity, resort to basic concepts of common sense and simple equity'. Finally, just as 'issues of war and peace are too important to be vested in the generals, . . . decisions as to antitrust regulation of business are too important to be lodged in arbitrators chosen from the business community—particularly those from a foreign community that has had no experience with or exposure to our law and values'. See *American Safety*, 391 F2d, at 826–827.

Initially, we find the second concern unjustified. The mere appearance of an antitrust dispute does not alone warrant invalidation of the selected forum on the undemonstrated assumption that the arbitration clause is tainted. A party resisting arbitration of course may attack directly the validity of the agreement to arbitrate. See *Prima Paint Corp., supra*. Moreover, the party may attempt to make a showing that would warrant setting aside the forum-selection clause—that the agreement was '[a]ffected by fraud, undue influence, or overweening bargaining power'; that 'enforcement would be unreasonable and unjust'; or that proceedings 'in the contractual forum will be so gravely difficult and inconvenient that [the resisting party] will for all practical purposes be deprived of his day in court'. *The Bremen*, 407

16. Act of July 31, 1970, Pub. L. 91–368, 84 Stat. 692, codified at 9 USC §§201–208.

US, at 12, 15, 18. But absent such a showing—and none was attempted here—there is no basis for assuming the forum inadequate or its selection unfair.

Next, potential complexity should not suffice to ward off arbitration. We might well have some doubt that even the courts following *American Safety* subscribe fully to the view that antitrust matters are inherently insusceptible to resolution by arbitration, as these same courts have agreed that an undertaking to arbitrate antitrust claims entered into *after* the dispute arises is acceptable. See, *e.g.*, *Coenen* v. *R. W. Pressprich & Co.*, 453 F2d 1209, 1215 (CA2), cert. denied, 406 US 949 (1972); *Cobb* v. *Lewis*, 488 F2d 41, 48 (CA5 1974). See also, in the present cases, 723 F2d, at 168, n. 12 (leaving question open). And the vertical restraints which most frequently give birth to antitrust claims covered by an arbitration agreement will not often occasion the monstrous proceedings that have given antitrust litigation an image of intractability. In any event, adaptability and access to expertise are hallmarks of arbitration. The anticipated subject matter of the dispute may be taken into account when the arbitrators are appointed, and arbitral rules typically provide for the participation of experts either employed by the parties or appointed by the tribunal.[17] Moreover, it is often a judgment that streamlined proceedings and expeditious results will best serve their needs that causes parties to agree to arbitrate their disputes; it is typically a desire to keep the effort and expense required to resolve a dispute within manageable bounds that prompts them mutually to forgo access to judicial remedies. In sum, the factor of potential complexity alone does not persuade us that an arbitral tribunal could not properly handle an antitrust matter.

For similar reasons, we also reject the proposition that an arbitration panel will pose too great a danger of innate hostility to the constraints on business conduct that antitrust law imposes. International arbitrators frequently are drawn from the legal as well as the business community; where the dispute has an important legal component, the parties and the arbitral body with whose assistance they have agreed to settle their dispute can be expected to select arbitrators accordingly.[18] We decline to indulge the presumption that the parties and arbitral body conducting a proceeding will be unable or unwilling to retain competent, conscientious and impartial arbitrators.

17. See, *e.g.*, Japan Commercial Arbitration Association Rule 26, reprinted in App. 218–219; W. Craig, W. Park & J. Paulsson, International Chamber of Commerce Arbitration §§25.03, 26.04 (1984); Art. 27, Arbitration Rules of United Nations Commission on International Trade Law (UNCITRAL) (1976), reprinted in II Yearbook Commercial Arbitration 167 (1977).
18. See W. Craig, W. Park & J. Paulsson, *supra*, §12.03, p. 28; Sanders, Commentary on UNCITRAL Arbitration Rules §15.1, in II Yearbook Commercial Arbitration, *supra*, at 203.

We are advised by Mitsubishi and *amicus* International Chamber of Commerce, without contradiction by Soler, that the arbitration panel selected to hear the parties' claims here is composed of three Japanese lawyers, one a former law school dean, another a former judge, and the third a practicing attorney with American legal training who has written on Japanese antitrust law. Brief for Petitioner 26; Brief for International Chamber of Commerce as *Amicus Curiae* 16, n. 28.

The Court of Appeals was concerned that international arbitrators would lack 'experience with or exposure to our law and values'. 723 F2d, at 162. The obstacles confronted by the arbitration panel in this case, however, should be no greater than those confronted by any judicial or arbitral tribunal required to determine foreign law. See, *e.g.*, Fed. Rule Civ. Proc. 44.1. Moreover, while our attachment to the antitrust laws may be stronger than most, many other countries, including Japan, have similar bodies of competition law. See, *e.g.*, 1, The Law of Transnational Business Transactions, ch. 9 (Banks, Antitrust Aspects of International Business Operations), §9.03[7] (V. Nanda ed. 1874); H. Iyori & A. Uesugi, The Antimonopoloy Laws of Japan (1983).

We are left, then, with the core of the *American Safety* doctrine—the fundamental importance to American democratic capitalism of the regime of the antitrust laws. See, *e.g.*, *United States* v. *Topco Associates, Inc.*, 405 US 596, 610 (1972); *Northern Pacific R. Co.* v. *United States*, 356 US 1, 4 (1958). Without doubt, the private cause of action plays a central role in enforcing this regime. See, *e.g.*, *Hawaii* v. *Standard Oil Co.*, 405 US 251, 262 (1972). As the Court of Appeals pointed out:

> "'A claim under the antitrust laws is not merely a private matter. The Sherman Act is designed to promote the national interest in a competitive economy; thus, the plaintiff asserting his rights under the Act has been likened to a private attorney-general who protects the public's interest".' 723 F2d, at 168, quoting *American Safety*, 391 F2d, at 826.

The treble-damages provision wielded by the private litigant is a chief tool in the antitrust enforcement scheme, posing a crucial deterrent to potential violators. See, *e.g.*, *Perma Life Mufflers, Inc.* v. *International Parts Corp.*, 392 US 134, 138–139 (1968).

The importance of the private damages remedy, however, does not compel the conclusion that it may not be sought outside an American court. Notwithstanding its important incidental policing function, the treble-damages cause of action conferred on private parties by §4 of the Clayton Act, 15 USC §15, and pursued by Soler here by way of its third counterclaim, seeks primarily to enable an injured competitor to gain compensation for that injury.

> 'Section 4 . . . is in essence a remedial provision. It provides treble damages to "[a]ny person who shall be injured in his business or property by reason of anything forbidden in the antitrust laws. . . ." Of course, treble damages also play an important role in penalizing wrongdoers and deterring wrongdoing, as we also have frequently observed. . . . It nevertheless is true that the treble-damages provision, which makes awards available only to injured parties, and measures the awards by a multiple of the injury actually proved, is designed primarily as a remedy.' *Brunswick Corp.* v. *Pueblo Bowl-O-Mat, Inc.*, 429 US 477, 485–486 (1977).

After examining the respective legislative histories, the Court in *Brunswick* recognized that when first enacted in 1890 as §7 of the Sherman Act, 26 Stat. 210, the treble-damages provision 'was conceived of primarily as a remedy for "[t]he people of the United States as individuals",' 429 US, at 486, n. 10, quoting 21 Cong. Rec. 1767–1768 (1890) (remarks of Sen. George); when reenacted in 1914 as §4 of the Clayton Act, 38 Stat. 731, it was still 'conceived primarily as "open[ing] the door of justice to every man, whenever he may be injured by those who violate the antitrust laws, and giv[ing] the injured party ample damages for the wrong suffered".' 429 US, at 486, n. 10, quoting 51 Cong. Rec. 9073 (1914) (remarks of Rep. Webb). And, of course, the antitrust cause of action remains at all times under the control of the individual litigant: no citizen is under an obligation to bring an antitrust suit, see *Illinois Brick Co.* v. *Illinois*, 431 US 720, 746 (1977), and the private antitrust plaintiff needs no executive or judicial approval before settling one. It follows that, at least where the international cast of a transaction would otherwise add an element of uncertainty to dispute resolution, the prospective litigant may provide in advance for a mutually agreeable procedure whereby he would seek his antitrust recovery as well as settle other controversies.

There is no reason to assume at the outset of the dispute that international arbitration will not provide an adequate mechanism. To be sure, the international arbitral tribunal owes no prior allegiance to the legal norms of particular states; hence, it has no direct obligation to vindicate their statutory dictates. The tribunal, however, is bound to effectuate the intentions of the parties. Where the parties have agreed that the arbitral body is to decide a defined set of claims which includes, as in these cases, those arising from the application of American antitrust law, the tribunal therefore should be bound to decide that dispute in accord with the national law giving rise to the claim. Cf. *Wilko* v. *Swan*, 346 US, at 433–434.[19] And so long as the prospective litigant effectively may vindicate its statutory cause of action in the arbitral forum, the statute will continue to serve both its remedial and deterrent function.

Having permitted the arbitration to go forward, the national courts of the United States will have the opportunity at the award enforcement stage to ensure that the legitimate interest in the enforcement of the antitrust laws has been addressed. The Convention reserves to each signatory country the right to refuse enforcement of an award where the 'recognition or enforcement of the award would be contrary to the public policy of that country'. Art. V(2)(b), 21 UST, at 2520; see *Scherk*, 417 US, at 519, n. 14. While the efficacy of the arbitral process requires that substantive review at the award-enforcement stage remain minimal, it would not require intrusive inquiry

19. In addition to the clause providing for arbitration before the Japan Commercial Arbitration Association, the Sales Agreement includes a choice-of-law clause which reads: 'This Agreement is made in, and will be governed by and construed in all respects according to the laws of the Swiss Confederation as if entirely performed therein'. App. 56. The United States raises the possibility that the arbitral panel will read this provision not simply to govern interpretation of the contract terms, but wholly to displace American law even where it otherwise would apply. Brief for United States as *Amicus Curiae* 20. The International Chamber of Commerce opines that it is '[c]onceivabl[e], although we believe it unlikely, [that] the arbitrators could consider Soler's affirmative claim of anti-competitive conduct by DISA and Mitsubishi to fall within the purview of this choice-of-law provision, with the result that it would be decided under Swiss law rather than the U.S. Sherman Act'. Brief for International Chamber of Commerce as *Amicus Curiae* 25. At oral argument, however, counsel for Mitsubishi conceded that American law applied to the antitrust claims and represented that the claims had been submitted to he arbitration panel in Japan on that basis. Tr. of Oral. Arg. 18. The record confirms that before the decision of the Court of Appeals the arbitral panel had taken these claims under submission. See District Court Order of May 25, 1984, pp. 2–3.

We therefore have no occasion to speculate on this matter at this stage in the proceedings, when Mitsubishi seeks to enforce the agreement to arbitrate, not to enforce an award. Nor need we consider now the effect of an arbitral tribunal's failure to take cognizance of the statutory cause of action on the claimant's capacity to reinitiate suit in federal court. We merely note that in the event the choice-of-forum and choice-of-law clauses operated in tandem as a prospective waiver of a party's right to pursue statutory remedies for antitrust violations, we would have little hesitation in condemning the agreement as against public policy. See, *e.g.*, *Redel's Inc.* v. *General Electric Co.*, 498 F2d 95, 98–99 (CA5 1974); *Gaines* v. *Carrollton Tobacco Board of Trade, Inc.*, 386 F2d 757, 759 (CA6 1967); *Fox Midwest Theatres* v. *Means*, 221 F2d 173, 180 (CA8 1955). Cf. *Lawlor* v. *National Screen Service*, 349 US 322, 329 (1955). See generally 15 S. Williston on Contracts §1750A (3d ed. 1972).

to ascertain that the tribunal took cognizance of the antitrust claims and actually decided them.[20]

As international trade has expanded in recent decades, so too has the use of international arbitration to resolve disputes arising in the course of that trade. The controversies that international arbitral institutions are called upon to resolve have increased in diversity as well as in complexity. Yet the potential of these tribunals for efficient disposition of legal disagreements arising from commercial relations has not yet been tested. If they are to take a central place in the international legal order, national courts will need to 'shake off the old judicial hostility to arbitration', *Kulukundis Shipping Co.* v. *Amtorg Trading Corp.*, 126 F2d 978, 985 (CA2 1942), and also their customary and understandable unwillingness to cede jurisdiction of a claim arising under domestic law to a foreign or transnational tribunal. To this extent, at least, it will be necessary for national courts to subordinate domestic notions of arbitrability to the international policy favoring commercial arbitration. See *Scherk*, *supra.*[21]

20. See n. 19, *supra.* We note, for example, that the rules of the Japan Commercial Arbitration Association provide for the taking of a 'summary record' of each hearing, Rule 28.1; for the stenographic recording of the proceedings where the tribunal so orders or a party requests one, Rule 28.1; and for a statement of reasons for the award unless the parties agree otherwise, Rule 36.1(4). See App. 219 at 221.

    Needless to say, we intimate no views on the merits of Soler's antitrust claims.

21. We do not quarrel with the Court of Appeals' conclusion that Art. II.1 of the Convention, which requires the recognition of agreements to arbitrate that involve 'subject matter capable of settlement by arbitration', contemplates exceptions to arbitrability grounded in domestic law. See 723 F2d, at 164–166; G. Gaja, International Commercial Arbitration: New York Convention I. B.2 (1984); A. van den Berg, The New York Convention of 1958: Towards a Uniform Judicial Interpretation 152–154 (1981); Contini, International Commercial Arbitration: The United Nations Convention on the Recognition and Enforcement of Foreign Arbitral Awards, 8 Am. J. Comp. L. 283, 296 (1959). But see A. van den Derg, *supra*, at 154, and n. 98 (collecting contrary authorities); G. Gaja, *supra*, at I. D., n. 43 (same). And it appears that before acceding to the Convention the Senate was advised by a State Department memorandum that the Convention provided for such exceptions. See S. Exec. Doc. E, 90th Cong., 2d Sess., 19 (1968).

    In acceding to the Convention the Senate restricted its applicability to commercial matters, in accord with Art. I.3. See 21 UST, at 2519, 2560. Yet in implementing the Convention by amendment to the federal Arbitration Act, Congress did not specify any matters it intended to exclude from its scope. See Act of July 31, 1970, Pub. L. 91–368, 84 Stat. 692, codified at 9 USC §§201–208. In *Scherk*, this Court recited Art. II.1, including the language relied upon by the Court of Appeals, but paid heed to the Convention delegates' 'frequent[ly voiced] concern that courts of signatory countries in which an agreement to arbitrate is sought to be enforced should not be permitted to decline enforcement of such agreements on the basis of parochial views of their desirability or in a manner that would diminish the mutually binding nature of the agreements'. 417 US, at 520, n. 15, citing G. Haight, Convention on the Recognition and Enforcement of Foreign Arbitral Awards: Summary Analysis of Record of United Nations Conference, May/June 1958, pp. 24–28 (1958). There, moreover, the Court dealt *arguendo* with an exception to arbitrability grounded in express congressional language; here, in contrast, we face a judicially implied exception. The utility of the Convention in promoting the process of international commercial arbitration depends upon the willingness of national courts to let go of matters they normally would think of as their own. Doubtless, Congress may specify categories of claims it wishes to reserve for decision by our own courts without contravening this Nation's obligation under the Convention. But we decline to subvert the spirit of the United States' accession to the Convention by recognizing subject-matter exceptions where Congress has not expressly directed the courts to do so.

Accordingly, we 'require this representative of the American business community to honor its bargain', *Alberto-Culver Co.* v. *Scherk*, 484 F2d 611, 620 (CA7 1973) (Stevens, J., dissenting), by holding this agreement to arbitrate 'enforce[able] . . . in accord with the explicit provisions of the Arbitration Act'. *Scherk*, 417 US, at 520.

The judgment of the Court of Appeals is affirmed in part and reversed in part, and the cases are remanded for further proceedings consistent with this opinion.

It is so ordered.

JUSTICE POWELL took no part in the decision of these cases.

SUPREME COURT OF THE UNITED STATES

NOS. 83–1569 AND 83–1733

MITSUBISHI MOTORS CORPORATION, PETITIONER 83–1569 *v.* SOLER CHRYSLER-PLYMOUTH, INC.

SOLER CHRYSLER-PLYMOUTH, INC., PETITIONER 83–1733 *v.* MITSUBISHI MOTORS CORPORATION

ON WRITS OF CERTIORARI TO THE UNITED STATED COURT OF APPEALS FOR THE FIRST CIRCUIT

[July 2, 1985]

JUSTICE STEVENS, with whom JUSTICE BRENNAN joins, and with whom JUSTICE MARSHALL joins except as to Part II, dissenting.

One element of this rather complex litigation is a claim asserted by an American dealer in Plymouth automobiles that two major automobile companies are parties to an international cartel that has restrained competition in the American market. Pursuant to an agreement that is alleged to have violated §1 of the Sherman Act, 15 USC §1, those companies allegedly prevented the dealer from transshipping some 966 surplus vehicles from Puerto Rico to other dealers in the American market. App. 92.

The petitioner denies the truth of the dealer's allegations and takes the position that the validity of the antitrust claim must be resolved by an arbitration tribunal in Tokyo, Japan. Largely because the auto manufacturers' defense to the antitrust allegation is based on provisions in the dealer's franchise agreement, the Court of Appeals concluded that the arbitration clause in that agreement encompassed the antitrust claim. 723 F2d 155, 159 (CA1 1983). It held, however, as a matter of law, that arbitration of such a claim may not be compelled under either the Federal Arbitration Act[1] or the Convention on the Recognition and Enforcement of Foreign Arbitral Awards.[2] 723 F2d, at 161–168.

This Court agrees with the Court of Appeals' interpretation of the scope of the arbitration clause, but disagrees with its conclusion that the clause is unenforceable insofar as it purports to cover an antitrust claim against a Japanese company. This Court's holding rests almost exclusively on the federal policy favoring arbitration of commercial disputes and vague notions of international comity arising from the fact

1. 9 USC §§4, 201.
2. 21 UST 2517, TIAS No. 6997.

that the automobiles involved here were manufactured in Japan. Because I am convinced that the Court of Appeals' construction of the arbitration clause is erroneous, and because I strongly disagree with this Court's interpretation of the relevant federal statutes, I respectfully dissent. In my opinion, (1) a fair construction of the language in the arbitration clause in the parties' contract does not encompass a claim that auto manufacturers entered into a conspiracy in violation of the antitrust laws; (2) an arbitration clause should not normally be construed to cover a statutory remedy that it does not expressly identify; (3) Congress did not intend §2 of the Federal Arbitration Act to apply to antitrust claims; and (4) Congress did not intend the Convention on the Recognition and Enforcement of Foreign Arbitral Awards to apply to disputes that are not covered by the Federal Arbitration Act.

I

On October 31, 1979, the respondent, Soler Chrsyler-Plymouth, Inc., ('Soler'), entered into a 'distributor agreement' to govern the sale of Plymouth passenger cars to be manufactured by the petitioner, Mitsubishi Motors Corporation of Tokyo, Japan ('Mitsubishi')[3] Mitsubishi, however, was not a party to that agreement. Rather the 'purchase rights' were granted to Soler by a wholly-owned subsidiary of Chrysler Corporation that is referred to as 'Chrysler' in the agreement.[4] The distributor agreement does not contain an arbitration clause. Nor does the record contain any other agreement providing for the arbitration of disputes between Soler and Chrysler.

Paragraph 26 of the distributor agreement authorizes Chrysler to have Soler's orders filled by any company affiliated with Chrysler, that company thereby becoming the 'supplier' of the products covered by the agreement with Chrysler.[5] Relying on

3. The distributor agreement provides, in part:

'This Agreement is made by and between CHRYSLER INTERNATIONAL S. A., a corporation organized and existing under the laws of the Swiss Confederation with its principal office in Geneva, Switzerland (hereinafter sometimes called CHRYSLER), and SOLER CHRYSLER-PLYMOUTH INC., . . . (hereinafter sometimes called DISTRIBUTOR), and will govern the sale by CHRYSLER to DISTRIBUTOR of PLYMOUTH PASSENGER CARS AND CAR DERIVATIVES MANUFACTURED BY MITSUBISHI MOTORS CORPORATION OF TOKYO, JAPAN and automotive replacement parts and accessories (said motor vehicles, replacement parts and accessories hereinafter sometimes called Products).' App. 18.

4. 'PURCHASE RIGHTS

'Subject to the provisions of this Agreement, CHRYSLER grants to DISTRIBUTOR the non-exclusive right to purchase Products from CHRYLER, and DISTRIBUTOR agrees to buy Products from CHRYSLER, for resale within the following described territory (hereinafter called Sales Area): METROPOLITAN SAN JUAN, PUERTO RICO. . . .' *Id.*, at 18.

This is the same company that is referred to as 'CISA' in the sales purchase agreement and in the Court's opinion.

5. Paragraph 26 of the distributor agreement provides:

'DIRECT SALES

'CHRYSLER and DISTRIBUTOR agree that CHRYSLER may, at its option, forward orders received from DISTRIBUTOR pursuant to this Agreement to its parent company, Chrysler Corporation, or to any subsidiary, associated or affiliated company (hereinafter called "SUPPLIER") which will then sell the Products covered by such order directly to DISTRIBUTOR, CHRYSLER and DISTRIBUTOR hereby acknowledge and agree that, unless otherwise agreed in writing, any such direct sales between SUPPLIER and DISTRIBUTOR will be governed by the terms and conditions contained on the order form and in this Agreement and that any such sales will not constitute the basis forming a distributor relationship between →

paragraph 26 of their distributor agreement,[6] Soler, Chrysler and Mitsubishi entered into a separate Sales Procedure Agreement designating Mitsubishi as the Supplier of the products covered by the distributor agreement.[7] The arbitration clause the Court construes today is found in that agreement.[8] As a matter of ordinary contract interpretation, there are at least two reasons why that clause does not apply to Soler's antitrust claim against Chrysler and Mitsubishi.

First, the clause only applies to two-party disputes between Soler and Mitsubishi. The antitrust violation alleged in Soler's counterclaim is a three-party dispute. Soler has joined both Chrysler and its associated company, Mitsubishi, as counter-defendants. The pleading expressly alleges that both of those companies are 'engaged in an unlawful combination and conspiracy to restrain and divide markets in interstate and foreign commerce, in violation of the Sherman Antitrust Act and the Clayton Act'. App. 91. It is further alleged that Chrysler authorized and participated in several overt acts directed at Soler. At this stage of the case we must, of course, assume the truth of those allegations. Only by stretching the language of the arbitration clause far beyond its ordinary meaning could one possibly conclude that it encompasses this three-party dispute.

Second, the clause only applies to disputes 'which may arise between MMC and BUYER out of or in relation to Articles I–B through V of this Agreement or for the breach thereof. . . .' *Id*, at 52. Thus, disputes relating to only five out of a total of 15 articles in the sales procedure agreement are arbitrable. Those five articles cover: (1) the terms and conditions of direct sales (matters such as the scheduling of orders, deliveries and payment); (2) technical and engineering changes; (3) compliance by Mitsubishi with customs laws and regulations, and Soler's obligation to inform Mitsubishi of relevant local laws; (4) trademarks and patent rights; and (5) Mitsubishi's right to cease production of any products. It is immediately obvious that Soler's antitrust claim did not arise out of Articles I–B through V and it is not a claim 'for the breach thereof'. The question is whether it is a dispute 'in relation to' those articles.

Because Mitsubishi relies on those articles of the contract to explain some of the activities that Soler challenges in its antitrust claim, the Court of Appeals concluded that the relationship between the dispute and those articles brought the arbitration clause into play. I find that construction of the clause wholly unpersuasive. The words 'in relation to' appear between the references to claims that arise under the contract and claims for breach of the contract; I believe all three of the species of arbitrable

→ SUPPLIER and DISTRIBUTOR. Further, DISTRIBUTOR acknowledges and agrees that any claim or controversy resulting from such direct sales by SUPPLIER will be handled by CHRYSLER as though such sale had been made by CHRYSLER.' *Id*., at 39–40.

6. 'WHEREAS, pursuant to Article 26 of the Distributor Agreement, CISA may forward orders received from BUYER to an associated company;

'WHEREAS, MMC and CISA have agreed that MMC, which is an associated company of CISA, may sell such MMC Products directly to BUYER pursuant to Article 26 of the Distributor Agreement.' *Id*., at 43.

7. Mitsubishi is jointly owned by Chrysler and by Mitsubishi Heavy Industries, Ltd, a Japanese corporation. *Id*., at 200–201.

8. That clause reads as follows:

'ARBITRATION OF CERTAIN MATTERS

'All disputes, controversies or difference which may arise between MMC and BUYER out of or in relation to Articles I–B through V of this Agreement or for the breach thereof, shall be finally settled by arbitration in Japan in accordance with the rules and regulations of the Japan Commercial Arbitration Association.' *Id*., at 52–53.

claims must be predicated on contractual rights defined in Articles I–B through V.

The federal policy favoring arbitration cannot sustain the weight that the Court assigns to it. A clause requiring arbitration of all claims 'relating to' a contract surely could not encompass a claim in restraint of trade. Cf. *Paramount Famous Lasky Corp.* v. *United States*, 282 US 30 (1930); see also *United States* v. *Paramount Pictures, Inc.*, 334 US 131, 176 (1948). Nor, in my judgment should it be read to encompass a claim that relies, not on a failure to perform the contract, but on an independent violation of federal law. The matters asserted by way of defense do not control the character, or the source, of the claim that Soler has asserted.[9] Accordingly, simply as a matter of ordinary contract interpretation, I would hold that Soler's antitrust claim is not arbitrable.

II

Section 2 of the Federal Arbitration Act describes three kinds of arbitrable agreements.[10] Two—those including maritime transactions and those covering the submission of an existing dispute to arbitration—are not involved in this case. The language of §2 relating to the Soler-Mitsubishi arbitration clause reads as follows:

> 'A written provision in . . . a contract evidencing a transaction involving commerce to settle by arbitration a controversy thereafter arising out of such contract . . . or the refusal to perform the whole or any part thereof, . . . shall be valid, irrevocable, and enforceable, save upon such grounds as exist at law or in equity for the revocation of any contract.'

The plain language of this statute encompasses Soler's claims that arise out of its contract with Mitsubishi, but does not encompass a claim arising under federal law, or indeed one that arises under its distributor agreement with Chrysler. Nothing in the text of the 1925 Act, nor its legislative history, suggests that Congress intended to authorize the arbitration of any statutory claims.[11]

9. Even if Mitsubishi can prove that it did not violate any provision of the contract, such proof would not necessarily constitute a defense to the antitrust claim. In contrast, in *Prima Paint Corp.* v. *Flood & Conklin Mfg. Co.*, 388 US 395 (1967), Prima Paint's claim of fraud in the inducement was asserted to rescind the contract, not as an independent basis of recovery.
10. Section 2 provides:
'A written provision in any maritime transaction or contract evidencing a transaction involving commerce to settle by arbitration a controversy thereafter arising out of such contract or transaction, or the refusal to perform the whole or any part thereof, or an agreement in writing to submit to arbitration an existing controversy arising out of such a contract, transaction, or refusal, shall be valid, irrevocable, and enforceable, save upon such grounds as exist at law or in equity for the revocation of any contract.' 9 USC §2.
11. In his dissent in *Prima Paint Corp.* v. *Flood and Conklin Mfg. Co.*, 388 US, at 415, Justice Black quoted the following commentary written shortly after the statute was passed:
'Not all questions arising out of contracts ought to be arbitrated. It is a remedy peculiarly suited to the disposition of the ordinary disputes between merchants as to questions of fact—quantity, quality, time of delivery, compliance with terms of payment, excuses for non-performance, and the like. It has a place also in the determination of the simpler questions of law—the questions of law which arise out of these daily relations between merchants as to the passage of title, the existence of warranties, or the questions of law which are complementary to the questions of fact which we have just mentioned.' Cohen & Dayton, The New Federal Arbitration Law, 12 Va. L. Rev. 265, 281 (1926).
In the *Prima Paint* case the Court held that the Act applied to a claim of fraud in the inducement of the contract, but did not intimate that it might also cover federal statutory claims. See n. 9, *supra*.

Until today all of our cases enforcing agreements to arbitrate under the Arbitration Act have involved contract claims. In one, the party claiming a breach of contractual warranties also claimed that the breach amounted to fraud actionable under §10(b) under the Securities and Exchange Actof 1934. *Scherk* v. *Alberto Culver Co.*, 417 US 506 (1974).[12] But this is the first time the Court has considered the question whether a standard arbitration clause referring to claims arising out of or relating to a contract should be construed to cover statutory claims that have only an indirect relationship to the contract.[13] In my opinion, neither the Congress that enacted the Arbitration Act in 1925, nor the many parties who have agreed to such standard clauses, could have anticipated the Court's answer to that question.

On several occasions we have drawn a distinction between statutory rights and contractual rights and refused to hold that an arbitration barred the assertion of a statutory right. Thus, in *Alexander* v. *Gardner-Denver Co.*, 415 US 36 (1974), we held that the arbitration of a claim of employment discrimination would not bar an employee's statutory right to damages under Title VII of the Civil Rights Act of 1964, 42 USC 2000e–2000e–17, notwithstanding the strong federal policy favoring the arbitration of labor disputes. In that case the Court explained at some length why it would be unreasonable to assume that Congress intended to give arbitrators the final authority to implement the federal statutory policy:

> '[W]e have long recognized that "the choice of forums inevitably affects the scope of the substantive right to be vindicated". *US Bulk Carriers* v. *Arguelles*, 400 US 351, 359–360 (1971) (Harlan, J., concurring). Respondent's deferral rule is necessarily premised on the assumption that arbitral processes are commensurate with judicial processes and that Congress impliedly intended federal courts to defer to arbitral decisions on Title VII issues. We deem this supposition unlikely.
>
> 'Arbitral procedures, while well suited to the resolution of contractual disputes, make arbitration a comparatively inappropriate forum for the final resolution of rights created by Title VII. This conclusion rests first on the special role of the arbitrator, whose task is to effectuate the intent of the parties rather than the requirements of enacted legislation. . . . But other facts may still render arbitral processes in the protection of Title VII rights. Among these is the fact that the specialized competence of arbitrators pertains primarily to the law of the shop, not the law of the land. *United Steelworkers of America* v. *Warrior & Gulf Navigation Co.*, 363 US 574, 581–583 (1960). Parties usually choose an arbitrator because they trust his knowledge and judgment concerning the demands and norms of industrial relations. On the other hand, the resolution of statutory or constitutional

12. 'The dispute between these parties over the alleged shortage in defendant's inventory of European trademarks, a matter covered by contract warranties and subject to pre-closing verification, is the kind of commercial dispute for which arbitration is entirely appropriate. In my opinion, the fact that the "fraud" language of Rule 10(b)(5) has been included in the complaint is far less significant than the desirability of having the Court of Arbitration of the International Chamber of Commerce in Paris, France, decide the various questions of foreign law which should determine the rights of these parties.' *Alberto-Culver* v. *Scherk*, 484 F2d 611, 619–620 (CA7 1973) (Stevens, J. dissenting), reversed 417 US 506 (1974).
13. It is interesting to note that in *Moses H. Cone Memorial Hospital* v. *Mercury Construction Corp.*, 460 US 1 (1983), the Court referred to the standard clause describing claims 'arising out of, or relating to, this contractor the breach thereof' as a provision 'for resolving disputes arising out of the contract or its breach'. *Id.*, at 4–5.

issues is a primary responsibility of courts, and judicial construction has proved especially necessary with respect to Title VII, whose broad language frequently can be given meaning only by reference to public law concepts.' 415 US, at 56–57 (footnote omitted).

In addition, the Court noted that the informal procedures which make arbitration so desirable in the context of contractual disputes are inadequate to develop a record for appellate review of statutory questions.[14] Such review is essential on matters of statutory interpretation in order to assure consistent application of important public rights.

In *Barrentine* v. *Arkansas-Best Freight System, Inc.*, 450 US 728 (1981), we reached a similar conclusion with respect to arbitrability of an employee's claim based on the Fair Labor Standards Act, 29 USC §§201–209. We again noted that an arbitrator, unlike a federal judge, has no institutional obligation to enforce federal legislative policy:

> 'Because the arbitrator is required to effectuate the intent of the parties, rather than to enforce the statute, he may issue a ruling that is inimical to the public policies underlying the FLSA, thus depriving an employee of protected statutory rights.
>
> 'Finally, not only are arbitral procedures less protective of individual statutory rights than are judicial procedures, see *Gardner-Denver*, *supra*, at 57–58, but arbitrators very often are powerless to grant the aggrieved employees as broad a range of relief. Under the FLSA, courts can award actual and liquidated damages, reasonable attorney's fees, and costs. 29 USC §216(b). An arbitrator, by contrast, can award only that compensation authorized by the wage provision of the collective bargaining agreement.... It is most unlikely that he will be authorized to award liquidated damages, costs, or attorney's fees.' 450 US, at 744–745 (footnote omitted).

The Court has applied the same logic in holding that federal claims asserted under the Ku Klux Klan Act of 1871, 42 USC §1983, and claims arising under §12(2) of the Securities Act of 1933, 15 USC §77*l*(2), may not be finally resolved by an arbitrator. *McDonald* v. *City of West Branch*, — US — (1984); *Wilko* v. *Swan*, 346 US 427 (1953).

The Court's opinions in *Alexander*, *Barrentine*, *McDonald* and *Wilko* all explain why it makes good sense to draw a distinction between statutory claims and contract claims. In view of the Court's repeated recognition of the distinction between federal statutory rights and contractual rights, together with the undisputed historical fact that arbitration has functioned almost entirely in either the area of labor disputes or in

14. 'Moreover, the factfinding process in arbitration usually is not equivalent to judicial factfinding. The record of the arbitration proceedings is not as complete; the usual rules of evidence do not apply; and rights and procedures common to civil trials, such as discovery, compulsory process, cross-examination, and testimony under oath, are often severely limited or unavailable. See *Bernhardt* v. *Polygraphic Co.*, 350 US 198, 203 (1956); *Wilko* v. *Swan*, 346 US, at 435–437. And as this Court has recognized, "[a]rbitrators have no obligation to the court to give their reasons for an award". *United Steelworkers of America* v. *Enterprise Wheel & Car Corp.*, 363 US, at 598. Indeed, it is the informality of arbitral procedure that enables it to function as an efficient, inexpensive, and expeditious means for dispute resolution. This same characteristic, however, makes arbitration a less appropriate forum for final resolution of Title VII issues than the federal courts.' 415 US, at 57–58 (footnote omitted).

'ordinary disputes between merchants as to questions of fact', see n. 11, *supra*, it is reasonable to assume that most lawyers and executives would not expect the language in the standard arbitration clause to cover federal statutory claims. Thus, in my opinion, both a fair respect for the importance of the interests that Congress has identified as worthy of federal statutory protection, and a fair appraisal of the most likely understanding of the parties who sign agreements containing standard arbitration clauses, support a presumption that such clauses do not apply to federal statutory claims.

III

The Court has repeatedly held that a decision by Congress to create a special statutory remedy renders a private agreement to arbitrate a federal statutory claim unenforceable. Thus, as I have already noted, the express statutory remedy provided in the Ku Klux Klan Act of 1871,[15] the express statutory remedy in the Securities Act of 1933,[16] the express statutory remedy in the Fair Labor Standards Act,[17] and the express statutory remedy in Title VII of the Civil Rights Act of 1964,[18] each provided the Court with convincing evidence that Congress did not intend the protection afforded by the statute to be administered by a private arbitrator. The reasons that motivated those decisions apply with special force to the federal policy that is protected by the antitrust laws.

To make this point it is appropriate to recall some of our past appraisals of the importance of this federal policy and then to identify some of the specific remedies Congress has designed to implement it. It was Chief Justice Hughes who characterized the Sherman Anti-Trust Act as 'a charter of freedom' that may fairly be compared to a constitutional provision. See *Appalachian Coals, Inc.* v. *United States*, 288 US 344, 359–360 (1933). In *United States* v. *Philadelphia National Bank*, 374 US 321, 371 (1963), the Court referred to the extraordinary 'magnitude' of the value choices made by Congress in enacting the Sherman Act. More recently, the Court described the weighty public interests underlying the basic philosophy of the statute:

> 'Antitrust laws in general, and the Sherman Act in particular, are the Magna Carta of free enterprise. They are as important to the preservation of economic freedom and our free-enterprise system as the Bill of Rights is to the protection of our fundamental personal freedoms. And the freedom guaranteed each and every business, no matter how small, is the freedom to compete—to assert with vigor, imagination, devotion, and ingenuity whatever economic muscle it can muster. Implicit in such freedom is the notion that it cannot be foreclosed with respect to one sector of the economy because certain private citizens or groups believe that such foreclosure might promote greater competition in a more important sector of the economy.' *United States* v. *Topco Associates, Inc.*, 405 US 596, 610 (1972).

The Sherman and Clayton Acts reflect Congress' appraisal of the value of economic

15. *McDonald* v. *City of West Branch*, — US — (1984).
16. *Wilko* v. *Swan*, 346 US 427 (1953).
17. *Barrentine* v. *Arkansas-Best Freight System, Inc.*, 450 US 728 (1981).
18. *Alexander* v. *Gardner-Denver Co.*, 415 US 36 (1974).

freedom; they guarantee the vitality of the entrepreneurial spirit. Questions arising under these Acts are among the most important in public law.

The unique public interest in the enforcement of the antitrust laws is repeatedly reflected in the special remedial scheme enacted by Congress. Since its enactment in 1890, the Sherman Act has provided for public enforcement through criminal as well as civil sanctions. The preeminent federal interest in effective enforcement once justified a provision for special three judge district courts to hear antitrust claims on an expedited basis, as well as for direct appeal to this Court by-passing the Courts of Appeals.[19] See, *e.g.*, *United States* v. *National Ass'n of Securities Dealers*, 422 US 694 (1975).

The special interest in encouraging private enforcement of the Sherman Act has been reflected in the statutory scheme ever since 1890. Section 7 of the original Act,[20] uses the broadest possible language to describe the class of litigants who may invoke its protection. 'The Act is comprehensive in its terms and coverage, protecting all who are made victims of the forbidden practices by whomever they may be perpetrated.' *Mandeville Island Farms, Inc.* v. *American Crystal Sugar Co.*, 334 US 219, 236 (1948); see also *Associated Genral Contractors* v. *Carpenters*, 459 US 519, 529 (1983).

The provision for mandatory treble damages—unique in federal law when the statute was enacted—provides a special incentive to the private enforcement of the statute, as well as an especially powerful deterrent to violators.[21] What we have described as 'the public interest in vigilant enforcement of antitrust laws through the instrumentality of the private treble damage action' *Lawlor* v. *National Screen Service Corp.*, 349 US 322, 329 (1955), is buttressed by the statutory mandate that the injured party also recover costs, 'including a reasonable attorney's fee'. 15 USC §15(a). The

19. See 32 Stat. 823 (1903), repealed 88 Stat. 1708 (1974), 98 Stat. 3358 (1984) (P. L. No. 98–620, §402(11)). The Act still provides an avenue for directly appealing to this Court from a final judgment in a Government antitrust suit. 15 USC §29(b).

20. 'Any person who shall be injured in his business or property by any other person or corporation by reason of anything forbidden or declared to be unlawful by this act, may sue therefor in any circuit court of the United States in the district in which the defendant resides or is found, without respect to the amount in controversy, and shall recover three fold the damages by him sustained, and the costs of suit, including a reasonable attorney's fee.' 26 Stat. 210.
The current version of the private remedy is codified at 15 USC §15(a).

21. 'We have often indicated the inappropriateness of invoking broad common-law barriers to relief where a private suit serves important public purposes. It was for this reason that we held in *Kiefer-Stewart Co.* v. *Seagram & Sons*, 340 US 211 (1951), that a plaintiff in an antitrust suit could not be barred from recovery by proof that he had engaged in an unrelated conspiracy to commit some other antitrust violation. Similarly, in *Simpson* v. *Union Oil Co.*, 377 US 13 (1964), we held that a dealer whose consignment agreement was canceled for failure to adhere to a fixed resale price could bring suit under the antitrust laws even though by signing the agreement he had to that extent become a participant in the illegal, competition-destroying scheme. Both *Simpson* and *Kiefer-Stewart* were premised on a recognition that the purposes of the antitrust laws are best served by insuring that the private action will be an ever-present threat to deter anyone contemplating business behavior in violation of the antitrust laws. The plaintiff who reaps the reward of treble damages may be no less morally reprehensible than the defendant, but the law encourages his suit to further the overriding public policy in favor of competition. A more fastidious regard for the relative moral worth of the parties would only result in seriously undermining the usefulness of the private action as a bulwark of antitrust enforcement. And permitting the plaintiff to recover a windfall gain does not encourage continued violations by those in his position since they remain fully subject to civil and criminal penalties for their own illegal conduct.' *Perma Life Mufflers, Inc.* v. *International Parts Corp.*, 392 US 134, 138–139 (1968).

interest in wide and effective enforcement has thus, for almost a century, been vindicated by enlisting the assistance of 'private Attorneys General';[22] we have always attached special importance to their role because '[e]very violation of the antitrust laws is a blow to the free-enterprise system envisaged by Congress'. *Hawaii* v. *Standard Oil Co.*, 405 US 251, 262 (1972).

There are, in addition, several unusual features of the antitrust enforcement scheme that unequivocally require rejection of any thought that Congress would tolerate private arbitration of antitrust claims in lieu of the statutory remedies that it fashioned. As we explained in *Blumenstock Brothers Advertising Agency* v. *Curtis Publishing Co.*, 225 US 436, 440 (1920), an antitrust treble damage case 'can only be brought in a District Court of the United States'. The determination that these cases are 'too important to be decided otherwise than by competent tribunals'[23] surely cannot allow private arbitrators to assume a jurisdiction that is denied to courts of the sovereign States.

The extraordinary importance of the private antitrust remedy has been emphasized in other statutes enacted by Congress. Thus, in 1913, Congress passed a special act guaranteeing public access to depositions in government civil proceedings to enforce the Sherman Act. 37 Stat. 731, 15 USC §30.[24] The purpose of that Act plainly was to enable victims of antitrust violations to make evidentiary use of information developed in a public enforcement proceeding. This purpose was further implemented in the following year by the enactment of §5 of the Clayton Act providing that a final judgment or decree in a Government case may constitute prima facia proof of a violation in a subsequent treble damage case. 38 Stat. 731, 15 USC §16(a). These special remedial provisions attest to the importance that Congress has attached to the private remedy.

In view of the history of antitrust enforcement in the United States, it is not surprising that all of the federal courts have considered the question have uniformly and unhesitatingly concluded that agreements to arbitrate federal antitrust issues are not enforceable. In a landmark opinion for the Court of Appeals for the Second Circuit, Judge Feinberg wrote:

> 'A claim under the antitrust laws is not merely a private matter. The Sherman Act is designed to promote the national interest in a competitive economy; thus, the plaintiff asserting his rights under the Act has been

22. Under the Panama Canal Act, any private shipper—in addition to the United States—may also bring an action seeking to bar access to the canal for any vessel owned by a company 'doing business' in violattion of the antitrust laws. 37 Stat. 567 (1912), 15 USC §31.
23. In *University Life Insurance Co.* v. *Unimarc Ltd.*, 699 F2d 846 (CA7 1983), Judge Posner wrote: 'The suit brought by Unimarc and Huff . . . raises issues of state tort and contract law and federal antitrust law. The tort and contract issues may or may not be within the scope of the arbitration clauses in the coinsurance and second marketing agreements but they are arbitrable in the sense that an agreement to arbitrate them would be enforceable. Federal antitrust issues, however, are nonarbitrable in just that sense. *Applied Digital Technology, Inc.* v. *Continental Casulty Co.*, 576 F2d 116, 117 (7th Cir. 1978). They are considered to be at once too difficult to be decided competently by arbitrators—who are not judges, and often not even lawyers—and too important to be decided otherwise than by competent tribunals. See *American Safety Equipment Corp.* v. *J. P. Maguire & Co.*, 391 F2d 821, 826–27 (2d Cir. 1968). The root of the doctrine is in the same soil as the principle, announced in *Blumenstock Bros. Adv. Agency* v. *Curtis Pub. Co.*, 252 US 436, 440–41 (1920), that federal antitrust suits may not be brought in state courts.' *Id.*, at 850–851.
24. See *United States* v. *Procter & Gamble Co.*, 356 US 677, 683 (1958).

likened to a private attorney-general who protects the public's interest. . . . Antitrust violations can affect hundreds of thousands—perhaps millions —of people and inflict staggering economic damage. . . . We do not believe that Congress intended such claims to be resolved elsewhere than in the courts. We do not suggest that all antitrust litigations attain these swollen proportions; the courts, no less than the public, are thankful that they do not. But in fashioning a rule to govern the arbitrability of antitrust claims, we must consider the rule's potential effect. For the same reason, it is also proper to ask whether contracts of adhesion between alleged monopolists and their customers should determine the forum for trying antitrust violations.' *American Safety Equipment Corp.* v. *J. P. Maguire & Co.*, 391 F2d 821, 826–827 (1968) (footnote omitted).

This view has been followed in later cases from that Circuit[25] and by the First,[26] Fifth,[27] Seventh,[28] Eighth[29] and Ninth Circuits.[30] It is clearly a correct statement of the law.

This Court would be well advised to endorse the collective wisdom of the distinguished judges of the Court of Appeals who have unanimously concluded that the statutory remedies fashioned by Congress for the enforcement of the antitrust laws render an agreement to arbitrate antitrust disputes unenforceable. Arbitration awards are only reviewable for manifest disregard of the law, 9 USC §§10, 207, and the rudimentary procedures which make arbitration so desirable in the context of a private dispute often mean that the record is so inadequate that the arbitrator's decision is virtually unreviewable.[31] Despotic decision making of this kind is fine for parties who are willing to agree in advance to settle for a best approximation of the correct result in order to resolve quickly and inexpensively any contractual dispute that may arise in an ongoing commercial relationship. Such informality, however, is simply unacceptable when every error may have devastating consequences for important businesses in our national economy and may undermine their ability to

25. *N. V. Maatschappij Voor Industriele Waarden* v. *A. O. Smith Corp.*, 532 F2d 874, 876 (CA2 1976) (*per curiam*).
26. 723 F2d, at 162 (Coffin, J., for the court) (opinion below).
27. *Cobb* v. *Lewis*, 488 F2d 41, 47 (1974) (Wisdom, J., for the court).
28. *University Life Insurance Co.* v. *Unimarc Ltd.*, 699 F2d, at 850–851 (1983) (Posner, J., for the court); *Applied Digital Technology Inc.* v. *Continental Casualty Co.*, 576 F2d 116, 117 (1978) (Pell, J., for the court).
29. *Helfenbein* v. *International Industries, Inc.*, 438 F2d 1068, 1070 (Lay, J., for the court), cert. denied, 404 US 872 (1971).
30. *Lake Communications, Inc.* v. *ICC Corp.*, 738 F2d 1473, 1477–1480 (1984) (Browning, C.J., for the court); *Varo* v. *Comprehensive Designers, Inc.*, 504 F2d 1103, 1104 (1974) (Chambers, J., for the Court); *Power Replacements, Inc.* v. *Air Preheater Co.*, 426 F2d 980, 983–984 (1970) (Jameson, J., for the court); *A. & E. Plastik Pak Co.* v. *Monsanto Co.*, 396 F2d 710, 715–716 (1968) (Merrill, J., for the court).
31. The arbitration procedure in this case does not provide any right to evidentiary discovery or a written decision, and requires that all proceedings be closed to the public. App. 220–221. Moreover, Japanese arbitrators do not have the power of compulsory process to secure witnesses and documents, nor do witnesses who are available testify under oath. *Id.*, at 218–219. Cf. 9 USC §7 (arbitrators may summon witnesses to attend proceedings and seek enforcement in a district court).

compete in world markets.[32] Instead of 'muffling a grievance in the cloakroom of arbitration', the public interest in free competitive markets would be better served by having the issues 'resolved in the light of impartial public court adjudication'. See *Merrill Lynch, Pierce, Fenner & Smith, Inc.* v. *Ware*, 414 US 117, 136 (1973).[33]

IV

The Court assumes for the purposes of its decision that the antitrust issues would not be arbitrable if this were a purely domestic dispute, *ante*, at 14, but holds that the international character of the controversy makes it arbitrable. The holding rests on vague concerns for the international implications of its decision and a misguided application of *Scherk* v. *Alberto-Culver*, 417 US 506 (1974).

International Obligations of the United States

Before relying on its own notions of what international comity requires, it is surprising that the Court does not determine the specific commitments that the United States has made to enforce private agreements to arbitrate disputes arising under public law. As the Court acknowledges, the only treaty relevant here is the Convention on the Recognition and Enforcement of Foreign Arbitral Awards. 21 UST 2517, TIAS No. 6997. The Convention was adopted in 1958 at a multilateral conference sponsored by the United Nations. This Nation did not sign the proposed convention at that time; displaying its characteristic caution before entering into international compacts, the United States did not accede to it until twelve years later.

As the Court acknowledged in *Scherk* v. *Alberto Culver Co.*, 417 US., at 520, n. 15, the principal purpose of the Convention 'was to encourage the recognition and enforcement of commercial arbitration agreements in international contracts and to unify the standards by which agreements to arbitrate are observed and arbitral awards are enforced in the signatory countries'. However, the United States, as *amicus curiae*, advises the Court that the Convention 'clearly contemplates' that signatory nations will enforce domestic laws prohibiting the arbitration of certain subject matters. Brief for the United States as *Amicus Curiae* 28. This interpretation of the Convention was adopted by the Court of Appeals, 723 F2d, at 162–166, and the Court declines to reject it, *ante*, at 24, n. 21. The construction is beyond doubt.

Article II(3) of the Convention provides that the court of a Contracting State, 'when seized of an action in a matter in respect of which the parties have made an agreement within the meaning of this article, shall, at the request of one of the parties,

32. The greatest risk, of course, is that the arbitrator will condemn business practices under the antitrust laws that are efficient in a free competitive market. Cf. *Northwest Wholesale Stationers, Inc.* v. *Pacific Stationery & Printing Co.*, — US — (1985), rev'g 715 F2d 1393 (CA9 1983). In the absence of a reviewable record, a reviewing district court would not be able to undo the damage wrought. Even a Government suit or an action by a private party might not be available to set aside the award.
33. The Court notes that some courts which have held that agreements to arbitrate antitrust claims generally are unenforceable have nevertheless enforced arbitration agreements to settle an existing antitrust claim. *Ante*, at 18. These settlement agreements, made after the parties have had every opportunity to evaluate the strength of their position, are obviously less destructive of the private treble damages remedy that Congress provided. Thus, it may well be that arbitration as a means of settling existing disputes is permissible.

refer the parties to arbitration'. This obligation does not arise, however, (i) if the agreement 'is null and void, inoperative or incapable of being performed', Art. II (3), or (ii) if the dispute does not concern 'a subject matter capable of settlement by arbitration', Art. II(1). The former qualification principally applies to matters of fraud, mistake, and duress in the inducement, or problems of procedural fairness and feasibility. 723 F2d, at 164. The latter clause plainly suggests the possibility that some subject matters are not capable of arbitration under the domestic laws of the signatory nations, and that agreements to arbitrate such disputes need not be enforced.

This construction is confirmed by the provisions of the Convention which provide for the enforcement of international arbitration awards. Article III provides that each 'Contracting State shall recognize arbitral awards as binding and enforce them'. However, if an arbitration award is 'contrary to the public policy of [a] country' called upon to enforce it, or if it concerns a subject matter which is 'not capable of settlement by arbitration under the law of that country', the Convention does not require that it be enforced. Art. V (2) (a) and (b). Thus, reading articles II and V together, the Convention provides that agreements to arbitrate disputes which are nonarbitrable under domestic law need not be honored, nor awards rendered under them enforced.[34]

This construction is also supported by the legislative history of the Senate's advice and consent to the Convention. In presenting the Convention for the Senate's consideration the President offered the following interpretation of Article II(1):

> 'The requirement that the agreement apply to a matter capable of settlement by arbitration is necessary in order to take proper account of laws in force in many countries which prohibit the submission of certain questions to arbitration. In some States of the United States, for example, disputes affecting the title to real property are not arbitrable.' S. Exec. Doc. E, at 19.

The Senate's consent to the Convention presumably was made in light of this interpretation, and thus it is to be afforded considerable weight. *Sumitomo Shoji America, Inc.* v. *Avagliano*, 457 US 176, 184–185 (1982).

International Comity

It is clear then that the international obligations of the United States permit us to honor Congress' commitment to the exclusive resolution of antitrust disputes in the federal courts. The Court today refuses to do so offering only vague concerns for comity among nations. The courts of other nations, on the other hand, have applied the exception provided in the Convention, and refused to enforce agreements to arbitrate specific subject matters of concern to them.[35]

34. Indeed, it has been argued that a State may refuse to enforce an agreement to arbitrate a subject matter which is nonarbitrable in domestic law under Article II(3) as well as under Article II(1). Since awards rendered under such agreements need not be enforced under Article V(2) the agreement is 'incapable of being performed'. Art. II(3). S. Exec. Doc. E, 90th Cong., 2d Sess. 19 (1968) (hereinafter S. Exec. Doc. E.); G. Haight, Convention on the Recognition and Enforcement of Foreign Arbitral Awards 27–28 (1958).
35. For example, the Cour de Cassation in Belgium has held that disputes arising under a Belgian statute limiting the unilateral termination of exclusive distributorships are not arbitrable under the Convention in that country, *Audi-NSU Auto Union A. G.* v. *S. A. Adelin Petit & Cie.* (1979), in 5 YB Commercial Arbitration 257, 259, and the Corte di Cassazione in Italy has held that labor disputes are not arbitrable under the Convention in that country, *Compagnia Generale Construzioni* v. *Piersanti*, [1980] Foro Italiano I 190, in 6 YB Commercial Arbitration 229, 230.

It may be that the subject matter exception to the Convention ought to be reserved—as a matter of domestic law—for matters of the greatest public interest which involve concerns that are shared by other nations. The Sherman Act's commitment to free competitive markets is among our most important civil policies. *Supra*, at 11–18. This commitment, shared by other nations which are signatory to the Convention,[36] is hardly the sort of parochial concern that we should decline to enforce the interest of international comity. Indeed, the branch of Government entrusted with the conduct of political relations with foreign governments has informed us that the 'the United States' determination that federal antitrust claims are nonarbitrable under the Convention . . . is not likely to result in either surprise or recrimination on the part of other signatories to the Convention'. Brief for the United States as *Amicus Curiae* 30.

Lacking any support for the proposition that the enforcement of our domestic laws in this context will result in international recriminations, the Court seeks refuge in an obtuse application of its own precedent, *Scherk* v. *Alberto-Culver Co.*, 417 US 506 (1974), in order to defend the contrary result. The *Scherk* case was an action for damages brought by an American purchaser of three European businesses in which it was claimed that the sellers fraudulent representations concerning the status of certain European trademarks constituted a violation of §10(b) of the Securities Exchange Act of 1934, 15 USC §78j(b). The Court held that the parties' agreement to arbitrate any dispute arising out of the purchase agreement was enforceable under the Federal Arbitration Act. The legal issue was whether the Court's earlier holding in *Wilko* v. *Swan*, 346 US 427—'that an agreement to arbitrate could not preclude a buyer of a security from seeking a judicial remedy under the Securities Act of 1933' see 417 US, at 510—was 'controlling authority'. *Ibid.*

The Court carefully identified two important differences between the *Wilko* case and the *Scherk* case. First, the statute involved in *Wilko* contained an express private remedy that had 'no statutory counterpart' in the statute involved in *Scherk*, see *id.* at 513. Although the Court noted that this difference provided a 'colorable argument' for reaching a different result, the Court did not rely on it. *Id.*, at 513–514.

Instead, it based its decision on the second distinction—that the outcome in *Wilko* was governed entirely by American law whereas in *Scherk* foreign rules of law would control and, if the arbitration clause were not enforced, a host of international conflict of laws problems would arise. The Court explained:

> 'Alberto-Culver's contract to purchase the business entities belonging to Scherk was a truly international agreement. Alberto-Culver is an American corporation with its principal place of business and the vast bulk of its activity in this country, while Scherk is a citizen of Germany whose companies were organized under the laws of Germany and Liechtenstein. The negotiations leading to the signing of the contract in Austria and to the closing in Switzerland took place in the United Stated, England, and Germany, and involved consultations with legal and trademark experts from each of those countries and from Liechtenstein. Finally, and most significantly, the subject matter of the contract concerned the sale of business enterprises organized under the laws of and primarily situated in

36. For example, the Federal Republic of Germany has a vigorous antitrust program, and prohibits the enforcement of pre-dispute agreements to arbitrate such claims under some circumstances. See Act Against Restraints of Competition §91(1), in Organisation for Economic Co-operation and Development, Guide to Legislation on Restrictive Business Practices, Part D, 49 (1980). See also 2 G. Delaume, Transnational Contracts §13.06, at 31 and n. 3 (1982).

European countries, whose activities were largely, if not entirely, directed to European markets.

'Such a contract involves considerations and policies significantly different from those found controlling in *Wilko*. In *Wilko*, quite apart from the arbitration provision, there was no question but that the laws of the United States generally, and the federal securities laws in particular, would govern disputes arising out of the stock-purchase agreement. The parties, the negotiations, and the subject matter of the contract were all situated in this country, and no credible claim could have been entertained that any international conflict-of-laws problems would arise. In this case, by contrast, in the absence of the arbitration provision considerable uncertainty existed at the time of the agreement, and still exists, concerning the law applicable to the resolution of disputes arising out of the contract.' *Id.*, at 515–516 (footnote omitted).

Thus, in its opinion in *Scherk*, the Court distinguished *Wilko* because in that case 'no credible claim could have been entertained that any international conflict of laws problems would arise'. That distinction fits this case precisely, since I consider it perfectly clear that the rule of American antitrust law must govern the claim of an American automobile dealer that he has been injured by an international conspiracy to restrain trade in the American automobile market.[37]

The critical importance of the foreign law issues in *Scherk* was apparent to me even before the case reached this Court. See n. 12, *supra*. For that reason, it is especially distressing to find that the Court is unable to perceive why the reasoning in *Scherk* is wholly inapplicable to Soler's antitrust claims against Chrysler and Mitsubishi. The merits of those claims are controlled entirely by American law. It is true that the automobiles are manufactured in Japan and that Mitsubishi is a Japanese corporation, but the same antitrust questions would be presented if Mitsubishi were owned by two American companies instead of by one American and one Japanese partner. When Mitsubishi enters the American market and plans to engage in business in that market over a period of years, it must recognize its obligation to comply with American law and to be subject to the remedial provisions of American statutes.[38]

The federal claim that was asserted in *Scherk*, unlik Soler's antitrust claim, had not been expressly authorized by Congress. Indeed, until this Court's recent decision in *Landreth Timber Co.* v. *Landreth*, — US — (1985), the federal cause of action asserted in *Scherk* would not have been entertained in a number of federal circuits because it did not involve the kind of securities transaction that Congress intended to regulate when it enacted the Securities Exchange Act of 1934.[39] The fraud claimed in *Scherk* was virtually identical to the breach of warranty claim; arbitration of such

37. Cf. *Compagnia Generale Construzioni* v. *Piersanti*, [1980] Foro Italiano I 190 (Corte Cass. Italy), in 6 YB Commercial Arbitration 229, 230; *Audi-NSU Auto Union A. G.* v. *S. A. Adelin Petit & Cie.* (Cour Cass. Belgium 1979), in 5 YB Commercial Arbitration 257, 259.
38. Cf. *Sumitomo Shoji America, Inc.* v. *Avagliano*, 457 US 176 (1982) (Japanese general trading company's wholly owned subsidiary which is incorporated in the United States is not exempt from obligations under Title VII under bilateral commercial treaty).
39. The Court's opinion in *Landreth Timber*, — US, at —, n. 7, does not take issue with my assertion, in dissent, that Congress never 'intended to cover negotiated transactions involving the sale of control of a business whose securities have never been offered orsold in any public market'. *Id.*, at —.

claims arising out of an agreement between parties of equal bargaining strength does not conflict with any significant federal policy.

In contrast, Soler's claim not only implicates our fundamental antitrust policies, *supra* at 11–18, but also should be evaluated in the light of an explicit Congressional finding concerning the disparity in bargaining power between automobile manufacturers and their franchised dealers. In 1956, when Congress enacted special legislation to protect dealers from bad faith franchise terminations,[40] it recited its intent 'to balance the power now heavily weighted in favor of automobile manufacturers'. 70 Stat. 1125. The special federal interest in protecting automobile dealers from overreaching by car manufacturers, as well as the policies underlying the Sherman Act, underscore the folly of the Court's decision today.

V

The Court's repeated incantation of the high ideals of 'international arbitration' creates the impression that this case involves the fate of an institution designed to implement a formula for world peace.[41] But just as it is improper to subordinate the public interest in enforcement of antitrust policy to the private interest in resolving commercial disputes, so it is equally unwise to allow a vision of world unity to distort the importance of the selection of the proper forum for resolving this dispute. Like any other mechanism for resolving controversies, international arbitration will only succeed if it is realistically limited to tasks it is capable of performing well—the prompt and inexpensive resolution of essentially contractual disputes between commercial partners. As for matters involving the political passions and the fundamental interests of nations, even the multilateral convention adopted under the auspices of the United Nations recognizes that private international arbitration is incapable of achieving satisfactory results.

In my opinion, the elected representatives of the American people would not have us dispatch an American citizen to a foreign land in search of an uncertain remedy for the violation of a public right that is protected by the Sherman Act. This is especially so when there has been no genuine bargaining over the terms of the submission, and the arbitration remedy provided has not even the most elementary guarantees of fair process. Consideration of a fully developed record by a jury, instructed in the law by a federal judge, and subject to appellate review, is a surer guide to the competitive character of a commercial practice than the practically unreviewable judgment of a private arbitrator.

Unlike the Congress that enacted the Sherman Act in 1890, the Court today does not seem to appreciate the value of economic freedom. I respectfully dissent.

6.6 — F2d — (2nd Cir., 1986).

6.7 28 USC 1602–1611.

6.8 *See* Section 2 of this Chapter; note such decisions as McMahon *v.* Shearson/American Express, Inc, 788 F2d 94 (2nd Cir., 1986); American Safety Equipment Corp. *v.* J. P. Maguire & Co, 391 F2d 821 (2nd Cir., 1968); and Wilcox *v.* Ho-Wing Sit, 586 F Supp 561 (ND Cal., 1984).

6.9 Ch 684 Fla Laws 1986, as set forth hereafter.

40. Automobile Dealer's Day in Court Act, 15 USC §1221–1225.

41. *E.g.*, Charter of the United Nations and Statute of the International Court of Justice, 59 Stat. 1031, TS No. 993 (1945); Constitution of the International Labor Organisation, 49 Stat. 2712, TS No. 874 (1936); Treaty of Versailles, Pt. 1, S. Doc. 49, 66th Cong., 1st Sess. 8–17 (1919) (Covenant of the League of Nations); I. Kant, Perpetual Peace (1795), in Kant's Political Writings (H. Reiss, ed. 1971).

Chapter 684. Arbitration: International Relationships

Part I. Title, Policy, Scope, and Definitions

684.01 Short title.—This chapter shall be known and may be cited as the 'Florida International Arbitration Act'.

History.—s. 1, ch. 86–266.

684.02 Policy.—

(1) It is the policy of the Legislature to encourage the use of arbitration to resolve disputes arising out of international relationships and to assure access to the courts of this state for legal proceedings ancillary to, or otherwise in aid of, such arbitration.

(2) Any person may enter into a written undertaking to arbitrate any dispute then existing or thereafter arising between that person and another. If the dispute is within the scope of this chapter, the undertaking shall be enforced by the courts of this state in accordance with s. 684.22 without regard to the justiciable character of the dispute. In addition, if the undertaking is governed by the law of this state, it shall be valid and enforceable in accordance with ordinary principles of contract law.

History.—s. 1, ch. 86–266.

684.03 Scope of this chapter.—

(1) This chapter shall only apply to the arbitration of disputes between:

(a) Two or more persons at least one of whom is a nonresident of the United States; or

(b) Two or more persons all of whom are residents of the United States if the dispute:

1. Involves property located outside the United States;

2. Relates to a contract or other agreement which envisages performance or enforcement in whole or in part outside the United States;

3. Involves an investment outside the United States or the ownership, management, or operation of a business entity through which such an investment is effected, or any agreement pertaining to any interest in such an entity; or

4. Bears some other relation to one or more foreign countries.

(2) Notwithstanding the provisions of subsection (1), this chapter shall not apply to the arbitration of:

(a) Any dispute pertaining to the ownership, use, development, or possession of, or a lien of record upon, real property located in this state, unless the parties in writing expressly submit to the arbitration of that dispute to this chapter; or

(b) Any dispute involving domestic relations or of a political nature between two or more governments.

(3) If, in any arbitration within the scope of this chapter, reference must, under applicable conflict of laws principles, be made to the arbitration law of this state, such reference shall be to this chapter.

(4) This chapter shall not apply to conciliation or mediation proceedings except as provided in s. 684.10.

History.—s. 1, ch. 86–266.

684.04 Definitions.—As used in this chapter:

(1) The term 'person' shall have the meaning set forth in s. 1.01(3) and shall include a government or any agency, instrumentality, or subdivision thereof.

(2) The term 'resident of the United States' means:

(a) A natural person who maintains his sole residence within a state, possession, or territory of the United States or within the District of Columbia; or

(b) Any person organized or incorporated under the laws of the United States or any state, possession, or territory thereof or of the District of Columbia.

(3) The term 'nonresident of the United States' means any person not a resident of the United States as defined in subsection (2).

(4) Any reference to a 'written undertaking to arbitrate' shall be to that writing by which a person undertakes to submit a dispute to arbitration, without regard to whether that undertaking is sufficient to sustain a valid and enforceable contract or is subject to defenses. A written undertaking to arbitrate may be part of a contract, or may be a separate writing, and may be contained in correspondence, telegrams, telexes, or any other form of written communication.

History.—s. 1, ch. 86–266.

PART II. CONDUCT OF ARBITRATIONS

684.05 Scope of part.—This part shall apply to any arbitration within the scope of this chapter, without regard to whether the place of arbitration is within or without this state, if:

(1) The written undertaking to arbitrate expressly provides, or the parties otherwise agree, that the law of this state shall apply;

(2) In the absence of a choice of law provision applicable to the written undertaking to arbitrate, that undertaking forms part of a contract the interpretation of which is to be governed by the law of this state; or

(3) In any other case, the arbitral tribunal decides under applicable conflict of laws principles that the arbitration shall be conducted in accordance with the law of this state.

History.—s. 1, ch. 86–266.

684.06 Conduct of the arbitration.—

(1) Except as provided in this chapter or in the written undertaking to arbitrate, the arbitral tribunal shall conduct the arbitration as it deems appropriate, including determination of the language to be used.

(2) The arbitral tribunal shall have the power to rule on all challenges to its jurisdiction. This shall include, without limitation, challenges based on the claim that the written undertaking to arbitrate does not exist or does not give rise to a valid and enforceable agreement, challenges asserting that the dispute is not within the scope of the questions referable to arbitration or is otherwise nonarbitrable, and challenges to the composition of, or method used in forming, the tribunal.

History.—s. 1, ch. 86–266.

684.07 Freedom of parties to fix rules for arbitration.—

(1) The parties may at any time agree in writing to conduct the arbitration in accordance with such rules as they may select, including any system of rules incorporated by reference in the written undertaking to arbitrate. In determining those rules, the parties may elect to exclude from the arbitration one or more provisions of this part. The provisions of this part shall not apply except to the extent consistent with and subject to the rules adopted by the parties. As used in this part, the term 'written undertaking to arbitrate' includes any system of rules selected by the parties.

(2) If any provision of this part or of the written undertaking to arbitrate is not complied with, any party who nevertheless proceeds with the arbitration without stating his objection without undue delay or, if a time limit is provided for stating such objection, within such time period may be deemed to have waived or be estopped from any right to object.

History.—s. 1, ch. 86–266.

684.08 Notice commencing arbitration; answer and notices during arbitration.—

(1) A party desiring to arbitrate a dispute pursuant to a written undertaking to arbitrate shall give or cause to be given to all parties to that undertaking written notice of the commencement of the arbitration. The notice shall set forth the nature of the dispute, the names and addresses of the parties, a reference to the written undertaking to arbitrate, a demand that the dispute be referred to arbitration under that undertaking, and a statement of the relief sought, including the amount claimed, if any. The notice may also include a proposal for the method of appointing the arbitral tribunal, if that method has not already been agreed upon, or may give notice of the appointment of an arbitrator.

(2) The notice commencing arbitration shall be served upon the other parties to the written undertaking to arbitrate in the manner provided in that undertaking or, in

the absence of such a provision, in a manner reasonably designed to give other parties actual notice of the proposed proceedings.

(3) If a party to a written undertaking to arbitrate dies or if a committee of the person or property of a party to such an undertaking is appointed, an arbitration under that undertaking may be commenced or continued by, or upon notice to, the personal representative or administrator of the deceased party; the committee of the person or property of that party; or, where the proceedings relate to real property, any distributee or devisee who has succeeded to the deceased party's interest in the property.

(4) Following its appointment, the arbitral tribunal shall fix a time within which any party served with a notice commencing arbitration must file with the tribunal such written answer, counterclaim, or cross-claim as that party determines appropriate. Such answer, counterclaim, or cross-claim shall also be served upon the other parties to the arbitration in the manner provided in the written undertaking to arbitrate or, in the absence thereof, in the manner fixed by the arbitral tribunal. Failure to file an answer shall constitute a general denial of the claim set forth in the notice commencing the arbitration.

(5) If in the course of an arbitration it becomes necessary or advisable for any party to give notice to or serve documents upon the arbitral tribunal or one or more parties to the arbitration, it shall do so in the manner provided in the written undertaking to arbitrate or, in the absence thereof, in the manner fixed by the tribunal.

History.—s. 1, ch. 86–266.

684.09 Appointment of the arbitral tribunal.—If the parties in the written undertaking to arbitrate or otherwise agree upon a method for appointing the arbitral tribunal or any member thereof or successor thereto, that method shall be followed. If, notwithstanding that undertaking, the parties agree upon named arbitrators, the arbitrators so named shall constitute the tribunal. If the parties shall fail to agree upon such a method or if the method selected shall fail and the parties shall not have otherwise named the tribunal, such appointment may be made as provided in s. 684.23(1). Unless the parties otherwise agree, the tribunal shall consist of a single arbitrator.

History.—s. 1, ch. 86–266.

684.10 Mediation, conciliation, and settlement.—

(1) If during the arbitral proceedings a party claims in writing that one or more of the parties has not complied with an agreement to submit a dispute to mediation or conciliation, the arbitral tribunal shall determine the validity and timeliness of that claim and, upon finding it valid and timely, shall hold the arbitral proceedings in abeyance pending submission of the dispute to mediation or conciliation as agreed. Thereafter, the tribunal shall proceed to arbitrate the dispute when satisfied that the attempt at mediation or conciliation has failed.

(2) If before a final award is issued the parties agree to settle their dispute, the arbitral tribunal shall either issue an order terminating the arbitral proceeding or, if requested by the parties and accepted by the tribunal, record the agreed settlement in the form of a final award.

History.—s. 1, ch. 86–266.

684.11 Majority action by the arbitral tribunal.—If the arbitral tribunal consists of more than one arbitrator, its powers shall be exercised by a majority of its members, except that the tribunal may authorize the presiding arbitrator to decide matters of procedure subject to review by the full tribunal.

History.—s. 1, ch. 86–266.

684.12 Consolidation of arbitrations.—

(1) If two or more disputes have common questions of law or fact or arise out of a single transaction or enterprise and if at least one of those disputes is to be arbitrated under this chapter, the disputes may be consolidated and determined by one arbitral tribunal if consolidation is not prohibited by the arbitral law or the rules otherwise applicable to the separate disputes and:

(a) All affected parties agree to the consolidation; or

(b) All of the disputes are to be submitted to the same tribunal, and the tribunal determines that consolidation will serve the interests of justicc and the expeditious resolution of the disputcs.

(2) The consolidated proceedings shall be conducted under such rules as the parties agree upon or, in the absence of agreement, as determined by the arbitral tribunal.

History.—s. 1, ch. 86–266.

684.13 Hearings; place of arbitration.—

(1) At the request of a party or upon its own initiative, the arbitral tribunal shall conduct one or more hearings for the purpose of examining witnesses, inspecting documents or other evidence, or entertaining oral arguments; however, if the parties shall request more than one hearing, the determination as to whether any hearings shall be held subsequent to the first hearing shall be made by the tribunal. A hearing may be held at any place within or without this state that the tribunal determines appropriate, whether or not that place is the place of arbitration. In the absence of a request for a hearing, the tribunal may proceed on the basis of documents and other materials. If a hearing is to be conducted, the tribunal shall cause notice to be given to each party not less than 14 days before the hearing, unless notice proves impossible after efforts reasonably designed to give actual notice. Appearance at a hearing without timely objection shall constitute a waiver of the notice requirement.

(2) Prior to a date certain established by the arbitral tribunal, any party may amend a claim, answer, counterclaim, or cross–claim previously filed by it or may assert additional claims, counterclaims, or cross–claims. After that date, all such additions and amendments shall be a the discretion of the tribunal.

(3) The place of arbitration, whether within or without this state, shall be determined by the parties or, in the absence of such determination, by the arbitral tribunal having regard to the circumstances of the arbitration. Selection of the place of arbitration shall not in itself constitute selection of the procedural or substantive law of that place as the law governing the arbitration.

(4) The arbitral tribunal may hold meetings at any place, whether or not it is the place of arbitration, and may use any means of communication it deems appropriate.

(5) The arbitral tribunal may adjourn its proceedings from time to time upon its own initiative and shall do so upon the request of a party for good cause shown; however, no adjournment shall extend the proceedings beyond the date fixed by the parties for issuance of a final award unless the parties extend that date.

(6) The arbitral tribunal may dismiss any claim, counterclaim, or cross–claim which the moving party fails to prosecute with reasonable diligence as determined by the tribunal. If a person against whom a claim, counterclaim, or cross–claim is filed

fails to appear or proceed with a defense against that claim without good cause shown, the tribunal shall decide the claim, counterclaim, or cross–claim on the basis of the evidence before it. No award shall issue based solely upon the default of a party, and the failure of any party to appear, proceed, or defend shall not in itself be treated as an admission.

History.—s. 1, ch. 86–266.

684.14 Representation by counsel.—A party to an arbitration shall have the right to be represented by counsel in any arbitral proceeding. A waiver of that right prior to any proceedings is ineffective.

History.—s. 1, ch. 86–266.

684.15 Evidence; witnesses; subpoenas; depositions.—

(1) The arbitral tribunal shall determine the relevance and materiality of the evidence and need not follow formal rules of evidence. The tribunal may take into account its own experience and any customs, usages of trade, or other facts and circumstances which it deems relevant. The tribunal may utilize any lawful method it deems appropriate to obtain evidence additional to that produced by the parties, and the parties shall comply with any request of the tribunal for additional evidence.

(2) The arbitral tribunal may issue subpoenas or other demands for the attendance of witnesses or for the production of books, records, documents, and other evidence, may administer oaths, may order depositions to be taken or other discovery obtained, without regard to the place where the witness or other evidence is located, and may appoint one or more experts to report to it.

(3) The arbitral tribunal may fix such fees for the attendance of witnesses as it deems appropriate.

(4) In exercising the power conferred upon it by this section, the arbitral tribunal may apply for assistance from any court, tribunal, or governmental authority in any jurisdiction.

History.—s. 1, ch. 86–266.

684.16 Interim relief.—

(1) Upon application by a party and after all other parties have been notified and given an opportunity to comment, unless notice proves impossible after efforts reasonably designed to give actual notice, the arbitral tribunal may grant such interim relief as it considers appropriate and, in so doing, may require the applicant to post bond or give other security. The power herein conferred upon the tribunal is without prejudice to the right of a party under applicable law to request interim relief directly from any court, tribunal, or other governmental authority, within or without this state, and to do so without prior authorization of the arbitral tribunal. Unless otherwise provided in the written undertaking to arbitrate, such a request shall not be deemed incompatible with, nor a waiver of, that undertaking.

(2) In lieu of an order granting interim relief, or in aid of any order granted, the arbitral tribunal may itself apply or may authorize a party to apply to any court, tribunal, or other governmental authority within or without this state for such assistance in securing the objectives intended by the order or request for interim relief as the arbitral tribunal determines appropriate.

(3) If the arbitral tribunal determines that participation by one or more parties in its review of an application for interim relief might jeopardize the effectiveness of the relief requested, it shall, notwithstanding the requirements of subsection (1), make its

decision without notice to, and in the absence of, such parties and shall also, without notice to such parties, take any action authorized by subsection (2); provided that immediately following the issuance of an order for interim relief by the arbitral tribunal or by a court, tribunal, or other governmental authority, whichever is the last to occur, the arbitral tribunal shall extend to all parties not notified of the application for interim relief adequate opportunity to seek termination of modification of any relief granted.

(4) The arbitral tribunal may at any time modify or terminate any interim relief granted by it.

History.—s. 1, ch. 86–266.

684.17 Applicable law.—The arbitral tribunal shall decide the merits of the dispute before it according to the law or other decisional principles provided for in the written undertaking to arbitrate, including acting ex aequo et bono or as amiables compositeurs. In the absence of such stipulation, the tribunal shall decide the merits of the dispute according to the law, including equitable principles, which it determines should control. In making that determination, the tribunal shall be free to employ the conflict of laws principles which it deems most appropriate to the circumstances of the arbitration.

History.—s. 1, ch. 86–266.

684.18 Interest.—The arbitral tribunal may award interest as agreed to in writing by the parties or, in the absence of such agreement, as the tribunal deems appropriate.

History.—s. 1, ch. 86–266.

684.19 Awards.—

(1) The arbitral tribunal shall issue its final award within such time as is specified by the parties in writing or, in the absence of such specification, within such time as the tribunal determines appropriate. In addition to a final award, a tribunal may issue interim, interlocutory, or partial awards. Each award shall be in writing, shall state the date and place of issuance, and shall be signed prior to issuance by each member of the tribunal unless, in the case of a tribunal consisting of more than one member, the award is signed by a majority of the members and an explanation for each missing signature is given. Members' signatures need not be affixed at the place of arbitration.

(2) The arbitral tribunal shall deliver, either personally or by registered or certified mail, a signed counterpart of the award to each party to the arbitration, unless such delivery proves impossible after efforts reasonably designed to assure actual delivery.

(3) A written statement of the reasons for an award shall be issued only if all parties agree to the issuance thereof or the tribunal determines that a failure to do so could prejudice recognition or enforcement of the award. An award may be made public by the tribunal or by a party only if:

(a) All parties to the arbitration consent thereto in writing;

(b) Disclosure is required by law; or

(c) Disclosure is necessary in connection with any judicial or other official proceeding concerning the award.

(4) The arbitral tribunal may award reasonable fees and expenses actually incurred, including without limitation, fees and expenses of legal counsel, to any party

to the arbitration and shall allocate the costs of the arbitration among the parties as it determines appropriate.

History.—s. 1, ch. 86–266.

648.20 Change of award.—Upon application by a party filed within 30 days of the issuance of an award, the arbitral tribunal may vacate, clarify, correct, or amend an award. A copy of the application shall be delivered to all parties to the arbitration personally or by registered or certified mail, unless such delivery proves impossible after efforts reasonably designed to assure actual delivery. Thereafter, the parties shall be given adequate opportunity to respond in writing. In reaching its decision, the tribunal may hold further hearings, take additional evidence, and accept written submissions from the parties.

History.—s. 1, ch. 86–266.

PART III. COURT PROCEEDINGS IN CONNECTION WITH ARBITRATION

684.21 Scope of this part.
684.22 Court proceedings to compel arbitration and to stay certain court proceedings.
684.23 Court proceedings during arbitration.
684.24 Court proceedings upon final awards.
684.25 Grounds for vacating an award or declaring it not entitled to confirmation.
684.26 Award in foreign currency.
684.27 Judgment or decree on a final award.
684.28 Judgment roll; docketing.
684.29 Application to circuit court; form and process.
684.30 Consent to jurisdiction.
684.31 Venue.
684.32 Appeals.
684.33 Transitional rule.
684.34 Severability and characterization.
684.35 Immunity for arbitrators.

684.21 Scope of this part.—This part shall apply to any arbitration within the scope of this chapter, whether or not the arbitration is subject to the provisions of part II of this chapter.

History.—s. 1, ch. 86–266.

684.22 Court proceedings to compel arbitration and to stay certain court proceedings.—

(1) A person may apply to a circuit court of this state for an order compelling arbitration if that person claims that another party to a dispute has entered into a written undertaking to arbitrate that dispute and after notice has refused or otherwise failed to arbitrate in accordance with the undertaking. If the court, sitting without a jury, finds that the party refusing or otherwise failing to arbitrate has, in fact, given the undertaking claimed, the order compelling arbitration shall issue without regard to whether the place of arbitration is within or without this state or the arbitration is subject to part II of this chapter, unless the court finds:

(a) That there was fraud in the inducement of the written undertaking to arbitrate;

(b) That submission of the dispute to arbitration would be contrary to the public policy of this state or of the United States; or

(c) That an arbitral tribunal empaneled in accordance with the written undertaking to arbitrate has previously determined that he dispute is not arbitrable or that the undertaking is invalid or unenforceable.

All other questions, including whether the dispute is arbitrable or whether the written undertaking to arbitrate is subject to defenses or is otherwise invalid or unenforceable, shall be for the arbitral tribunal to decide. If any part of a dispute which cannot be submitted to arbitration for the reasons stated in paragraphs (a)–(c) is severable from the remainder of the dispute, the court may order arbitration to proceed with regard to the remainder.

(2) Upon timely application by a party, an action or proceeding in a court of this state involving a dispute that is subject to arbitration shall be stayed by the court if an order compelling arbitration of the dispute could issue under subsection (1). Upon application by a party, the stay may be accompanied by an order compelling arbitration. This subsection shall not apply to any court proceeding pursuant to s. 684.23 or s. 684.24.

(3) Upon timely application by a party, a circuit court of this state may enjoin another party from proceeding with an action before any court within or without this state involving a dispute that is subject to arbitration if an order compelling arbitration of the dispute could issue under subsection (1). The injunction may, upon application by a party, be accompanied by an order compelling arbitration. This subsection shall not apply to any court proceeding pursuant to s. 684.23 or s. 684.24.

(4) Upon timely application by a party, a circuit court of this state may stay the arbitration of a dispute if an order compelling arbitration could not issue under subsection (1). Such stay shall issue whether the place of arbitration is within or without this state.

History.—s. 1, ch. 86–266.

684.23 Court proceedings during arbitration.—

(1) Upon application by a party to a written undertaking to arbitrate, a circuit court of this state may appoint an arbitral tribunal or any member thereof or successor thereto, if the parties have failed to agree upon a method of appointment or if the method agreed upon fails or cannot be followed and, in either case, the parties have not otherwise agreed upon a named arbitrator or arbitrators. Any arbitrator so appointed shall exercise all powers and functions provided for in the written undertaking to arbitrate.

(2) Upon application by an arbitral tribunal or by a party authorized by the tribunal, a circuit court of this state:

(a) Shall enforce any subpoena, demand, or order of the tribunal for:

1. The attendance of witnesses,
2. The production of books, records, documents, or other evidence,
3. The taking of depositions, or
4. The obtaining of other discovery,

in the manner provided by law for the enforcement of subpoenas, demands, or other such orders in civil actions; and

(b) Shall, to the extent of its powers, render such other assistance as the movant may request, including issuance of letters rogatory or other requests for foreign judicial assistance.

(3) Upon application by an arbitral tribunal or by a party authorized by a tribunal to make the application, a circuit court of this state may grant any interim relief, including, without limitation, temporary restraining orders, preliminary injunctions, attachments, garnishments, or writs or replevin, which it is empowered by law to grant. All actions under this subsection shall be subject to such procedural requirements and other conditions as would apply in a comparable action not pertaining to an arbitration.

(4) The provisions of subsection (3) are without prejudice to the right of a party to an arbitration to seek interim relief directly from any court of competent jurisdiction, provided that no such relief shall be granted by the courts of this state unless the moving party shows that an application to the arbitral tribunal for that relief would prejudice the party's rights and that interim relief from the court is necessary to protect those rights. The tribunal shall be deemed a party in interest in any such action. Any court of this state that issues an order for interim relief as provided in this subsection shall, upon application by the tribunal, modify or terminate its order as appropriate.

(5) Upon application by a party showing that the arbitral tribunal has unduly delayed issuance of its final award, a circuit court of this state may fix a time within which a final award must issue, but only if the place of arbitration is within this state or the arbitration is subject to part II of this chapter. The tribunal shall be deemed a party in interest in any such action.

(6) The powers conferred upon the courts by this section may be exercised without regard to whether the place of arbitration is within or without this state, unless otherwise expressly provided.

History.—s. 1, ch. 86–266.

684.24 Court proceedings upon final awards.—

(1) Any party to an arbitration within the scope of this chapter may apply to a circuit court of this state for an order to confirm or vacate any final award or to declare that the award is not entitled to confirmation by the courts of this state. The court shall dispose of all such applications as provided in paragraphs (a)–(c) without regard to the law of the place of arbitration, the law governing the award, or whether a court of law or equity would apply the law or decisional principles applied by the arbitral tribunal or would grant the relief provided for in the award.

(a) The court shall confirm the award without regard to the place of arbitration unless one or more of the grounds set forth in s. 684.25 is established by way of an affirmative defense. If such a defense is established and the conditions set forth in paragraph (b) are met, the court, upon application, shall vacate the award without regard to any time limit contained in paragraph (3)(b); otherwise, it shall issue an order declaring that the award is not entitled to confirmation by the courts of this state.

(b) The court shall grant an application to vacate the award if:

1. The applicant establishes one or more of the grounds set forh in s. 684.25; and

2. Either the place of arbitration was in this state or the arbitration was subject to part II of this chapter.

If the applicant fails to establish one or more of the grounds set forth in s. 684.25, the court, upon application by any party, shall enter an order confirming the award.

(c) The court shall declare that the award is not entitled to confirmation by the courts of this state if the applicant establishes one or more of the grounds set forth in s. 684.25, but the place of arbitration was outside this state and the arbitration was not subject to part II of this chapter.

(2) In any action under subsection (1), the judgment of a court in a foreign country determining whether one or more of the grounds set forth in s. 684.25 is established shall be accorded the effect normally given the judgment of a court in a foreign country by the courts of this state.

(3) The applications referred to in subsection (1) shall be brought within the following time limits:

(a) An application to confirm an award shall be brought within the time provided in s. 95.051(1) for the enforcement of judgments.

(b) An application to vacate an award or for a declaration that the award is not entitled to confirmation by the courts of this state shall be brought within 90 days of receipt of the final award by the applicant or, in the case of an application based on s. 684.25(1)(d) or (e), within 90 days of the date when the circumstances giving rise to the application were discovered or, with the exercise of due diligence, should have been discovered by the applicant.

(c) If any party to an arbitration shall die or become incompetent, a court may extend the foregoing time limits.

(4) In considering an application filed under subsection (1), a court may request the arbitral tribunal to clarify its award and may modify or correct the award for any evident miscalculation or mistake in the description of any person or property or for any imperfection of form not affecting the merits.

(5) A judgment or decree of a court of this state confirming an award may, upon application, be vacated at any time on the grounds set forth in s. 684.25(1)(d) and (e), provided the application is made within 90 days of the date when the circumstances giving rise to the application were first discovered or, with the exercise of due diligence, should have been discovered by the applicant.

(6) If a final award has been reduced to judgment or made the subject of official action by any court, tribunal, or other governmental authority outside the United States, the courts of this state shall, except as provided in subsection (2), confirm, vacate, or declare the award not entitled to confirmation by the courts of this state without regard to any term or condition of the foreign judgment or official action and without regard to whether the award may be deemed merged into the judgment.

(7) For purposes of this section and of s. 684.25, an arbitral award shall be deemed a final award unless:

(a) It is expressly designated an interim or interlocutory award or by its terms is not final;

(b) An application to vacate, clarify, correct, or amend the award is pending before the arbitral tribunal; or

(c) Under the rules applicable to the arbitration, it is subject to further review by any arbitral authority.

For purposes of the law of this state, an award which is final as described above shall be deemed final regardless of whether judicial confirmation or other official action is necessary to render that award final within the contemplation of any foreign law which may be applicable to the arbitration.

History.—s. 1, ch. 86–266.

684.25 Grounds for vacating an award or declaring it not entitled to confirmation.—

(1) A final award shall be vacated or declared not entitled to confirmation by the courts of this state only if one or more of the following grounds is established:

(a) There was no written undertaking to arbitrate, there was fraud in the inducement of that undertaking, or an arbitral tribunal empaneled in accordance with the undertaking had previously determined that the dispute was nonarbitrable or that the undertaking was invalid or unenforceable, unless the party challenging the award participated on the merits in the arbitral proceedings leading to the award without first having submitted such questions to the arbitral tribunal;

(b) The party challenging the award was not given notice of the appointment of the arbitral tribunal or of the arbitral proceedings, unless notice proved impossible after efforts reasonably designed to give actual notice or such part waived notice or participated in those proceedings on the merits of the dispute;

(c) The arbitral tribunal conducted its proceedings so unfairly as to substantially prejudice the rights of the party challenging the award;

(d) The award was obtained by corruption, fraud, or undue influence or is contrary to the public policy of the United States or of this state;

(e) Any neutral arbitrator had a material conflict of interest with the party challenging the award, unless that party had timely notice of the conflict and proceeded without objection to arbitrate the dispute;

(f) The award resolves a dispute which the parties did not agree to refer to the arbitral tribunal, unless the party objecting shall have arbitrated the dispute without objection, and the tribunal's decision that such dispute was referred to it for arbitration was clearly erroneous, provided that a court may determine instead to vacate or to declare not entitled to confirmation only that portion of the award dealing with the excluded dispute; or

(g) The arbitral tribunal was not constituted in accordance with the agreement of the parties, unless the party challenging the award waived the irregularity or participated in the arbitral proceedings without first objecting thereto.

(2) The courts of this state shall not make an independent factual determination concerning whether the grounds described in paragraph (1)(c), paragraph (1)(f), or paragraph (1)(g) are present if the arbitration leading to the award was conducted under the rules of, or was subject to supervision by, an arbitral authority and such grounds were submitted to such authority as a basis for challenging the validity of the award or the conduct of the arbitration. In such a case, the determination of the arbitral authority concerning such grounds shall be final. In addition, if under the rules applicable to an arbitration the grounds described in paragraph (1)(c), paragraph (1)(f), or paragraph (1)(g) could have been but were not submitted to an arbitral authority as a basis for challenging the validity of the award or the conduct of the arbitration, the courts of this state shall not declare an award not entitled to confirmation or vacate that award or deny it confirmation on such grounds.

(3) A court issuing an order to vacate an award or to declare that an award is not entitled to confirmation by the courts of this state may also order that all or part of the dispute between the parties be resubmitted to the same or a new arbitral tribunal as it deems appropriate.

History.—s. 1, ch. 86-266.

684.26 Award in a foreign currency.—The courts of this state shall confirm a final award, notwithstanding the fact that it grants relief in a currency other than

United States dollars. In such case, the court shall, in addition to entering the order in the foreign currency designated by the award, upon application by a party also enter that order in United States dollars determined by reference to the market rate of exchange prevailing in this state on the date the award was issued, unless the award itself fixes some other date. If no such market rate of exchange is available, the court shall fix the rate it deems appropriate. Judgment or decreee may be entered upon such an order as provided in s. 684.27.

History.—s. 1, ch. 86–266.

684.27 Judgment or decree on a final award.—Once an order confirming or vacating an award or declaring that an award is not entitled to confirmation by the courts of this state has been rendered, a judgment or decree shall be entered in conformity with that order to be enforced like any other judgment or decree. Upon entry of a judgment or decree, the court may also, in its discretion, award costs and disbursements.

History.—s. 1, ch. 86–266.

684.28 Judgment roll; docketing.—

(1) Upon entry of a judgment or decree, the clerk shall prepare the judgment roll consisting, to the extent filed, of the following:

(a) The final award;

(b) A copy of the order; and

(c) A copy of the judgment or decree.

(2) The judgment or decree may be docketed as if rendered in a civil action.

History.—s. 1, ch. 86–266.

684.29 Application to circuit court; form and process.—An application to a circuit court of this state pursuant to this chapter shall be by motion and shall be heard in the manner provided by law or rule of the court for the making and hearing of motions. Process in connection with such an application shall be served as provided in s. 48.196.

History.—s. 1, ch. 86–266.

684.30 Consent to jurisdiction.—The conduct of an arbitration within this state, or the making of a written undertaking to arbitrate which provides for arbitration within this state or subject to part II of this chapter, shall constitute a consent to the exercise of in personam jurisdiction by the courts of this state in any action authorized by this part.

History.—s. 1, ch. 86–266.

684.31 Venue.—An application under this chapter shall be made to the circuit court for the county in which any party to the arbitration resides or has a place of business or in which the place of arbitration is located. If no such party resides or has a place of business within this state and if the place of arbitration is outside this state, then the application may be made to any circuit court of this state. All applications made subsequent to an initial application under this chapter shall be made to the court hearing the initial application, unless it shall order otherwise.

History.—s. 1, ch. 86–266.

684.32 Appeals.—

(1) An appeal may be taken from any of the following:

(a) An order under s. 684.22 granting or denying an application to compel or to stay arbitration or to stay judicial proceedings.

(b) An order granting or denying an application under s. 684.23(2) for assistance in obtaining evidence or an application under s. 684.23(3) for interim relief.

(c) An order under s. 684.24 confirming or vacating a final award or declaring that an award is not entitled to confirmation by the courts of this state.

(d) A judgment or decree entered pursuant to s. 684.27.

(2) Appeals shall be taken in the same manner and be subject to the same scope of review as appeals from orders or judgments in civil actions. All appeals shall be confined to questions within the competence conferred by this chapter upon the court from which the appeal is taken or to the question of whether such court exceeded that competence.

History.—s. 1, ch. 86–266.

684.33 Transitional rule.—This chapter shall apply to all written undertakings to arbitrate within the scope of this chapter, whether entered into before or after October 1, 1986; however, part III of this chapter shall not apply to any judicial proceedings commenced prior to that date, and part II of this chapter shall not apply to any arbitration commenced prior to that date unless the parties agree to the contrary in writing.

History.—s. 1, ch. 86–266.

684.34 Severability and characterization.—

(1) If any provision of this chapter or its application to any particular person or circumstance is held invalid, that provision or its application shall be deemed severable and shall not affect the validity of other provisions or applications of this chapter.

(2) If any arbitral, judicial, or other official proceeding within or without this state it shall become necessary to classify any provision of this chapter as substantive or procedural within the meaning of those terms in the conflict of laws, all provisions of this chapter relating to the obligation of the parties to arbitrate, to the conduct of the arbitral proceedings, and to the validity of arbitral awards shall be classified as substantive.

History.—s. 1, ch. 86–266.

684.35 Immunity for arbitrators.—No person may sue in the courts of this state or assert a cause of action under the law of this state against any arbitrator when such suit or action arises from the performance of such arbitrator's duties.

History.—s. 1, ch. 86–266.

7. 15 USC 1 to 7 (1982).
8. 417 US 506 (1974).
9. 723 F2d 155 (1st Cir, 1983).
10. 105 S Ct 3346 (1985).
11. *Id*, at p. 3355.
    American Construction Machinery & Equipment Corp *v*. Mechanized Construction of Pakistan Ltd, —F Supp—(Dkt. 85–3765, SDNY, 28 Feb 1986) upheld a waiver of immunity on the part of an agency of the Pakistan government with respect to

plaintiff's effort to enforce an arbitral award. Based upon the Pakistan entity's participation in an ICC decision in Geneva, and Pakistan's engagement in commercial activities in the US, the court readily found the waiver of immunity under 21 USC 1605(a)(1) and (2). Implicit in the decision was the defendant's awareness that enforcement of the arbitral award might be sought against it in the United States. The court appeared to state that there was no other need to establish a jurisdictional *nexus* between the underlying transaction and the United States.

12. 9 USC 1 to 14 (1982).
13. *Infra* note 48.
14. 21 UST 2517, TIAS No 6997 (10 June 1958).
15. 391 F2d 821 (2nd Cir, 1968).
16. I.e., (1) the enforcement role of private party treble damage actions, (2) the possibility that an arbitration clause was the result of a contract of adhesion, (3) the sophisticated legal and economic analysis required for the resolution of antitrust claims, and (4) the disinclination of an arbitral panel composed of businessmen to enforce the antitrust laws.
17. *Supra* note 12.
18. *Supra* note 14.
19. *Supra* note 10.
20. 18 USC 1961 to 1986.
21. 617 F Supp 55 (SDNY, 1985).
22. 576 F Supp 566 (SDNY, 1983), aff 745 F2d 190 (2nd Cir, 1984).
23. *See* Chapter 10 herein.
24. 87 L Ed2d 346 (1985).
25. *Supra* note 3.
26. *Supra* note 12.
27. 622 F Supp 1505 (SDNY, 1985).
28. 643 F2d 863 (1980) at p. 889.

28.1—F Supp—(DKT. 84CIV. 7170, SDNY, 8 May 1986).

29. Pub La 91–368, 84 Stat 692 (1970), codified at 9 USC 201–208.
30. *See* Murray Oil Products Co *v.* Mitsui & Co Ltd, 146 F2d 381 (2nd Cir, 1944).
31. *See generally* 80 Am J Internat L (1986) at pp. 24 *et seq.*
32. 427 F Supp 2 (SDNY, 1975).
33. 451 F Supp 1044 (ND Cal, 1977).
34. *Id*, at p. 1052.
35. *Id.*
36. 57 NY2d (1982).
37. *Id*, at p. 414.
38. *See* 1985 NY Laws, Ch 253; subparagraph (c) of Section 7502 of the CPLR reads as follows:

> '(c) Provisional remedies. The supreme court in the county in which an arbitration is pending, or, if not yet commenced, in a county specified in subdivision (a), may entertain an application for an order of attachment or for a preliminary injunction in connection with an arbitrable controversy, but only upon the ground that the award to which the applicant may be entitled may be rendered ineffectual without such provisional relief. The provisions of articles 62 and 63 of this chapter shall apply to the application, including those relating to undertakings and to the time for commencement of an action (arbitration shall be deemed an action for this purpose) if the

application is made before commencement, except that the sole ground for the granting of the remedy shall be as stated above. The form of the application shall be as stated above in subdivision (a).'

39. Section 6201 of the NY CPLR requires a person seeking a prejudgment attachment to make one of the following showings:

> '(1) that the defendant is a nondomiciliary residing without the state or is a foreign corporation not qualified to do business in the state; (2) that the defendant, although a resident or domiciliary of the state, cannot be served despite diligent efforts, or, (3) that the defendant is attempting to defraud creditors or frustrate the enforcement of a judgment by assigning, disposing, encumbering, secreting or removing property from the state.'

40. Under Section 6301 of the NY CPLR the plaintiff had to show that the defendant was threatening or was about to do an act in violation of plaintiff's right respecting the subject of the action tending to render the judgment ineffective; also plaintiff had to prove the likelihood of injury from an act or omission of the defendant.

The New York legislature in July 1984 enacted laws designed to overcome problems with respect to choice of law or choice of forum by amending Article 5 of the New York General Obligations Law and by adding a new Title 14:

TITLE 14.
ENFORCEABILITY OF CLAUSES RESPECTING
CHOICE OF LAW AND CHOICE OF FORUM IN
CERTAIN TRANSACTIONS

Section 5-1401. Choice of law
5-1402. Choice of forum

§ *5-1401. Choice of law* 1. The parties to any contract, agreement or undertaking, contingent or otherwise, in consideration of, or relating to any obligation arising out of a transaction covering in the aggregate not less than two hundred fifty thousand dollars, including a transaction otherwise covered by subsection one of section 1-105 of the uniform commercial code, may agree that the law of this state shall govern their rights and duties in whole or in part, whether or not such contract, agreement or undertaking bears a reasonable relation to this state. This section shall not apply to any contract, agreement or undertaking (a) for labor or personal services, (b) relating to any transaction for personal, family or household services, or (c) to the extent provided to the contrary in subsection two of section 1-105 of the uniform commercial code.

2. Nothing contained in this section shall be construed to limit or deny the enforcement of any provision respecting choice of law in any other contract, agreement or undertaking.

§ *5-1402. Choice of forum* 1. Notwithstanding any act which limits or affects the right of a person to maintain an action or proceeding, including, but not limited to, paragraph (b) of section thirteen hundred fourteen of the business corporation law and subdivision two of section two hundred-b of the banking law, any person may maintain an action or proceeding against a foreign corporation, non-resident, or foreign state where the action or proceeding arises out of or relates to any contract, agreement or undertaking for which a choice of New York law has been made in whole or in part pursuant to section 5-1401 and which (a) is a contract, agreement or undertaking, contingent or otherwise, in consideration of, or relating to any obligation arising out of a transaction covering in the aggregate, not less than one million dollars, and (b) which contains a provision or provisions whereby such foreign corporation or non-resident agrees to submit to the jurisdiction of the courts of this state.

2. Nothing contained in this section shall be construed to affect the enforcement of any provision respecting choice of forum in any other contract, agreement or undertaking.

Section 2. Rule three hundred twenty-seven of the civil practice law and rules, as added by proposal two of the judicial conference of nineteen hundred seventy-two, is amended to read as follows:

Rule 327. Inconvenient forum. (a) When the court finds that in the interest of substantial justice the action should be heard in another forum, the court, on the motion of any party, may stay or dismiss the action in whole or in part on any conditions that may be just. The domicile or residence in this state of any party to the action shall not preclude the Court from staying or dismissing the action.

(b) Notwithstanding the provisions of subdivision (a) of this rule, the court shall not stay or dismiss any action on the ground of inconvenient forum, where the action arises out of or relates to a contract, agreement or undertaking to which section 5-1402 of the general obligations law applies, and the parties to the contract have agreed that the law of this state shall govern their rights or duties in whole or in part.

Section 3. This act shall take effect immediately and shall apply to contracts entered into after the effective date hereof and shall apply to contracts entered into on or before the effective date hereof in connection with any action or proceeding commenced on or after the effective date hereof.

41. 501 F2d 1032 (3rd Cir, 1974).
42. 558 F Supp 1372 (SDNY, 1983).
43. The court quoted the dissent in Cooper *v.* Ateliers, etc, *supra* note 37:

> '(2) [I]n the light of . . . the fact that the UN Convention does not specifically address the subject of preaward attachment, the UN Convention cannot properly be said to have proscribed such an attachment by implication; and (3) the use of attachment in maritime contract cases arbitrated under the Federal statute cannot properly be distinguished from arbitration-related attachment permitted under State statutory and decisional law, for the UN Convention makes no distinction; it either permits or proscribes both. In my view, absent more specific language of proscription in the UN Convention, it permits both.'

44. 598 F Supp 754 (SDNY, 1984).
45. —F Supp— (SDNY, 1985).
46. *Supra* note 12 at Section 3 thereof.
47. *Supra* note 6.2 hereinbefore and note 48.1 hereinafter.
48. —AD2d—, (NYS2d— (1986).
48.1 330 UNTS No 4739, TIAS No 6997 (1958).
48.2 *See* 14 ILM 336 (1975).
48.3 Among the signatories are Chile, Costa Rica, El Salvador, Honduras, Mexico,

Panama, Paraguay, Uruguay, and Venezuela. *See generally* NYLJ (18 Nov 1986) at pp. 1 *et seq.*
48.4 *See* Section 5 hereinafter.
48.5 The text of the IACICA, signed in Panama on 30 January 1975, follows:

'The Governments of the Member States of the Organization of American States, desirous of concluding a convention on International commercial arbitration, have agreed as follows:

Article 1. An agreement in which the parties undertake to submit to arbitral decisions any differences that may arise or have arisen between them with respect to a commercial transaction is valid. The agreement shall be set forth in an instrument signed by the parties, or in the form of an exchange of letters, telegrams, or telex communications.

Article 2. Arbitrators shall be appointed in the manner agreed upon by the parties. Their appointment may be delegated to a third party, whether a natural or juridical person.

Arbitrators may be nationals or foreigners.

Article 3. In the absence of an express agreement between the parties, the arbitration shall be conducted in accordance with the rules of procedure of the Inter-American Commercial Arbitration Commission.

Article 4. An arbitral decision or award that is not appealable under the applicable law or procedural rules shall have the force of a final judicial judgment. Its execution or recognition may be ordered in the same manner as that of decisions handed down by national or foreign ordinary courts, in accordance with the procedural laws of the country where it is to be executed and the provisions of international treaties.

Article 5. 1. The recognition and execution of the decision may be refused, at the request of the party against which it is made, only if such party is able to prove to the compentent authority of the State in which recognition and execution are requested:

a. That the parties to the agreement were subject to some incapacity under the applicable law or that the agreement is not valid under the law to which the parties have submitted it, or, if such law is not specified, under the law of the State in which the decision was made; or

b. That the party against which the arbitral decision has been made was not duly notified of the appointment of the arbitrator or of the arbitration procedure to be followed, or was unable, for any other reason to present his defence; or

c. That the decision concerns a dispute not envisaged in the agreement between the parties to submit to arbitration; nevertheless if the provisions of the decision that refer to issues submitted to arbitration can be separated from those not submitted to arbitration, the former may be recognized and executed; or

d. That the constitution of the arbitral tribunal or the arbitration procedure has not been carried out in accordance with the terms of the agreement signed by the parties or, in the absence of such agreement, that the constitution of the arbitral tribunal or the arbitration procedure has not been carried out in accordance with the law of the State where the arbitration took place; or

e. That the decision is not yet binding on the parties or has been annulled or suspended by a competent authority of the State in which, or according to the law of which, the decision has been made.

2. The recognition and execution of an arbitral decision may also be refused if the competent authority of the State in which the recognition and execution is requested finds:

a. That the subject of the dispute cannot be settled by arbitration under the law of that State; or

b. That the recognition or execution of the decision would be contrary to the public policy ('ordre public') of that State.

Article 6. If the competent authority mentioned in Article 5.1.e has been requested to annul or suspend the arbitral decision, the authority before which such decision is invoked may, if it deems it appropriate, postpone a decision on the execution of the arbitral decision and, at the request of the party requesting execution, may also instruct the other party to provide appropriate guaranties.

Article 7. This Convention shall be open for signature by the Member States of the Organization of the American States.

Article 8. This Convention is subject to ratification. The instruments of ratification shall be deposited with the General Secretariat of the Organization of American States.

Article 9. This Convention shall remain open for accession by any other State. The instruments of accession shall be deposited with the General Secretariat of the Organization of American States.

Article 10. This convention shall enter into force on the thirtieth day following the date of deposit of the second instrument of ratification.

For each State ratifying or acceding to the Convention after the deposit of the second instrument of ratification, the Convention shall enter into force on the thirtieth day after deposit by such State of its instrument of ratification or accession.

Article 11. If a State Party has two or more territorial units in which different systems of law apply in relation to the matters dealt with in this Convention, it may, at the time of signature, ratification or accession, declare that this Convention shall extend to all its territorial units or only to one or more of them.

Such declaration may be modified by subsequent declarations, which shall expressly indicate the territorial unit or units to which the Convention applies. Such subsequent declarations shall be transmitted to the General Secretariat of the Organization of American States, and shall become effective thirty days after the date of their receipt.

Article 12. This Convention shall remain in force indefinitely, but any of the State Parties may denounce it. The instrument of denunciation shall be deposited with the General Secretariat of the Organization of American States. After one year from the date of deposit of the instrument of denunciation, the Convention shall no longer be in effect for the denouncing State, but shall remain in effect for the other States Parties.

Article 13. The original instrument of this Convention, The English, French, Portuguese and Spanish texts of which are equally authentic, shall be deposited with the General Secretariat of the Organization of American States. The Secretariat shall notify the Member States of the Organization of American States and the States that have acceded to the Convention of the signatures, deposits of instruments of ratification, accession, and denunciation as well as of reservations, if any. It shall also transmit the declarations referred to in Article 11 of this Convention.'

49. 22 Bankr Rep 763 (1982).
49.1 The ICC Court of Arbitration handles between 250 and 300 requests for arbitration each year, according to the International Lawyers' Newsletter, Vol VII, No. 1 (1985). Eighty-five per cent of these arbitrations took place in Western Europe and only 7.5 per cent in the US and Canada. *See generally* 24 Va J Internat. L 4 (Summer 1984).
50. *Id*, at p. 765.
51. 711 F2d 845 (8th Cir, 1983).
52. 40 UN GAOR Supp (No 17), UN Doc A/40/17.

United Nations Commission on International Trade Law: Model Law on International Commercial Arbitration [Adopted, 21 June 1985]

UNCITRAL Model Law on International Commercial Arbitration

(as adopted by the United Nations Commission on International Trade Law on 21 June 1985]

Chapter I. General Provisions

Article 1. Scope of Application

(1) This Law applies to international commercial arbitration, subject to any agreement in force between this State and any other State or States.
(2) The provisions of this Law, except articles 8, 9, 35 and 36, apply only if the place of arbitraton is in the territory of this State.
(3) An arbitration is international if:
   (a) the parties to an arbitration have, at the time of the conclusion of that agreement, their places of business in different States; or
   (b) one of the following places is situated outside the State in which the parties have their places of business:
      (i) the place of arbitration if determined in, or pursuant to, the arbitration agreement;
      (ii) any place where a substantial part of the obligations of the commercial relationship is to be performed or the place with which the subject-matter of the dispute is most closely connected; or
   (c) the parties have expressly agreed that the subject-matter of the arbitration agreement relates to more than one country.
(4) For the purposes of paragraph (3) of this article:
   (a) if a party has more than one place of business, the place of business is that which has the closest relationship to the arbitration agreement;
   (b) if a party does not have a place of business, reference is to be made to his habitual residence.

(5) This Law shall not affect any other law of this State by virtue of which certain disputes may not be submitted to arbitration or may be submitted to arbitration only according to provisions other than those of this Law.

Article 2. Definitions and rules of interpretation

For the purposes of this Law:

(a) 'arbitration' means any arbitration whether or not administered by a permanent arbitral institution;

(b) 'arbitral tribunal' means a sole arbitrator or a panel of arbitrators;

(c) 'court' means a body or organ of the judicial system of a State;

(d) where a provision of this Law, except article 28, leaves the parties free to determine a certain issue, such freedom includes the right of the parties to authorize a third party, including an institution, to make that determination;

(e) where a provision of this Law refers to the fact that the parties have agreed or that they may agree or in any other way refers to an agreement of the parties, such agreement includes any arbitration rules referred to in that agreement;

(f) where a provision of this Law, other than in articles 25(a) and 32(2)(a), refers to a claim, it also applies to a counter-claim, and where it refers to a defence, it also applies to a defence to such counter-claim.

Article 3. Receipt of written communications

(1) Unless otherwise agreed by the parties:

(a) any written communication is deemed to have been received if it is delivered to the addressee personally or if it is delivered at his place of business, habitual residence or mailing address; if none of these can be found after making a reasonable inquiry, a written communication is deemed to have been received if it is sent to the addressee's last-known place of business, habitual residence or mailing address by registered letter or any other means which provides a record of the attempt to deliver it;

(b) the communication is deemed to have been received on the day it is so delivered.

(2) The provisions of this article do not apply to communications in court proceedings.

Article 4. Waiver of right to object

A party who knows that any provision of this Law from which the parties may derogate or any requirement under the arbitration agreement has not been complied with and yet proceeds with the arbitration without stating his objection to such non-compliance without undue delay or, if a time-limit is provided therefor, within such period of time, shall be deemed to have waived his right to object.

Article 5. Extent of court intervention

In matters governed by this Law, no court shall intervene except where so provided in this Law.

Article 6. Court or other authority for certain functions of arbitration assistance and supervision

The functions referred to in articles 11(3), 11(4), 13(3), 14, 16(3) and 34(2) shall be performed by . . . [Each State enacting this model law specifies the court, courts or, where referred to therein, other authority competent to perform these functions.]

CHAPTER II. ARBITRATION AGREEMENT

Article 7. Definition and form of arbitration agreement

(1) 'Arbitration agreement' is an agreement by the parties to submit to arbitration all or certain disputes which have arisen or which may arise between them in respect of a defined legal relationship, whether contractual or not. An arbitration agreement may be in the form of an arbitration clause in a contract or in the form of a separate agreement.
(2) The arbitration agreement shall be in writing. An agreement is in writing if it is contained in a document signed by the parties or in an exchange of letters, telex, telegrams or other means of telecommunication which provide a record of the agreement, or in an exchange of statements of claim and defence in which the existence of an agreement is alleged by one party and not denied by another. The reference in a contract to a document containing an arbitration clause constitutes an arbitration agreement provided that the contract is in writing and the reference is such as to make that clause part of the contract.

Article 8. Arbitration agreement and substantive claim before court

(1) A court before which an action is brought in a matter which is the subject of an arbitration agreement shall, if a party so requests not later than when submitting his first statement on the substance of the dispute, refer the parties to arbitraton unless it finds that the agreement is null and void, inoperative or incapable of being performed.
(2) Where an action referred to in paragraph (1) of this article has been brought, arbitral proceedings may nevertheless be commenced or continued, and an award may be made, while the issue is pending before the court.

Article 9. Arbitration agreement and interim measures by court

It is not incompatible with an arbitration agreement for a party to request, before or during arbitral proceedings, from a court an interim measure of protection and for a court to grant such measure.

Article 10. Number of arbitrators

(1) The parties are free to determine the number of arbitrators.
(2) Failing such determination, the number of arbitrators shall be three.

Article 11. Appointment of arbitrators

(1) No person shall be precluded by reason of his nationality from acting as an arbitrator, unless otherwise agreed by the parties.
(2) The parties are free to agree on a procedure of appointing the arbitrator or arbitrators, subject to the provisions of paragraphs (4) and (5) of this article.
(3) Failing such agreement,
 (a) in an arbitration with three arbitrators, each party shall appoint one arbitrator, and the two arbitrators thus appointed shall appoint the third arbitrator; if a party fails to appoint the arbitrator within thirty days of receipt of a request to do so from the other party, or if the two arbitrators fail to agree on the third arbitrator within thirty days of their appointment, the appointment shall be made, upon request of a party, by the court or other authority specified in article 6;
 (b) in an arbitration with a sole arbitrator, if the parties are unable to agree on the arbitrator, he shall be appointed, upon request of a party, by the court or other authority specified in article 6.
(4) Where, under an appointment procedure agreed upon by the parties,
 (a) a party fails to act as required under such procedure, or
 (b) the parties, or two arbitrators, are unable to reach an agreement expected of them under such procedure, or
 (c) a third party, including an institution, fails to perform any function entrusted to it under such procedure,

 any party may request the court or other authority specified in article 6 to take the necessary measure, unless the agreement on the appointment procedure provides other means for securing the appointment.
(5) A decision on a matter entrusted by paragraph (3) or (4) of this article to the court or other authority specified in article 6 shall be subject to no appeal. The court or other authority, in appointing an arbitrator, shall have due regard to any qualifications required of the arbitrator by the agreement of the parties and to such considerations as are likely to secure the appointment of an independent and impartial arbitrator and, in the case of a sole or third arbitrator, shall take into account as well the advisability of appointing an arbitrator of a nationality other than those of the parties.

Article 12. Grounds for challenge

(1) When a person is approached in connection with his possible appointment as an arbitrator, he shall disclose any circumstances likely to give rise to justifiable doubts as to his impartiality or independence. An arbitrator, from the time of his

appointment and throughout the arbitral proceedings, shall without delay disclose any such circumstances to the parties unless they have already been informed of them by him.

(2) An arbitrator may be challenged only if circumstances exist that give rise to justifiable doubts as to his impartiality or independence, or if he does not possess qualifications agreed to by the parties. A party may challenge an arbitrator appointed by him, or in whose appointment he has participated, only for reasons of which he becomes aware after the appointment has been made.

Article 13. Challenge procedure

(1) The parties are free to agree on a procedure for challenging an arbitrator, subject to the provisions of paragraph (3) of this article.

(2) Failing such agreement, a party who intends to challenge an arbitrator shall, within fifteen days after becoming aware of the constitution of the arbitral tribunal or after becoming aware of any circumstances referred to in article 12(2), send a written statement of the reasons for the challenge to the arbitral tribunal. Unless the challenged arbitrator withdraws from his office or the other party agrees to the challenge, the arbitral tribunal shall decide on the challenge.

(3) If a challenge under any procedure agreed upon by the parties or under the procedure of paragraph (2) of this article is not successful, the challenging party may request, within thirty days after having received notice of the decision rejecting the challenge, the court or other authority specified in article 6 to decide on the challenge, which decision shall be subject to no appeal; while such a request is pending, the arbitral tribunal, including the challenged arbitrator, may continue the arbitral proceedings and make an award.

Article 14. Failure or impossibility to act

(1) If an arbitrator becomes *de jure* or *de facto* unable to perform his functions or for other reasons fails to act without undue delay, his mandate terminates if he withdraws from his office or if the parties agree on the termination. Otherwise, if a controversy remains concerning any of these grounds, any party may request the court or other authority specified in article 6 to decide on the termination of the mandate, which decision shall be subject to no appeal.

(2) If, under this article or article 13(2), an arbitrator withdraws from his office or a party agrees to the termination of the mandate of an arbitrator, this does not imply acceptance of the validity of any ground referred to in this article or article 12(2).

Article 15. Appointment of substitute arbitrator

Where the mandate of an arbitrator terminates under article 13 or 14 or because of his withdrawal from office for any other reason or because of the revocation of his mandate by agreement of the parties or in any other case of termination of his mandate, a substitute arbitrator shall be appointed according to the rules that were applicable to the appointment of the arbitrator being replaced.

Chapter IV. Jurisdiction of Arbitral Tribunal

Article 16. Competence of arbitral tribunal to rule on its jurisdiction

(1) The arbitral tribunal may rule on its own jurisdiction, including any objections with respect to the existence or validity of the arbitration agreement. For that purpose, an arbitration clause which forms part of a contract shall be treated as an agreement independent of the other terms of the contract. A decision by the arbitral tribunal that the contract is null and void shall not entail *ipso jure* the invalidity of the arbitration clause.

(2) A plea that the arbitral tribunal does not have jurisidiction shall be raised not later than the submission of the statement of defence. A party is not precluded from raising such a plea by the fact that he has appointed, or participated in the appointment of, an arbitrator. A plea that the arbitral tribunal is exceeding the scope of its authority shall be raised as soon as the matter alleged to be beyond the scope of its authority is raised during the arbitral proceedings. The arbitral tribunal may, in either case, admit a later plea if it considers the delay justified.

(3) The arbitral tribunal may rule on a plea referred to in paragraph (2) of this article either as a preliminary question or in an award on the merits. If the arbitral tribunal rules as a preliminary question that it has jurisdiction, any party may request, within thirty days after having received notice of that ruling, the court specified in article 6 to decide the matter, which decision shall be subject to no appeal; while such a request is pending, the arbitral tribunal may continue the arbitral proceedings and make an award.

Article 17. Power of arbitral tribunal to order interim measures

Unless otherwise agreed by the parties, the arbitral tribunal may, at the request of a party, order any party to take such interim measure of protection as the arbitral tribunal may consider necessary in respect of the subject-matter of the dispute. The arbitral tribunal may require any party to provide appropriate security in connection with such measure.

Chapter V. Conduct of Arbitral Proceedings

Article 18. Equal treatment of parties

The parties shall be treated with equality and each party shall be given a full opportunity of presenting his case.

Article 19. Determination of rules of procedure

(1) Subject to the provisions of this Law, the parties are free to agree on the procedure to be followed by the arbitral tribunal in conducting the proceedings.

(2) Failing such agreement, the arbitral tribunal may, subject to the provisions of this

Law, conduct the arbitration in such manner as it considers appropriate. The power conferred upon the arbitral tribunal includes the power to determine the admissibility, relevance, materiality and weight of any evidence.

Article 20. Place of arbitration

(1) The parties are free to agree on the place of arbitration. Failing such agreement, the place of arbitration shall be determined by the arbitral tribunal having regard to the circumstances of the case, including the convenience of the parties.
(2) Notwithstanding the provisions of paragraph (1) of this article, the arbitral tribunal may, unless otherwise agreed by the parties, meet at any place it considers appropriate for consultation among its members, for hearing witnesses, experts or the parties, or for inspection of goods, other property or documents.

Article 21. Commencement of arbitral proceedings

Unless otherwise agreed by the parties, the arbitral proceedings in respect of a particular dispute commence on the date on which a request for that dispute to be referred to arbitration is received by the respondent.

Article 22. Language

(1) The parties are free to agree on the language or languages to be used in the arbitral proceedings. Failing such agreement, the arbitral tribunal shall determine the language or languages to be used in the proceedings. This agreement or determination, unless otherwise specified therein, shall apply to any written statement by a party, any hearing and any award, decision or other communication by the arbitral tribunal.
(2) The arbitral tribunal may order that any documentary evidence shall be accompanied by a translation into the language or languages agreed upon by the parties or determined by the arbitral tribunal.

Article 23. Statements of claim and defence

(1) Within the period of time agreed by the parties or determined by the arbitral tribunal, the claimant shall state the facts supporting his claim, the points at issue and the relief or remedy sought, and the respondent shall state his defence in respect of these particulars, unless the parties have otherwise agreed as to the required elements of such statements. The parties may submit with their statements all documents they consider to be relevant or may add a reference to the documents or other evidence they will submit.
(2) Unless otherwise agreed by the parties, either party may amend or supplement his claim or defence during the course of the arbitral proceedings, unless the arbitral tribunal considers it inappropriate to allow such amendment having regard to the delay in making it.

Article 24. Hearings and written proceedings

(1) Subject to any contrary agreement by the parties, the arbitral tribunal shall decide whether to hold oral hearings for the presentation of evidence or for oral argument, or whether the proceedings shall be conducted on the basis of documents and other materials. However, unless the parties have agreed that no hearings shall be held, the arbitral tribunal shall hold such hearings at an appropriate stage of the proceedings, if so requested by a party.
(2) The parties shall be given sufficient advance notice of any hearing and of any meeting of the arbitral tribunal for the purposes of inspection of goods, other property or documents.
(3) All statements, documents or other information supplied to the arbitral tribunal by one party shall be communicated to the other party. Also any expert report or evidentiary document on which the arbitral tribunal may rely in making its decision shall be communicated to the parties.

Article 25. Default of a party

Unless otherwise agreed by the parties, if, without showing sufficient cause,
(a) the claimant fails to communicate his statement of claim in accordance with article 23(1), the arbitral tribunal shall terminate the proceedings;
(b) the respondent fails to communicate his statement of defence in accordance with article 23(1), the arbitral tribunal shall continue the proceedings without treating such failure in itself as an admission of the claimant's allegations;
(c) any party fails to appear at a hearing or to produce documentary evidence, the arbitral tribunal may continue the proceedings and make the award on the evidence before it.

Article 26. Expert appointed by arbitral tribunal

(1) Unless otherwise agreed by the parties, the arbitral tribunal
  (a) may appoint one or more experts to report to it on specific issues to be determined by the arbitral tribunal;
  (b) may require a party to give the expert any relevant information or to produce, or to provide access to, any relevant documents, goods or other property for his inspection.
(2) Unless otherwise agreed by the parties, if a party so requests or if the arbitral tribunal considers it necessary, the expert shall, after delivery of his written or oral report, participate in a hearing where the parties have the opportunity to put questions to him and to present expert witnesses in order to testify on the points at issue.

Article 27. Court assistance in taking evidence

The arbitral tribunal or a party with the approval of the arbitral tribunal may request from a competent court of this State assistance in taking evidence. The court may execute the request within its competence and according to its rules on taking evidence.

Chapter VI. Making of Award and Termination of Proceedings

Article 28. Rules applicable to substance of dispute

(1) The arbitral tribunal shall decide the dispute in accordance with such rules of law as are chosen by the parties as applicable to the substance of the dispute. Any designation of the law or legal system of a given State shall be construed, unless otherwise expressed, as directly referring to the substantive law of that State and not to its conflict of laws rules.
(2) Failing any designation by the parties, the arbitral tribunal shall apply the law determined by the conflict of laws rules which it considers applicable.
(3) The arbitral tribunal shall decide *ex aequo et bono* or as *amiable compositeur* only if the parties have expressly authorized it to do so.
(4) In all cases, the arbitral tribunal shall decide in accordance with the terms of the contract and shall take into account the usages of the trade applicable to the transaction.

Article 29. Decision-making by panel of arbitrators

In arbitral proceedings with more than one arbitrator, any decision of the arbitral tribunal shall be made, unless otherwise agreed by the parties, by a majority of all its members. However, questions of procedure may be decided by a presiding arbitrator, if so authorized by the parties or all members of the arbitral tribunal.

Article 30. Settlement

(1) If, during arbitral proceedings, the parties settle the dispute, the arbitral tribunal shall terminate the proceedings and, if requested by the parties and not objected to by the arbitral tribunal, record the settlement in the form of an arbitral award on agreed terms.
(2) An award on agreed terms shall be made in accordance with the provisions of article 31 and shall state that it is an award. Such an award has the same status and effect as any other award on the merits of the case.

Article 31. Form and contents of award

(1) The award shall be made in writing and shall be signed by the arbitrator or arbitrators. In arbitral proceedings with more than one arbitrator, the signatures of the majority of all members of the arbitral tribunal shall suffice, provided that the reason for any omitted signature is stated.
(2) The award shall state the reasons upon which it is based, unless the parties have

agreed that no reasons are to be given or the award is an award on agreed terms under article 30.

(3) The award shall state its date and the place of arbitration as determined in accordance with article 20(1). The award shall be deemed to have been made at that place.

(4) After the award is made, a copy signed by the arbitrators in accordance with paragraph (1) of this article shall be delivered to each party.

Article 32. Termination of proceedings

(1) The arbitral proceedings are terminated by the final award or by an order of the arbitral tribunal in accordance with paragraph (2) of this article.

(2) The arbitral tribunal shall issue an order for the termination of the arbitral proceedings when:
  (a) the claimant withdraws his claim, unless the respondent objects thereto and the arbitral tribunal recognizes a legitimate interest on his part in obtaining a final settlement of the dispute;
  (b) the parties agree on the termination of the proceedings;
  (c) the arbitral tribunal finds that the continuation of the proceedings has for any other reason become unnecessary or impossible.

(3) The mandate of the arbitral tribunal terminates with the termination of the arbitral proceedings, subject to the provisions of articles 33 and 34(4).

Article 33. Correction and interpretation of award; additional award

(1) Within thirty days of receipt of the award, unless another period of time has been agreed upon by the parties:
  (a) a party, with notice to the other party, may request the arbitral tribunal to correct in the award any errors in computation, any clerical or typographical errors or any errors of similar nature;
  (b) if so agreed by the parties, a party, with notice to the other party, may request the arbitral tribunal to give an interpretation of a specific point or part of the award.

  If the arbitral tribunal considers the request to be justified, it shall make the correction or give the interpretation within thirty days of receipt of the request. The interpretation shall form part of the award.

(2) The arbitral tribunal may correct any error of the type referred to in paragraph (1)(a) of this article on its own initiative within thirty days of the date of the award.

(3) Unless otherwise agreed by the parties, a party, with notice to the other party, may request, within thirty days of receipt of the award, the arbitral tribunal to make an additional award as to claims presented in the arbitral tribunal to make an additional award as to claims presented in the arbitral proceedings but omitted from the award. If the arbitral tribunal considers the request to be justified, it shall make the additional award within sixty days.

(4) The arbitral tribunal may extend, if necessary, the period of time within which it shall make a correction, interpretation or an additional award under paragraph (1) or (3) of this article.

(5) The provisions of article 31 shall apply to a correction or interpretation of the award or to an additional award.

Chapter VII. Recourse against Award

Article 34. Application for setting aside as exclusive recourse against arbitral award.

(1) Recourse to a court against an arbitral award may be made only by an application for setting aside in accordance with paragraphs (2) and (3) of this article.
(2) An arbitral award may be set aside by the court specified in article 6 only if:
(a) the party making the application furnishes proof that:
(i) a party to the arbitration agreement referred to in article 7 was under some incapacity; or the said agreement is not valid under the law to which the parties have subjected it or, failing any indication thereon, under the law of this State; or
(ii) the party making the application was not given proper notice of the appointment of an arbitrator or of the arbitral proceedings or was otherwise unable to present his case; or
(iii) The award deals with a dispute not contemplated by or not falling within the terms of the submission to arbitration, or contains decisions on matters beyond the scope of the submission to arbitration, provided that, if the decisions on matters submitted to arbitration can be separated from those not so submitted, only that part of the award which contains decisions on matters not submitted to arbitration may be set aside; or
(iv) the composition of the arbitral tribunal or the arbitral procedure was not in accordance with the agreement of the parties, unless such agreement was in conflict with a provision of this Law from which the parties cannot derogate, or, failing such agreement, was not in accordance with this Law; or
(b) the court finds that:
(i) the subject-matter of the dispute is not capable of settlement by arbitration under the law of this State; or
(ii) the award is in conflict with the public policy of this State.
(3) An application for setting aside may not be made after three months have elapsed from the date on which the party making that application had received the award or, if a request had been made under article 33, from the date on which that request had been disposed of by the arbitral tribunal.
(4) The court, when asked to set aside an award, may, where appropriate and so requested by a party, suspend the setting aside proceedings for a period of time determined by it in order to give the arbitral tribunal an opportunity to resume the arbitral proceedings or to take such other action as in the arbitral tribunal's opinion will eliminate the grounds for setting aside.

Chapter VIII. Recognition and Enforcement of Awards

Article 35. Recognition and enforcement

(1) An arbitral award, irrespective of the country in which it was made, shall be recognized as binding and, upon application in writing to the competent court, shall be enforced subject to the provisions of this article and of article 36.
(2) The party relying on an award or applying for its enforcement shall supply the

duly authenticated original award or a duly certified copy thereof, and the original arbitration agreement referred to in article 7 or a duly certified copy thereof. If the award or agreement is not made in an official language of this State, the party shall supply a duly certified translation thereof into such language.

Article 36. Grounds for refusing recognition or enforcement

(1) Recognition or enforcement of an arbitral award, irrespective of the country in which it was made, may be refused only:
  (a) at the request of the party against whom it is invoked, if that party furnishes to the competent court where recognition or enforcement is sought proof that:
    (i) a party to the arbitration agreement referred to in article 7 was under some incapacity; or the said agreement is not valid under the law to which the parties have subjected it or, failing any indication thereon, under the law of the country where the award was made; or
    (ii) the party against whom the award is invoked was not given proper notice of the appointment of an arbitrator or of the arbitral proceedings or was otherwise unable to present his case; or
    (iii) the award deals with a dispute not contemplated by or not falling within the terms of the submission to arbitration, or it contains decisions on matters beyond the scope of the submission to arbitration, provided that, if the decisions on matters submitted to arbitration can be separated from those not so submitted, that part of the award which contains decisions on matters submitted to arbitration may be recognized and enforced; or
    (iv) the composition of the arbitral tribunal or the arbitral procedure was not in accordance with the agreement of the parties or, failing such agreement, was not in accordance with the law of the country where the arbitration took place; or
    (v) the award has not yet become binding on the parties or has been set aside or suspended by a court of the country in which, or under the law of which, that award was made; or
  (b) if the court finds that:
    (i) the subject-matter of the dispute is not capable of settlement by arbitration under the law of this State; or
    (ii) the recognition or enforcement of the award would be contrary to the public policy of this State.

(2) If an application for setting aside or suspension of an award has been made to a court referred to in paragraph (1)(a)(v) of this article, the court where recognition or enforcement is sought may, if it considers it proper, adjourn its decision and may also, on the application of the party claiming recognition or enforcement of the award, order the other party to provide appropriate security.

53. For other acts of the parties authorized by the Model Law, *see* Articles 3(1), 11(2), 13(1), 21, 22(1), 23(1), 25, 26, 28(1) and 28(3).

54. *See* 24 Va T Internat L 4 (Summer 1984) in which the authors David J. Branson and W. Michael Tupman supported these conclusions.

Chapter 10. The Racketeering Influenced and Corrupt Organizations Act, or RICO, and the Foreign Plaintiff

Section 1. A New and Unique Cause of Action

The foreign plaintiff, along with the US plaintiff, has in recent years found a new entry into US courts in the form of a cause of action under the Racketeering Influenced and Corrupt Organization Act, or RICO.[1] This federal statute, admittedly designed to seek eradication of organized crime in the United States, has opened the US court to a unprecedented number of civil suits by civil fraud plaintiffs seeking to recover treble damages and attorneys' fees in an ordinary business dispute.[2] There are four separate bases of liability set forth in 18 USC 1962, and the most popular theory of violation is that the defendant was a person 'employed by or associated with' an 'enterprise' that conducted or participated in the conduct of the affairs of the 'enterprise' through a pattern of racketeering activity or collection of unlawful debt.[3] The second base of liability concerns the receiving of income from a pattern of racketeering activity or from the collection of an unlawful debt and investing that income or its proceeds to establish, operate or acquire an interest in an 'enterprise'.[4] The third base of liability under RICO is acquiring or maintaining an interest in, or control of, an enterprise through a pattern of racketeering or collection of an unlawful debt.[5] Finally, the fourth base of liability is a 'conspiracy' to violate any of the three prior provisions of RICO.[6] A 'person' is defined under RICO as 'any individual or entity capable of holding a legal or beneficial interest in property'.[7] An 'enterprise' is defined as 'any individual, partnership, corporation, association or other legal entity, and any union or group of individuals associated in fact although not a legal entity'.[8] However, the defendant 'person' may not also be the 'enterprise', as illustrated by Masi *v*. Ford City Bank and Trust Co,[9] where the bank used plaintiff's funds to pay a loan to itself. 'Pattern of racketeering activity' is defined under 18 USC 1961 (5) as requiring 'at least two acts of racketeering activity' which occur within 10 years of one another, at least one act having occurred after the effective date of the RICO statute. Examples of 'racketeering activity' are set forth in statute, to wit: mail fraud,[10] wire fraud,[11] interstate transportation of money or property taken by fraud,[12] bribery and extortion punishable under state law by imprisonment for more than one year;[13] bankruptcy fraud;[14] fraud in the sale of securities;[15] and the myriads of examples delineated within 18 USC 1961(1):

'racketeering activity' means (A) any act or threat involving murder,

> kidnaping, gambling, arson, robbery, bribery, extortion, dealing in obscene matter, or dealing in narcotic or other dangerous drugs, which is chargeable under State law and punishable by imprisonment for more than one year; (B) any act which is indictable under any of the following provisions of title 18, United States Code: Section 201 (relating to bribery), section 224 (relating to sports bribery), sections 471, 472, and 473 (relating to counterfeiting), section 659 (relating to theft from interstate shipment) if the act indictable under section 659 is felonious, section 664 (relating to embezzlement from pension and welfare funds), sections 891–894 (relating to extortionate credit transactions), section 1084 (relating to the transmission of gambling information), section 1341 (relating to mail fraud), section 1343 (relating to wire fraud), sections 1461–1465 (relating to obscene matter), section 1503 (relating to obstruction of justice), section 1510 (relating to obstruction of criminal investigations), section 1511 (relating to the obstruction of State or local law enforcement), section 1951 (relating to interference with commerce, robbery, or extortion), section 1952 (relating to racketeering), section 1953 (relating to interstate transportation of wagering paraphernalia), section 1954 (relating to unlawful welfare fund payments), section 1955 (relating to the prohibition of illegal gambling businesses), sections 2312 and 2313 (relating to interstate transportation of stolen motor vehicles), sections 2314 and 2315 (relating to interstate transportation of stolen property), section 2320 (relating to trafficking in certain motor vehicles or motor vehicle parts), sections 2341–2346 (relating to trafficking in contraband cigarettes), sections 2421–24 (relating to white slave traffic), (C) any act which is indictable under title 29, United States Code, section 186 (dealing with restrictions on payments and loans to labor organizations) or section 501(c) (relating to embezzlement from union funds), (D) any offense involving fraud connected with a case under title 11, fraud in the sale of securities, or the felonious manufacture, importation, receiving, concealment, buying, selling, or otherwise dealing in narcotic or other dangerous drugs, punishable under any law of the United States, or (E) any act which is indictable under the Currency and Foreign Transactions Reporting Act.'

It is self-evident that just about any business fraud will involve use of the mails or telephone so that liability can clearly be predicted upon violation of RICO. The federal district court in Massachusetts in Hunt *v.* Weatherbee[16] upheld the validity and propriety of a claim for sexual harassment and discrimination under RICO. Here plaintiff was a female carpenter who alleged that she was coerced into buying raffle tickets for a political functon and also coerced into dropping criminal charges of assault and battery against a co-worker after sexual intimidation and physical threats. Her suit against union officials alleged that they maintained control over the local union and engaged in threats and acts intended to quell any dissension or conflict in the workplace as well as to harass and discriminate against female members of the union. The court found that the coercion to buy raffle tickets and to drop the criminal charges against a co-worker satisfied the requirements of 18 USC 1961(1). The 'events' were more than isolated acts, according to the court; these 'events' represented instances 'in a longstanding effort by union officials to maintain the status quo' and to 'quell any dissension or conflict within the work setting'. The court found that the two or more 'events' alleged by the plaintiff occurred within 10 years of each other and after the enactment of RICO, thus demonstrating a 'pattern of racketeering activity' as required by 18 USC 1961 (5).

It should be observed that most state courts have stated that the structure, language and legislative history of RICO mandates exclusive federal court jurisdiction over all RICO claims.[17] However, it is apparent that the states will and have enacted RICO-type legislation and thus expand the likelihood that the foreign plantiff (and the US plaintiff) will have another entry into courts in the United States.

Another interesting point is that the expected civil action prerequisites to a civil action under RICO that the defendant has been criminally convicted for the acts underlying the civil RICO suit, that plaintiff allege a special kind of racketeering injury, and that there was a *nexus* between the challenged activity and organized crime, were all swept away by the US Supreme Court on 1 July 1985 in its decision in Sedima SPRL *v.* Imrex Company, Inc.[18] In a 5–4 decision the highest court explicitly rejected these very prerequisites to the civil RICO suit on the ground that these restrictions or constraints were not justified by the language or the legislative history of RICO. According to the Court, Section 1962(c) requires only 'conduct of an enterprise through a pattern of racketeering activity', and 'racketeering activity' means any act or threat chargeable under a wide variety of state laws, or any act or threat indictable under a host of provisions in the US Code, including fraud.[19] In Brener *et al v.* BeckerParibas, Inc *et al*,[20] the federal district court for the Southern District of New York observed: 'The majority of civil RICO claims do not impact on the general society or involve vital national interests. . . . Indeed, it appears that most civil RICO claims are being asserted against respected and legitimate enterprises, rather than the archetypal, intimidating mobster. . . . In its private civil version RICO is not generally being used to eradicate organized crime as it was originally designed to do. . . . Because of the breadth of RICO's language it has become a federal business tort statute.' The foreign plaintiff has not always fared well with RICO complaints, as illustrated in Guildford Mills, Inc *v.* Torf[20.1] where the federal district court for the Southern District of New York dismissed a complaint which sought to predicate RICO liability upon allegations that plaintiff had been fraudulently induced to sell textiles for resale in Nigeria: 'A RICO pattern is not alleged by a plaintiff's mere identification of two related predicate acts; some aspect or threat of continuity of the criminal enterprise is required.' But in Beck *v.* Manufacturers Hanover Trust Co[20.2] the Second US Court of Appeals found two related predicate acts in defendant's wrongdoing in connection with the payment of interest on certain mortgage bonds held by Mexico. In Zaveri *v.* E. F. Hutton & Co[20.3] the defendant had argued that it commenced in the United

Arab Emirates a prior action against the foreign plaintiff allegedly to recover $1.3 million in funds which the foreign plaintiff allegedly owed defendant on gold contracts; the federal district court for the Southern District of New York dismissed the suit on *forum non conveniens* grounds because the foreign plaintiff's choice of the New York forum deserved 'less deference than usual because he is a foreigner.' The court concluded that 'if Zaveri could not literally pursue claims under that RICO statute in the United Arab Emirates', the foreign plaintiff could still seek relief in a separate fraud action; Section 1965(a) of RICO did not deprive the court of its discretion to dismiss the suit on *forum non conveniens* grounds.

One of the prime questions in interpretation of Section 1962(a) of RICO is whether or not the pleading can name the same entitiy as both the 'person' and 'enterprise'. According to De Muro *et al. v.* E. F. Hutton[21] the answer was 'yes', i.e., the 'person' and 'enterprise' need not be distinct. But in Rush *v.* Oppenheimer & Co, Inc[22] the same court came to an opposite conclusion: 'One can interpret the lack of a required *nexus* between person and enterprise in Section 1962(a) to indicate the need for a more distinct pleading of enterprise and statute violator because the statute contemplates an enterprise which can be entirely unrelated to the predicate acts. While Section 1962(c) contemplates a perpetrator working through the legitimate or illegitimate enterprise in furtherance of a racketeering scheme, a Section 1962(a) "enterprise" can be the bounty purchased with the racketeering profits, the entity used to "launder" the ill-gotten gains. Therefore, if it is inappropriate to plead identity in Section 1962(c), it is then inappropriate to plead it under Section 1962(a), particularly in light of our knowledge that the statute was not intended to convict the infiltrated enterprise but the violator of the predicate acts.'

Another thorny issue is what constitutes a 'pattern' of racketeering activity for purposes of pleading under RICO. In Northern Trust Bank/O'Hare NA *v.* Inryco Inc[23] the defendant allegedly participated in a construction contract kickback scheme and received a series of kickback payments totaling about $265,000 in the course of one year; a subcontractor was hired by defendant and allegedly permitted to perform in an unsatisfactory manner. On these facts, the federal district court for the Northern District of Illinois, Eastern Division, found no 'pattern' of racketeering activity, even though at least two indictable acts of mail fraud had occurred in connection with the first kickback payment, and probably more indictable acts had occurred in connection with subsequent kickback payments. The court viewed this activity as a 'single fraudulent effort' and a 'single fraudulent scheme'. In Rush *v.* Oppenheimer & Co, Inc[24] the federal district court for the Southern District of New York sustained the complaint against an individual defendant, finding that a sufficient 'pattern of racketeering activity' had been pleaded where the complaint alleged distinct acts of 'churning' an account as well as misrepresentation over a period of almost two years. In February 1986 in Soper *v.* Simmons International, Ltd[25] the same court set forth an excellent analysis of what constitutes adequate pleading of a 'pattern' of racketeering activity. Judge Sand dismissed the complaint and stated that the 'pattern' requisite necessitated 'more than two related acts'. Here RICO liability was predicated upon an alleged conspiracy to deprive plaintiffs of a sales commission, but the court found that the predicate acts were merely ministerial acts performed in the execution of a single allegedly fraudulent scheme: 'The mere failure of a promised performance has never permitted a factual finding that defendants never intended to perform.' And in First Federal Savings and Loan Association *v.* Oppenheimer[26] Judge Lasker of the same federal district court opined that general allegations that the 'mails and means and instrumentalities of interstate commerce were employed' were 'insufficient to notify (defendant) of what use of the wires plaintiffs claim it made.' But a RICO claim was adequately pleaded because allegations of defendant's mass mailing of audit confirmations, taken together with allegations of defendant's oral misrepresentation as to Comark's financial status were sufficient to plead a 'pattern'. Also, according to the court, while defendant could not be both the 'enterprise' and the 'person', the complaint sufficiently charged defendant with being part of an 'association in fact' comprising his partners.

In Zaveri *v.* E. F. Hutton & Co[27] the defendant argued that it had commenced in the United Arab Emirates a prior action against the plaintiff to recover $1.3 million which plaintiff allegedly owed defendant on gold contracts. Plaintiff's suit in the federal district court was grounded upon commodities fraud and upon RICO violations. The court dismissed the action on *forum non conveniens* grounds because the foreign plaintiff's choice of forum deserved 'less deference than usual because he is a foreigner'. The court observed that 'if Zaveri could not literally pursue claims under that RICO statute in the Arab Emirates action, this would not deprive Zaveri of presenting the essence of his position—fraud.' The court concluded that Section 1965(a) of RICO did not deprive the court of its discretion to dismiss for *forum non conveniens*.[28]

The arbitrability of RICO claims has been well established, as illustrated by Development Bank of the Philippines *v.* Chemtex Fibers Inc.[29] Here the US defendant had contracted with a Philippines corporation for the dismantling and reassembly of a synthetic fiber plant; the contract called for arbitration of any disputes in New York under the auspices of the International Chamber of Commerce. Defendant agreed to provide the financing for the project, and the foreign plaintiff bank guaranteed the loans made by defendant to the Philippines corporation. When the corporation defaulted on some of the notes due the defendant, the foreign plaintiff bank made the payments, and then filed suit against defendant, alleging that defendant had submitted false accounts as well as violations of RICO. Defendant moved for arbitration of the dispute in accordance with the contract, and plaintiff resisted on the grounds that it was not a party to that contract and therefore not bound to arbitrate. The court found, however, that the foreign plaintiff bank was in fact a signatory to the contract and was involved at every stage of contract negotiations, and therefore was bound to arbitrate. The court further ruled that RICO claims raised in an international setting are arbitrable under the holding of the US Supreme Court in Mitsubishi Motors Corp *v.* Soler Chrysler-Plymouth, Inc.[30] Another example is West *v.* Drexel Burnham Lambert, Inc[31] wherein plaintiff contracted with defendant for investment, only to discover that defendant had been 'churning' the account in violation of RICO. The defense moved to compel arbitration of the dispute under the brokerage contract, and the court agreed because the claim 'touches upon no great societal or public interest, the policy of enforcing arbitration agreements should prevail'.[32]

The RICO civil suit resembles the private antitrust suit at least with respect to treble damages and attorney's fees[33] as well as the liberal pre-trial discovery. This private right of action to redress statutory violations only requires the usual civil standard of proof, not the criminal standard of proof.[34] In the field of products liability it would appear that repeated misrepresentations of the safety or efficacy of a product should constitute mail fraud or wire fraud;[35] but unfortunately Drake *v.* B. F. Goodrich Co[36] construed Section 1964(c) as barring recovery for personal injuries. The Sixth US Court of Appeals decision in Great Lakes Concrete Pole Co *v.* Eash,[37] however, sanctioned recovery under RICO for damage to property from a misrepresented defective product such as the corrosive mortar and concrete additive. Dilatory and misleading conduct on the part of an insurance carrier in handling claims of the insured may be delineated as 'bad faith' and may constitute misrepresentations by mail or telephone in violation of RICO.[38] Even misconduct in federal discovery procedures may constitute a violation of RICO if the misconduct rises to destruction of documents or intimidation of witnesses, for example.[39]

Insurance carriers have utilized RICO offensively [standing in the shoes of the plaintiff], as illustrated by Schacht *v.* Brown [39.1], involving the insolvency of another carrier, and Fireman's Fund Insurance Co *v.* The Plaza Oldsmobile, Ltd [39.2], where the carrier sued various defendants allegedly engaged in a conspiracy to obtain monies fraudulently from automobile insurance claims. In Heritage Insurance Company of America *v.* First National Bank of Cicero [39.3], the defendant bank allegedly used escrow funds to the detriment of the insurance carrier. See generally For the Defense magazine (Fall 1986) at pp. 24 *et seq.* In United States *v.* Teitler and Schultz [39.4] the defendant lawyers were convicted under RICO for defrauding insurance companies by manipulating claims arising out of automobile accidents. The jury, during its deliberations, inquired whether a defendant could be convicted of RICO conspiracy if convicted on only one mail fraud count, and the trial judge answered affirmatively. The appellate court affirmed: 'We find no authority for the proposition that a person must commit two predicate acts of racketeering to be convicted of a RICO conspiracy. . . . The crime of conspiracy does not require actual commission of the substantive crime.'

In Bankers Trust Co. *v.* Feldesman, [39.5] the court ruled that the New York three-year statute of limitations applied to all civil damage actions brought under RICO. The Fifth Amendment privilege against self-incrimination is applicable to RICO cases because any civil RICO case requires proof of criminal predicate acts; see Fonseca *v.* Regan [39.6].

Section 2. Jurisdiction of State Courts over RICO Complaints

The RICO complaint, whether brought by a foreign or US plaintiff, need not be brought exclusively in the federal courts. The California Supreme Court in Cianci *v.* Superior Court[40] pointed out that, although RICO 'takes aim at a national problem', to wit: organized crime in the United States, that fact does not imply that state courts are unable to apply the statute; nor are federal judges uniquely qualified to handle RICO claims since a list of predicate offenses under RICO includes violations of state laws as well as federal laws, and state courts would be uniquely qualified to handle violations of state laws. Furthermore, since civil RICO claims includes the common variety of business fraud, the claim that RICO deals with federal interests is untenable since state courts have always dealt with the common variety of business interests. Federal courts in Wisconsin[41] and in Pennsylvania,[42] for example, allow state court RICO suits; the Seventh US Court of Appeals in County of Cook *v.* Midcon Corp[43] favored state court jurisdiction over RICO suits: 'We would be reluctant to conclude from congressional silence that Congress intended to depart from the usual rule' of concurrent jurisdiction.

The opposite view against state court jurisdiction over RICO complaints is seen in Kinsey *v.* Nestor Exploration, Ltd[44] a determination by the federal district court for the Eastern District of Washington, and in Maplewood Bank & Trust Co *v.* Acorn, Inc[45] a decision by a New Jersey Superior Court. It would appear that since the language of Section 1964(c) of RICO closely parallels that of Section 4 of the Clayton Act which limits jurisdiction to the federal courts, it can be argued that RICO is similarly restricted to the federal courts.

Under the civil provisions of the RICO statute[46] venue is proper in any district in which the defendant resides, is found, has an agent, or transacts his affairs.[47] Venue is also proper in the district where the cause of action arose.[48] RICO also provides that a party residing in another judicial district may be summoned into the forum district where the 'ends of justice' may require.[49] Thus, RICO provides in effect nationwide service of process over defendants even though the forum court would not ordinarily have personal jurisdiction over those defendants and venue would be improper.

RICO does not contain a statute of limitations for instituting the private civil action, so that the nearest analogous state statute of limitations will be applied.[50] However, the determination as to when plaintiff's cause of action accrued as well as the determination of which state statute of limitations is applicable, is a matter of federal law, not state law.[51] In A. J. Cunningham Packing Corp *v.* Congress Financial Corp[52] the Third US Court of Appeals ruled that Pennsylvania's 6-year statute of limitations governed the RICO fraud claim rather than the 2-year federal statutory period governing fraud claims. However, it has been held that state law may not incorporate a discovery rule for determining the accrual date of a cause of action, for the federal rule of when the claimant knew or should have known of the injury or loss, governs the RICO claim.[53]

Section 3. Indirect Defendants in the RICO Action

The decision of the Eighth US Court of Appeals in Bennett *v.* Berg[54] points up the necessity of suing indirect defendants such as professional persons and insurance companies who were associated with the primary tortfeasor in the RICO business fraud. Here the owner of a religious retirement community mismanaged its finances and used fraud to get new residents to sign 'life care contracts'; the plaintiffs also sued the indirect defendant Prudential Insurance Company, which held a mortgage on the community, and that was the tortfeasor's business and it allegedly knew of the primary tortfeasor's fraudulent scheme. (Indeed, the primary tortfeasor was in jail as a result of an unrelated securities fraud.) Section 1962(c) of RICO states that it is illegal 'for any person . . . associated with any enterprise engaged in interstate commerce to conduct or participate, directly or indirectly, in the conduct of such enterprise's affairs through a pattern of racketeering'. The indirect defendant Prudential Insurance Company apparently settled the case for $62.8 million: Prudential agreed to forgive $48.3 million in mortgage payments by the residents of the community, and to pay $13 million to 380 plaintiffs, $1 million to the community itself, and $500,000 in attorneys' fees.[55]

Notes

1. 18 USC 1961 to 1986.
2. *See generally* NLJ (12 Nov 1985) at p. 6.
3. 18 USC 1962(c).
4. 18 USC 1962(a).
5. *Id.*
6. 18 USC 1962(d).
7. 18 USC 1961(3). Attorneys have also been implicated in RICO claims, as indicated in Bennett *v.* Berg, 685 F2d 1053 (8th Cir, 1982), aff 710 F2d 1361 (8th Cir, 1983), cert den 464 US 1008 (1983). Here former and present residents of a retirement community brought a RICO action against the not-for-profit corporation which owned the community, the community founder, the mortgage lender, the former accountant, two attorneys, and others, charging all defendants with false statements as to the financial soundness of the community and the promise of an affordable 'life care'. Apparently, the defendants breached their fiduciary duties by operating the community through a pattern of self-dealing and profit-making. The federal district court, however, dismissed the complaint on the basis that the complaint failed to allege an 'enterprise' (supra note 3) within the meaning of RICO. But the federal appellate court reversed, holding that an allegation of commercial or competitive injury is not required, and that the not-for-profit corporation that owned the retirement community and the other defendants had an existence apart from the predicate acts of mail fraud and thus constituted an 'enterprise'.
8. 18 USC 1961(4).
9. 779 F2d 397 (7th Cir, 1985).

10. 18 USC 1341.
11. 18 USC 1343.
12. 18 USC 2314.
13. 18 USC 1961(1).
14. *Id.*
15. 18 USC 1961(1).
16. 626 F Supp 1097 (Mass, 1986).
17. *See* Waldschmidt *v.* Crosa, 177 Ga App 707, 304 SE2d 664 (1986).
18. 105 S Ct 375 (1985); for lower court opinion, 741 F2d 482 (2nd Cir, 1984).
19. 18 USC 1961(1).
20. —F Supp—(SDNY, 1986).
20.1 —F Supp— (SDNY, 1987).
20.2 —F2d— (2nd Cir, 1987).
20.3 632 F Supp 254 (SDNY, 1986).
21. *See* Haroco *v.* American Bank & Trust Co, 747 F2d 284 (7th Cir, 1984), aff 105 S Ct 3291 (1985).
22. —F Supp—(SDNY, 1986), aff 779 F2d 885 (2nd Cir, 1986).
23. —F Supp—(ND Ill, 1985).
24. *Supra* note 22.
25. —F Supp—(SDNY, 1986).
26. —F Supp—(SDNY, 1986).
27. *Supra* note 20.3 hereinbefore.
28. *See* Chapter 4, Section 2, herein.
29. 617 F Supp 55 (SDNY, 1985); *also note* Chapter 9 herein.
30. 105 S Ct 3346 (1985); *See* Chapter 9 herein for a delineation of this important case.
31. 623 F Supp 26 (WD Wash, 1985).
32. *Id* at p. 29.
    In Jacobson *v.* Merrill Lynch, Pierce, Fenner & Smith, Inc, —F2d—(3rd Cir, 11 Aug 1986) arbitrability of RICO claims was upheld so long as the predicate offenses on which the RICO suit is based could also have been subject to arbitration. A contrary position was taken by the Second US Court of Appeals in McMahon *v.* Shearson/American Express, Inc, 788 F2d 94 (2nd Cir, 1986), holding that no RICO claims were arbitrable, regardless of the predicate offenses.
33. 18 USC 1964(c).
34. *See* Armco Industrial Credit Corp *v.* SLT Warehouse Co, 782 F2d 475 (5th Cir, 1986).
35. *Supra* notes 10 and 11.
36. 782 F2d 638 (6th Cir, 1986).
37. —F2d—(6th Cir, 1985).
38. *See* Elliott *v.* Chicago Motor Club Insurance Co, F Supp (ND Ill, 1986).
39. *See* Malley-Duff & Associates *v.* Crown Life Insurance Co, —F2d—(3rd Cir, 1986).
    39.1 711 F2d 1343 (7th Cir, 1983), cert den 464 US 1002 (1983).
    39.2 600 F Supp 1452 (EDNY, 1985).
    39.3 629 F Supp 1412 (ND Ill, 1986).
    39.4 —F2d—(2nd Cir, 25 Sept 1986).
    39.5 —F Supp—(SDNY, 1 Sept 1986).
    39.6 98 FRD 694 (EDNY, 1983).
40. 40 Cal3d 903 (1985).
41. *See* Luebke *v.* Marine National Bank of Neenah, 567 F Supp 1460 (ED Wis, 1983).
42. *See* Chas Kurz Co *v.* Lombardi, 595 F Supp 373 (ED Pa, 1983).
43. 773 F2d 892 (7th Cir, 1985).

44. 604 F Supp 1365 (ED Wash, 1985).
45. —NJ Super—, —A2d—(1986).
46. *Supra* note 1.
47. 18 USC 1965(a).
48. *See* DeMoss *v.* First Artists Production Co, Ltd, 571 F Supp 409 (ND Ohio, 1983).
49. 18 USC 1965(b).
50. *See* Seawell *v.* Miller Brewing Co, 576 F Supp 424 (MDNC, 1983).
51. *See* State Farm Fire & Casualty Co *v.* Estate of Caton, 540 F Supp 673 (ND Ind, 1982).
52. —F2d—(3rd Cir, 1986).
53. *See* Compton *v.* Ide, 732 F2d 1429 (9th Cir, 1984).
54. 710 F2d 1361 (8th Cir, 1983).
55. *See* Lawyers Alert (24 Feb 1986) at p. 5.

Index

The numbers refer to Chapters and to Sections respectively